A FARMER'S YEAR

The Cresset Library

Cover: *Interior of an Old Barn* by Sir George Clausen RA
Courtesy of the Royal Academy of Arts

A FARMER'S YEAR

BEING

HIS COMMONPLACE BOOK FOR 1898

BY

H. RIDER HAGGARD

New introduction by Ronald Blythe

" Who minds to quote
Upon this note
    May easily find enough:
What charge and pain,
To little gain,
    Doth follow toiling plough.

" Yet farmer may
Thank God and say,
    For yearly such good hap,
' Well fare the plough
That sends enough
    To stop so many a gap ' "

THOMAS TUSSER, 1558

THE CRESSET LIBRARY

London   Melbourne   Sydney   Auckland   Johannesburg

The Cresset Library

An imprint of Century Hutchinson Ltd

62–65 Chandos Place, London WC2N 4NW

Century Hutchinson Australia Pty Ltd
PO Box 496, 16–22 Church Street, Hawthorn,
Victoria 3122, Australia

Century Hutchinson New Zealand Ltd
PO Box 40–086, Glenfield, Auckland 10,
New Zealand

Century Hutchinson South Africa (Pty) Ltd
PO Box 337, Bergvlei 2012, South Africa

First published in Longman's Magazine 1898–9
First published as a book 1899
This edition first published 1987

Introduction © Ronald Blythe 1987

Made and printed in Great Britain by
Richard Clay Ltd, Bungay, Suffolk

British Library Cataloguing in Publication Data

Haggard, H. Rider
   A farmer's year.
   1. Country life—England—Norfolk
   2. Norfolk—Social life and customs
   I. Title
   942.6'1081'0924   S522.G7

ISBN 0 09 170841 9

DEDICATION

MY DEAR HARTCUP,

Had your mother—who found interest in these pages and who to the end was fond of quiet reading about country things—lived to see them finished, I should have asked, as some small token of their author's affection and respect, to be allowed to set her name upon a book that tells of the home where she was born and the fields in which she spent her distant youth.

But it cannot be; so to you, as a friend and fellow inhabitant of Arcady, to you who also have had experience of the frowning face of adverse agricultural balance sheets, I venture to offer them.

Believe me

Ever sincerely yours,

H. RIDER HAGGARD.

DITCHINGHAM : 1899.

HERBERT HARTCUP, ESQ.

INTRODUCTION TO THE CRESSET LIBRARY EDITION

'Nowadays the novel is almost everything. If a matter is to be read of, it must be spiced and tricked out with romance. But, rightly or wrongly, I imagine that the generations to come will study our facts rather than our fiction.' So declared Henry Rider Haggard at the close of the nineteenth century as he exchanged the hat of a bestselling novelist for that of a worried Norfolk farmer. The prognostication would not prove accurate where he was concerned. *King Solomon's Mines*, *She* and a number of his tales bear both reading and examination to this day. Their narrative strength and brilliant imaginative atmosphere, like those of Stevenson and Ballantyne, have kept Haggard's fictions from being carried away on the usual tides. His Africa and his East Anglia were equally potent forces in his literary development, though in severely divided interests. Africa made him an Empire romance-writer of the first water in ordinary popular terms, but two small farms on the Suffolk–Norfolk border made him an agricultural historian not unworthy a place near Arthur Young, William Cobbett and Lord Ernle. Was Haggard himself divided, a part colonialist, part squire? An administrator of the Cape and a JP and churchwarden of his English village, a family man and a wanderer, a progressive abroad and a Tory at home, a man of action in Pretoria and a dreamer in West Dereham – was his a double life? Curiously not. His personality combining an earthy level-headedness with that uniquely Victorian adventurousness and fantasy was all of a confident piece. Which is why his two 'state of the land' books, *A Farmer's Year* and *Rural England*, are now recognized as key reading for anyone who wants to know how and why the countryside we see today has emerged. Perhaps more novelists should be set to producing reports on social change.

Haggard took as a blueprint for *A Farmer's Year* Thomas Tusser's *Hundredth Good Pointes of Husbandrie*, a practical guide to farming written by a professional musician in the year in which Elizabeth I came to the throne. Tusser wrote his famous advice at Cattiwade, Suffolk, where he was sowing and ploughing fields very close to those which would be worked by John Constable's family in the eighteenth century. It is the source of a great number of the rural proverbs, saws and platitudes which are still in use today. Tusser later farmed at West Dereham, Norfolk, which is why he attracted Haggard. Here was a kind of artist whose duty, like his own, it was to understand and explain man's primal toil, the growing and harvesting of crops, and the herding of animals. Except that, unlike Tusser's agricultural scene, Haggard's was one of stagnation, collapse and abandonment. The tragedy was what the politicians and newspapers of his time were calling 'the flight from the land'. When he wrote *Rural England*, he placed a text from the Book of Judges on the title-page – 'The highways were unoccupied . . . and inhabitants of the villages ceased.'

The quote on the title-page of *A Farmer's Year*, the bitter-sweet journal of what was happening on his own farms as the great agricultural depression descended upon them 'during the last year but one of an eventful and wondrous century' comes from Tom Tusser, the musician-farmer struggling along in the 1550s by the River Stour:

> Who minds to quote
> Upon this note
>   May easily find enough:
> What charge and pain,
> To little gain
>   Doth follow toiling plough.

Haggard called *A Farmer's Year* 'His commonplace book for 1898' and illustrated it with maps, statistical tables and melancholy sepia pictures. A master of 'atmosphere', that here is no less powerful in its way than that which surrounds Ayesha and Umslopogaas. He was in his early forties when he wrote it and was taking stock of his future after having unsuccessfully contested the local parliamentary seat. His career so far had been extraordinary – thrilling even – combining as it did the Victorian virtues of action and the ability to describe it. At nineteen he sailed to South Africa to be secretary to the Governor of Natal, Sir Henry Bulwer. Two years later he was on the staff of Sir Theophilus Shepstone and had himself raised the Union flag in Pretoria's main square. Revered by the Africans, detested by the Boers, Shepstone had annexed the Transvaal for Britain almost single-handed – and without consulting the government. The resulting turmoil ended an extraordinary career. Shepstone's psychological approach to native Africa and his great adventures – he had himself crowned Cetewayo King of Zululand – entranced the young Haggard and fed his imagination. Although he was still only twenty-four when he returned to England for good, Africa and daring radicals like Shepstone continued to influence his vision and made him a very unusual member of Norfolk's farming and sporting gentry. Most curious of all was his ability not to allow his reputation as a popular romancer in any way to compromise that which he was soon to gain as the tough and realistic recorder of Britain's worst agricultural slump. Thus his *Farmer's Year*, a format frequently used by poets, diarists and country-calendarists, is a village book with a difference.

Haggard began farming in 1889, a time when many of those who could were getting out of the industry, and especially the farm-labourers. Throughout East Anglia 'Our American relations were bringing villages to poverty by swamping the markets' – i.e. newly-invented iron grainships, the oil tankers of their day, were flooding Europe with cheap corn from the prairies of the United States and Canada. And if this wasn't bad enough, a run of wet summers which culminated in 'the fearful year of 1879' washed out what was left of harvests and hope. For Haggard, not long married and also by now fast becoming one of England's most popular writers of adventure fiction, it was not just a question of truthfully documenting the collapse of farming, but a sincere need to reawaken in country people their belief in nature, in the patterns of field-work and of craftsmanship, and most of all a belief in the superiority of village existence to that of the city. 'What kind places are these cities to live in, for the poor?' What kind of places in the late nineteenth century were Bedingham and Ditchingham for thirteen shillings a week farm labourers and near bankrupt farmers? *A Farmer's Year* provides answers that are both earthily practical and filled with Haggard's deep love for the land. A few months before he wrote it he had visited Egypt and had seen the paintings and reliefs on the royal tombs at Sakkara, and had thought how very like he was to 'the gentlemen-farmers of the Fifth and Sixth Dynasties who, whilst yet alive, caused their future sepulchres to be adorned with representations of such scenes of daily life and husbandry as to them were most pleasant and familiar'. Egypt had had plagues, but they passed and the joy of the cornfields remained. So he makes his plea to the English countryman to stand firm, 'although how the crisis will end it is not possible for the wisest among us to guess today'. We now know that this crisis ended in the 1940s, when the nation's food requirements inaugurated the second agricultural revolution – and, subsequently, today's embarrassing food mountains.

In all Haggard farmed 365 acres, some two-thirds of which were near his house at Ditchingham, a big village of 1100 inhabitants, and a third in Bedingham, a village 5 miles distant. Some of the Ditchingham land was rented. These farms are immensely ancient and are mostly on 'loving' or heavy land which clings to boots and wheels. When such farms go down it can take years to drain and weed them and bring them back to good working order, and he records his struggles with the dereliction at Bedingham.

Ditchingham, where the young Haggards lived in the Lodge, was a very different matter for the situation was one of the most beautiful in Norfolk, where the Bath Hills and the Waveney Valley spread towards Bungay and the grounds of the Lodge were bordered by the river. Close to the village were the extensive woodlands owned by Lord de Saumarez but whose shooting rights belonged to Haggard. The scene here is that of the successful Empire-builder come home to rest on his laurels – except that it happens to be a scene whose underlying difficulties are preoccupying a landowner–novelist whose idealism and expert grasp of agricultural economy were tearing him apart, emotionally speaking. In time he would produce the kind of report which make governments act, although those of his own day scarcely raised a finger to help the farmer and his men. But now, as the scale of what was happening became clear, Haggard decided that a personal farming diary in the classic form, a book which everybody connected with the land would be warned and inspired by, was essential.

A Farmer's Year holds nothing back. The profit and loss of Ditchingham and Bedingham are given to the last halfpenny. So in another sense are those of Haggard's personality as he swings over from being a typical conservative to a highly candid radical. Much of what he longed to happen has happened, a great deal of what he was sensibly proposing nearly a century ago still hasn't been done. The one thing in particular which the modern reader must be struck by is the gulf which stretches between a gentleman-farmer and his labourers. As magistrate, employer, church-warden and workhouse guardian, Haggard is in total control of them and not at that date less possessive of them than were those Nile farmers of their slaves whose seasonal tasks he saw carved around the doors of Sakkara. He admires their skills and strength, their stoicism and their character but with all his imagination he cannot get into their situation, and his book is the better, if the more bitter, for his never attempting to do so. Suitably in the December chapter he describes a visit to Heckingham Workhouse and it sums up his absolute honesty.

What do these old fellows think about, I wonder, as they hobble to and fro round those measureless precincts of bald brick? The sweet-eyed children that they begot and bred up fifty years ago, perhaps, whose pet names they still remember, dead or lost to them for the most part; or the bright waving cornfields whence they scared birds when they were lads from whom death and trouble were yet a long way off. I dare say, too, that deeper problems worry them at times in some dim half-apprehended fashion; at least I thought so when the other day I sat behind two of them in a church near the workhouse. They could not read, and I doubt if they understood much of what was passing, but I observed consideration in their eyes. Of what? Of the terror and the marvel of existence, perhaps, and of that good God whereof the parson is talking in those long unmeaning words. God! They know more of the devil and all his works; ill-paid labour, poverty, pain, and the infinite unrecorded tragedies of humble lives. God? They have never found Him. He must live beyond the workhouse wall – out there in the graveyard – in the waterlogged holes which very shortly – . . . .

In all Haggard employs fifteen men on his farm and gives meticulous descriptions of their many skills. Their dogged strength astounds him. In January he watches two of them bush-draining a huge expanse of clay land. It takes ten weeks and at the end 'such toilers betray not the least delight at the termination of their long labour'. Similarly with dyke-drawing, the toughest of all the winter jobs. This is a book which reminds one that, the ploughing apart, most of Britain's landscape was fashioned by men with spades. Haggard's men work a twelve-hour day in summer and every daylight hour in winter, and without holidays. Minimal though their education is, it 'teaches them that there are places in the world besides their own Little Pedlington' and makes them aspiring and restless. More and more of them disappear, making for the army, the colonies, the Lowestoft fishing smacks, anywhere preferable to a Norfolk farm. It grieves him. *A Farmer's Year* is his apology for agriculture as man's natural activity, the noblest of tasks, and he cites its improved conditions. Now and then, as in Africa, he joins in the labour, although this he finds separates him further from the workers than if he merely sat his horse and made notes. Whatever he sees or feels or does is written down with total candour, and his journal is at once an important and authoritative compendium of farming practice, a private confessional, a history of turn of the century Norfolk and, in its way, an entertainment. The scene he paints is darker than he wants it to be and, for something which set out as an autobiographical rural calendar about the state of the land at a given date, balance sheets and all, there are highly emotional and intellectual tensions of an unexpected kind.

Sir Henry Rider Haggard's then radical exposure of agrarian decline in this and other books disturbed the profoundly conservative rural society to which he belonged, and, getting on for a hundred years later, it is still capable of upsetting us. But capable of delighting us too, for this is a rich picture of the old landscape and the 'old' people as they were before modern farming and other developments transformed both. It is unlikely to make anyone nostalgic but it will, like a tale by Thomas Hardy, remind us of the tensions, and of the idyll, which not so very long ago were interlocked, as it were, the fields.

A Farmer's Year first appeared as a serial before it was published in book form in 1899. Its purpose was to hearten the yeomen of England during a time of utter hopelessness and to check the abandonment of the villages by their employees. Haggard pours into the narrative everything which would fascinate the farmer and his men, legends, local history, flowers, sport, the church, games, gossip, weather, prices, customs, country pleasures, hard-nosed profits and losses – nothing is left out. He said that 'it mirrors faithfully . . . the decrepit and even dangerous state of farming and attendant industries in eastern England during the great agricultural crisis of the last decade of the nineteenth century', and it does.

Ronald Blythe
1986

AUTHOR'S NOTE

AMONGST a great deal of very kindly criticism that has reached him during their publication in serial form (for which hereby he tenders his best thanks) the author of these pages has read one or two notices complaining that they are not sufficiently technical. He wishes to explain, therefore, that he never intended them to be a manual of farming, but rather what their title implies—the record of one year of the daily experiences and reflections of an individual farmer. With the many existing and admirable works upon the subject he has neither the desire to enter into competition nor, in truth, the scientific and detailed knowledge necessary to such a task.

Outside of descriptions of rustic scenes and events, which to some quiet minds are often pleasing, any interest that this book may possess, indeed, for the present or for future time, must be due in the main to the facts that it is a picture, or perhaps a photograph, of one facet of our many-sided modern life, and that it mirrors faithfully, if incidentally, the decrepit and even dangerous state of the farming and attendant industries in eastern England during the great agricultural crisis of the last decade of the nineteenth century. That is to say, its pages describe those industries with their surroundings as they presented themselves in the year 1898 to the eye and mind of a landowner and farmer of the smaller and therefore more representative sort ; a man who chanced to have had the advantage of visiting other countries, and to the best of his ability to have observed the conditions, social, agricultural and political, which prevail in them.

How that crisis will end it is not possible for the wisest among us to guess to-day. Thus, in obedience to some little understood and subtle law of averages and economic retaliation, Agriculture the starved and neglected, may yet avenge itself upon the towns full-fed with cheap and foreign produce, by swamping them with the competition of the inhabitants of the hamlets who troop thence to find a higher wage than 'the land that dies' can pay them. This movement, indeed, perhaps one of the most significant if the most silent and unnoticed of our time, is already in rapid progress, and when—should no unforeseen event, accident or political change, such as the revival of some modified form of Protection, not expected now, but still possible as an expedient of despair, occur to stay it—the exodus is completed, and the rural districts are desolate, then it may be asked : Must not the numbers, health, and courage of our race in their turn pay a portion of the price of the ruin of its wholesome nurseries?

When the 'highways were unoccupied' and the 'inhabitants of the village ceased' Deborah the Prophetess and a wise Mother in Israel did not think the omen good.

Perhaps it is a superstition and no more ; yet it seems hard to credit that a country will remain prosperous for very long after it has ceased to be even moderately remunerative to till any but its choicest fields for food, and when for the lack of a reasonable reward, the tillers themselves, abandoning the free air their fathers breathed for centuries, have swarmed to inhabit the grim and sweltering courts of cities. Under like circumstances at least Rome did not remain prosperous.

Heretofore John Bull has been depicted as a countryman and nothing else, a comparison with meaning. If henceforth he is to forsake the soil that bred him, how will he be pictured by our children, drawing from a changed and shrunken model?

Indeed to the millions who follow it, and therefore to the nation at large, although few seem to understand that this is so, the practice of Agriculture—that primæval occupation and the cleanest of them all—means more than the growing of grass and grain. It means, among other things, the engendering and achievement of patient, even minds in sound enduring bodies, gifts of which, after the first generation, the great towns rob those who dwell and labour in them. And when those gifts are gone, or greatly lessened, what does history teach us of the fate of the peoples who have lost them?

When, too, the countryman has put on a black coat, or, for that matter, kept to his corduroys, what welcome has the city he craves for him? What kind of places are these cities to live in, for the poor? What mercy do they show to those who fall sick or fail? Ask the labouring man who seeks work after the cheap hair-dye ceases to conceal that he is turned of fifty. Ask the clerk, competent, blameless (and married, with a family), but on the wrong side of forty-five. Ask the widow derelict and tossing upon that bitter sea. They will reply with a paraphrase of the famous saying of the Emperor Charles V., or would if they knew it, 'Cities are women, who reserve their favours for the young.'

There the hideous grinding competition of the age leaves little room for those from whom the last possible ounce of brain or body work can be no longer pressed. They go to the wall, they sink to the slum, and the Dock gate, and the House, and the hospital ward. I say that from these great towns with their aggregated masses of mankind, there rises one eternal wail of misery— the hopeless misery that with all its drawbacks the country does not know, of those who, having fallen, are being trampled by those who stand.

Such are the things of the cities, with their prizes for the few, their blanks, their despairs for the many. And all the while —that is why I speak of them and their pomps and poverties— outside these human hives lie the wide, neglected lands of England, peopled often enough but by a few struggling farmers, and in the course of desertion by a dwindling handful of labouring folk. And yet here should be—not palaces with deer parks only, though sometimes these have their uses—but tens and twenties of thousands of quiet homes, where, given easier conditions as regards carriage, taxation and markets, families might live, not in riches indeed, but in ample comfort; in health of body and of mind, with pure air, pure thoughts, pure sights. Oh! who will so handle matters as to make this enthusiast's dream a possibility, who will turn the people to the land again and thus lessen the load of a nation's sorrows? And from the empty waste of half-tilled acres floats back the echo 'Who?'

Most of us pass such problems with a shrug; they do not concern us we think.

It is an unnatural war between the cities and the land which bore and nurtured them, if that can be called a war where the mother lies prostrate for the daughters to tread out her life. When the towns are full what do they care to-day if the fields be empty? 'Bear our burdens, feed, educate, give us the best of your blood and brain—your hungry Realty can meet the bill. Then you may go starve,' say they; 'what is that to us who have enough? Send us your stalwart men and women :—we will pay you back in sparrows!'

Indeed, the masses of the population, and therefore the governments who seek their suffrages, whatever they may pretend, at heart interest themselves little in the welfare of rural England. It is troublesome with its complaints, half bankrupt, divided by class prejudice, and therefore politically impotent—let it take its chance —that is their attitude—secret if not declared. Countries in China, Central Africa, anywhere, must be seized or hypothecated to provide 'new markets'—even 'at the cost of war'—for this is fashionable and imperialistic, and, it is hoped, will bring profit to the people with the most votes and influence, the traders and dwellers in the towns. For these, money, men, everything they ask ; but for the home earth and its offspring, small help, no, scarce the most naked justice. 'Gentlemen, the Cities would never stand it,' runs the accustomed formula of repulse.

'Open doors abroad' is the cry—what does it matter if the old-fashioned door at home is shut, that door which in bygone ages has so often stood between the wolf and the Englishman? It matters nothing at all, is the answer of our masters (short-sighted as some of us think), for British-grown products are no longer of great importance to the community except, perhaps, to an enterprising section of it, those of the meat-salesmen and traders who use the title as a veil for fraud.

In short, British agriculture on its appropriate journey to
Jericho resembles that Biblical traveller who fell among acquisitive
and self-seeking characters. At least the parallel holds to a certain
extent. The Pharisee, the Scribe, the Priest and the Levite—
townsfolk all of them—pass by with a jest and a curse—sometimes
they add a kick—but the good Samaritan has yet to appear. When
he comes, if ever, and proves successful in his work of healing;
when he has emptied the anæmic, enervated cities back on to the
land and caused the vanished yeoman class to re-arise, he will
be the greatest man of his age, and as a reward will earn the
gratitude of healthy country-nursed posterities, who, without him,
would not have been.

Where is he—this son of consolation?

But with reference to the above opinions and sundry others
expressed from time to time throughout this book, some of them
unconventional perhaps, its student is asked to remember, in
conclusion, that they are only the unimportant though sincerely
held views of a private observer of events; intended, it is true, to
convert as many as possible to their author's way of thinking, but,
should they fail in this, at least to give offence to no one; to be
taken, indeed, at such value as the reader pleases, much, or little,
or none at all.

DITCHINGHAM : 1899.

PREFACE TO SILVER LIBRARY EDITION

IN ancient Egypt the gentlemen-farmers of the Fifth and Sixth Dynasties whilst yet alive caused their future sepulchres to be adorned with representations of such scenes of daily life and husbandry as to them were most pleasant and familiar.

The study of these paintings and reliefs has delighted me much to-day as it did when first I visited them in 1887. Whilst considering them it occurred to me that in this book, by means of the methods of my own age, I have unconsciously attempted to follow the example of the authors of those rock-hewn manuscripts who lived some fifty centuries ago.

Perhaps, I thought to myself, in times to be, when all is changed again save the eternal ways of Nature that are the ways of God, the word-pictures of my pages also may thus interest and instruct unborn men of tastes akin to mine.

Such is my hope.

H. RIDER HAGGARD.

(Written near the Pyramids of Gizeh on March 24, 1904, after revisiting the tombs at Sakkara in Egypt.)

Since the publication of this book my remarks about Lord Nelson and Lady Hamilton have given rise to a considerable amount of controversy which necessitates some short explanation.

On August 10, 1905, on the occasion of the laying, by the present Lord Nelson, of the foundation stone of a Memorial Hall which is to be erected in honour of the great Admiral, in the parish of Woodton, in Norfolk, I made a speech in the course of which I alluded to the finding, in 1881, at the Paston School at North Walsham, of the Nelson brick spoken of in the text. In the *Eastern Daily Press* of August 14, 1905, appeared an article in which it was stated that 'a gentleman of excellent standing in the neighbourhood of North Walsham called at these offices to assure us, on his own direct testimony, that the initials (*i.e.* those carved on the brick) originated in a boyish fraud, and that he and some other Pastonians still living had been all along aware of it. For the present he wishes to remain anonymous ; but he authorises us to disclose his name if his credit should be seriously impugned.'

Then follows the gentleman's story, in which he says that he perfectly well remembers the publication of a letter from my late father, Mr. Haggard, stating that somewhere or other there was a brick in the school wall with Nelson's initials thereon. He adds that it occurred to a boy from Oswestry 'to cut the initials just for a lark,' and that 'I with others saw him do it.'

In commenting upon this gentleman's evidence (as he has not revealed his name I cannot give it) in a letter, or rather two letters to the *Eastern Daily Press*, I pointed out that my father never published any such communication as that of which he speaks, but that, in 1895, many years after my visit with him to the school, I did publish a letter in the *Times* on this and other matters, which is doubtless that which he had in his mind. Further, I showed that whether or no the boy from Oswestry cut Nelson's initials on a brick in preparation for a visit from my father, which visit neither my father nor anyone else knew would be made until within half an hour of its occurrence, certainly such a brick with such initials was to be seen in the school wall over eighty years ago, when my father was a little boy, as he well remembered its existence.

.It was, however, elucidated in the course of the correspondence that my memory was at fault when I stated that my father personally found the brick. It seems, as indeed I now recollect, that failing to find it he went with me and the head master into the schoolroom and asked if any of the boys knew of this brick. One little boy replied that he did, and, coming into the yard, pointed out the initials in the broken wall by the light of a lantern. To this boy my father gave a tip of half-a-crown.

To these explanations the critic of the event, whose remarks had meanwhile been copied into sundry other papers, made no reply, and so matters stood until, on August 22 and 24, 1905, I received two letters from Mr. Gerard J. Buxton, of Icklingham, Mildenhall. In these letters he informs me that this little boy was his late brother, a great admirer of Nelson, and that he well remembers his leaving the schoolroom to point out the brick to my father, and his delight at receiving the half-crown, although, until Mr. Buxton read the correspondence all these years afterwards, he had no knowledge of the identity of the donor. He says further : 'I am perfectly convinced that the H. N. was not cut on the brick during the time I was at the Paston School, from 1880 to 1884. At that time it had every appearance of being thoroughly "weathered." Had it been the result of a schoolboy's "lark," as suggested, I should have been among the first to have known it.'

It seems to me that this testimony, taken in conjunction with that of my father's memory, goes far to establish the genuineness of this relic. Also the latter seems to prove that if these initials were forged, that forgery was executed over eighty years ago.

If, however, I am right upon this point—as I believe—on another I and my informant, old Canham, are presumably wrong. I stated on my own authority, which was based upon local tradition, that 'in or about the year 1804 Mrs. Bolton, who was Nelson's sister, and her husband hired Bradenham'; and, on that of Canham, that it was part of his duty 'from time to time to take out the coat in which he (*i.e.* Nelson) was killed at Trafalgar, and to air it on the lavender bushes that grow by the kitchen garden railings.' Also I said that after Nelson's death ' all his sea-going belongings were sent to Bradenham.'

Now, in the autumn of 1905, at the time of the Nelson Centenary, Mrs. Nelson-Ward, wife of the last surviving son of Horatia, kindly wrote to me enclosing various documents, which are too long to print here, that seem to prove beyond doubt that the Boltons did not move from Cranwich to Bradenham Hall (with which by the way, that had an hereditary connection, since Edmund, Lord Nelson's father, was born at East Bradenham in 1722, during his father's tenancy of the living) until the year 1811, and that it was after this date that Lady Hamilton visited them there. Also it would seem that the coat which Canham used to hang out on the railings was not that in which Nelson was killed at Trafalgar, since before 1811 Lady Hamilton had sold it to Alderman Smith, and that Nelson's belongings from the Victory were sent to Merton and not to Bradenham. When Mrs. Nelson-Ward wrote me her first letter she was of opinion that this coat belonged to Sir William Bolton, the son-in-law of Mrs. Susannah Bolton, a naval officer with whose history I am not acquainted. In a subsequent letter, however, she states that the Misses Girdlestone, who are relatives of the Boltons, have now a coat in their possession which appears to have been the one that old Canham used to air upon the railings. Here are her words : 'The Misses Girdlestone also mentioned the coat we have been in correspondence about. They say they now possess the coat ; it is one that belonged to the Admiral, but was not the Trafalgar coat ; it has always been called the Copenhagen coat, and has no hole in it. They possess the coat through their great grandmother, Susannah, and their grandmother Katherine, wife of Sir William Bolton.'

I should add that my late friend, Mr. Cordy Jeaffreson, in his book 'Lady Hamilton and Lord Nelson,' vol. ii. p. 266, writes as follows : 'Whilst Nelson was at sea, Lady Hamilton lived upon affectionate terms with his brothers and sisters, receiving them at Merton for staying visits, and making trips to their homes in different parts of the country. "I long," Nelson wrote to her, on July 12, 1803, "to hear of your Norfolk excursion, and everything that you have been about, for I am ever most warmly interested in your actions." *In the autumn of the following year (1804) she was again with the Boltons at Bradenham Hall, co. Norfolk*, the wooded home of the Norfolk Haggards.'

The italics, I should state, are mine ; but if, as I have every reason to suppose, Mrs. Nelson-Ward is right in believing that the Boltons did not go to Bradenham until 1811, it seems strange that Mr. Jeaffreson should have made this curious error in dates in a serious biographical work. The truth is that, after the lapse of a hundred years, such points are very difficult to unravel with certainty.

H. R. H.

CONTENTS

CONTENTS

Canvassing—Politics of the Labourer—Heat or Pheasants—Courtship among Turkeys—The Last of the Irish Cattle—A Bad Balance Sheet—The Low Price of Butter—The Foreign Article—A Margarine Factory—Home-grown Hams—An Election Tale—Snake Bite in Norfolk—Gathering Orchids at Bedingham—The Vitality of Seed—Political Meetings—School Board Cases—Sir J. Gorst on Education—Laying down Grass at Kessingland—The Result of the Election—Backwardness of the Season—The End of Newborn Pride—Benacre Broad—The Habits of Peewits—The Closing of the Broads—May sayings 178

JUNE

Grass in Iceland—Njäl's Hall at Bergsthorsknoll—Backwardness of the Season—Crops and Stock at Bedingham—A June Frost—Preparing to Steam-saw—Sheep-shearing—The Humour of Shearers—Weight of Fleeces—Lights and Colours—Bees in the Beans—The Ways of Swallows—Weeds and Carrots—The Decay of Bungay Market—Low Price of Wool—Striking a Bargain—Lucky Pigs—A Use for Oak Butts—Steam-sawing—Spoke Setting—Curlew on the Common—Farming with the Hoe—Flat Hoeing—Cracked Shoulder-blades—A Tale of the Zulu War—Fairy Rings—Adventure with the Porch Swallows—Egg-Stealing—Resale of the King's Head Hotel—Price of Lambs—The Uses of the Dock—About Hawks—The Work of the late Mrs. Scudamore—The Keeper and the Owl—Moorhens and their Young—The Cold and the Swallows—Sheep Dipping—Life on the Lawn—The Refusal of Christian Burial—Cutting the Layer—Hen and Ducklings—Swifts on the Bath Hills—Dragging Twitchgrass—Curiosities of the Bedingham Registers—Dan and Sheep Murder—A Solemn Sky—Naturalism—Wanted, a Kicking-strap—Allotment Crops—Price of Garden Stuff—Good Blood *versus* Bad—Docks on the Marshes—Hoeing under Difficulties—Drying Wet Hay—The Blooming of Wheat—The First Breath of Summer—Female Labour—Transplanting Mangold—Machine-mowing Laid Grass—Barleys at Bedingham—The Fly—Flowers and Birds in Websdill Wood . . 211

JULY

The Season Up to Date—The Shed at Baker's—Woodton Hall and Church—The Infamous Dowsing—Forgotten Brides—Epitaphs—Wealth of the Georgian Era—The Hay on Nos. 5 and 11—Effect of Sheeping Pastures—Treading of Land by Sheep—Weaning Lambs—Haysel at Bedingham—Kohl-rabi and Pigeons—A Wicked Pony—A

DECEMBER

APPENDIX

A FARMER'S YEAR

IT IS WITH VERY REAL HUMILITY that I take up my pen to write
of farming, following the excellent example of Thomas Tusser,
who, more than three hundred years ago, as I do, tilled the land
in Norfolk. The subject is so vast and the effort seems so pre-
sumptuous. I propose, however, that this book shall be the
journal of a farmer's year rather than a work about farming,
setting forth with other incidental things the thoughts and reflections that occur to him, and what he sees day by day in field or
wood or meadow, telling of the crops and those who grow them,
of the game and the shooting of it, of the ways of wild creatures
and the springing of flowers, and touching, perhaps, on some of
the thousand trivial matters which catch the eye and occupy the
attention of one who lives a good deal in the company of Nature,
who loves it and tries to observe it as best he may.

I wrote 'of the trivial matters,' but at times I think that these
natural phenomena : the passage of the seasons, the sweep of the
winds and rain, the play of light upon the common, the swell and
ebbing of the flood water, and all the familiar wonders which happen
about us hour by hour, for those who take note of them have more
true significance than the things we seek so eagerly in cities and
in the rush of modern life. There is no education like that
which we win from the fellowship of Nature ; nothing else
teaches us such true lessons, or, if we choose to open our minds

to its sweet influence, exercises so deep an effect upon our inner selves—an effect that is good to its last grain. I say 'if we choose,' for there are many in all classes of life who pass their days in the fields and yet never open their minds. Of the inner mystery and meaning of things they see nothing; they do not understand that to win her favours Nature is a mistress who must be worshipped with the spirit as well as admired with the eyes. Such folk miss much.

Let the reader of utilitarian mind have patience, however, for there will be a practical side to this book. I am a farmer, and engaged in a desperate endeavour to make my farming pay. Perhaps the chronicle of my struggles may have interest for others so situated; may at least—if one man's experience in agriculture or anything else is ever of any use to others—teach them what to avoid. To prove that I set out the exact truth, moreover, at the end of this chapter I shall print, amongst other things, a statement of the financial conditions under which my farming is carried on, and of its pecuniary results up to the present time.

One more word of warning. This is not to be the history of the working of a great farm run by some rich man regardless of expense, with model buildings, model machinery, and the rest.

On the contrary, here is but a modest place, modestly, if sufficiently, furnished with the necessary buildings, capital, instruments, and labour. Possibly for this very reason the details connected with it may prove of the more value to readers interested in the subject. After all, few people have to do with large and perfectly equipped farms, whereas many—to their sorrow —are weighted with small holdings thrown on their hands in wretched order. How often indeed has a reader been annoyed after purchasing a manual on some sport or amusement in which he is interested—let us say on shooting—to find that, to all appearance, it has been written by a millionaire for millionaires. Very few people can base their estimate of sport on five or eight thousand acres of the best game country in England, or look on 100 brace of driven partridge as a small day. Something humbler in scale would be more useful to them. Perhaps the same consideration applies to a book dealing with the land.

In all I am now farming 365 acres of land or thereabouts, of which 261 are situated in this parish of Ditchingham, and 104 in the parish of Bedingham, five miles away. Of the 261 acres at Ditchingham I hire about 110 acres, and am therefore, as regards this proportion of the land, a tenant farmer holding under three separate landlords. This may seem a large amount of land to hire, being considerably more than a third of the total acreage, but the explanation is twofold. First, these pieces of land cut into my own holding; and, secondly, as I find from experience that it is more economical to farm on a considerable scale than on a small one, it suited my purpose to take these acres as they came into the market, rather than to disturb old tenants on other land in my own possession in the parish.

This 110 acres is rented, some of it at a high price (for the times), and some moderately, the net total payable being 111*l*. 10*s*., or about 1*l*. an acre. But on the turnover of a farm of this size even 111*l*. for rent makes no enormous figure. The wise people who are continually shouting into our ears that the real remedy for agricultural depression is a further reduction of rents are indeed very much mistaken. Let farming become once more a fairly remunerative business, and we farmers shall not grumble at a reasonable rent; but let it remain in the condition in which it has been for the last ten years, and, save in very exceptional instances, the abolition of rent altogether would not enable it to pay a living profit.

At Bedingham none of the land is hired, the farm, which belongs to this estate, having been thrown upon my hands four years ago. I might have relet it, but found out in time that the applicant's capital was small indeed. As, but a short while before, I had experienced the joys of such a tenant in another farm—at an expense to myself of a loss of several hundred pounds—I declined the offer, and took over the land. Perhaps it will be more convenient if I describe this place first.

The name of it is the Moat Farm, but whether it is so called
from a large pond in the meadow in front of the house, or because
it was once a 'Mote' or meeting place, a gathering-ground perhaps
of long-forgotten parish councils, is more than I can say. The
origin of the name of the village itself—Bedingham—gives food for
conjecture. Blomefield informs us that it is derived from a rivulet
in Sussex called the Beding ; but why a village in Norfolk should
take its title from a streamlet in Sussex he does not explain. If
he be right, the christening took place some time ago, for the
'town' seems to have been called Bedingham in the days of
William the Conqueror, who owned the greater part of it, which
was in the charge of his steward, one Godric. Quite close also,
in the neighbouring village of Hedenham, the Romans had a brick
kiln ; there is one there still, so probably they were acquainted
with Bedingham.

There are few things which give rise to reflections more melancholy—since the fate of those bygone worthies who owned it is
the same that awaits us all—than the contemplation of any piece of
ground to which we chance to be attached and to see and walk
upon day by day. We may know its recent history, traditions
may even survive of old So-and-so, and how he farmed 'sixty
years gone' ; but before that ! How many generations of them
have taken exactly the same interest in those identical fields?
How many dead eyes week by week, as ours do, have dwelt upon the
swell of yonder rise, or the dip of the little valley? How many
dead hands have tilled that fallow, or mown that pasture?

Look at the long procession of them—savages herding battle
and hogs, scores of generations of these ; slaves under the charge of
a Roman overseer ; Saxons, Danes, Normans, monks, English of all
the dynasties, our immediate predecessors, and, last of all, ourselves.

And the land itself? Scarcely changed, as I believe. Any portion of it that chanced to be forest in his day excepted, the Saxon
Thane, Hagan, who farmed it in the time of Edward the Con-
fessor, would know it again at once, for every little rise and fall of
it is the same as in his generation ; the streamlet is the same, the

roads follow precisely the same winds and turns, taking the course dictated to them in the beginning by the occurrence of boggy land or the presence of groves of ancient oaks. The land is more generally enclosed, and the trees upon it would seem to have moved themselves into unfamiliar places—these would be the principal differences in his eyes. But when it came to the question of soil, probably he could tell us the nature of almost every acre. Yonder it would never do to plough after wet lest it should 'kill' the land. That piece is 'scaldy' because the gravel comes near to the top earth, and corn would not 'cast' on it in a dry season. And so forth. Doubtless his information would be correct to the letter, except where some swamps are concerned, for in this part of Norfolk they have all been drained. Things move slowly in our temperate clime, and more than a thousand years are needful to alter even the character of the soil of a field—or so I believe.

Well, Hagan the Thane has gone to his rest in the churchyard yonder, whither since his day, although the population of the hamlet is small, he must have been followed by over six thousand of the inhabitants of Bedingham. They are all forgotten, every man of them, but the names of the more recent generations are recorded in registers which few ever open, though about these I shall have a word or two to say. Yet some of them were people of importance in their day. For instance, there were the de Gournays in the time of Henry II. Nicholas de Stutvile, who married Gunnora, an heiress of the de Gournays, lost his lands in Bedingham for rebellion against King John. The wrath of that monarch was not very long-lived, however, for in 1206 he restored to Nicholas the son that which he had taken from Nicholas the father. Then there were Bigods and de Udedales, and Gostlings and Sheltons, one of whom, by the way, in the time of Henry VIII. conveyed an estate here to Thomas Hauchet, of Upp Hall, Braughing, Herts, now the property of the writer's friend, Mr. Charles Longman, the publisher of this book. The Stanhow family were here also for some two hundred and fifty years. Then came the Stones, one of whom married Catherine, the heiress of the Stanhows, who dwelt on at Bedingham Hall till within the memory of folk still alive. At last they died out, and the old Hall was pulled down, and with it departed such glory as Bedingham possessed, for now, with the exception of that of the clergyman (who is expected to exist on about 140*l.* a year), no gentle family lives in the parish.

Of all these faint and far-off ghosts that once were men and women (and owned or cultivated my farm) the one who interests me most is that member of the Bruce or Brews family who died 'beyond sea' and caused his heart to be sent back to Bedingham for burial. The heart still lies in the chancel, enclosed, so says tradition, in a casket of silver. Tradition tells us also that its owner fell in the Crusades, but I can find no confirmation of the report. Perhaps the story has become mixed with that of the heart of a more famous Bruce, and its adventures in the Crusades.

There was another Brews also, the merry Margery, who writes from Topcroft by Bedingham in February 1477 to her 'Voluntyn' (valentine), John Paston (*see* the Paston Letters). 'No more to yowe at this tyme, but the Holy Trinitie have yowe in kepyng. And I besech yowe that this bill be not seyn of none erthely creatur save only your selffe. And thys letter was indyte at Topcroft with full hevy herte, By your own Margery Brews.'

Poor dead Margery! she did not anticipate the art of printing or foreknow the eyes that would read her sweet love-laden valentine.

There was a priory at Bedingham, for Sir John de Udedale granted the manor to the Canons of Walsingham in 1318. So the priory must have existed for something more than two centuries when Henry VIII. seized it and gave it to one Thomas Gawdy. All that is left of the monks to-day is an ancient building, said to have been part of the monastery, which is now used as a farmhouse. It stands close to the church, a long and beautiful building, which used to be called the 'Mother' church of this district, probably built, or rebuilt, by the monks. If so, this is the only monument they have left behind them; but I often wonder what their life was like in the grey old priory, and, when they were not praying in the church, what they did with their time during their long peaceful day of more than two centuries. I am not aware that the commissioners reported their establishment for riotous or unseemly practices; indeed it seems difficult to connect such fast doings with Bedingham or its inhabitants, clerical or lay, although this may be mere Arcadian prejudice. Therefore, as there is no fishing in the neighbourhood, I have come to the conclusion that the old monks must have been great farmers, and probably very good ones according to their lights and opportunities.

I make no excuse for these remarks on the history of Bedingham, introduced into a description of a farm in the parish, since I believe that most readers will agree with me that there is something almost fascinating about such records and the speculations to which they give rise. The crown and charm of rural England is its antiquity. Our American relations may bring these villages to poverty by swamping the markets and thus destroying our agricultural prosperity, but in a certain sense we are avenged upon them. I wonder what they would give for a few hamlets with a pedigree like that of Bedingham. Here such places and their pasts are quite unnoticed; yonder, where they have more taste and sympathy for what is bygone, they would be prized indeed. But so it is. If, like the present writer, a man has lived in new countries, and been more than satisfied with their unshaped crudity, he turns home again with a quickened appetite for things hoar with age, and with a gathered reverence towards that which has been hallowed by the custom of generations. Indeed the lives of us individuals are so short that we learn to take a kind of comfort in the contemplation of communities linked together from century to century by an unbroken bond of blood, and moulded to a fixed type of character by surroundings and daily occupations which have scarcely varied since the days of Harold.

The Moat Farm at Bedingham is a heavy-land farm, in fact it would be difficult to find a heavier. Walk over it in wet weather, and five minutes of hard work will scarcely clean your boots, so 'loving' is the country; walk over it in dry before the frost has broken up the clods in winter, or rain has slaked them in summer, and you must be careful lest you twist your ankle. But heavy land, unless it be very 'thin in the skin,' does not necessarily mean bad land. Indeed, if I were given the choice, I would more lightly undertake a heavy-land farm in good order than one liable to 'scald,' which refuses to produce a crop of hay or roots unless deluged day by day with rain. Perhaps, however, this conviction owes something to the three years of drought which we have just experienced. The clay of Bedingham laughs at drought; as an old fellow there said to me, 'It didn't never take no harm from it since Adam,' and on it during these dry years I have grown some good barleys. For example, my Bedingham barley of 1896 fetched the highest price of any produced in this district that year.

Several causes have combined to give the stiff soils so bad a name, and to knock down the value of such land in East Anglia to about 10*l.* the acre. First and foremost among these is the ruinous cheapness of corn. The heavy lands are corn-growing lands, and if it no longer pays to grow the corn they are supposed to be of no further value. I say 'supposed to be,' for reasons which I will give presently. Then they are expensive to stock and work properly; the farmer must have good horses and enough of them, the draining must be attended to in its proper rotation, and so forth. Lastly, when once they are thoroughly foul and neglected it is a long and costly business to bring them straight again. When a ditch has not been cleaned, or a pond 'fyed,' or a field drained, or a hedge cut on such a farm for years, as is often the case, it is no child's task to overtake the work; indeed, it cannot be done, without great expense for labour, under a period of time, probably two four-year shifts. This state of affairs means, moreover, that the land is foul with docks and other weeds, and to clean it is a labour of Hercules. Consequently, a heavy-land farm in this condition, or anything approaching to it, is practically valueless to a yearly tenant, as it would take him several years to 'right-side' it, during which time, unless he chanced to be a man of substance, probably he would starve.

Here is an instance of the extraordinary drop in the value of

heavy land in this neighbourhood. Major John Margitson, my
father-in-law, and predecessor in this property, about thirty-five
years ago purchased a farm of 195 acres of heavy land for a sum
of 6,000*l*., or including certain necessary improvements 6,500*l*. In
1868 this farm was let for 252*l*., the tenant paying the tithe of 35*l*.
In 1881 the rent had fallen to 200*l*. Then came the bad seasons,
indeed they had already begun with the fearful year of 1879, and
the tenant, a worthy man of the old school who felt his age, had
neither the energy nor the capital to stand up against them. He
drifted into insolvency, and the farm was relet to another tenant
at a greatly reduced rent. This gentleman, although it was not
discovered at the time, was already practically insolvent. In the
end he went bankrupt also, and the estate lost several hundred
pounds. Now I was anxious to take the farm in hand, as at the
time I chanced to be able to command the 2,000*l*. capital which
would have been necessary to the venture. But my late friend and
agent, Mr. William Simpson, the well-known and respected Norfolk
auctioneer and valuer, dissuaded me from that course. By this
time, like everybody else, he was thoroughly frightened at the
outlook for farming, and assured me that I should certainly lose
1,000*l*. over the transaction. I bowed to his judgment and
experience and the farm was relet, this time for 50*l*. a year—as he
could only value the land at 8*l*. the acre I declined to go further
and attempt to sell it. Out of this magnificent revenue I am
expected to repair the house and extensive buildings, to bear the
ordinary landlord's charges, to find the seed for laying down
permanent pastures, and pay the tithe, which now, I believe,
has declined to about 25*l*., or half the gross rental. Also, I am
called upon for subscriptions to local charities. By the way, can
it ever have been contemplated that the system of tithe should
work thus? When the farm let for 252*l*. the tithe seems to have
been about 35*l*.; now, when the rent is 50*l*. the tithe is about 25*l*.,
a large proportion—to the profits I was about to write, but, of
course, there are none. To own that farm costs a considerable
sum out of pocket annually.

To return to the Moat Farm at Bedingham. It is very stiff, although not so stiff as some in this neighbourhood, that is, if common repute and nomenclature go for anything. 'Muck and Misery' one is called, and another 'Stark-Naked Farm.' They are heavy land both of them. For a good many years before I began to work it the land had been farmed 'off-hand,' that is to say, the tenant did not live on the farm, but put in a working bailiff. The result of this kind of arrangement is generally apparent in the outward aspect of the homestead. When the farmer lives on a place himself, in most cases it is kept tidy. His wife or daughters look to the flowers; one of them is sure to grow a few roses, wallflowers, dahlias, or hollyhocks. Vegetables for the family use are cultivated also, either by the tenant himself, though farmers are generally very bad gardeners, or by one of his men in their spare time, when the weather is unsuitable for other jobs. Often enough, however, the labourer in charge of an 'off-hand' farm takes little interest in such matters. The garden grows up, the apple trees are unpruned, and a briar bush or two alone remain to show where once the roses were which they have choked.

Such was the case at Bedingham. The buildings, moreover, were dilapidated and the yards like pit-holes. Year by year the litter had been carted out of them, together with a portion of the bed on which it lay; but rarely, indeed, if ever, were any stones put in to make them good. In these clay lands stones are scarce. A certain number of flints are ploughed up and gathered on the layers, but these are used for more urgent repairs, such as that of the round where the horse walks when at work on the chaffing-machine, or to mend the gate openings. The yards are left to take their chance, and the muck in them to soak in a pond of water till it could better be described as dirty straw than good manure.

Thus too often it is with everything; so long as it will possibly serve the thing is neglected, unless indeed it is some damage that the landlord can be forced or worried into repairing. Especially is this the case with gates, that on such a farm are often represented by a rickety ledge or two, and a broken back leaning against a post so rotten that a strong man could push it over, or, rather, break it just where it enters the ground. Here it is that a post gets the 'wets and drys,' and here the best of them go in time. Even if a tenant is bound by lease to leave the gates in good repair the case is much the same. This was so at Bedingham, and I remember when it came 'in hand' seeing a carpenter engaged in tinkering at the gates. Yet since I have had it I have been obliged to renew some of them altogether, and many others are worn out. Another thing much neglected by most tenants of late years is the periodical 'fying,' or cleaning out of pit-holes, and even of large ditches. If the pits are not cleaned animals feeding in the fields are liable to get 'laid,' or bogged, but their owners take the risk of that rather than go to the expense of fying, although in truth the mud thrown from the ponds almost repays this cost, since it is most valuable for the refreshing of pastures. Again, if the ditches are neglected on heavy land, the mouths of the drains get blocked and the soil becomes sour and sodden with water, after which its owner will soon hear that 'the mucky old land won't grow northin' at all, not enough to feed a cow on ten acres of it,' or something equally depressing. Since I took over the Moat Farm in 1894 I have 'fyed' every pond upon it. Out of one of them, that in front of the homestead, there were drawn more than two hundred loads of mud. According to the testimony of the 'oldest inhabitant' it had not been touched for over fifty years.

Still, on the whole, the Bedingham farm was not in such bad order when I took charge of it, as may be judged by the fact that one field proved clean enough to lay down in pasture. It used to be very well farmed by a worthy man who understood heavy soil. He died of consumption ; and, after his death, his executors carried on his business, but the land was not quite so well done by. Still, if judged by the state of the larger farm at Ditchingham, of which I shall have to speak presently, its condition was good—a comparative term, however.

The Moat Farm, as may be seen from the map upon the

opposite page, has in all an area of about 104 acres, whereof
twenty-five acres or thereabouts were permanent pasture in 1894.
Of this grass, however, fourteen acres (No. 20 in the accompanying
map) is land cleared by the stubbing up of a covert known as
Websdill Wood.   This appears to have been done within the last
fifty years, for old men still living in the parish remember it, but the
ground was left thickly covered with oaks, rather small in size,
owing to the poverty of the sub-soil.   Indeed, I am told that they
have scarcely altered in girth for a generation, although their timber
is of good quality.   Of these oaks I have cut down about seventy
within the last few years, and used them in farm repairs.   Underneath them many brambles still cumber the soil in little clumps.
These are now removed annually, and the surface-drains having
been reopened, the pasture is improving, for last year a considerable head of young things, about ten in all, together with two colts,
found a living on this fourteen acres during the summer months.
That it cannot have been a bad one was evident from their condition in the autumn, the colts especially showing as fat as butter.

The rest of the old pasture is good, and produces excellent hay.
All the land round the wood is heavy, cold, and very flat, especially
the pieces numbered respectively 19, 15, 16, 21, and 22.   When
negotiations were going on for the reletting of this farm, the tenant
would offer no rent at all for them, alleging them to be worthless.
I was of a different opinion ; and I hope to be able to bring the
reader to my way of thinking.   The land, it is true, had many
disadvantages.   Indeed, however carefully it was cultivated, it is
doubtful whether one root crop in four, on the pieces in question,
would repay the trouble and expense of tillage.   Either the
roots suffered from a 'wet stunt' in rainy weather, or the soil would
'set hard,' or, for some reason unexplained, the seedlings received
a 'check' from which they never could recover.   In good seasons,
which at Bedingham mean very dry seasons, corn did fairly upon
these lands, but the crop could scarcely be ensured.

Now, from the first, I had seen that if a farm of this character
is to be made to pay in these days, it would be necessary to keep

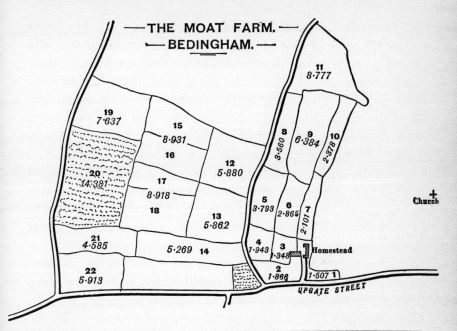

THE MOAT FARM.
BEDINGHAM.

Pastures	Arable	Present Crop (1898)	Last Year's Crop (1897)
1. 1·507	5. 3·793	Barley	Tares and Kohlrabi
2. 1·866	6. 2·865	Wheat	Beans
3. 1·348	8. 3·560	Wheat	Pease
4. 1·943	9. 6·384	Wheat	Clover Layer
7. 2·101	12. 5·880	Barley	Swedes
10. 2·378 [1]	13. 5·862	Pease and Oats	Barley
11. 8·777	14. 5·269	Beans	Barley
15. } 8·931 [2]	17. } 8·918	Root	Barley
16.	18.	Swedes and Kohlrabi	Wheat
19. 7·637 [2]	21. 4·585	Barley and Permanent Pasture	Roots and Cabbage
20. 14·381 [3]	22. 5·913	Root	Barley
50·869	53·029		

TOTAL ACREAGE

Pasture 50·869 }
Arable   53·029 } Homestead

103·898

[1] Laid last year.   [2] New pasture.   [3] Websdill Wood rough pasture.

the labour bill as low as possible, and to reduce the number of horses necessary to its working, which, by the way, if I remember right, was four for the first two years. To do this, it was essential that a good deal more land should go down to grass, and for grass accordingly I set apart pieces numbered 10, 19, 15, 16, 21, and 22. As might be expected, my idea of laying land of this character down to grass at all met with considerable criticism. The late tenant had informed me, when I made the suggestion to him, that it was futile, as the grass would never stand more than three years ; and other authorities were not much more encouraging. It was at this juncture that I happened to read in the *Times* a letter from Mr. Elliot, of Clifton Park, describing his method of dealing with bad thin-skinned lands which he wished to lay down, by mixing with the permanent grass seeds a proportion of deep-rooting herbs—weeds, some would call them— such as chicory, burnet, lucerne, and yarrow, the object being to pierce the hard pan of clay sub-soil with their roots, and let the air down into it to do its fertilising work. This experiment, after some correspondence with Mr. Elliot, who most kindly replied to my queries, I determined to try upon the worst piece of all, about seven acres of land next to the wood, numbered 19 on the map.

Accordingly, having first been thoroughly 'bush-drained,' a process which I shall have occasion to describe later, down it went, the permanent pasture seeds, plus the deep-rooted 'rubbish,' being sown in a crop of barley.[1] In the two following years, 1895 and

---

[1] This is the mixture of seeds with which No. 19 was sown down four years ago, and that has been sown for permanent pasture with the barley on No. 21 this year (1898).

PROPORTIONS PER ACRE

Fiorin	1½ lbs.	Common Yellow Clover or Trefoil	1 lb.
Meadow Foxtail	3 ,,	Timothy or Meadow Catstail	2 lbs.
Crested Dogstail	1½ ,,	Rough Stalked Meadow Grass	3 ,,
Rough Cocksfoot	3 ,,	Alsike Clover	2 ,,
Hard Fescue	2 ,,	Perennial Red Clover	3 ,,
Tall Fescue	2 ,,	Perennial White Clover	2 ,,
Sheep's Fescue	2 ,,	Chicory	2 ,,
Meadow Fescue	3 ,,	Burnet	2 ,,
Perennial Rye Grass	3 ,,	Lucerne	2 ,,
Greater Birdsfoot Trefoil	4 ,,	Yarrow	1 lb.

45 lbs. in all. The four last mentioned are the deep-rooted herbs.

1896, Nos. 15 and 16 were also laid down respectively; but, fearing to put all our eggs into one basket, my steward, Hood, and I agreed to very largely modify the proportion of deep-rooted herbs. Last spring also the narrow two and a half acres marked No. 10 was laid down, as I desired to connect pasture No. 7 with the eight-acre far meadow, No. 11, so as to form a continuous belt of grass at this end of the farm. As this two acres (No. 10) is very good land, none of the herbs were sown with the grass seeds.

Now for the results so far as they have gone. Of the three heavy-land pieces, that which received the full dose of deep-rooted herbs (No. 19) looks far the best, although of course it must be remembered that it is older than No. 15 by one year, and than No. 16 by two years. Last summer, however, it threw up an abundant supply of herbage, on which, eked out with some cake, seven yearling steers and in-calf heifers lived for several months, although the season was exceptionally dry and distressing to pastures, especially to young pastures. No. 15, on the contrary, did not look or do very grandly, although it was laid down clean and drained, and its soil is no worse than that of No. 19. It was set for hay, but the grass seemed so short and poor that we determined to let it stand until the seeds were almost ripe, and then to feed it instead. This was done; with the result that the field is now a mat of tiny seedlings, sprung from the seeds knocked out by the cattle as they fed. Off No. 16 we took a crop of hay, as it is usual to do in the first year of a pasture; but, owing to the drought, it gave a poor return.

The general result of the experiment, it may interest Mr. Elliot to learn, should he ever chance to read of it, up to the present is strikingly in favour of his system; so much so, that I intend to lay down field No. 21 this spring exactly on the same principle. There is, however, one drawback which should be mentioned. These herbs—or perhaps it is only the chicory, the most valuable of them for this particular purpose of aëration, because, as I am told, the most deep-rooted—throw up tall and unsightly heads, which cattle feed round and sometimes refuse, with the result that a pasture sown with them looks as though it were infested by a crop of peculiarly vigorous docks. The best remedy for this unsightliness is, about midsummer, to send a man over the field with a scythe, charged to mow them down— after all, no great or costly task.

This year the field No. 19 is to come for hay ; and I hope to record in these pages the details of its progress, and of the success or failure of the crop. This pasture has now arrived at that age when, according to the prophets of ill, it might be expected to begin to die away, and its future is therefore of interest. I may add that it has never been manured, as have most of the new pastures here at Ditchingham, of which I shall speak when I come to write of this Home Farm, for the reason that we have never had any muck to spare. Most of it, however, has now received a coating of mud dug out from ponds and ditches, the best that I have to give it, and a great deal better than nothing at all.

Bordering my land is other land. I know not, or have forgotten, who farms it or owns it, but on this land are fields which, as I presume, have been 'laid down.' To me, looking over a neighbouring lane, the herbage seems to consist chiefly of water grass, black grass, elm suckers, and various weeds whereon even a rabbit would scarcely find a living. So far, at any rate, my new meadows are better, although the soil, presumably, is the same.

The truth is that in these parts, and under the present conditions of farming, it is, in many cases, quite useless to entrust the laying down of permanent pastures on difficult soils to tenants. The landlord finds the seed, no light expense, for it costs 30s. the acre, the tenant sows it, but from that hour nothing goes well Perhaps the land is not clean or drained, and with wet weed-infested soil a pasture is doomed from the beginning, for the moss and water grass will kill out the finer herbage. More probably, however, it is remorselessly mown, or sheep and horses are turned on within the first year or two, which bite and nibble the crowns out of the springing grass plants, causing them to die. Cattle only should be allowed to feed young pastures, for they sweep the herbage into their mouths with their tongues, and do not nip it down close. At least, the result is too frequently the same : a complaint that the pasture has 'gone off,' with a suggestion that the seed provided at so great a cost was bad. The truth is that the tenant has no personal interest in the success of the experiment ; it is the landlord's money he is 'kicking down,' not his own, and if that lot of seed fails, well, the landlord can find more. Moreover, it is probable that in his heart he does not believe in the laying down of heavy lands. It was not done in his father's time, or in his own youth, and so it must be wrong. Heavy lands were intended to grow corn. Therefore if the landlord has a fad on the point and wishes to make them grow grass instead, let him indulge it at his own expense—he at least is more wise, and is not going to bother about the matter.

The remainder of the land on the Moat Farm, excluding the pieces that have been or are to be laid down, is a heavy soil of fair quality, such as, with careful tillage, draining, and manuring, in all ordinary seasons should produce good crops of whatever is grown upon it. The particulars of the use to which each field is to be put this year will be given in due course (see Map, p. 13), also of the labour and horses employed upon the holding.

THE HOME FARM

I turn now to describe the land I farm here at Ditchingham. Ditchingham is a parish of about eleven hundred inhabitants, containing something over two thousand acres of land. In shape it is large and straggling, but the most of the population live at the Bungay end, for the village and the town meet at the bridge over the Waveney ; indeed, were it not for the sundering river it would be difficult to say where the one finishes and the other begins. The village, in the course of ages, must have shifted away from the church, which, in the beginning, was presumably its central point ; at least, not a single cottage now stands near to it. Here we have little difficulty in tracing the origin of the name of the place, since down on the 'Dam' are many ditches, and doubtless it was from some ancient dyke, cut in an age when dykes were few, that the village was christened Ditchingham, or the Hamlet of the Ditch. Not that the parish is all low land ; on the contrary, most of it is high. For instance, here where I live the wells are over ninety feet deep, at which depth in some dim age the sea once rolled. This I know, for when a few years since I was engaged in cleaning out a disused well, and in order to do this effectually caused it to be deepened by a few feet, we came upon sea sand containing thousands of shells, all of them common and familiar to us to-day. It was curious to look at them and wonder how many ages had gone by since they were washed to the lip of the tide and left there by the retreating waves. Very many, I suppose, for ninety feet of clay and other substances take a long time to deposit. But whenever it was, the climate was the climate of England as we know it, for had it been either tropical or arctic the shells would have differed in character.

From the northern part of the parish there is a gradual fall of the ground, till the level of the marshes is reached at its southern end. To the south-west however lies the great feature and beauty of the village, the lofty bank or incline known as the Bath Hills, and in more ancient times as the Earl's Vineyard, a slope eighty or ninety feet high, which without doubt was once the bank of an inland fiord or tidal water. Now the space beneath is drained by the gentle winding Waveney, beyond whose stream lies a wide expanse of 400 acres of pasturage and gorse known as Outney, or Bungay Common. On the opposing slopes above the Waveney, which encircles this common, lie Stow Park, once a home of the King's deer, and the wooded fields of Earsham, while to the south appear the red roofs of Bungay. I have travelled a great way about the world in my time and studied much scenery, but I do not remember anything more quietly and consistently beautiful than this view over Bungay Common seen from the Earl's Vineyard, or, indeed, from any point of vantage on its encircling hills. For the most part of the year the plain below is golden with gorse, but it

is not on this alone that the sight depends for beauty, or on the
green of the meadows and the winding river edged with lush
marshes that in spring are spotted by yellow marigolds and
purple with myriads of cuckoo flowers.   They all contribute to it,
as do the grazing cattle, the gabled distant roofs, and the church
spires, but I think that the prospect owes its peculiar charm to the
constant changes of light which sweep across its depths.   At every
season of the year, at every hour of the day it is beautiful, but
always with a different beauty.   Of that view I do not think that
any lover of Nature could tire, because it is never quite the same.

The lamentable thing is that with such a prospect at our
doors only one house in the neighbourhood, Upland Hall, has
any benefit from it, except indeed Ditchingham Lodge, which
is the property of this estate, and stands at the bottom of the
hill almost on a bend of the river.   Had the builders of this
house where I write, for instance, chosen to place it 400 yards
further back, as they might very easily have done, it would have
commanded what I believe to be the finest view in Norfolk, since
from that spot the eye travels not only over the expanse of Bungay
Common and its opposing slopes, but down the valley of the
Waveney to Beccles town and tower.   But it would seem that in
the time of the Georges the people who troubled their heads
about beautiful prospects were not many.   The country was
lonely then, and the neighbourhood of the Norwich road had
more attractions than any view.   Along that road passed the
coaches, bringing a breath of the outer world into the quiet
village, and the last news of the wars ; also, did any member of
the household propose to travel by them, it was easy for one of
the men-servants to wheel his baggage in a barrow to the gate.

But people did not travel much or far from home.   The constant intermarriages amongst neighbouring families in those days
show this plainly.   Also, even such a small place as Bungay, with its
population of three or four thousand, had a winter season.   An aged
relative, who still lives close by, tells me that she can well remember
as a young lady being carried in a sedan chair to card parties at

the assembly rooms in the Tuns Inn, also how gentle families living so near as the Rectory at Hedenham, that is within three miles, used to migrate to a town house at Bungay for the winter ! [1]

To return to the Bath Hills. Scenery is not the only advantage of these slopes, which are also the warmest and most sheltered spot in this part of Norfolk. It is no exaggeration to say that there are days in spring when, here on the top of the hill, a man needs an ulster, whereas he may sit in the Lodge garden coatless, and listen to the east wind howling and moaning in the Scotch firs on the crest of the hill above. Any farmer will understand the value of such a place for sheltering early lambs in spring, the only question being whether the land with its singular advantages of situation could not be put to a better use. There is little doubt but that one of the Earl Bigods had a vineyard here, for the traditional name still lingers. Also that vineyard was growing in the thirteenth century, as Blomefield quotes a deed uuder which William de Pirnho, in the 24th of Henry III., released to Roger, Earl of Norfolk, by fine, his right of fishery ' from the mill of Cliff and the Bridge of Bungay,' and the Earl granted to him a fishery ' from Bungay Bridge to the Earl's Vineyard.' Often I have wondered what kind of wine they made at this vineyard, and who was so bold as to drink it ; but since I have heard that some enterprising person has taken to the cultivation of the grape in Wales with such success that—so says the wondrous tale—he sells his home-made champagne for 84*s*. the dozen, it has occurred to me that the Bigods knew more than we imagine about the possibilities of vine-growing in England. Or it may chance that the climate was more genial in those days, although this is very doubtful.

It is, however, by no means certain that there was not a vineyard on these slopes so late as 1738. In that year a certain John King, an apothecary of Bungay, wrote a very curious essay on hot and cold bathing. It appears from this scarce tract, of

[1] Mrs. Jane Hartcup, *née* Margitson, the lady alluded to above, died in October 1898.

which I have been so fortunate as to secure a perfect copy, that Mr. King was then the owner of the Vineyard Hills, and of some of the further slopes now belonging to Captain Meade, of Earsham. Here, a hundred yards or so beyond the boundary of this property, he discovered a mineral spring, 'which,' he says, 'at length I found in my own Land, at the foot of a large and deep Hill, whose oblique Height is not common; it's most curiously adorn'd with many Sorts of Trees standing in so handsome a Manner, as form of themselves a beautiful Landskip, the opposite side is a fine delightful Stream, encompassing a large spacious Common, whose Prospect is little inferior to any.' It will be observed that here there is no mention of a vineyard, but in the illustration of Bungay Common and the Bath House as they appeared in 1738, which is here reproduced from the frontispiece of Mr. King's book, (please observe the double gallows and the fine coach), can be seen vines planted on the hillside slope. Also in an Appendix a letter is quoted written (apparently) to Mr. King by 'a certain Gentleman of superior abilities,' who does not sign his name. This gentleman in turn quotes from a 'letter to a young lady by a Gentleman at your *Bath*, whither, amongst many arguments to invite her thither, he describes the Beauties of the Place in the following Manner :

' "Those Lovely Hills which incircle the flowery Plain are variegated with all that can ravish the astonish'd Sight; they arise from the winding Mazes of the River Waveney, enriched with the utmost variety the watry Element is capable of producing. Upon the Neck of this Peninsula the Castle and Town of Bungay (now startled at its approaching Grandeur) is situated on a pleasing Ascent to view the Pride of Nature on the other Side, which the Goddesses have chose for their earthly Paradise, where the Sun at its first Appearance makes a kindly Visit to a steep and fertile Vineyard, richly stored with the choicest Plants from *Burgundy*, *Champaigne*, *Provence* and whatever the *East* can furnish us with.

' "Near the Bottom of this is placed the Grotto or Bath itself, beautified on one side with Oziers, Groves and Meadows, on the other with Gardens, Fruits, shady Walks and all the Decorations of a rural Innocence.

' "The Building is designedly plain and neat, because the least attempt of artful Magnificence would by alluring the Eyes of Strangers, deprive them of those profuse Pleasures which Nature has already provided.

' "As to the Bathing there 'tis a Mixture of all that *England, Paris* or *Rome* could ever boast of; no one's refused a kind Reception, Honour and Generosity reign throughout the whole, the Trophies of the Poor invite the Rich, and their more dazzling Assemblies compel the Former." '

I make no apologies for transcribing 'the Former,' since it deserves *Preservation* even in an age rich in *Style*. Did a young man write it who sincerely desired that his adored should share with him the pleasures of nature at Bungay, and at the same time benefit her health in its peerless baths? Or did the late Mr. King, with the mundane view of advertising the said baths, put these glowing words into the mouth of an imaginary swain writing to a fancied mistress? Alas! now that Mr. King, baths, lover and lady have alike vanished, and only the hillside and the spring remain, the question never can be answered.

But in this superb epistle a vineyard is mentioned; moreover the kinds of grapes planted therein are specified. Was this vineyard, furnished with the fruits of the ' East,' an effort of the imagination suggested by the traditional name of the place (now oddly enough superseded by a new name taken from the tradition of Mr. King's bath), or did it, as the picture suggests, really exist in the year 1738? *Quien sabe?* as they say in Mexico. There have, in my time, been several old men in Ditchingham whose grandfathers may have been living in 1738, yet I never heard from them any tale of a vineyard on the Bath Hills. But this proves nothing.

Whether or not the vineyard was there, certainly the spring was, whose healthful properties (according to Mr. King, who gives his cases) wrought so many cures a hundred and seventy years ago, for it still bubbles from the foot of the hillside. Even in my day some traces of the bath remained, but they have vanished now, and nothing is left but the excavation which once held the water. That this water is mineral there can be no doubt, for it leaves a red stain on the mud, caused, I suppose, by the presence of iron. It is moreover peculiarly delicious to drink ; but notwithstanding these advantages, no one has ever taken the trouble to have it analysed. If this were done, possibly Bungay might once more be 'startled at its approaching grandeur,' and property in these parts would increase in value—a consummation devoutly to be wished.

But Bungay has bygone grandeurs of its own. Its name has been supposed to be derived from Bon Gué or Good Ford, but as the town was called Bungay before ever a Norman set foot in England, this interpretation will not hold. More probable is that suggested to me by the Rev. J. Denny Gedge, that the origin of the name is Bourne-gay or Boundary Ford. Or the prefix 'Bun' may, as he hazards also, have been translated from 'placenta,' a sacred cake, indicating, perhaps—but this is my suggestion—that in old times Bungay was the town that pre-eminently 'took the cake.' Mayhap, for in philology anything might chance ; but if so, alas ! it takes it no longer.

Bungay Castle, whereof the ruins are now part of an inn garden, was built by one of the Bigods. Here King Stephen besieged Hugh Bigod and took the castle. This Hugh was a second time besieged at Bungay by Henry II., to whom, his garrison of five hundred men having deserted him, he was forced to surrender. Suckling prints in full the spirited old ballad that tells the tale of this defeat. Here are a few verses of it :

> The King had sent for Bigod bold
> In Essex whereat he lay,
> But Lord Bigod laughed at his Poursuivant,
> And stoutly thus did say :
> Were I in my castle of Bungay,
> Upon the River of Waveney,
> I would no care for the King of Cockney.

. . . .

When the news was brought to London town,
How Sir Bigod did jest and sing,
Say you to Lord Hew of Norfolk,
Said Henry, our English King,
Though you be in your castle of Bungay,
Upon the River of Waveney,
I'll make you care for the King of Cockney.

At last comes the lamentable end of Sir Bigod's boasting :

Sir Hugh took three score sacks of gold,
And flung them over the wall,
Says go your ways in the Devil's name,
Yourself and your merry men all !
But leave me my castle of Bungay,
Upon the River of Waveney,
And I'll pay my shot to the King of Cockney.

His shot he paid sure enough—one thousand marks of gold and the destruction of his 'castle of Bungay.' This, however, was rebuilt by his descendant, Roger Bigod, in 1289, about a hundred years after its demolition, under special license from Edward I., and it is the ruins of the second castle which we see to-day.

There was also a Benedictine Nunnery at Bungay dedicated to God and the Holy Cross, of which some few fragments still remain, founded in the year 1160 by Roger de Glanville and his wife Gudruda, the widow of Roger Bigod. I have in my possession a deed executed by Roger de Huntingfeld about 1295, under which he 'settles, gives, and concedes, and by this charter confirms to God and the Church of the Holy Cross of Bungaie and the holy people who serve God in it, Alveva, the wife of Roger Brunllan, and Thomas, his firstborn son, with the tenement which he holds of me in this town of Medefeld . . . for the health of the souls of my father and mother and of my ancestors and successors.'

Here I append a translation of the full text of this document, which is worth transcribing, although the original Latin, with its curious contractions beautifully written out by some thirteenth-century lawyer, is interesting only to antiquaries :

To all Christ's faithful, to whom this present writing comes, Roger of Huntingfield wishes health. Let our whole acquaintance know that I have given and granted, and by this present charter of mine have confirmed, to God and to the Church of the Holy Cross at Bungay and to the nuns there serving God, Alveva, the wife of Roger Brunllan, and Thomas his firstborn son, with their whole tenement which they held of me in the village of Metfield, of the purtenances of Mendham, for free, and pure, and perpetual charity for the salvation of the soul of my father, and of my mother, and of my ancestors and successors. Saving the service of (our) lord the King, to wit, for ward, one penny a year on a thousand shillings, and for scutage of (our) lord the King on twenty shillings two pence, and on more, more, and on less, less.

And that this donation and confirmation may remain firm and settled I have strengthened it by the muniment of my seal for myself and for my heirs.

These being witnesses: William of Huntingfield, Walter Malet, Peter Walter, Robert of Huntingfield, William of Corton, Hubert Walter, Alan of Withersdale, William Cantelow, G(eoffrey?) of Drokes, Adam the son of Walter, Walter King, Adam the monk, William the monk, Martin the monk, Godfrey of Linburne.

Strange times indeed when a woman and her son could be given as serfs to a nunnery to benefit various souls, disembodied or still to be embodied. This ancient and most interesting document still carries the perfect seal of Roger de Huntingfeld, which, as he states, he affixes to it to bind himself and his heirs. On the next page is a reproduction of it as it came from his hand—all that remains to-day of the pious and once upon a time very important Roger. Well, six centuries hence, of how many of us will there be left even as much as this? Few, indeed, I think.

This deed passed to me in a curious manner. Some years ago I went into the shop of a chemist at Kensington with a prescription, and left my address, to which it was to be posted. In due course the medicine arrived, and with it the original charter of Roger de Huntingfeld. The chemist, Mr. W. H. Stickland, into whose hands the parchment had come, I forget how, knowing that it had to do with Bungay, and that I lived in the neighbourhood, most kindly sent it to me. I can assure him that his gift was appreciated; indeed, I would swallow many potions to win such another.

Bungay in the old days was famous as the seat of an industry for the copper bottoming of ships, though what sort of ships they were that could sail up the Waveney to Bungay staithe I know not. Certainly they could not have drawn much water ; but then, even

SEAL OF ROGER DE HUNTINGFELD

the ocean-going vessels of three hundred years ago were very small. Had they not been so Queen Elizabeth could scarcely have spoken of her 'seaport of Norwich,' as she does when giving leave to Hollanders of the reformed faith to take refuge there from religious persecution. The stranger of to-day, contemplating the muddy waters of the Wensum, with its burden of wherries, would scarcely think of describing Norwich as a seaport. But the ships that used it in those times were large enough to help to beat back the Armada.

There still lingers, or lingered a few years ago, a vague belief that the devil is on rare occasions to be met with in these parts, and especially on Hollow Hill in this parish, in the concrete shape of the black dog of Bungay. Indeed, once I met him myself at this very spot, looking saucer-eyed in the twilight and clanking an appropriate chain, but he turned out to be an escaped retriever. The original animal, however, was a dog or a devil of mettle. His most striking recorded appearance was in the midst of a terrific thunderstorm on Sunday, August 4, 1577, in the church of St. Mary. Hear what one Abraham Fleming says on the subject, or rather a short extract from his voluminous report :

'This Black Dog or the Divel in such a likeness (God hee knoweth all who worketh all) running all along down the body of the Church with great swiftness and incredible haste among the people, in a visible forme and shape, passed between two persons as they were kneeling on their knees and occupied in prayer as it seemed, wrung the necks of them bothe at one instant clene backward, insomuch that even in a moment where they kneeled they stra'gely died. This is a wonderful example of God's wrath, no doubt to terrfie us, that we might feai him for his justice, or putting back our footsteps from the paths of sin, to love him for his mercy.'

After this the Black Dog, pursuing his violent career, gave another membei of the congregation 'such a gripe in the back that therewithall he was presently drawn togither and shrunk up,' as it were a piece of lether schorched in a hot fire ; or as the mouth of a purse or bag drawn togither with a string.'

Next the Dog went up to the roof, where he greatly alarmed the clerk, who was cleaning out the gutter, and so away. 'O Lord,' ends the worthy but credulous Fleming, 'how wonderful art Thou in all Thy works.' Wonderful indeed ! Still, there is some truth in the story, since the registers of St. Mary record that in this year 'John Fuller and Adam Walker slayne in the tempest, in the belfry in the tyme of prayer, upon the Lord's Day, ye 11th of August.'

To return to the Bath Hills, from which I have wandered a full mile. Beyond the site of the Earl's Vineyard and the kitchen garden of the Lodge are some acres of woodland. This, which has for many years been the constant haunt of trespassers, boys bird-nesting, foot passengers escaping into it from the muddy right of way above, poachers seeking pheasants' eggs, and amorous couples, I have now enclosed with a veritable fortification of the strongest and most prickly barbed wire that money will buy, whereby I hope to abate the nuisance. My chief object, however, is to keep the place perfectly quiet, so that it may become the home of all

sorts of birds and wild things. In this attempt I think I ought
to be successful, since this warm slope, with the stream at its foot,
is already favoured by them, and beasts and birds very soon collect
where they find none to do them harm. Already there are otters
on the river, and I thought of putting down some badgers, but have
not done so, as I am told that they are somewhat destructive to
gardens. At least the birds, of which there are already many
varieties, will multiply, as the wood is not too deep for them.
Birds do not like a large wood, and rarely build in its centre,
whence they have far to fly for food.

By the foot of the Vineyard Hills, at a little distance from the
garden, stands the Lodge, a quaint red-brick residence of which
some part at least is very ancient. Indirectly this house is connected with the famous French writer and politician, the Vicomte
de Chateaubriand, and directly with a young lady whom he admired
or who admired him. She was the daughter of the Reverend Mr.
Ives, who was rector of St. Margaret's, Ilketshall, but lived in
Bungay. This excellent shepherd of souls, by the way, is reported
to have been one of the hardest-headed men of his time, that is,
he could drink almost anybody else under the table. So great was
his fame that it excited the envy of a Duke of Norfolk of that day,
who also had a reputation to keep up. They met, they drank;
bottle after bottle of port disappeared, till at length towards
midnight victory declared for the Church, and his conquered
Grace bowed and fell, yes, he slid senseless beneath the board.
Then came the marvel which, when he recovered, impressed the
Duke so much that it moved him, so says the story, to present his
reverend victor with a living. Clear-eyed and steady, Mr. Ives
rose from his chair, rang the bell, ordered of the astonished butler
a glass of *brandy and water*, *hot and stiff*—after all the port, hot
and stiff, by Bacchus !—drank it, and strolled quietly home.

This tale was told to me many years since by an aged gentleman now dead, and I have no doubt but that in substance, at any
rate, it is true. Seventy or eighty years ago even it does not seem
to have been common for the élite of the Bungay neighbourhood

to return sober from a dinner-party. On these festive occasions each man's wife, indeed, was expected to support and see him home.

When in 1793 Chateaubriand, whom, so says local tradition, his pupils used to call Monsieur 'Shatterbrain,' came to England as a refugee in the days of the Terror, he drifted down to Bungay, how or why I do not know, where he supported himself by giving French lessons in the neighbourhood. Amongst his pupils was Charlotte Ives, the daughter and only child of the hard-drinking parson, a very pretty and charming young lady with large dark eyes which are still remembered in this neighbourhood. The exiled Frenchman was tender, and Charlotte, it seems, was impressionable; at any rate, she welcomed his advances, and being a young woman of determined mind, persuaded her well-to-do parents to overlook the *émigré's* lack of means and position and to put no obstacle in his amorous path. Time went on, but although the attentions continued, as nothing tangible came of them, Mrs. Ives, the mother, thinking that he did not speak because of a natural delicacy that sprang from his lack of fortune, took Chateaubriand aside in the old red house in Bridge Street, and explained to him frankly that as they were mutually attached, and as their daughter would be well provided for, his misfortunes need be no obstacle to their union. The gallant Frenchman looked up and sighed, then he looked down and murmured : ' Hélas ! Madame, je suis désolé ; *mais je suis marié* ! ' For all the time this poetic soul could boast a wife in France !

In the end the young lady, getting over her disappointment, married a sailor who became Admiral Sutton, and lived for many years as a wife and widow at the Lodge. When in after days Chateaubriand returned to England as the Ambassador of France, a meeting took place between him and his old love, Mrs. Sutton. At first it was arranged that they should see each other here at Ditchingham, but in the end she went to London, and what passed at the interview I do not know.

About this Mrs. Sutton is told another rather interesting story. When she was a widow at the Lodge she engaged for her sons a certain tutor named Colonel A., who for various reasons became very distasteful to the lads in question. In his habits Colonel A. was free and easy, and as the dark stain upon the white marble still shows, or showed not long ago, it was his graceful habit while instructing the mind of youth to rest his head against the mantel-piece and prop his legs upon a chair. In due course Colonel A., the tutor, died, and, much against the will of her sons, Mrs. Sutton, who, as I have said, was of a determined character, insisted upon burying him in the Sutton vault in Ditchingham churchyard. Time went on and Mrs. Sutton died also, whereon the sons, taking the opportunity of the vault being opened, dragged out the body of their unfortunate mentor by night, and thrust it into a hole which they had dug somewhere in the graveyard. That this tale is substantially correct I have satisfied myself by inquiry.

The rest of the Bath Hills to the south of the Lodge dwelling-house are clothed with Scotch firs and other trees, below which lies a stretch of grass land running down to the river. This grass, most of which I let, is not of first-rate quality, though good enough in dry seasons, because of the floods which spread over it in times of heavy rain. In 1879, the first of our really bad years, the floods were so high that many of the trees were killed, though some of them took a dozen years to die. Last year also we had a heavy flood in February, but it was of brief duration. Indeed the floods are neither so frequent nor so prolonged as they used to be, either because the millers below are more merciful in the matter of holding up the water with their sluice-gates, or because the bridge at Beccles has been widened, allowing the stream to escape quicker to the sea. Round Beccles itself, however, I believe that the water has been out more than usual, owing to the high tides, which dam up the mouth of the river. Never has such a time for high tides been known, and the gale of December last will long be remembered on the east coast for its terrible amount of damage. The sight close to a house which I possess at Kessingland, a place near Lowestoft, was something to remember, for here and at Pakefield the high cliff has been taken away by the thousand tons. In such a tide the fierce scour from the north licks the sand cliff and hollows it out till the clay stratum above it falls, and is washed into the ocean. Fortunately for me, my house is protected by a sea-wall, and though the water got behind the end of this, it did no further damage ; but with property that was not so fortified the case was very different —it has gone in mouthfuls. Old residents on the coast declare that no such tide has been known within the present century, and it is to be hoped that there will not be another for the next century. But these phenomenal events have an unpleasant way of repeating themselves, and if this happens, the loss and desolation will be very great—greater even than that of the December gale.

For generations the sea has been encroaching on this coast. So long ago as the time of Queen Elizabeth it is said that three churches went over the cliff at Dunwich in a single Sunday afternoon, yet during all this time no concerted effort has been made for the common protection. If we were Dutchmen the matter would have been different, but here in rural England, unless they are forced to it by Act of Parliament, it is almost impossible to oblige people to combine to win future profits or ward off future dangers. It is chiefly for this reason that I do not believe that creameries and butter factories will be successfully established in our time—at any rate in this part of East Anglia—for to secure success I imagine that common effort and mutual support would be necessary, and to such things our farmers are not accustomed. Many of them, to all appearance, would prefer individual failure to the achievement of a corporate victory.

The great tide of the December gale was followed by other high tides, luckily unaccompanied by north winds of unusual strength, and therefore not so destructive ; but the effect of these tides does not reach so far as Bungay. Here our floods result from rain only, and of rain we have had little to speak of since the beginning of last spring.

Although there is a proportion of heavy soil on it, but none so heavy that it cannot be drained with pipes, the land which I culti-

vate in this parish is comparatively speaking light. Not that it is
a light-land farm in the sense that some of the Norfolk country is
light—that in the neighbourhood of Brandon, for instance—but on
the whole it is soil that would do better in a wet season than in a
dry one. And for the last few years it has been dreadfully dry, at
least at those periods of the season when rain was most wanted.

This land at Ditchingham, of which I propose to treat in the
following pages, is made up of four separate holdings: 1. That
portion of my own property which I farm, amounting to about one
hundred and forty-six acres, whereof about ninety-six are pasture;
2. The hired farm known as Baker's, taken on this last November,
and amounting to about fifty-six acres, of which eight acres are
pasture; 3. The hired farm known as All Hallows, of nearly forty-
four acres, of which about seven are pasture; 4. Glebe land
amounting to fourteen acres, no pasture. Therefore, with sundry
enclosures, in Ditchingham I am farming about two hundred and
sixty acres of land, of which one hundred and twelve acres are
pasture, some of it laid down within the last few years. On this
farm the stock at the beginning of the year 1898 was:

Cattle above two years old, including twenty cows	34
Other cattle, including calves	18
Sheep, including two rams	50
Pigs	33
Horses and colts	11
Total head	146

The labour employed here at Ditchingham at the beginning of the
year was one working steward, eight men, one boy.

My farming began in the year 1889, when, letting off the rest
of it in small parcels, I took about a hundred and twenty acres in
hand on the occasion of the tenant giving up the farm. Then the
land which I took over, naturally good for the most part, was in so
scandalous a condition that now, after eight years' cleaning and
manuring, it has only just recovered its fertility. The heart had
been dragged out of it and very little put into it in return; for

instance, if I remember right, the back lawn had been mown nine years in succession. Moreover, the arable was for the most part a mass of docks and other weeds—indeed, such was its condition that after vainly attempting to clean one piece for two years, we had to abandon the effort and 'summer till' it. Another field of four and a half acres I let off. Meeting the tenant a while afterwards, I asked him how he was getting on, whereon he informed me, almost with tears, that he had spent *fourteen pounds* in labour in getting the docks out of that field ! In proof of his words he showed me the docks themselves, with salt thrown over them, heaped in a long 'hale,' like beet, where in due course they rotted, to be put back on to the land as manure. To-day that close is a pleasure to look at. The occupier farms it in four shifts, as though it were a tiny farm, and not a weed can I discover on it, for every bit of black grass even is forked out. The result is that he grows more on his four acres than many people do on six or eight.

Farms coming on their owners' hands in the condition of that which I am describing are not rare nowadays, having been reduced to it by the poverty of the tenant or by deliberate 'land-sucking.' Even in these times a deal of money can be made in four years or so out of a farm, provided that it is in good heart at the time when the 'land-sucker' commences operations. Let us say that he has taken on a four years' lease a holding which has been worked for a long period by its former owner, some gentleman deceased, or that he has decided to give up his tenancy after the expiration of another three or four years. From that moment, if he be a person of this sharp-dealing order, the land will be run with its labour bill brought down to an irreducible minimum ; the hay and straw will be sold off it instead of going back into the soil as manure, weeds will be left to seed and drains to choke and 'holls' uncleared, and many other things will be done, or left undone, that are known only to the experienced land-sucker.

Then Heaven help the unfortunate landlord who finds himself in the possession of acres so deteriorated that nobody will pay a rent for them, for it will need capital, skill, and six or eight years of time to bring them round; acres which, very possibly, he cannot afford to face the loss of farming himself.

There is a great deal of talk about compensation by the landlord for the unexhausted improvements of tenants, but one never hears anything about compensation to the landlord for their inexhaustible dis-improvements. Doubtless that unfortunate and much-abused person has a theoretic remedy, but evidently it is one which in practice cannot be enforced. Even with my present experience I could undertake to leave the land I hire in a scandalous condition without giving any of my various landlords a cause of action against me which would be recognised as worthy of damages by an ordinary jury. Obviously this sort of interpretation of agreements is a new thing that came in with the bad times. The old stamp of tenant would have starved before he treated the land and its owner thus, or, if here and there one found a man of a different kidney, the landlord would have given him notice promptly, assured that his place could be filled by a person of different views. But those days have gone, and other days have come, when the majority of landlords are not in a position to turn away a tenant, however bad he is, so long as he pays something resembling a rent. It is a case of *væ victis*, at any rate in our Eastern Counties, although fortunately there are still tenants who, being men of probity, take a different view of their obligations.

But however bad the state of the farm, the landlord who is called upon to take it in hand will find that the valuation upon it amounts to a very considerable sum of money. This 'valuation,' it may be explained, is the amount due to the outgoing tenant. If he is under 'Norfolk covenants' he is paid by the crops, if he is under the 'Suffolk covenants' he is paid by the ploughings. In the first case he will generally find that the farm has been singularly productive during the preceding year, for with skill and knowledge even a holding in the worst of order can be made temporarily productive. Thus a boy with a bag of certain sorts of artificial manure, such as nitrate of soda, and a teaspoon in any ordinary season can go far towards securing a large total of bulky root, however coarse and watery in fibre. One way and another also a very considerable tonnage of hay may be reckoned on, and if the tenant has not found it necessary to muck his fields for the last twelve or fifteen months, there are piles of manure, most of it mere dirty rain-washed straw, which will add up satisfactorily. For instance, on this farm of about two hundred acres, when I took it over, the valuations paid in cash amounted to 382*l.* I suggest that it would be equitable if the docks and other dis-improvements had been valued *per contra.*

When I had farmed about one hundred and thirty to one hundred and forty acres of my own land for some five years I hired the small farm of forty-three acres known as All Hallows, which runs into mine. This land, belonging as it does to an institution in the parish which had been working it, was in good heart and order; for which reason, and because from its position it was convenient to me to take it, I consented to pay for it the high rent, as things are here, of 70*l.* Of this sum, however, about 19*l.* comes back from the rent of the farmhouse, which I let off as a dwelling, and of two cottages that go with it. So the net rent of the land is about 23*s.* 6*d.* per acre. At the same time I hired about fourteen and a half acres of glebe, very light and gravelly soil, though not unproductive in a wet season. This land, which for years had been farmed by a poor old gentleman who had not the means to work it, was in an awful condition; indeed, it is only just beginning to recover heart. I think that I am now paying for it a rent of 12*l.*

Also, last autumn I hired from a neighbour, a gentleman who bought it on the double bankruptcy of its former owner and of the tenant who worked it, another small farm in the parish known as 'Baker's.' This farm on the whole is very fair land, with good buildings, but it has been sadly dealt by for the last few years; therefore docks and other weeds are many, and its general condition is low, with scarcely a sound gate or a holding fence in it. On every acre of it, indeed, is written the old story of borrowed capital and insufficient stock and labour. Yet I remember that six or seven years ago, when a former owner, now dead, had it in hand, this land used to be some of the best farmed and most productive in the parish, as, if I live and continue to work it, I trust it may be again.   At the least, however, it will take four years to pull

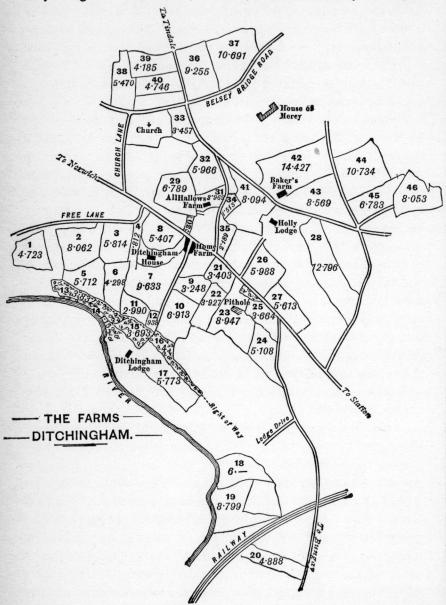

Pastures	Arable	Present Crop (1898)	Last Year's Crop (1897)
1. 4·723	21. 3·403	Vetches	Oats
2. 8·062	22. 3·927	Root	Wheat
3. 5·814	23. 8·947	Wheat and Roots	Beans and Oats
4. ·812	24. 5·108	Sheep's Feed	Layer
5. 5·712	25. 3·664	Barley	Root
6. 4·298	26. 5·988	Beans	Barley
7. 9·633	27. 5·613	Barley	Root
8. 5·407	28. 12·796	Root and Barley	Wheat and Root
9. 3·248			
10. 6·913			
11. 2·990			
12. ·938			
13. 3·832			
14. 1·162			
15. 3·693			
16. 4			
17. 5·773			
18. 6			
19. 8·799			
20. 4·888			
96·697	49·446		

Total, 146·143   Homestead, ·78

Pastures	Arable	Present Crop (1898)	Last Year's Crop (1897)
30. { ·705 [1]	29. 6·789	Root	Wheat
& { 1·088 [1]	32. 5·966	Wheat	Beans
31. { 1·100 [1]	33. 3·457	Barley	Beet and Carrot
34. 1·076	36. 9·255	Barley	Root
35. { 1·513	37. 10·691	Layer and Pease	Barley
{ 2·189			—
7·671	36·158		

[1] Orchard, stackyard, meadow, &c.

Pasture . . . 7·671
Arable . . . 36·158
Total . . . 43·829 and Homestead
House let at 10l.   Two Cottages let 9l.
Rent 70l.

GLEBE LAND

Arable	Present Crop	Last Year's Crop
38. 5·470	Root and Potato	Barley
39. 4·185	Oats	Layer
40. 4·746	Oats	Layer
14·401		

Rent, 12l.

BAKER'S FARM

Pastures	Arable	Present Crop	Last Year's Crop
	41. 8·094	Barley	Roots
	42. 14·427	Wheat and Oats	Pease and Layer
	43. 8·569	Pease and Beans	Corn
	44. 10·734	Roots	Corn
	45. 6·783	Layer	Barley
46. 8·053	48·607		

Pasture . . . 8·053
Arable . . . 48·607
Total . . . 56·660
Homestead, ·512
Rent, 44l.

SUMMARY

	Pastures	Arable	Total Acreage
Ditchingham Home Farm . . .	96·697	49·446	146·143
All Hallows . . .	7·671	36·158	43·829
Glebe Land . . .	—	14·401	14·401
Baker's . . .	8·053	48·607	56·660
Bedingham . . .	112·421	148·612	261·033
	50·869	53·029	103·898
	163·290	201·641	364·931

Net rent paid, 111l. 10s.

it round. For this land I pay 15*s*. per acre, or about 40*l*. for the first year, and 17*s*. 6*d*. an acre, or about 46*l*. 10*s*. for future years.

Lastly I hire the shooting rights over a large wood of 120 acres, known as Tindale Wood and belonging to Lord de Saumarez. This is not strictly a farming item, but as a little shooting is generally included in the record of 'A Farmer's Year' (if the state of agriculture supplies him with means to pay for it) it may as well be mentioned in the schedule.

And now after these introductory remarks, and before we proceed to follow the fortunes of my farming month by month, I give here (*vide* p. 36) a sketch map of the Ditchingham farms, whereon each field is numbered and marked with the various areas. By means of this map any reader, who cares to trouble to do so, can trace the fate of each individual close throughout the year, and see which of the crops succeed and which of them fail. The book, I trust, will tell him why they succeeded and why they failed.

Next follows an important statement. A record of a farm such as I propose would have little practical value unless the reader were informed of the amount of capital invested, and instructed generally as to the financial position. Therefore I print here a profit and loss account for Bedingham and Ditchingham since I took over each holding, and cash accounts showing the amount of capital invested.

Ditchingham. Cash Account. Michaelmas, 1897

DR.				CR.			
To Capital :	£ s. d.	£ s. d.		By Valuation at Michaelmas, 1897 :			
Oct. 1889	1,000 0 0				£ s. d.	£ s. d.	
Jan. 1890	250 0 0			Covenants	283 4 6		
Jan. 1895	250 0 0			Horses .	187 0 0		
				Stock, &c.	611 2 6		
	1,500 0 0			Implements	145 0 0		
Less paid to				Corn . .	276 8 0		
Estate Account July						1,502 15 0	
2, 1897 . .	200 0 0			,, Cash at Bank . . .		228 17 7	
		1,300 0 0		,, Mr. Haggard's account, 1896[2] . . .		54 13 9	
,, Balance from Profit and Loss Account . . .		540 13 7		,, Mr. Haggard's account, 1897[2] . . .		54 7 3	
		1,840 13 7[1]				1,840 13 7	

[1] To this total must now be added 103*l*. paid last November for valuation on Baker's, bringing it to 1,943*l*. 13*s*. 7*d*. [2] Since paid.

DITCHINGHAM
Profit and Loss on each year

	Profit £ s. d.	Loss £ s. d.
1890	—	140 17 5
1891	98 3 8	—
1892	62 11 1	—
1893	—	32 11 10
1894	114 19 8	—
1895	—	0 10 6
1896 . . . . . :	186 5 9	—
1897 . , ...	252 13 2	—
	714 13 4	173 19 9
Loss .	173 19 9	

Net profit on eight years . . 540 13 7

Bedingham.   Cash Account.   Michaelmas, 1897

Dr. £ s. d.		Cr. £ s. d.
To Capital 700 0 0	By Valuation of Live and Dead Stock, Covenants, and Corn, Michaelmas, 1897	655 17 0
	,, Cash at Bank . . .	6 17 11
	,, Mr. Haggard's account[1]	20 6 7
	,, Balance (loss) . . .	16 18 6
700 0 0		700 0 0

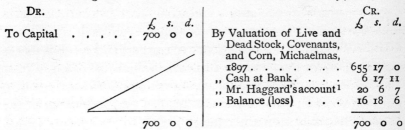

BEDINGHAM
Profit and Loss on each year

	Profit £ s. d.	Loss £ s. d.
1895	—	119 3 5
1896	26 5 8	—
1897	75 19 3	—
		102 4 11

Net loss on three years 16 18 6

From these accounts it will be seen that in my three years' farming at Bedingham I have up to Michaelmas 1897 incurred a net loss of 16*l.* 18*s.* 6*d.*   To this deficit, however, should be added loss of rent at say 10*s.* per acre for three years—153*l.* (in 1868 it let for 135*l.* *a year* !), and loss of interest on 700*l.* at 5 per cent. for three years—105*l.*   So, without the advantage of winning a daily

---

[1] Since paid.

livelihood out of the place, as a farmer is supposed to do—at any rate, to a very large extent—the loss on this farm for the three years is 274*l*. 18*s*. 6*d*.

When we come to the Ditchingham Farm the case is a little better, for, as the statement shows, there is a net profit on eight years' farming of 540*l*. 13*s*. 7*d*. But here, again, things are not so good as they look. Thus the rent on 146 acres (the amount of my own land that I farm in this parish, for the rent of the rest appears and is included in the accounts, and must not be reckoned) at 1*l*. per acre for eight years amounts to 1,168*l*., and the interest at 5 per cent. of 1,250*l*. for eight years, plus the interest on 250*l*. for two and a half years, amounts to 531*l*. 5*s*., just about the net profit shown. Therefore, again without allowing anything for living, since, together with the cost of all carting, &c., every article I have from the farm is religiously paid for at market prices, it would seem that the net loss for the eight years is 1,158*l*. 11*s*. 5*d*. But that is not all of it, for here and at Bedingham there has been at least 500*l*. expended on the buildings, or, writing off the 200*l*. paid to the estate account in July last against that expenditure, let us say 300*l*. This brings up the total out-of-pocket amount to 1,458*l*. 11*s*. 5*d*., or, adding on the Bedingham loss of 274*l*. 18*s*. 6*d*., to a grand total of 1,733*l*. 9*s*. 11*d*.

This result does not seem encouraging to those about to farm.

Of course, however, it would be easy to pick holes in these figures. Thus the 300*l*. for buildings ought to go to capital account; moreover, at Michaelmas last there was about 228*l*. 17*s*. 7*d*. cash in bank. Further, the valuations at that date about equal the total of cash invested, so that, theoretically, if the business were wound up, there should be no actual loss of capital as distinguished from interest. It may be objected also that I have no right to reckon on a rent; that nowadays in these counties rent is too often a mere ideal which cannot be grasped ; and no doubt when I took the farms in hand this was the case, for its condition was so deplorable, at any rate at Ditchingham, that nobody would have given anything for the land. But the rents suggested are modest in its present state, and could, I think, be obtained.

Still, with every deduction and allowance, the loss remains heavy, although I think I may say that the holding has been farmed with economy and not without intelligence. The agricultural position in our part of England, however, is such that unless the land is sound, if not good, and in heart and order, it cannot be made to pay at the prices which have prevailed for the last few years, that is, if it is properly done by and honestly farmed as a man would farm his own. There is no margin left for loss or for a mistake, and, as everybody reminds us, even we farmers make mistakes ! One bit of bad luck, such as a disease among the stock, or a drought or a flood, will swallow all the profit.

All things combine against the great British industry of farming, because that industry, in our circumstances, cannot combine to protect itself. One man's vote is as good as that of another, therefore the labourers, being in the majority, have the majority of votes, and for the most part they cannot be made to see that their interests are one with those of the landowner and the farmer, with whom they must stand or fall. Often enough, in what I hold to be their blindness, they will vote for those pledged to injure these interests rather than for those pledged to help them. Therefore the seven millions of people concerned in agriculture get little real help from Governments of either party, for soft words, oratorical tears, and Royal Com missions are not help. They get little help because, being a house divided against itself, they cannot force their will upon them, and turn them out if they will not listen.

Thus, by way of illustration, without going into the vexed question of Protection, if we who are interested in the land were the citizens of any other country, or even if we were Irishmen, who understand how to deal with Governments, should we be so disproportionately rated and taxed as we are still, in comparison with the burdens laid upon personal property, or should we be obliged to see the products of the foreigner carried by the railway

companies at easier rates than our own, as, whatever the letter of
the law may be, in fact they are? Or, to take another instance,
for the want of a simple preventive Act should we be forced to
stand helpless while foreign meat is sold by dishonest butchers
as best home-grazed and at the prices which home-grazed
commands? 'Reduce the rents is a favourite answer from a
certain section of politicians to all the complaints of farmers;
but as one who both pays rent and farms land of his own, I
say again : It is not the rent that crushes us ; it is the prices we
receive for our produce, and the unjust taxation, frauds and harsh
dealing of which we are the victims.

To turn from these lamentations to the cause of them. The
statements of account that I have given above must fill any
sympathetic reader with awful reflections on the fate of those
unfortunate persons who, having land in bad condition thrown
upon their hands, have been forced to borrow money to farm it.
Then, in addition to the various outgoings enumerated above,
there would be five per cent. to the bank for the loan of the capital,
and probably another five per cent. or so to meet the premiums of
the insurance which the bank requires as extra security to cover
its advance. Under these circumstances, the working of a 300-acre
farm would bring any but a rich man to bankruptcy in ten years.
Happily, however, I escaped the necessity of borrowing, so the
loss is only the loss of possible rent and interest, of which neither
might have been realised. Indeed, the capital itself might perhaps have been invested away in some other direction ; for at
least remember this, O reader—one loses money more slowly in
farming than in any other fashion.

After some experience, at my present age, I have come to the
conclusion that, were I a rich man, there are only two things
in which I would invest my wealth at prevailing prices : land
(including farming on *a very large scale*), and the various forms
of life insurance. Perhaps Chippendale furniture, discreetly
purchased, might be added to the list, but this is a business for
the instructed only. If any reader of this book will act upon the

above advice (even should he go wrong on the Chippendale), it will, I believe, prove the most profitable work to him for which he ever paid money. Yet, under the existing conditions of agricultural affairs, in advising the purchase of East Anglian land at any price, on reflection, I feel that I may be wrong.

And now, having sufficiently contemplated the cloud, let us look at its silver lining. If I am somewhat out of pocket over my farms for the period that they have been in hand, it is largely due to exceptional circumstances, such as the state of the land when I took it over that necessitated an unusual outlay, and, so far as the light soil is concerned, the persistent droughts of the last few years, which have made it very unproductive. Moreover, it would seem that at last the corner has been turned, seeing that on separate balance sheets struck for 1897, by which I mean balance sheets that do not carry on the trading losses of earlier years, a profit was earned on the Bedingham Farm of 75*l.* 19*s.* 3*d.*, and on the Ditchingham Farm of 252*l.* 13*s.* 2*d.* It must, however, be understood that this money remains in the land—one cannot draw it out and spend it; though, on the other hand, there is a substantial cash balance at the bank, over and above the amount originally belonging to the farm. Moreover, there is now a total of sixty-two acres of my own land laid down in permanent pasture, thirty-eight and a half at Ditchingham, and twenty-three and a half at Bedingham, all of which, in time, as I trust, will make good sound meadows, worth from a pound to thirty shillings the acre.

Also this farm, which eight years ago was in so desperate a condition, is to-day, with the exception of certain docks in the marsh meadows, in good heart, and where necessary pipe-drained. At Bedingham, too, the tall fences that I found there have gone under the soil in the shape of bush-drains, and the land generally is not in such a state that I should be ashamed for a farming friend to walk over it, though there remain jobs to be done to the buildings. Notably a new stable is wanted, but the present old hovel still serves its purpose, and must hang for a few more years.

So on the whole I face the new farming year with a somewhat lighter heart, although it is true that I am again hampered with over fifty acres of foul, half-starved land on Baker's Farm. There is a more hopeful feeling in the air, but whether the season will end in prosperity and, glorious possibility, something in the bank that can actually be drawn and spent, or with a swollen deficit, I know not. The reader, if such a man there be who is willing to accompany me from spring to winter in the adventures of the year, can form his own opinion. At least, I promise him that the whole truth shall be told; nothing shall be glozed over, or made to seem better than in reality it is.

As I write, the fear takes me that such a journal as I propose of agricultural and countryside events, and of reflections arising out of them, may prove monotonous; but if so, doubtless it will be my skill that is to seek, since nature is never monotonous. Even the history of a single hedgerow daily recorded would be full of interest to those who cared about hedgerows. But if my artless tale is dull, I trust that to some extent it may prove useful to those who are weary of text-books and yet wish to learn something about rural ways and life upon the land in this era of dreadful depression, when the fate of British agriculture hangs quivering in the balance. At the worst, a year spent moving in fancy from field to field and watching all that lives and grows therein, with the wind and the wet in his face, and the smell of the earth and the corn in his nostrils, can scarcely be unwholesome to the town-held reader.

JANUARY

January 1, 1898.—Never within my recollection have we experienced so mild and open a winter as that of the year which died yesterday. There has been no rain, and until the 24th of last month, when it froze for a few hours, practically no frost, nor in my recollection has the land for a single day been too hard or too wet to plough. Christmas Day, with one exception, was the most beautiful that I can remember in this country. That exception was a certain Christmas five or six and twenty years gone, which I spent at my father's house in another part of Norfolk. There had been a heavy snowfall during the preceding night, followed by frost, so that in the morning the snow lay inches thick upon the fir-boughs, bending them down in deep arches till they almost touched the earth, while the sun shone upon the glittering surface of the white world till the eyes ached to look at it. One often hears of a mad hare, but this long dead Christmas Day was the only occasion upon which I ever saw one, for I recollect that as we were walking to church we perceived a hare tearing round and round in a circle through the snow in a neighbouring field. Being young in those days, of course I went to catch it, and succeeded. On examination the creature showed no sign of having been shot or otherwise injured, so I can only suppose that it was suffering from some sort of a fit.

This last Christmas Day differed from that which I have described, since there was no snow and only a few degrees of frost. But after its own fashion it was as beautiful, for in the morning every branchlet of the trees showed thick with a wonderful white rime, more perfect than any I have seen of late, because of the extraordinary calmness of the air. By the time that we came out of church this rime had melted in the bright sunshine, but the day remained frosty and windless. The best part of it, however, was the sunset as seen from the Bungay Road—a huge ball of fire that vanished gradually behind a deep background of spreading wreaths of vapour, smoky red in hue, roll upon roll of them covering the western sky. Against this sombre and glorious pall the trees in the foreground stood out nakedly, every bough, and indeed each separate twig, outlined and accentuated with fire, as in the morning they had been outlined and accentuated by frost. Then, to complete the picture, in the clear blue-black of the heavens above hung the crescent moon. Altogether it was an evening to be remembered.

That night promised sharper cold, but the promise was not to be fulfilled, for on Sunday the 26th the frost began to break and the moon came ringed into a clear sky. Moreover, I heard curlew calling over Bungay Common—it is impossible for anyone who knows it to mistake that wild and melancholy note, although I cannot recall hearing it here before. This I took as a sign of bad weather ; nor was I wrong, for on the morrow the frost had departed and half a gale blew from the sou'-west, which on the 30th developed into a full gale. But like some worn-out old man, the year died quietly. I was shooting pheasants in Tindale Wood on the 31st, and there could not have been a better day for the purpose of that pastime.

As the old year died so the new year was born, in peace and beauty, a mild southerly wind barely stirring the black trees. There is only one plough going on the farm to-day, turning up the five acres of glebe land, No. 40 on the plan. This piece, together with its companions, Nos. 38 and 39, is very stony and light, the sort of land that would be the better for rain three days a week. Last year it and No. 39 were clover layers, but owing to the persistent drought the crop they yielded was poor indeed. I remember finding patches of them at times absolutely brown and shrivelled, as though they had been exposed to the heat of a fire. Now they are being ploughed for oats.

The ploughman, Peachey, tells me that on this land, where the friction against stones is so constant, the share of the plough (not the breast) only lasts about a week. In heavy land it will last from three weeks to a month. The breast of a plough, or that part of it which turns the furrow, ought to wear from one to two years, according to the nature of the soil.

To-day two carts are carrying refuse from the undrained town of Bungay to be scattered on that part of the nine acres of land, No. 23, which is coming for root, or on so much of it as we can spare time and horses to cover. We have been at the task for nearly a week, sometimes with two and sometimes with three carts, and, I think, have spread about fifty loads upon the root land. This compost, disagreeable as it is in many ways and mixed with troublesome stuff, such as old tins and broken glass, is the best manure which I have ever used; but I think that to get its full value it should be spread upon the land and ploughed in at once, leaving it to decompose beneath the surface. I adopted this plan last year on the piece of rootland at All Hallows Farm, No. 33, and with the most excellent results. The field is small, but, notwithstanding the drought, the piece of beet which resulted was the finest that I have yet grown. The cost of this manure is about two shillings the load as it lies upon the heap, and I suppose that the carting would come to as much more. Against this expense, however, it must be remembered that it spares the farm-yard, upon which the calls are heavy and continuous; also for a root crop I would rather use it than any expensive artificial dressing on the market.

January 2.—To-day being Sunday I have confined my farming operations to looking over the young stock in the yard. One of the calves there is the first-born of a heifer, and therefore doomed to die. Hood, my bailiff, a man of strong opinions, is convinced that it is useless to keep the first calves of heifers, which, as he alleges, always grow up weak and puny. In vain have I pointed out that this is not the case with the offspring of other mammals, beginning with man. His opinion remains unshaken, but I should much like to learn whether it is based upon any ascertained fact. Once I made the experiment here under the following circumstances. When I began to farm I determined to start a small herd of pedigree red polls, and with this view bought a couple of in-calf heifers at the sale of a Suffolk herd. They were beautiful animals, but rather smally made and remarkable for their fine mottled hides. One of them turned out to be barren and was fatted, but the other in due course produced a cow-calf, which Hood was most anxious to fat and sell to the butcher. Indeed, he would have done so had not Mr. Simpson discovered his purpose and told him that the creature was too valuable. In time this calf grew up, and is now a middle-aged cow, and a very good one. It cannot be denied, however, that she is somewhat small-boned and finely built, but then so is her mother, and so, I expect, were all the herd. Indeed, I believe that this story about heifers' calves is more of a superstition than a reality.

January 6.—There has been little to chronicle this week. Yesterday, Wednesday, it rained without ceasing at night from a singularly clear sky, but to-day is very fine and mild. I walked down to the farm called Baker's, which I took over last November, and found two ploughs going in the eight-acre cottage field, No. 43 on the plan, which is being made ready for spring beans and pease. Thence I went down the lane to the brook pasture, No. 46, to see the man who was engaged in clearing out the dykes ; a task, by the way, that cannot often be undertaken at this time of the year.

Of all the forms of manual labour, I think that this dyke-drawing must be about the hardest, since the strain upon the muscles of the arms and back, continuously endured for a long day's work of lifting heavy forkfuls of mud and weeds, cannot but be great.

Indeed, I suspect that any man, however strong, who was not accustomed to this kind of toil, would be utterly exhausted long before his eight or ten hours were finished.

In the lane leading to this meadow I found the wildflower called green-arrow in bloom in the hedgerow ; also, nestling under the shelter of the bank and white-thorn roots, the bright green leaves of the vigorous black parsley (*Smyrnium Olusatrum*). For years I have noticed that such signs of coming spring show first in this lane, and very welcome is the sight of the shining leaf of that weed after the long and dreary months of winter. The reason that vegetation appears here so soon is that at this spot the fall of the land is steep, and the rain of hundreds, or very possibly of thousands, of years, has by degrees lowered the road-way—once, no doubt, a bridle track—till at places it lies eight or nine feet below the surface level of the fields that border it. Therefore the banks are very sheltered, and those herbs and flower roots that nestle in them can thrust out their new growths a month before their companions unprotected by the bank dare even to wake from the winter sleep. This year, however, vegetation is at least three weeks before its time ; thus, on my way home I noticed bees working busily at the hives in the farm orchard, and by the east windows of this house I found the *Pyrus Japonica* in bud and bloom. This, I think, is something of a record for Norfolk on the 6th of January.

January 7.—To-day was my rent audit. It is held at an inn in Bungay, where the tenants of this estate, which, although not large, is scattered, assemble once a year to pay their rent and dine. Rent audits of late years, in the Eastern Counties, have been something like the play of 'Hamlet' without the Prince of Denmark ; that is to say, their first cause, the rent, has been, if not conspicuous by its absence, at least very painfully diminished. The accounts of any Norfolk estate for the year 1897 are indeed a melancholy document if compared with those, let us say, of the year 1867. This property is no exception.

I doubt even if it returns in net profit more than a third of what it produced thirty years ago. Indeed, in some ways its case is particularly unfortunate, seeing that it is purely agricultural in character, and being, as I have said, dispersed, brings in nothing in the way of shooting rents, on which nowadays so many landlords are compelled to exist, together with the proceeds of the letting of the Hall, if they are fortunate enough to find some successful South African or business man to hire the mansion house.

In truth, few people, except those who are more or less behind the scenes, know the straits to which the owners of land, and especially of entailed land, have been put of late years, at any rate in East Anglia. Even if they are totally unencumbered, most of such properties barely produce enough to pay outgoings and keep up 'the place' upon a very modest scale. And if they are encumbered, as is the case in eight out of ten of them, either by mortgages or with jointures and charges in favour of younger children executed on a scale of liberality dictated by prosperous times, then the position is bad indeed. In nearly every instance their history is the same—a long and pitiful struggle on the part of the sinking family, then at last foreclosure, ruin, and sale at any sacrifice. Who does not know cases of parishes where the property has been held for centuries by a single family? But long as their day may be, at length it comes to an end, and the lands which they owned from father to son for so many generations, the home that their forefathers built and the woods which they planted, are put up to auction and sold for whatever they will fetch. Well, as it has been with them, so in the fulness of appointed time it shall be with those who supplant them, for against this ultimate fate the hoarding of moneys and the laying of field to field are no sure defence.

Soon or late the stock, like the individual, must decay and vanish, and no doubt it is all for the good of the State that the bankrupt family should be replaced in due season by the family with a large bank balance. Yet to my mind there is something infinitely pathetic about the process—this sad sequence of the death and departure of a race. To understand the thing and appreciate it fully it is necessary to take the registers of any given parish, and to read them through from their beginnings about the year 1550. At that beginning, in such cases as I have instanced, we shall already find the family in possession, for here are entries of their births, their marriages, their burials—nearly all of them make these three formal appearances in that record which no one studies once in a century.

And so it goes on through the long generations, this tale of the considerable dead—so important in their own day, looming so large for a while upon the little world of the village which they ruled, and now so utterly forgot that their bones are tossed about, as I have seen happen, by the man from London who fits the hot-water pipes in the parish church, unrecognised, uncared-for, and unknown—till at length we come to the entries of the baptisms of the past owners, still living, perhaps, but ' gone away, leaving no address,' as they say on letters that follow us from forsaken lodg-ings. The time of their race has come; they and the soil that bred them—yes, the very earth, chemically changed indeed, but still the earth of which the bodies of those of them who survive are built up—have been divorced for ever, unless indeed they creep, or rather are carried, back to claim the hospitality of burial in some ancestral vault, as those possessing a family grave have the right to do. In this particular the villager is more fortunate than his dispossessed and ancestral lord. Having nothing to lose, he loses nothing, but from generation to generation lives on where his fathers lived, earning his daily bread by the sweat of his daily toil. Indeed, if all the truth were known, in the case of most vanished families, doubtless the race, or some part of it, still survives in him, for from the highest to the lowest, in past ages at any rate, the blood of our English villagers was curiously mixed.

For the benefit of those unacquainted with the function I will describe a rent audit of the local type. The ceremony begins about twelve o'clock, when the agent takes his seat in a small room in the King's Head at Bungay, and makes ready his papers and book of printed receipts. To him presently enters a tenant who produces—or does not produce, as the case may be—the rent he owes. Also in these times he generally takes the opportunity to point out that a further reduction upon the attenuated sum payable is absolutely necessary to enable him to live. In most instances his story is true enough, although the landlord could wish that he would show as great a readiness to call attention to the fact whenever times or prices improve. Such an instance of almost superhuman virtue has just come to my notice. A tenant of a relative of mine in this neighbourhood appeared the other day and paid his rent, plus an extra sum of 9*l*. Being asked for what the 9*l*. was owing, he answered that when he took the farm he came to a verbal understanding with its owner, since deceased, that if ever times improved his rent should be increased. There was no written statement to this effect, and the other party to the arrangement can no longer bear witness to it ; but as this pearl among tenants considered that times had improved with him to the exact extent of 9*l*., he handed over that amount unasked. ' Comment is superfluous.'

In the old days it was customary to discharge the rent in coin, a practice which some tenants still keep up, but now most of them have a banking account and pay by cheque. From the sum due is deducted the amount disbursed out of pocket by the tenant, but properly chargeable to the landlord, on account of rates and taxes or repairs. Then the cheque is drawn out, often slowly and with labour, unless, indeed, it has been brought ready prepared, in which case the agent gives a cross cheque for the difference, plus any allowance that may have been agreed upon. Next, having been offered and drunk a glass of sherry, that tenant departs with a sense of duty done, a lighter pocket, and the instruction to send up Mr. So-and-so.

Of course there are tenants and tenants. There is the specious and horsey young man with a glib tongue, from which flow reasons innumerable why he should not pay his just debts, or plausible explanations as to how he came to be found selling straw off the farm. This sort is at one end of the scale. At the other stands the silver-haired old gentleman who has been a tenant on the estate for fifty years, and all that time has never failed to meet his rent. To such a one to 'get behind' is a real grief; indeed I have seen a man of this stamp almost break into tears because the times had at last proved too much for him. The most remarkable tenant that ever I had to do with, however, was an old gentleman, now dead, who had occupied a farm belonging to this estate for no less than seventy-seven years. The time seems long, but he was born in a certain room in that homestead, for seventy-seven years he slept every night of his life in the room, and there finally he died. He was a man who drove about the country a good deal to markets and other places, but, at any rate during the latter part of his life, no earthly consideration would have induced him to be away from home for a single night. Indeed, the dread of such a thing obtained a complete mastery of his mind, and I believe that on one or two occasions, when accident detained him at a distance, he spared no expense, and journeyed incessantly to reach his farm before the following dawn. In these days of frequent and distant travel it is certainly curious to hear of a man of some position who has slept in a single house for seventy-seven years, but among the lower classes such cases are not exceptional. Thus, a few years ago, one day when I chanced to be at a village called Spexhall, about six miles from Bungay, where I have a farm, I lost my way in a lane and asked a labouring man to show it to me. He proved almost as uncertain about it as I was myself, which puzzled me till I discovered that, although he must have been sixty years old and had lived in Spexhall all his life, he had never yet visited Bungay, a few miles from his door.

When the tenants have been interviewed, or most of them, dinner is announced, about three o'clock generally, and everybody adjourns to a long, old-fashioned room. Here the landlord takes the head of the table, and the agent the foot, while the tenants range themselves in solemn lines on either side, in order of seniority and social precedence. Then grace is said and the meal begins; and an excellent meal it is, by the way, though perhaps it would not recommend itself to the guests at a London dinner party. Here is the menu, which never varies from year to year:

Clear Ox-tail Soup.

Fried Soles.   Boiled Cod.

Roast Beef.   Boiled Mutton.

Chicken and Tongue.

Roast Turkey.

(For this festival is always celebrated early in January.)

Plum Pudding.   Mince Pies.

Cheese.

Beer, Port, and Sherry.

Such is the feast, most admirably cooked in the good old English fashion with the old English accessories, and it is one to which hungry men who have eaten nothing since the morning certainly do justice.

After the meal is finished glasses are filled and the landlord proposes 'The Queen,' which is loyally drunk, but in silence, as though to her Majesty's memory. Then comes a solemn pause, till the largest tenant present at the feast—as regards his holding, not his person—his eyes fixed sternly upon vacancy, rises and proposes the health of the landlord in a few brief but kindly sentences.

Another pause and the landlord rises to reply. How well he knows that speech! It begins invariably with a solemn wail or lament over the shocking bad times, which, as a general rule, he is obliged to confess are even worse than they were at the last gathering. Then, while his audience shake their heads and sigh, he rises to a more cheerful note and talks of the inherent pluck and nobility of the character of Englishmen, which, as he firmly believes, will, if persisted in, enable them in the end to put up the price of corn—how, he prefers not to specify. He also discourses hopefully of signs of better fortune upon the horizon of the year, if he can find any, and points out (which is perfectly true) that the interests of the landlord, the tenant, and the labourer, and indeed of all who live by the land, are one interest, whatever agitators and mischief-makers may say to the contrary. Then he gives some account of the farming of whatever country he may last have visited, America, or Iceland, or Egypt, or the Hebrides, or Mexico. This is generally the most popular part of the speech, as there is a slight novelty about it, the rest being somewhat of a formula. Finally he ends with the best peroration that occurs to him and resumes his seat amidst the jingling of glasses, to rise again presently and propose the health of the agent, to whose many virtues he delicately alludes.

Next the agent replies, paying him back full measure and running over in the coin of compliment, and exhorting the tenants to make up their minds that the bad times are done with, and to pay their rent like men and Britons. Finally he ends by proposing their healths, calling on two of them to respond. This does not take long, for the average farmer is no great speaker, and when the last of them sits down with a sigh of relief the oratorical programme is exhausted.

Then the songs begin—the pipes, long clay churchwardens, have been lit already. These songs are generally three in number, and always the same. One, a very long one, is of a local character, for it describes the glories of Bungay, the chorus at the end of each verse being, 'For old Bungay is a wonderful town.' Another is a melancholy ditty descriptive of the ills of life and the dangers and disasters that beset each profession; even the lawyer, who, so says the song, is invariably rich and happy in every other way, must beware of the spite of Fate, since, while he is comfortably fleecing his clients, his clerk 'is a-kissing of his wife.' The third song is of a patriotic nature, and has for a refrain something about 'twisting the lion's tail.' Perhaps it was written in America.

While the sound of music lingers still the agent rises and,

going to the door, beckons mysteriously at some individual whose rent is yet to pay. This is generally the signal for the departure of the landlord, and so far as he is concerned another rent audit is gathered to the many which he remembers in the past.

This year some of the tenants were absent, from death and other causes. Of one of those who did not appear a good story is told, a true one as I believe. Physically a splendid man and very powerful, it is said that he can do, and does, as much hard work as anyone in the county Also he is an early riser and hates to waste time. Normally he breakfasts at five o'clock off a pound and a half of cold pork, but on one occasion, as he had to start away at half-past three on the following morning, he determined that he would not spend any time over breakfast. Feeling, however, that he would need his usual amount of nourishment, he overcame the difficulty by eating his supper, waiting half an hour, and then break-fasting on the fixed ration of pork before he went to bed. He him-self admits, however, that the experiment did not succeed, since, for the first time in his life, his digestion rose in violent rebellion.

By the way, after dinner one of the tenants kindly fetched from the shop of a neighbouring saddler for my inspection an ancient bridle that had been found in a loft. This bridle has its date of manufacture, 1722, stamped upon it, and the leather, which remains in perfect preservation, is most beautifully worked, while rising from the head-band is a ball-shaped crest of red wool. Evidently this headpiece was part of the harness used upon the fore horse of a team on grand occasions, such as a journey to Bungay fair. I had never before seen a bridle so old or so elaborately ornamented.

An interesting conversation was started at dinner as to the storage of beet, and nearly all present declared that roots which are placed in the hale dry, ferment much more quickly than if heaped there wet. This seems curious, but I believe it to be true.

January 8.—My first two lambs were born to-day. When I began to keep sheep last year, before which we had not sufficient grass lands to run them on and leave enough for a herd of cows, I started with about forty black-faced Suffolk ewes in lamb to a Southdown ram. These lambs did exceedingly well; I remember that I sold the first lot of them at Easter for about thirty shillings a head, and all the rest were fatted up and disposed of during the summer at reasonable prices. Indeed, we had good luck with them throughout, for I think that only one died; also I lost an ewe from inflammation of the lungs, but none during the lambing. This year I took a fancy to try some Southdowns, and bought about a score of well-bred ewes of that breed together with two rams. The result of the experiment remains to be seen, but I incline to the opinion that in this district it is best to keep to the Suffolk ewes, crossing them perhaps with the Southdown rams to get quality in the mutton. Pure-bred Southdowns no doubt furnish the best meat, but they are too small. It is true that they eat somewhat less than the black-faced breed, but, on the other hand, the difference between the excellence of their mutton and that of the Suffolks crossed with the Southdown is slight, whereas the difference in weight is considerable. Where the Southdowns really have the pull is in their appearance. The Suffolks, heavy by comparison and hungry-looking, are at a disadvantage here when compared with the nimble, shapely Southdowns, with their game-like heads ; but after all, even in the case of sheep, handsome is as handsome does, and the local butcher cares nothing about looks. He goes by weight, and will give most for the heaviest lamb.

With so small a flock on a mixed farm like mine, where there are many things to attend to, I have no shepherd, nor can I boast any proper lambing folds. In place of them a barn on the All Hallows Farm is divided off into little pens with hurdles, where the ewes are placed in comfort as they come on to lamb. The steward, Hood, attends to them at that critical time, and certainly hitherto his ministrations have met with considerable success.

As the weather keeps so open the cows are let out for a few hours every day to take exercise in one or other of the meadows and pick up what food they can, which is not much. This morning I was watching their behaviour to one of their number that, for domestic reasons, had been in seclusion for about a fortnight. Now she reappeared for the first time, and, forgetful of her calf, which no doubt had been removed from her a week or so before, testified her joy at finding herself in the open air again by gambolling about the field with the awkwardness peculiar to the race, kicking up her heels and lowing. The strange point of the performance was that the other cows were much annoyed at her appearance, for every one of them, as they found a chance, butted her and knocked her about in a fashion which made me glad that the breed is hornless. Clearly the memory of cows is short. This sister of theirs had been separated from them for a few days, therefore they treated her as an intruder, a slight which she seemed to resent, for whenever she could spare time from her gambols she gave her last assailant battle, pushing at it with her head till one or the other got the better of the war. This cow-play went on for twenty minutes or more, when it was given up apparently by mutual consent, and the stranger, as it were, readmitted into the fellowship of the herd with all the rights and privileges thereto pertaining.

Here I may as well explain that my cows, of which I keep about twenty at the Home Farm in Ditchingham, are all regis-tered pedigree animals of the Norfolk red-poll breed, that as yet is not so well known throughout Great Britain as it deserves to be. Looked at with the most critical eye it cannot be doubted that red-polls have many advantages, though, of course, there may be other tribes which have even more. To begin with, their looks are in their favour. What can be more beautiful than the appearance of a herd of these bronze-red, shining-coated cattle as they wander over a pasture in the summer, or stand chewing their cud in the cool shadow of the trees, gazing at the intruder with wide-opened, sleepy eyes? Indeed, so fine are their limbs, and, espe-cially in the case of the young things, so deer-like their heads, that they might almost be taken for wild creatures which know not man, although, as a matter of fact, they are singularly docile in character. Of course, as their name implies, they are hornless, a great point where it is desired to keep a number of cattle in small or medium-sized yards. Another advantage is their great hardiness—with ordinary care it is not common to lose a red-poll from sickness, or even in calving. During the seven or eight years that I have been farming, indeed, I can only remember the loss of two, and both by accident; one of them, a fine young bull, doing himself to death last year by getting his head fixed between the hawthorn stems of a fence and struggling until he broke his neck. Lastly, they ripen early for the butcher—as a rule I sell mine at about two years of age, when, without undue forcing, they average over forty stone dead weight—and for tenderness and general quality their beef is not to be surpassed by any that I know.

The points urged against red-polls are: that they lack size, and that their milk, although very rich, is scant in quantity. To the first of these points I answer that they are quite large enough. Nowadays few people want great-boned cattle, indeed the demand is all for small beef. As to the second, I cannot speak with authority myself, for it is not my practice to weigh and keep a record of the milk of each individual cow, as is very properly done in large herds, where they have more labour and better facilities at command. Indeed, even if I could do so, the test would not be a fair one, since I have only kept red-polls for a short time, whereas it takes at least twenty years of weeding out and careful selection to establish a herd of the very best milking qualities. As specimens of what red-polls will do as milkers, however, I take the record from the 'Red-Poll Herd-Book' for 1897 of the two best cows of a few herds as set down therein for one year.

Aspall Hall Herd

Sappho	.	.	.	9,716 lbs. weight of milk.
Susan	.	.	.	9,135 ,, ,, ,,

Cirencester Park Herd

Frump	.	.	.	9,599 lbs. weight of milk.
Sloe .	.	.	.	8,793 ,, ,, ,,

Melton Constable Herd

Davy 87th .	.	.	.	8,714½ lbs. weight of milk.
May Queen	.	.	.	7,335½ ,, ,, ,,

Necton Hall Herd

Rosina 3rd	.	.	.	7,472 lbs. weight of milk.
Sheba 3rd .	.	.	.	7,177 ,, ,, ,,

Rendlesham Herd

Fresh Fuss	.	.	.	9,296¼ lbs. weight of milk.
Sweet Pear 2nd .	.	.	8,339 ,, ,, ,,

Tring Park Herd [1]

Elmham Rosebud 9th	.	10,159 lbs. weight of milk.
Moth	.	.	.	10,210 ,, ,, ,,

I might quote from other herds, especially the noted one of Mr. Colman, but the above are sufficient for my purpose.

I cannot find in Stephens' 'Book of the Farm,' or elsewhere, a comparative table of the milk-producing powers of different breeds of cows, but I doubt whether any breed, except perhaps the Short-horn, will show very much better returns than those quoted above. It must be remembered, however, that these are the picked cows of picked herds, and that the majority even of pedigree red-polls give a much inferior yield.

The points of the first-class red-poll as defined in the 'Herd-Book' are : That it must be of a deep red hue, white being allowed only on the tip of the tail. The nose must not be dark-coloured. The throat and head must be finely modelled, the eye full, and a tuft of hair should hang over the forehead. There must be no trace of horns, developed or undeveloped, but the frontal bones should contract into a narrow peak at the summit of the head.

January 12.—The weather for the last three days has been damp, mild, and misty. On the farm we have been ploughing and

---

[1] In this herd thirty-seven cows gave an average of 6,939 lbs. and a fraction per cow. But then they are owned by a Rothschild, so doubtless much is expected of them.

hedge-trimming. I was talking yesterday to Buck, my milkman, at the All Hallows Farm—where I keep nearly half my cows—who, as is the custom with such men when not milking or attending to the cattle, is employed on odd jobs about the land. He was trimming the fence of the back lawn, which ever since I have had the farm in hand has been kept neatly clipped with shears, and took the opportunity to remark that in another twenty years there would not be a hedge left alive in this country. I asked him why; to which he answered that farmers have entirely given up the old custom that was in force when he was a boy, of cutting the thorns off right down by the roots and ‘ditching’ the crown of the fence by coating it with mud out of the holl. He informed me that in the old days it was usual for a provision to be inserted in leases enforcing this custom.

But nowadays we have no leases, and, if we had, the face of the farmer who was asked to bind himself to keep his fences in a particular way, or indeed to do anything except to follow his own sweet will, would probably be a study. I can remember when it was the custom of my father's tenants at Bradenham at the other side of Norfolk to cart all the coals required for the use of the Hall, and I think—but of this I am not sure—to provide a certain amount of straw gratis. Within the last fifteen years, even, tenants have carted gravel for me here; but these old customs are dying out, more's the pity. It is a pity not only because the landlords have lost the advantage of what was a convenience to them, but also for the reason that one of the bonds of good feeling induced by the ungrudging performance of a neighbourly service has been broken away. As regards the hedges, I am inclined to think that Buck is too pessimistic in alleging that they will all die. I have, however, myself observed that hawthorns have a natural tendency to get thin at the bottom, however much they may be trimmed at the top, no doubt because their nature is to grow into trees and not into bushes.

I noticed to-day while walking over the new pasture by the stackyard, No. 6 on plan, that the suckling is already thick in the grass, making patches of green carpeting, a very unusual thing at this time of year. I am glad to see it there, however, for this pasture has now reached the critical period, about its fifth year, when the young clovers and finer grasses are only too apt to die out. I have already made some remarks as to the laying down of pastures, and now I would add to them a question to those who argue that these cannot be successfully established upon such lands as are generally supposed to be unsuitable to them. How is it, then, that even on most of these soils the banksides or ditches bordering the head-lands are good sound turf, not black grass, or water-grass, or twitch, but herbage such as a beast can fatten on? Doubtless the grasses going to form that herbage are those natural to the neighbourhood, and I believe that in almost every case, if a botanist could be found to classify them and to estimate even roughly in what proportions they occur, the difficulty of laying down grasses which would prove quick to establish themselves as permanent would be very much lessened.

In a paper written by one of the most esteemed of our Norfolk farmers, Mr. Clare Sewell Read, I read recently that when he was a lad he remembers pastures being very successfully established on light land by a system of inoculation, that is, by cutting turf from the roadside or other waste places, and planting it in lumps over the surface of a field, leaving spaces of bare soil between the lumps. Across these spaces the grass spread quickly, till in a few years it formed a compact turf, the trouble being to prevent the rooks and other birds from pulling up the planted squares before they had time to get hold. I can well believe that this plan is an excellent one, although too slow, perhaps, for our modern habits. Anyone who has observed such matters will be aware how quickly growing things spread in soil that is suitable to them. Thus I am certain that were it left uncultivated much of the land in England would become dense thorn scrub within a single generation.

Indeed, I have seen the process going on in a neglected

meadow on the heavy-land farm at Spexhall, belonging to this property, which a few years ago was dotted thickly with thorn-bushes. Also, when shooting in Hertfordshire last year over fields from which a corn crop had been taken that autumn, I noted thousands of bramble seedlings. Can it be doubted that if this land were left unploughed for a few seasons it would become nothing but a briar scrub spreading from the hedgerows?

The sheep are now penned upon part of No. 42, the fourteen-acre on Baker's Farm, which was layer last year. The land is foul and poor, and as we have no manure to put on it, we are folding it with the ewes before ploughing it for oats in order to freshen it up as much as possible under the circumstances. Fortunately I have still a fair supply of white turnips with which to feed them. These are said to be a better food for ewes in the lambing time than beet, which are supposed to make them miscarry; and indeed beet at this time of year are still very lush. These white turnips were a catch crop grown on a portion of the twelve-acre, No. 28, commonly known as the Thwaite field.

Last year, or rather the year before, the top part of this Thwaite field was sown for winter wheat, but for some unexplained reason, perhaps because of the bitter spring winds, which strike this exposed situation with great force, the crop was the worst that I ever grew. I drilled vetches in the spring into the greater part of it, in the hope that it would give me a breadth of cheap feed after such corn as there was had been cut, but these vetches failed also, owing to the drought. Indeed, that part of the field produced more poppies than anything else—red weed we call it, which, although picturesque in appearance, is not satisfactory to the farmer. About three acres of the worst of it, however, we folded off for sheep, which throve very well upon the young wheat until, towards the end, the straw grew too tough for them. After they had done with it the land was ploughed and drilled with white turnips, and from these, although the season has been so dry,

I have had an excellent return, more indeed than could have been expected. This is another testimony, if any were needed, to the value of sheep as fertilisers of the soil.

January 14.—The weather to-day is again dull, mild, and quite windless. There are three ploughs going on the farm, one of them at work in the nine-acre on All Hallows Farm, No. 36 upon the plan, a good but rather scaldy bit of land. This field was under beet and swedes last year, the beet being sown on the lower half of it, where the soil is somewhat deeper. There was a very full plant of swedes, which would have produced a fine crop had it not been for the drought that stunted them. The beet, standing on the cooler soil, did well; indeed beet do not mind dry weather in moderation. The whole field is now coming for barley, and I hope will only need this one ploughing. Peachey, the plough-man, who is at work on it, a person of experience, tells me that he prefers 'the first earth' for barley, and I believe that this preference is general, though if the land has been ploughed early in the autumn and gone down tight, a second ploughing is very beneficial. Also barley land that has been sheeped is best ploughed twice, once skimmed only to cover the 'tether,' and once for crop.

This afternoon I went to Bedingham and inspected the stock. There are four red-poll steers tied up fatting in a shed, and three others in the yard, all looking very well. Also there is a two-year-old bullock which promises to make such a beauty that I am keeping him over with a view of showing him next Christmas, a thing I have never done before. I might have disposed of him at a good price to the agent of a much larger breeder who is looking out for promising beasts to be shown by his employer next Christmas, but I have declined the offer. Probably I shall regret this ere the year is out, as eight out of ten of these animals, before their time comes to go to the show bench, develop some imper-fection or other which proves fatal to their chances of prize-taking. In fact the showing of cattle is an unprofitable business to any except the largest breeders, who make it a part of their routine in order to advertise their herds and thus to obtain large prices for their young bulls and heifers. Success is very much a matter of outlay, for not only, as a rule, must the bulls and dams be costly animals, but the expense of preparing their progeny for the ring is considerable. Thus, they must be kept on a cow much longer than is usual, and afterwards receive more ample food and attention. Also, the sending of them and their attendants backwards and forwards to shows always means money. It is not wonderful, therefore, that many owners of good cattle do not think that the game will pay for the candle.

Besides these steers there are ten young things running in the big meadow, whence they come up at night and are fed with a mixture of hay, chaff, and swedes. Also there are the farm-horses (we are managing with two at Bedingham now, one of them in foal), colts and ponies, so it will be seen that for the size of the place there is a good proportion of stock.

After inspecting the animals I walked down to the six-acre, No. 18 on plan, which is being bush-drained, a process that is perhaps worth describing for the benefit of the uninitiated.

Bush-draining is a system used upon very heavy clay lands where it would be of doubtful advantage, if not mere waste, to go to the expense of pipes. It is done thus. First the lines of the drains are drawn with a plough. This sounds simple enough, and perhaps it is simple to the experts who do it, but to the uninstructed the difficulties, especially on a perfectly flat piece of land, seem enormous. Of course the land is not perfectly flat; if it were, while hesitating to express a positive opinion, I presume that it would not be possible to drain without the help of a pump. Still, to take the instance of this field at Bedingham, it is so flat that the eye, or rather my eye, can detect no variation of level. In fact, however, there is a slight rise in the centre of the field, forming its watershed, so that the drains must run and discharge in two directions, starting from the watershed; or, to put it more clearly, although the drain trenches are cut straight from one side of the field to the other, the water does not flow the whole length of them, but does flow to the top or bottom ditch, according to the side of the watershed upon which it is collected in the soil. Now this and many other facts have to be mastered and borne in mind by the man who draws the drains; above all he has to know the exact slope of the various falls and the best spots for the outlets of the water. Further, he must make no mistake, or much money and labour may be wasted; and the curious part of it is that he does not make any mistake, at least in my experience I have never known him to do so. By 'him' I may explain that I mean the ordinary ploughman who is set to draw the drains, not an expert employed for that purpose. Theoretically, and perhaps actually, he is provided with a spirit-level, but I do not think that he often uses that instrument.

It may be asked, then, how he accomplishes his task; to which I answer that I do not know, for nothing is more difficult than to get a clear explanation of anything to do with their art from men of this stamp. I conclude, however, that on a difficult field the thing is done partly by eye and partly by watching the natural trickle of the water, but most of all by tradition. Very likely the man has drawn the drains before, perhaps several times upon this very field; or if he has not, his father has, or, failing him, someone else about the place.

In this country, where such labourers as remain on the land are practically *adscripti glebæ*, there are always men who know the history of a particular field for the last one or two generations. Thus, when I was draining the eight-acre, No. 2, here, with tile drains before it was laid down to permanent pasture, I remember some old pipes, of the sort that were used many years ago, measuring about an inch and a half in diameter, being turned up by the drainers, filled, each of them, with a core of stiff clay. An old man was standing beside me watching the operations. 'Ah!' he said, addressing the pipe, I remimber a-carrying of yow when I wore a lad more nor seventy yir ago. It transpired afterwards that in this remote period the old gentleman had been employed to place these narrow pipes—then, I believe, a new-fangled agricultural luxury—in little heaps ready to the hand of the man who laid the drains. He also told me, by the way, that in those days the field in question was common land, which someone enclosed and drained.

It is the fashion, especially in the comic papers, to talk of the agricultural labourer as Hodge—a term of contempt—and to speak of him as though he had about as much intelligence as a turnip. As a matter of fact, after a somewhat prolonged experience of his class, I say deliberately that, take it all in all, there are few sections of society for which I have so great an admiration. Of course, I am excepting black sheep, brutes, drunkards, and mean fellows, of whom there is an ample supply in every walk of life. But, on the other hand, I am excepting also any specimens palpably above the general level, and talking of the man as one meets him everywhere upon whatever farm one likes to visit.

Let us take the problem of life as it presents itself to that *rara avis*, the stay-at-home agricultural labourer of to-day. He has received some education—for, supposing him to be a man on the right side of forty, the Board schools had begun in his time—but he does not trouble himself much about learning. As soon as he was out of school he began work on a farm in his parish, and at nineteen or twenty, following a natural and proper impulse, he took to himself a wife. From that day, earlier than is the case with any other class of society, his responsibilities began. Being still so young he would not be trusted in any of the higher positions on a farm, such as that of horseman, but his work would be that of a general labourer earning, let us say, an average wage of about thirteen shillings a week, including his harvest. Within five years he would have at least three children, perhaps more, and within twelve years seven or eight living, all of whom must be supported by the daily labour of his hands, and who, in nine cases out of ten, are so supported. Besides providing for these children, he pays the rent of his cottage, 3*l.* or 4*l.* a year, and, if he is a prudent man, a subscription towards an Oddfellows or other benefit society, which makes him an allowance on the rare occasions when he falls sick

or is disabled by accident.   It is during these first seventeen or
eighteen years of his married life that the burden of existence falls
most heavily upon him, since there are many mouths to feed and
only one pair of hands to provide the food.   Still, in the vast
majority of instances, it is provided, and, what is more, if his wife
be a managing woman blessed with fair health, the children are
sufficiently, and in many instances neatly, clothed.   Often, when
passing the school of this parish as the scholars are coming out
of it, I have noticed and wondered at their general tidiness and
good appearance.   Not one of them looks starved, not one of
them seems to be suffering from cold ; indeed, any delicate
youngster is provided with a proper coat or comforter.

Afterwards, when his family is growing up, our labourer's long
struggle against want becomes less severe, for the boys begin to
earn a little, some of which finds its way to the general fund, and
the girls go out as servants, kitchen-maids, or ' generals,' in situations where they are well fed and paid enough to dress themselves,
leaving a pound or two in their pockets at the end of the year.   So
matters go on until our friend becomes old, which common misfortune overtakes him about the age of seventy.   Then it is that
too frequently the real tragedy of life strikes him.   He is no
longer able to do a full day's work, and in these times, when the
best of farmers can scarcely make both ends meet and earn a
living, it is not to be expected, indeed it is not possible, that they
should continue to pay him for what he cannot perform.   Therefore, if help is not forthcoming from his children or other sources,
he must sink to the workhouse, or at least upon the rates.

Such but too often, though by no means universally, is the
bitter end of his long life of useful and strenuous labour.   Is it a
necessary end?   I think not.   I know all the pitfalls and difficulties that surround the question of Old-Age Pensions.   This is
not the place to discuss them fully, but for my part I believe that
the case of a deserving labouring man ought not to be beyond the
reach of some system of insurance, though whether it should be
national insurance—that is to say, inaugurated, managed, and

guaranteed by the nation—or conducted in the ordinary way by private enterprise, I do not know. Any such insurance, however, necessarily presupposes a steady contribution that the beneficiary can ill afford to the fund which provides it, and it is here that the trouble comes in. It is difficult, if not impossible, to force free men to contribute to such a fund by Act of Parliament; yet, if they are not forced, would the bulk of them keep up their payments through a long life of penury? Would they, even if they so desired, be able to keep them up? Even the strongest man is sometimes sick; even the most deserving is sometimes out of work. Moreover, it seems to me that it is of the essence of the thing that this provision should not be a mere dole provided by the State or by charities, for such a system could never stand. To be effective, to be appreciated, and to be generally adopted, it must, under the common law of life, be provided by the labour and self-sacrifice of the person benefited.[1]

The problem before society is to discover by what method—State-guaranteed or otherwise—this can be done without crushing the wage-earner into the dirt during his long years of contribution, and in such a fashion as will assist him without debasing the great principles of self-help and self-reliance. Again I say that however difficult this problem may appear, I do not believe it to be insoluble, indeed I hope to live long enough to see it on the way to solution.

[1] Recently I have insured all the men in my employ, farm and domestic servants together, with a policy under which, in case of death or disablement by illness or accident, they or their representatives obtain certain advantages. This policy, I may explain, has nothing to do with the Employers' Liability Acts, under the provisions of which farmers are not liable, except in the case of misfortunes resulting from the use of steam machinery, although it covers all such possible risks. Yet, although, *faute de mieux*, I have adopted it, the system in my opinion is bad. A man ought to insure himself out of his own earnings, or if he will not, then the State should force providence upon him. Other trades (unless the law intervenes) do not provide for their servants in this fashion. For instance, so far as I am aware, my literary employers have not found themselves called upon to insure me against the results of accident, breakdown, or premature imbecility.

Money is deducted from dividends or other earnings to satisfy income-tax. Would it not be possible by some similar legislative regulations to oblige the employer to pay over a certain percentage of all wages to a great insurance fund for the benefit of the person who is temporarily deprived of such percentage, and, that these laws might not appear invidious, to apply their principle to the earnings of every class of society? Of course this would be an interference with the liberty of the subject to do what he likes with what he has earned, but then so is the income-tax. *That* goes to support the nation; *this* would go to support the individual, his family, or his representatives. I cannot see that there is more degradation in being forced to contribute towards a pension fund than in being forced to contribute towards the income-tax. In fact, I believe that this system already obtains in the Indian Civil Service and elsewhere, but I never heard that Indian civil servants felt themselves degraded or aggrieved because they were obliged to comply with it. I am sure, indeed, that most of us would be deeply grateful to any Government that from the beginning had insisted on collecting, say, ten per cent. of our earnings for our own benefit.

Of course many would object in every walk of life, and especially among the labouring classes — that section of them who, from improvidence or idleness, are pretty certain to end upon the rates. Of course, also, because any such measure would not only be difficult in its details, but unpopular among a large number of voters, no Government is likely to undertake it at present. Even were it convinced that it was for the welfare of the nation, it is doubtful whether any Government would undertake it, because as a general rule Governments think of their own welfare first. And it may be argued that it is *not* for the welfare of the nation. All the old saws as to the natural and proper ruin and disappearance of the unfit, the unlucky, and the improvident, would certainly be trotted out. Life, we should be told, and the good things thereof, are to the strong and the rich, and to those who know how to save or to transfer

the savings of others to their own pockets. As to the thought-
less or indeed wicked person who has neglected to put by sufficient for his old age out of twelve shillings a week, well, he must
take the consequences and go to the workhouse with any dependent upon him. To force him to provide for himself would be to
emasculate the race and to deprive it of the instinct of thrift and
the stimulus of self-denial.

Well, if this be so, I should like to see the race emasculated.
I think that the object of all good government ought to be to
provide for the greatest happiness of the greatest number in
every legitimate way that does not involve interfering with the
established rights of others. I think that the 'survival of the
fittest' theory can be pushed too far. It is very well to point to
Nature; but I answer that I do not approve of Nature—that in fact
all our life as a race, as communities, as individuals, is one long
struggle against Nature. Of course Nature must win in the end,
but at least we can mitigate her cruelties. My sympathies go out
to the weak, the unfortunate, and even to the improvident. I am
more moved by the sight—let us say—of the drayman who, with
his family, sinks to the workhouse because of a too frequent indul-
gence in bad beer (bought at a 'tied house') than by that of the
glory of his employer, the brewer, who (having had opportunity
and being strong and provident), because he has mastered the art
of making that beer cheaply and selling it dear, is now a noble
lord with an estate that will pay death-duties on a million. I
would not interfere with the brewer and his million, except perhaps
by way of a graduated income-tax, but I would try to protect the
drayman against himself, for his family's sake if not for his own.
Moreover, I would see, by the way, that the beer with which he
fuddles his brain *was* beer, not the mixture of quassia chips, sugar,
and other foreign ingredients which in some instances, perhaps,
has helped to make a millionaire of his master, and that the
public-house where he deals has liberty to sell him whatever brew
he may prefer.

Doubtless these ideas are very radical, but there are points upon which some of us grow more radical as we grow older. Also I am sure that they have been better argued by others. Still, they are my own, not got from books, but the honest result of my private observations, and there can therefore be no harm in setting them down here. I believe, moreover, that posterity will ratify them.

To return to our labourer. Most people unacquainted with the routine of a farm have a notion that his duties are of the simplest description. To these I would say—let them try any one of them, even the easiest, such as 'drawing' a ditch, and I think that they will change their views. In truth, there is no single operation on the land that does not require a very considerable amount of skill to perform it properly, and this skill, acquired by years of practice, the agricultural labourer puts at the service of anyone who will pay him thirteen shillings a week. Moreover, there is no nonsense about eight hours a day with him. With brief intervals for food he labours from six to six, or more, and in winter from daylight to dark. Indeed, horsemen and cattlemen work longer; moreover, when calves or foals are expected they have often to sit up all night, perhaps for the best part of a week, and this without extra charge. Likewise, holidays are for them practically non-existent, and if the weather should be such that it is impossible for farm-work to continue, the labourer goes home and is docked of his wage.

The sympathetic, on reading these details, may possibly say to the writer of them, 'We hope that *you* pay your men a higher wage, and don't send them home when the weather is bad?' As regards the last, certainly I do bid my steward to try always to find them a job of some sort or other, however hard it may freeze, or snow, or rain. As regards the first, like Mr. Curzon in the House of Commons, I say that the answer is in the negative. The man who, from philanthropic or other motives, began to pay his labourers more than the local rate of wage would bring down upon himself the concentrated curse of his entire neighbourhood. Moreover, if, like myself, he is a farmer farming as a business, he cannot possibly afford to do so. Nobody runs a large farm and

pays away several hundreds per annum in wages as a mere amusement for long, or if 'nobody' is a large term, very few do so.   In
short, the labourer is paid according to the value of his labour, and
owing to the dreadful depression in farming, and the nominal
price of produce, its value is not great.   I hope to see his wage
rise, but it cannot rise appreciably unless the price of produce
rises also.   Meanwhile he is taking the matter into his own hands,
and deserting the land.

If you argue this question of the labourer's lot with farmers,
who, as a class, are very severe critics of the actual tillers of
the soil, they will point out that, owing to the fall in the price
of provisions, although wages are so low, his circumstances are
better than they were fifty or a hundred years ago.   This is
doubtless true, but they neglect to explain what his position was
at the beginning of the century.   Those interested in the question
can easily study it in the pages of various writers, but to my mind
the marvel is that when wheat was selling for 5*l.* or 6*l.* a quarter,
and cottages were mere mud-hovels, the race continued to exist.
On this property, not a quarter of a mile from my house, there
stands a shed built of clay-lump, and roofed, I think, with faggots ;
it may measure sixteen feet in length by about ten in breadth, and
inside is divided into two parts, now tenanted by calves.   In that
shed an old lady—not of the poorest, for she planted a large
orchard—reared a numerous family, one of whom was for many
years my groom.   Nowadays the cottage which I provide upon
the holding contains two sitting and several bed rooms, with ample
offices—an instance that shows how in this respect things have
changed for the better.

Sometimes I wonder whether any labourers will be content to
stick to the soil at the present scale of remuneration.   Doubtless the
older men at present employed upon it will do so because they must,
but how about their sons ?   The education which they receive at
the schools teaches them that there are places in the world
besides their own Little Pedlington, with the result that already
there is an enormous influx into the towns, where wages are higher
—for those who can get them—and life is more lively.

That the people go somewhere is proved by the fact that, in spite of its great increase throughout England, the population of our villages is rapidly waning, and that really skilled farm hands, men who can plough, thatch, drain, and milk, are becoming more and more difficult to find. At present, however, I do not think that the surplus gets much further than the cities. In the future, as their minds become accustomed to the idea, and they grow to understand how great are the opportunities of the British Colonies, perhaps the young men will drift thither. At present bricklayers in Bulawayo are being paid a pound and an ordinary labouring man ten shillings a day, and were he less stay-at-home these are prices that might tempt Mr. Hodge to travel, especially as in those lands Jack is as good—or rather better—than his master.

Up till now, if the inhabitant of a Norfolk village emigrates, it is generally to America, and very often he does not like America when he gets there. I remember a blacksmith with whom I was well acquainted going to the States, but in a couple of years he was to be seen working at the old forge in his native village. I asked him why he had come back, and he told me that he earned plenty of money out there, but he 'didn't like it.' When I was in New York a tailor came to see me who had been an apprentice here in Bungay. He told me the same story. Plenty of money, especially at times, but he 'meant to get back as soon as he could.' Also I had a conversation with an English coachman, whose tale was much the same. His wages were large, but 'there weren't no society for such as him'; in the States they were all 'gents or niggers.'

When the labouring classes come to know it, circumstances are different in the British Colonies, where a hard-working, respectable man still has a chance of rising to almost any position, and of seeing his sons and daughters in the same social station as the gentry of the country parish which he has left at home. Of course, however, these lands will fill up, and such opportunities become rare. In the meanwhile two potent considerations above all others prevent the young men of our villages from availing themselves of them : First, their innate horror of change and of the unknown ; and, secondly, reasons not unconnected with the other sex. To emigrate with a family is difficult, and if they emigrate as unmarried men, in nineteen cases out of twenty they must leave some girl with whom they are more or less mixed up behind them. Therefore, as such affairs begin early among this class, they do not emigrate as yet—except to London ; at least, not in any great numbers. With the Irish, who have gone out to people many lands, it is a different matter.

Thus it comes about that the towns still leave us a decreasing number of labourers who are content to stop in the village which has been inhabited by their ancestors for hundreds of years, and to till the fields that their forefathers tilled from the times of the Tudors or Plantagenets, although, as I have said, it is very noticeable that among the younger men can be found few good ploughmen or yardmen. Indeed the lack of these skilled hands is becoming one of the most serious questions, if not the most serious, that the farmer has to face.

In our part of the world a certain proportion of the lads go for soldiers, and a still larger number become amphibious ; that is to say, they take service on Lowestoft smacks during the herring season. As a rule the smacksmen do better than the soldiers, for the latter almost invariably return after their eight years' service to find themselves absolutely unfitted at six-and-twenty or so to follow the avocation of an agricultural labourer. A few get situations as grooms—I have two such men in my employment at this moment ; but there is a general, though frequently a very unjust, prejudice against them. The farmers will have nothing to do with them, for they say, perhaps rightly, that they have lost touch with the land, and are of little use upon it.

I remember trying to persuade my bailiff to take on a young fellow, the son of one of my horsemen, who had come home from his spell of short service, but without result. He was physically a fine man, and very willing, but the answer was that though he might be all very well for odd jobs, he was no good as a labourer. Failing to find employment— I tried to get him admitted into the police, but he was a little over age—he went to sea as a smacksman, and was drowned on his first voyage. His brother, who had also been a soldier, hung about his parents' house without employment till, as it was said, he took to drinking. At any rate, his mind became unhinged, and he committed suicide a few days before the ex-soldier was lost at sea. The worst thing that a young fellow from a country village can do is to enlist, unless he means to make soldiering the profession of his life. It is all very well to take on an eight years' engagement at forty years of age; at eighteen, with your life before you, it seems a folly.

My remarks upon the rural labourer have led me away from the subject of bush draining at Bedingham, to which I now return.

After the furrows are drawn all loose soil is neatly cleared from them with a shovel. Then the drainers begin their task. Generally they labour in pairs, agreeing to drain the field by piece-work on payment of so much *per* rod. In this fashion hardy, untiring men can earn a good deal more than the usual daily wage, although, draining being so laborious, they are in any case somewhat better paid for it than for other kinds of work. It is curious to watch them at their toil. They seldom do anything hurriedly or seem to over-exert themselves. I have never seen a labourer employed about his work show any sign of physical distress, however hard it may chance to be; that is to say, his colour does not change or his breathing come quicker, nor does he turn faint or weaken about the knees. This is because he knows how to use his strength—how much, in short, he can expend daily without overdrawing the account.

Now, one unaccustomed to labour who has suddenly to undertake it will almost invariably make the mistake of working too hard, or too quickly, and thereby exhausting himself. When I was a young fellow I owned a farm in South Africa, and as my partner and I were determined to show a good example to the Kaffirs and wished to earn as much as we could, we laboured with our own hands, a thing which very few white men do out there if they are in a position to make anyone else labour for them. Our work consisted principally in building sod walls, making bricks, and cutting hay with a machine.

The bricks were heavy enough, but it was the wall-building that exhausted me, as those awful sods never seemed to weigh less than half a hundredweight and there was an infinite supply of them. In fact, sod-walling knocked me up, and this I attribute to the fact that I worked too hard through want of training to the game. An ordinary labourer no stronger than I was would have placed sods all day without feeling more than comfortably tired at the end of it, but he would have placed them more slowly. Mine was the old mistake of *trop de zèle*.

Grass-cutting was the lightest work of these various pastoral occupations, although in Africa even grass-cutting has its risks. Our custom was to yoke four oxen on to the machine. This team was led by my partner, while I sat on the seat and managed the lever that lifts the knives—an anxious task, for the flat top of the mountain where we cut the hay was peppered over with large stones which, if struck full by the knife-sheaths, might have smashed the machine—a valuable thing in those days—all to fragments. The stones, however, were not so bad as the ant-bear holes, which in some cases it was impossible to see, although very often they were several feet in diameter. Into these from time to time one of the iron wheels would fall with a bump, and then the problem was for the operator to prevent himself from being thrown off the seat on to the knives and hacked to pieces by them.

Once cut, the process of haymaking was simple. We never attempted to turn the grass, but left it to dry for a day in the hot sun. Then, as we lacked carts, by the help of a horse-rake of our own manufacture we dragged the stuff into large cocks about the size of a Kaffir hut, and covered it with old waggon-cloths. In this way, as the grass was plentiful and we worked hard, on one occasion we made in about three weeks a bulk of hay which we sold to the Commissariat for over 200*l.* ; for, as a war was in progress at the time, fodder was in considerable demand. This proved the most profitable bit of farming that ever I did, and I am always proud to remember that I once earned 240*l.*, or the half of it, by the labour of my own hands.

To return from Rooi Point to Bedingham. The drains having been cleared, the *modus operandi* is as follows : First one man goes down the line digging out a spit of soil with his draining-spade, a narrow, heavy tool furnished with a projecting bar upon which the foot is set. It takes three cuts of this spade, each of them driven home up to the projecting bar, to loosen the spit, that with a slow heave of the labourer's body and a quick movement of his arm is then thrown out to one side. After him comes his mate, armed with a still narrower tool, who, in like fashion, cuts out and removes a deeper spit. This work is even harder than that of the first man, since No. 2 is now digging in primæval clay, which at Bedingham is about the toughest stuff that I ever saw. If anyone doubts it, let him get some upon his boots on a wet day and then try to get it off again. When a suitable length of drain has been done out thus to the depth of a double spit, No. 2 man takes another instrument called a scoop, something like a trowel with the handle set more or less at right angles, and with it cleans the bottom of the drain, into which it exactly fits, till it is quite neat and level. Then, having first removed with his fingers any little clods or other obstructions that may have fallen into it, he lifts bushes from the heaps that are laid at intervals along the course of the drain, and packs a sufficient quantity of them into the cutting, thrusting them down to the narrow bottom of the V by means of a forked stick. These bushes, by the way, must not be mere hedge trimmings, but good stout stuff of five or six years' growth, otherwise they will rot long before their time.

When the bushes have been thrust home clods of clay are thrown loosely into the cutting to fill it up, and practically the drain is finished. These drains, by the way, are generally cut about six or eight yards apart. They do not, for the most part, run direct into the receiving ditch, but into another drain drawn at right angles, which is called a 'lead,' and in the case of tile drains is furnished with larger pipes. From this lead 'eyes' open into the ditch wherever may be convenient.

To contemplate the spectacle of two men commencing to drain a great expanse of six or eight acres of stiff clay land on some dull and cheerless day in January is to understand the splendid patience of developed man, that gift by which he has been able to lift himself from the level of the savage, or as some believe (although I am not one of them) from the moral and physical status of the gorilla. The task looks so vast in the miserable grey light; it seems almost impossible, indeed, that two men should find the strength to dig out all those long lines of trenches, or at least that they should have the spirit to attempt it. Yet if you speak to them you will find that they are not in the least depressed at the prospect, in fact the only thing which troubles them is the fear lest frost or heavy snow should force them to pause in their monotonous labour. Go away, and return in about ten weeks' time, and, if the weather has kept open, probably you will find them engaged in finishing the last cut, with dozens of long rough furrows on the hither side of them, each of which shows a completed drain.

The strange part of the thing is that such toilers betray not the least delight at the termination of their long labour. I have come to the conclusion that the agricultural labourer cares little for change or variety in his work; that if he were paid what he considered a satisfactory wage he would be content to go on till he grew old digging drains in the same flat clay field through the same miserable January weather. Perhaps this is because so little change and variety come his way, poor fellow! except that of the mutable face of Nature, whereof, so far as one can discover, very often he takes but small account.

January 15.—The mild, windless weather continues, bringing with it a great deal of influenza and other sickness. It is, however, a splendid open time for farmers; thus, to-day, at a season of the year when very often everything is frost-bound, I have three ploughs going on the farm, while carts are carrying dead leaves from the shrubbery to the yards, and mud 'fyed' from a pond is being dumped into heaps to be spread upon the back lawn. To-day also we have begun felling the undergrowth on the Bath Hills, most of which has not been cut for the last twelve or fourteen years. In properly managed woodlands the fell ought to be taken every seven years ; indeed, in considerable woods it is divided into seven portions for this purpose, one portion being cut each year, when the stouter stuff is split for hurdles, and the rest, of less substance, twisted into another form of hurdle which is known as a ' lift,' the remaining brushwood being tied for faggots.

In another part of Norfolk, where I was born, I remember my father taking a visitor who had been bred in London round the Big Wood, and elaborately explaining to her how one-seventh of it was cut down each year. ' Dear me ! ' she exclaimed, staring at some oaks in the fell which might have seen between two and three hundred winters, 'I never knew before that trees grew so big in seven years.' The story reminds me of that of another lady whom I escorted to a field where we were drilling wheat. I showed her some of the grain, and, as she did not seem to recognise it, explained to her that it was the origin of the common or domestic loaf. ' What ! ' she exclaimed incredulously, ' do you mean to tell me that bread is made out of those little hard things ? I always thought that it came from that fine white stuff which grows in flowers ! ' Evidently there was some confusion in the lady's mind between flour and flowers. Exactly what it was it is not now safe to ask her to explain. Indeed, she boldly repudiates the story.

It will be observed that of these various agricultural operations which are now in progress, only one, the felling, can be carried on in frost, while even that must cease during snow or heavy rain. Well-to-do people often express a wish for a ' good old-fashioned winter,' but they do not understand what hardship this means to the poor, with whom fuel is scanty, and who have to earn their daily bread by labouring on the land. The poor, who do not skate or make snowballs, pray for an open winter; although, indeed, frost in moderation is a good thing for the land, as it pulverises the earth and destroys noxious insects by the thousand.

To-day I saw the first snowdrops blooming in the garden.

In walking over the eight-acre meadow on Baker's to look at the dykes which the man has now finished drawing, I heard the partridges calling to each other on the neighbouring layer for the first time this year. I have not, however, seen any pairs as yet. This meadow is full of docks, the result of long neglect, and it will cost much trouble and expense to get rid of them. On our marshes, indeed, it is impossible to keep clear of these weeds, for as fast as you pull them out new ones establish themselves, sprung from seed brought down by the flood water. The vitality of the dock is something dreadful. (Query: Why are all evil things, even among herbs, more vigorous and easier of propagation than good things? He who could answer this question would, I suppose, know the riddle of the world!) To-day I picked up one on the wheatland, of which the root stood several inches above the surface of the soil. On pulling it out of the earth I discovered that its head was buried deep in the ground. Yet, in that unnatural position, even thus early in the year, it was growing vigorously, for from the crown of the plant were springing thick tufts of leaves, which on their journey to the surface had bent themselves into the shape of a hook. Another week or two and that dock would have been completely re-established, with the difference that what had been its head would henceforth be its tail.[1]

Ever since I began to observe the ways of plants I have been trying to discover what useful part a dock can perform in the economy of Nature, but hitherto without the slightest result. It is a great exhauster of the land, since, if left undisturbed, it will grow to the dimensions of a moderate-sized carrot; no animal,

---

[1] Where will a dock not live? On the shore of the Island of Coll in the Hebrides I found one recently flourishing in a cranny of rock, almost without soil, and exposed to the washing of sea spray and the full fury of the northern gales.

so far as I can learn, will touch its foliage, and I think that even grubs and insects avoid the root, at least I never remember seeing it at all eaten.   If anyone knows what its real use may be I shall be obliged if he would inform me.[1]

By the way, taking into consideration the extraordinary re-productive powers of this and other noxious plants, how does it come about that when left to themselves they do not absolutely and entirely possess the land?   According to all the rules of arithmetical progression it would be easy to prove that if you started one dock in the middle of a hundred-acre field, in so many months or years that field must be nothing but a tangled mass of docks.   Yet this would not be the case; docks and other weeds there would be in plenty, also a proportion of wholesome grasses.   What regulates the proportion and keeps the balance? How is it that one thing does not obtain the mastery?   The same problem confronts us in the animal world.   There is no apparent reason why any particular noxious pest or insect should not increase to such an extent as must make all other life im-possible.   Yet it never does.   Even a bacillus knows where to stop, for the Black Death was satisfied with killing *half* the population.

On my way home I stopped to see the cart being filled from the lower clamp of swedes in the twelve-acre known as the Thwaite field.   For some reason or other these swedes have rotted considerably.   I can only suppose that the mild weather has caused them to ferment; and, indeed, in such a season as we have had, they would have kept just as well, or better, not earthed up at all, or left quite open at the top to allow the heat to escape. Perhaps, if the theory advanced by my friend at the audit is correct, it applies to swedes as well as to beet, and these were 'haled' too dry.   Swedes grown with artificial manure are said to rot more readily than others, but these in question were treated with farmyard muck.   Curiously enough, there are many more decayed bulbs in the middle than at either end of the hale.

January 19.—A day of woe and desolation !   My best ox is

[1] For an answer to the above question see p. 230.

dead. When, somewhat unexpectedly, I took on Baker's Farm last November, not having sufficient cattle to stock it, I was obliged to buy ten head on Norwich market, which I did at a price of thirteen pounds apiece. I have never done this before, and, unless it is absolutely necessary, I never mean to do it again, as I look upon these market cattle with great distrust. For the most part they come from Ireland, and then are hawked about from sale to sale until their owner gets what he considers an advantageous offer. Thus they might begin at Lynn and go to Dereham, and thence to Norwich, on each occasion standing for a whole day in the market-place. Consequently, when they leave these pens the brutes are ravenous, and pick up and swallow any rubbish that they can find, thus laying the foundation of internal disorders ; also often enough, although they may not show the result of it till afterwards, they have been knocked about upon board ship, or in the trucks, or on the road by brutal drovers.

The cruelty which this class of men will sometimes show to animals in their charge is almost incredible, especially if they happen to have had a glass too much beer and the beasts are obstinate or troublesome. A year or so back, when I was wait-ing at Forncett Station for a train on market day, I saw two drovers driving pigs up an inclined plank into a truck. One of these pigs refused to go up the plank and ran away once or twice, whereupon the men beat it about the head with their heavy sticks till it was three-parts stunned and the blood came from its ears and nostrils. Fortunately I had a minute or two to spare before the train came in, and was able to employ it in a rapid visit to the police. These men were afterwards prosecuted for cruelty to animals, but I do not know with what result, as I was away from home at the time.

A few days after their arrival here one or two of these pur-chased oxen, which were fine-grown but rather poor Irish beasts, showed signs of not being very well. Hood and I were afraid lest they might be about to develop an infectious disease, for that risk he who buys cattle on the market must take also. They recovered, however, and went on fairly until to-day. Then, as Hood was on his way to visit them, he met the boy whose business it is to feed the beasts at Baker's running to seek him in great fright with the news that one of the oxen (of course the biggest and best) was 'blown.' Blown he was sure enough, for there he lay on his back, swollen to almost twice his size, his legs feebly kicking in the air. He must have been in this condition for some time, perhaps the best part of an hour, and, had the case been reported at once, probably he could have been cured by means of a drink such as all cattle-owners keep at hand. But lads are not so observant as they might be, and thus it came about that the youth in charge never noticed his condition until too late, though I think that he will be more careful in future. Blowing, or 'hoven,' it may be explained for the benefit of the uninitiated, results from the gluttony of cattle, that sometimes fill themselves so full with food that in the fermentation which ensues there is no room for the gases to escape. Then the pressure seems to close the pipes, and they fall upon their backs, where they lie kicking violently until the gases, pushing upon the heart, stop it, and the interesting sufferer expires, like one of the early English kings, from 'a surfeit of good cheer.'

Finding that the beast was dying, Hood, having nothing at hand with which to despatch him, drove as hard as he could to Bungay and brought back the butcher. Then, not without difficulty, the dead animal was hauled on to a cart and taken to the town to be opened. It was curious to watch the demeanour of the other oxen in the yard while these melancholy scenes were in progress. They sniffed at the carcass, whisked their tails, and gambolled awkwardly as though they were experiencing some gentle and pleasing excitement. I have often heard it said that cattle are terrified at the smell of blood, but in this case I could not see a sign of fear about them, although undoubtedly they understood that something unusual was going on.

It would be interesting if anyone could discover what is the exact measure of an ox's intelligence. Here, where they are confined in yards, fatting, it would seem to be almost entirely limited to matters connected with the food which they gorge so persistently. But that oxen are not altogether fools will be evident to anyone who, like myself, has had considerable experience of them in Southern Africa, where they are the draught animals of the land. Notably they are very clever in finding their way across country to the place where they were bred, or where they have lived a long while, sometimes for a distance of hundreds of miles, though I very much doubt whether, in the case of oxen, this is not instinct rather than intelligence.

That in the case of horses it is intelligence I think I can prove by the following story : When I lived in Africa I had a hunting horse called Moresco, a remarkable beast, of great speed, endurance, and sure-footedness. This creature was so clever that I have known him resort to extraordinary artifices to obtain food, such as lying down and wriggling himself upon his side underneath a waggon till he could reach the sack where the mealies were kept and gnaw a hole in it with his teeth. Then, still lying on his side, he devoured most of the contents. Also, once he broke open a door to get at the forage stored behind it. When I was travelling with him on circuit through New Scotland, the great horse-breeding district of the Transvaal, Moresco one night broke the *riem* with which he was tied to the waggon and made off after a troop of mares. We searched for him without avail, and at length, as it was absolutely necessary that we should open Court in a certain town on a fixed day, we were obliged to abandon him. I think it was three mornings afterwards that I climbed out of the waggon at daylight to find Moresco standing untied among our other horses. As roads in this part of South Africa in those days were nothing but tracks wandering hither and thither across the veldt, of which we had crossed many during the time while he was lost, I can only suppose that this horse, when he was tired of the company of the mares, had deliberately taken up our spoor and followed it till he found us forty or fifty miles away.

A year or two afterwards Moresco was stolen from Newcastle, in Natal, where I was then living, and for six months we mourned him as lost beyond redemption. One day, however, the poor creature, a mere scaffolding of skin and bones, with a dreadful hole almost through his withers produced by neglected sore back, was found wandering about upon the farm. Subsequent inquiries went to show that the man who stole Moresco had ridden him into the Cape Colony, nearly a thousand miles away, and that the horse had escaped thence and found a path back to his home.

The end of this horse, the most remarkable which I ever knew, was so pathetic that I will tell it. He was what is called salted, that is to say, he had survived the horse-sickness, and it was supposed, therefore, that he could not catch it again. This, however, proved to be an error ; indeed, my experience goes to show that very few horses are so thoroughly salted that they will not re-develop the sickness, generally in a different form, under conditions favourable to that disease. Moresco's state when he escaped from the thief in the Cape Colony was such that had he been any other animal I should have shot him. As an old favourite and companion he was kept and nursed, however, in the hope that he might ultimately recover. But 1881, the year of the Boer war, was a dreadful season for sickness ; I remember that we lost two hundred pounds' worth of horses by it in a single week. At last the plague seized upon poor old Moresco also. We did what we could for him—which was little enough, for, though animals occasionally recover, there is no real remedy for horse-sickness—and then were obliged to leave him to take his chance.

At the rear of my house at Rooi Point stood a wall of loose stones nearly four foot high, with a gate in it which was shut in the evening. About midnight we were awakened by the sound of a clumsy knocking upon the back door. On investigating the cause it was found that poor Moresco, feeling himself dying, had contrived to climb the wall and was seeking our assistance and calling attention to his sad state by the only means in his power, namely, by knocking at the door. Nothing could be done for him, so he was driven through the gate, and in the morning we found him dead not far away.

By way of illustration of this story I may add that I remember, when I lived in Pretoria, another instance of a horse belonging to an acquaintance, which, on feeling itself mortally stricken with sickness, came and pawed at the door of his house. Also, the animal of which I have spoken, Moresco, was an exception among his kind—they say that every man owns one perfect beast in his life, and Moresco was mine. It is by no means wise, however, always to trust to the instinct of horses, and especially to their supposed faculty of finding their way home upon a dark night. Once I did this near Maritzburg, in Natal, with the result that presently I found myself, with the horse, at the bottom of a stone-pit!

To return to the case of the oxen. Although in some particulars they show undoubted intelligence, in many ways they are great fools. Thus they seem to have no knowledge of what is or is not good for them to eat. In Natal there grows a herb called 'tulip,' which is almost certain death to cattle, a fact with which they must have been acquainted for generations. Yet they seem to eat it greedily whenever they get the chance. Once I lost about twenty valuable trek-oxen from this cause alone. This incident, and the tale of horse-sickness, to say nothing of the recent record of rinderpest, will show the reader that farming in South Africa is not without its risks. Indeed, I am acquainted with no country where the waste of animal life is so constant and tremendous, although doubtless as the land becomes enclosed and proper buildings and winter food are provided it will greatly lessen.

Returning to the Home Farm after watching the funeral procession of the departed ox, I found the pork-butcher, who had arrived there to execute a pig. He informed me that he had cured blown cattle by giving them salt and water, and drawing a sack over their heads, making it fast about their necks. The salt and water might do something, but I confess that I do not understand the sack. Another local recipe is to shut them up in a loose-box, exclude all air, and heap sacks upon them. My own opinion is that animals which recover under this treatment would not have died in any case. I believe also that the best preventive against 'blowing' is to have the root they feed on pulped and mixed with the chaff twelve hours before it is given to the cattle. This excellent plan allows fermentation to take place and the gases to escape before the food reaches the stomach of the ox. It is, however, very difficult to persuade farmers and bailiffs to adopt it, partly because they are prejudiced about the matter, and partly because it requires a little more thought and trouble, and a proper place is necessary where the pulped root can be kept safe and clean until it is wanted.

January 20.—To-day is extraordinarily mild for the time of year, and all the birds are singing with a full voice as though spring were already come. The garden, too, shows many signs of life, and one crocus has just opened its gold cup upon the north slope of the lawn bank. Three ploughs are going upon the eight-acre on Baker's Farm, No. 41, turning back the soil which was ploughed for barley a few weeks ago. This is a stiffish bit of land, and, if the weather holds fairly dry, a second ploughing will no doubt do it a great deal of good. Should it chance to come on wet, however, it may probably work it harm, as the freshly turned soil will then run together into a kind of cake. Still, since the season holds so dry, it seems worth while to take the risk.

This afternoon I saw the butcher who despatched the blown ox. He told me it is so bruised from long struggling on its back after it 'went down' that the meat is of little value, and added that he dared not send it to London for fear lest we should all get into trouble. I begged him on no account to do anything of the sort, as I do not wish to appear before a metropolitan magistrate in the character of a vendor of doubtful meat. He assured me that he will not, but as a matter of curiosity I should like to know what becomes of this class of beef. So far as I can gather it is consumed on board the herring-smacks; smacksmen, it would seem, are not dainty feeders.

January 23.—To-day, Sunday, is one of the most beautiful imaginable, very mild, with a fresh west wind and bright sunshine. I walked over Baker's Farm and found the wheat looking wonderfully well, while the grass seems to be growing visibly. The sunset to-night was especially lovely—a large glowing ball of fire without a cloud to dim it.

On Friday, the day after my last entry, we had more bad luck, for another of the bullocks at Baker's was taken sick ; he did not seem to be blown, but stood by himself, his back humped, his eye dull and his head hanging. The farrier says that he is suffering from obstruction in his third stomach—it was news to me that oxen are endowed with *three* of these useful organs. If the veterinary thinks so I suppose that he is right, but so far as I can judge the animal might just as well be suffering from anything else. Had we been in Africa I should say that he had contracted red-water, of which he has certainly many of the symptoms.

Hood is very indignant that another of this Irish lot should have gone wrong, and attributes it to the hay that we took over by valuation on Baker's, which undoubtedly is sticklike and mouldy, whereof he speaks in terms more forcible than polite. When the ox dies, as I presume he will sooner or later, although he was better yesterday, we shall find out whether it is to his third stomach or to his liver, or to something else, that his decease is due. Having satisfied myself that under no circumstances can these brutes return a halfpenny of profit, I await the issue in gloomy calm.

January 25.—The lambs are beginning to come faster ; yesterday I had two doubles. As I returned from looking at them I saw the first pair of partridges which I have noticed this year ; also I observe that the sparrows are beginning to build in the banksia rose on the south side of the house. These sparrows, which breed in millions in the towns, whence they migrate to the country, are a perfect pest to us, and I know not how to keep them under. In some parts of the farm they move about in flocks a hundred strong, and while the damage that they do is very great, I have been unable to discover in them a single redeeming virtue. They take coombs of corn out of some of the fields of wheat, spoiling even more than they devour, as they seem to like to pick the ears to pieces for mere mischief's sake. Also they are very destructive to young beet, especially if the crop has been planted in a small close, as they issue from the hedges on every side and tear the tender leaves to bits with their strong bills. As a climax to their crimes they attack the swallows and martins, driving them away and taking possession of their nests. Indeed, sometimes they kill them, for I have picked up the corpses of the poor things with a hole pecked through their skulls.

In former times Sparrow Clubs used to exist in these parts, under the provisions of which the farmers of a district banded themselves together to destroy the common enemy in any way possible, but with the decline of agriculture the clubs have vanished. Now we are obliged to rely upon the destructive instincts of youth, paying so much a score to boys for sparrows' eggs or young sparrows. Occasionally also in hard weather a good many can be killed by laying a trail of corn, and when the sparrows are feeding in flocks, firing down it with a charge of dust-shot. But the worst of this plan is that the shooter is very apt to massacre harmless birds, such as chaffinches and robins, which come to pick up any crumbs that may fall from the sparrows' table and are involved in their doom. Of late patent basket sparrow-traps have been largely advertised, and with them testimonials from gentlemen who say they have caught great numbers by their means. I purchased one of these wicker traps for five shillings, but the result showed that I might as well have kept my money in my pocket, as not one single sparrow have I been able to catch with it. I suppose, therefore, that the race must be more artful about here than in the neighbourhood of those gentlemen who give the testimonials. According to the directions, grain or crumbs should be sprinkled at the bottom of the trap, whereon the birds will go down the little hole in the middle and find themselves unable to get out again. My experience of the working of the thing has been that, whereas they will use the trap as

a perch gladly enough, not even the youngest and most inexperienced sparrow evinces the faintest intention of hopping down
the hole to investigate its inside and devour the dainties spread
to entice the unwary.

The only really effectual way of keeping these birds under is
by means of poisoned wheat, but this, unless spread with great
care in places frequented by sparrows alone, such as eaves and
water-troughings, is highly dangerous to all life. Also the sale of
it is illegal; indeed, we have convicted men for this offence
before my own Bench. Still, farmers use it a good deal under
the rose, and, I am sorry to say, not for sparrows only, but for
pigeons and rooks also, with the result that a great deal of game
and many harmless birds are poisoned. On the whole, taking
one farm with another, the bold, assertive, conquering sparrow,
that Avian Rat, as someone has aptly named him, pursues his career
of evil almost unchecked, producing as many young sparrows as
it pleases him to educate. Indeed, I do not understand how it
comes about that we are not entirely eaten up with these mischievous birds, except for the reason, as I have said on a previous
page, that there is some mysterious power which preserves a
balance amongst all things that live and grow.

I observed also, in the course of my walk, that the moles seem
to be very numerous this year, possibly on account of the mildness
of the season, for some of the meadows, and especially the lands at
the foot of the Vineyard Hills, are dotted all over with the brown
heaps of soil thrown up by them. Farmers dislike moles, and allege
much evil against them; but I believe that they do more good
than harm, at least on pastures, by bringing up so many tons
of quite fresh earth from the subsoil, which, when harrowed and
brushed, gives the grasses a dressing of new mould that must
benefit them much. Indeed, I doubt whether some pastures
which are frequently mown and never manured would keep their
fertility half as well as they do were it not for the action of moles
and worms. In his remarkable book upon earth-worms Darwin
has shown how great is the work they do upon the surface of the
world, and I believe that one part of it is to promote its fertility.

When entering the house after walking about the garden, the door shut behind me with a bang. As it chanced, I wished to go out again for some reason, and on reaching the steps I saw a curious sight. A little rough terrier dog, called Di, hearing the door slam—usually a signal to her that I am starting on my rounds—had run to seek me from some hole or corner where she was engaged in her hourly occupation of hunting a quite uncatchable rat. Not being able to see me, for I had gone into the house, not come out of it—a solution of the mystery which did not strike her—she set to work to trace my spoor, following every loop and turn that I had made as I wandered about the garden, and finally striking out across the tennis-court and over the lawn beyond, which I had crossed on my homeward way. The curious thing was not her following my spoor, for I have often seen her do this before, but the persistence and cleverness with which she followed it *backwards*. What I should like to know—and perhaps some reader of this book can inform me on the matter—is whether there is anything about the scent left by man or beast to enable a dog or other creature on the spoor to tell which way it runs. This instance of Di would seem to show that there is none ; but, after all, it is only one example, and she may be an undiscerning little dog. Also, it must be remembered that her mind was full of the preconceived idea that I had gone out of the house. It never occurred to her that I might have returned into it.

This morning I met Hood as he was driving the unlambed ewes from the little All Hallows farm meadow, where they are now confined at night, to the hay-stubble on Baker's, which we are folding before sowing it with oats. I stood talking with him for a minute or two, while the sheep went through the gateway on to the main road. When we followed, presently, not one of them was to be seen, till an ominous sound of munching caused me to look over a neighbouring fence. There were the ewes, the whole lot of them, in the well-kept garden of one of my men—at least it had been a garden, but that five minutes had sufficed to reduce it to a trodden wilderness with cabbage-stalks sticking up here and there.

I shouted aloud to Hood, whereupon the ewes, of their own accord, and without waiting to be driven, stopped gobbling the remains of the cabbages and ran to a hole, which they must have made in the thick fence with considerable effort and difficulty while we were talking, and through it, one by one, back into the road. This spontaneous retreat seems to prove that they knew perfectly well that they were doing what they should not. Indeed, I think that sheep are nothing like so foolish as they are supposed to be, though nearly all their intelligence seems to concentrate itself upon matters connected with their provender, for of the ovine race it may be said with truth, ' their god is their belly.' It is curious to notice how seldom they stop eating while there is anything left that excites their appetite, and how, after having fed heavily for hours in one place, on the gate being opened, they will rush to another in the hope of finding more food there. Thus this very morning, so soon as they had escaped from the ruined garden, they set off down the road, round the proper turn, to the gate of the field where they are penned in the daytime, about a quarter of a mile away. Here, heavy as they are in lamb, they broke into a full gallop in their eagerness to reach the turnips heaped on the land and steal some before their shepherd arrived to put them in the pen.

This afternoon I went to Bedingham, and found the wheats looking wonderfully green and thick, so much so that in the case of two of the pieces, Nos. 6 and 8 on the plan, they will, I think, have to be thinned by harrowing. The crops on these fields last year were respectively beans and pease, and doubtless we owe this fine prospect to the nitrogen collected from the atmosphere by these leguminous plants. The remaining piece of wheat, No. 9, is not nearly so strong, I suppose because it is grown on flag-land, this field having been a clover layer last year, off which a cut of hay was taken, followed, as the autumn proved suitable to its ripening, by a crop of seed.

I found Moore, who is in local charge of this farm, baulking or earthing up for root. He said, and I agreed with him, that the land had never been known to work so well at this time of year since we had to do with it, the long-continued drought having made it friable and tender, whereas in other Januaries often it is hard with frost or so stiff with wet that, if an attempt is made to stir the soil, it comes up in lumps as large as horses' heads.

The open season has been very fortunate for me upon this farm, as, owing to the taking over of Baker's, I was obliged to draw a horse from Bedingham, leaving two only, and one of these an old mare in foal. Therefore, had not the weather remained so clement that work could be attended to as it pressed, week in, week out, I might have been forced to buy another horse, which I do not wish to do, as I have several growing animals in stock. But, however dry the season, water is never far off in these stiff clays. Thus I could see it standing at the bottom of the trenches being cut by the drainers on field No. 18, and especially wherever they chanced to have crossed the line of an old drain and bled it. By the way, it is getting difficult to find enough bushes with which to finish this draining, almost all the suitable stuff having been used. There was plenty of it when I took over this farm, but since then the fences have gone underground.

To-day I have been making a plan for roofing in the horse and cattle yard at Bedingham with galvanised iron supported by oak posts. If possible, and if it is not too costly, I am anxious to deal thus with all my open yards, as I believe that the expense of closing them in, which, if one can provide the necessary timber, is not so very great, will be repaid in three years by the manure saved and the increase in its fertilising value. I have already three such sheds erected over yards, and there is no comparison between the stuff which comes from beneath them and that from the open pen which is frequently little better than dirty, rain-washed straw. Another thing is that roofed-in yards mean a great saving of the amount of litter used, and consequently less carting both in and out. I doubt—but this is, of course, only conjecture, as it is difficult to arrive at the exact quantities—whether the beasts in a closed-in yard will make away with much more than half the quantity of straw necessary to the wellbeing of an equal number of animals in an open pen during a wet season. Lastly, the cattle do far better under shelter.

January 28.—The day before yesterday I rode to Kessingland, fifteen miles away, on a bicycle, and beyond Beccles I stopped to talk with an old labourer who was hedge-trimming. He told me that he was seventy years of age and had worked in that neighbourhood all his life, but that never yet had he known such a season for the time of year, or the water in dykes, ponds, and springs to be so low.

Yesterday was mild and dry, and all my three ploughs were at work 'thwarting'—that is cross-ploughing—root-land on the Nunnery Farm.

A good many more lambs have been born, and, with their mothers, are established in comfortable little hurdle-made pens in the old barn at All Hallows. The worst of this plan is that the lambs get through the hurdles and become inextricably mixed in their vain attempts to find their own mothers. It is curious to notice the behaviour of the ewes when the wrong lamb comes to them. First they sniff at it, for to all appearance they are guided in this matter by the sense of smell alone ; then, if the result is unsatisfactory, they simply put down their heads and with a vicious butt knock the poor little creature into space. Evidently they have no affection for lambs as a class ; it is only their individual offspring that claims their sympathy. Yesterday we had to try one old ewe with about a dozen different lambs, each of which she knocked over in the most cold-blooded fashion. A cautious sniff at the thirteenth satisfied her that at length her missing infant had returned, whereon she baa-ed contentedly, and with a smile of maternal pride allowed it to partake of refreshment.

I noticed for the first time the brilliant but tiny scarlet blooms open upon the filbert bushes ; by the number of them it should be a good nut-year. My drill was hired out to a neighbour to put in his spring beans ; the man in charge of it told me that they went in very well.

To-day I have begun drilling my own spring beans and pease on the eight acres on Baker's, No. 43. This field has had a good coat of the manure which I took over by valuation, supplemented, as there was not enough available, by a few loads of Bungay compost, road scrapings, &c., in the far corner. Like the rest of the farm, it is foul, and will, I fancy, give plenty of work to the hoe, for the plough and harrows turn up docks like carrots, to say nothing of countless minor weeds. The tilth, however, is very good, and the beans, with as much of the pease as we could sow to-day, went in beautifully, not a single seed being visible after the drill had dropped them, for the soil ran in behind it almost like dry sand. We only use six 'coulters' on the drill, a seven-foot instrument, in planting beans, as against twelve or thirteen for pease, which are set much closer. Coulters, I may explain, in case there should be any who do not know them, are the shares connected with the body of the machine, whence the seed is lifted and dropped by wheels set with cups through a number of flexible funnels fitting one into the other. Down these funnels the seed trickles at a given rate, to fall grain by grain into the trench cut with the coulters. Preceding the drill, a rig or two ahead of it, goes a set of iron harrows dragged by two horses, tearing down the rough surface of the plough and breaking the clods into mould. Next comes the drill itself, dragged by three horses, with two men in charge of it. It is followed by the wood harrow, with a pair of horses, which fills in the furrows made by the coulters of the drill, burying the seed in the mould and completing the process.

It is still early to drill spring beans and pease, but I think it wise to get them in while the soil is in such good order, as in our uncertain climate it is impossible to say what kind of weather awaits us.

Some more lambs were born to-day, and my two Southdown rams were sold at Bungay market, the large one for forty shillings, and the smaller for twenty-five. I was sorry to part with the big ram, as he is a good-looking pedigree animal, but these creatures are a nuisance to keep through the summer; they cannot be allowed to run with the ewes, as they would knock about and perhaps kill the lambs, and if penned up they are apt to develop foot-rot. Of course, in large flocks, where there are proper provisions for keeping rams by themselves, it is another matter, but in the case of a little lot of sheep like mine it is best to get rid of them, and buy or hire others when they are wanted.

January 29.—This morning we finished drilling the pease on Baker's, No. 43, and also drilled four acres of pease on All Hallows, No. 37, the ten-acre which was under barley last year and is now divided into six acres of layer and four of pease. Like those sown on the other piece, they went in very well. In drilling with a number of coulters it is very necessary to watch that nearest to the wheel, since the earth lifted by it in its revolutions is apt to fall into the funnel and choke the lower exit. This happened to-day, with the result that the centre funnels filled with pease which could not escape, and necessitated the following backwards of the line cut by the coulter by a man who sowed with the hand the seed that had missed.

In the afternoon I went to Bedingham, where I found the men getting on very well with the draining of field No. 18. Bushes by now, however, have become scarce indeed, and as there is no fence left which we can cut, we have been obliged to fall back on the stout growth springing from the crowns of pollards. Here I found Moore splitting back the baulks on one of the fields which he had earthed up for root. Yesterday he horse-hoed No. 14, the five acres of winter beans. I should think that this is almost the first time within the memory of living man that beans have been horse-hoed at Bedingham on January 29. The immediate object of the operation was to get rid of some of the barley which dropped from last year's crop before it was carried. Two years ago we learnt a lesson in this matter of barley here at Ditchingham on the brick-kiln field, No. 22. The season before had been very dry, causing the grain to shed in quantity, with the result that in the following spring it came up thick among the beans. For some reason or other we were unable to horse-hoe it sufficiently early, and in the end, in order to prevent the beans from being smothered, we were obliged to pull the usurping barley by hand, for the hoe could not deal with it—a tedious and a costly process.

I have seldom seen beans looking better than those on this piece at Bedingham.

January 31.—Yesterday, Sunday, it rained sharply during the morning but cleared in the afternoon, when a gale came up from the south-west; at night also there were flaws of rain. The large ox, which was supposed to have recovered from the derangement of its third stomach, is sick again. Now it grinds its teeth and is foaming at the mouth as though it had hydrophobia. My own opinion is that none of them know from what the poor animal is suffering.

I find that I am now employing fifteen hands in all on the two farms, not reckoning Mrs. Hood, who makes the butter, or Mrs. Moore, who attends to the fowls at Bedingham. This allows for nine men and one boy on the home farms, with four men and one boy at Bedingham. One of these, however, is an extra man employed by piece-work on the draining.

To-day, the last of the month, is lovely and spring-like, with a drying north-west wind. This morning we drilled three acres of sheep's-feed on No. 24. This field has stood for two years under layer, and as it is light land, before the flag was broken up we gave it a dressing of heavy clay from the pit in this garden which was enlarged last autumn. Also, it has been more or less manured with road and yard scrapings, and anything else that we could find to put upon it. The rain of yesterday has not done much more than damp this light land, so the seed went in very well. We were using fifteen coulters on the drill, and one coomb, that is four bushels, of seed to the acre.

It looked a curious mixture as it lay in the boxes or hoppers of the drill, oats for the most part, mingled with wheat, tares, and a few beans, but doubtless the sheep will appreciate it in due course.

> He who would fill his pouch with groats
> In Januair must sow his oats,

runs the old saw—by the way, the word 'groats' shows that it must be a very old one—but these are the only oats that I have drilled as yet. To-morrow, however, if it is fine, we are sending five horses to Bedingham to drill oats, pease, and barley. Never before have we drilled barley so early, and both Hood and I (especially Hood) are rather doubtful of the wisdom of so doing on heavy land. The fact is that the fine, indeed the extraordinary weather we have had this month has made us a little 'winter-proud,' as they say of wheat that has grown too vigorously during the dead months of the year, and it is quite possible that before the sweet surprises of the English spring are done with our high hopes, like the wheat, may meet with an unexpected check. Still, I am for going straight ahead, as though the spring were, in truth, already with us, and sowing barley, or anything else if the land is fit to drill.

And so good-bye to January. Here are one or two saws collected from various sources for those who care for proverbial wisdom:

> If January has never a drop,
> The barn will need an oaken prop;

which certainly is comforting news to the farmer in this year of grace. Lest he be too elated, however, I append another:

> In January if the sun appear,
> March and April pay full dear.

Also a third of still more evil import:

> If grass do grow in Januair or Februair,
> It will grow the worse for it all the year.

FEBRUARY

February 1.—Last night there was a sharp rain, but the month has opened with a beautiful day, more like April than February weather, the thermometer marking 53 degrees in the shade and on a north wall. In the afternoon I went over to Bedingham, where the oats were being drilled, four bushels of them to the acre. They went in rather indifferently, for last night's rain has already affected this cold and sticky soil; also the long manure, which, having no other available, we were obliged to use for this field, No. 13, interfered somewhat with the action of the drill. The pease, with which the remaining half of the same field is sown, went in well this afternoon, when the land had dried somewhat in the stiff west wind. To-morrow, if the rain holds off, we propose to drill barley at Bedingham.

February 3.—Yesterday was much colder, with a strong nor'-west wind, increasing to a gale, and a good deal of bright sunshine. There is one plough going on All Hallows Farm, thwarting for root, but all the other horses are at Bedingham drilling, or trying to drill, barley, except one that is carting root into the shed. We have set a fold for sheep on the three-acre pasture, No. 11. This was the first field that I laid down for permanent grass, and is the worst land that I have on the farm, the seven-acre, No. 10, opposite to it not excepted. It has now been down for about six years, and has reached a rather critical stage in the life-history of a meadow. As a good deal of moss and many daisies have appeared in places among the herbage, we have come to the conclusion that the best chance of turning it into a really sound pasture is to sheep it heavily, and afterwards to harrow it and give it a good sprinkling of clover seed.

The sky last night looked heavy and grey, as though snow were coming. There was a very fine sunset, the lights upon the Common reflected in long lines and arrows from the clouds above being unusually beautiful. I know of few more curious and dreary sounds—though in a way it is an attractive music enough—than that of the wind rushing through the pine-trees on the Vine-yard Hills as it comes to the ear of the listener standing on the slope below. I can only compare it to that of Æolian harps ; there is the same sweet dreariness about the quality of the note.

Yesterday was Candlemas Day, and again, if we may trust to proverbs, the farmer's outlook is black enough. For what say the wise saws ?

> The hind had as soon see his wife on her bier
> As on Candlemas Day that the sun should shine clear ;

which suggests that the average hind is, or used to be, deeply interested in agriculture and not much in his wife. The shepherd, indeed, is, or was, still more decided on the point, for of him it is said :

> If Candlemas day be bright and clear,
> The shepherd had *rather* see his wife on her bier.

It is a wise proverb that urges,

> Lock in the barn on Candlemas Day
> Half your corn and half of your hay,

calling attention as it does to the fact that in this climate the 2nd of February is often for all practical purposes mid-winter. Here is another saying :

> If Candlemas Day be fair and bright,
> Winter will have another flight ;
> But if it be dark with clouds and rain,
> Winter is gone and will not come again.

And another :

> As far as the sun shines in on Candlemas Day,
> So far the snow will blow in afore May.

Two more, and good-bye to Candlemas :

> Where the wind is on Candlemas Day,
> There it will stick till the end of May.

> Si sol splendescat Maria purificante,
> Major erit glacies post festum quam fuit ante.

Of all of which proverbs we shall learn the truth or falsity if we live long enough to prove them.

To-day the weather is squally, with cold rain and fine intervals. We began to thrash this morning, but were obliged to give up about eleven o'clock. It is very curious to observe how absolutely indifferent the lambs seem to cold. One would think that the icy blasts of wind blowing on their wet skins would freeze them through, but they appear to mind these very little. Sheep are naturally cold-loving animals. Occasionally they shiver when penned up wet in a high wind, but it is heat that really makes them miserable, and flies, which are worse to them even than the heat. Were they left untended in many parts of the country, however plentiful and good their food, I believe that sheep would soon die out, if only from this plague, against which they seem quite unable to protect themselves. I suppose that in places where their race thrives naturally, as on the mountains of Scotland and Wales, the flies are much fewer, perhaps owing to the constant movement of winds at those altitudes.

It may be asked how sheep manage in the East, where flies are many, and I can only answer that I do not know, for although I think that I have seen them in Egypt and Cyprus, I neglected to make inquiries. Nor did I ever keep any sheep when farming in South Africa, so am ignorant of their treatment in that country; but I am sure that if they are as susceptible to the fly pest there as here, great numbers must die unless they are very strictly looked after. Last year, notwithstanding constant dressing, I nearly lost two ewes out of my small flock from this cause. One got a sore upon her neck, which it was vain to bandage, for so fast as the cloths were tied on the foolish thing tore them off with her sharp hoofs, with the result that she went about all the summer tormented by black lumps of flies which feasted on her wounds. Another suffered from an abscess behind, produced by flies, the pain of which seemed to drive the poor creature almost mad. I remember that on one occasion she left the flock and returned to the back lawn from nearly a mile away, breaking through the fences in order to get there. Here I found her lying panting on her side. When disturbed, she would stagger to her feet, run a hundred yards or so like a demented thing, and then lie down again. I thought that she must die, but with care she recovered, and, indeed, has recently lambed.

In the afternoon I went to Bedingham, where I found the men opening the water-furrows on field No. 5, which they had drilled with barley yesterday, the seed going in fairly well. To-day nothing has been drilled, as most of the six acres to be sown has proved intractable. Three times did the horses drag the land with the heavy harrows, until they were quite exhausted, indeed ; but the chief result seemed to be that they rolled over the tough clods instead of breaking them. As it chanced, however, about an acre and a half of this field was got up before Christmas and received the benefit of the only frosts that have fallen this season. The results serve to show how necessary is the action of frost to the securing of a good tilth on land of this character, for whereas there was plenty of mould on the acre and a half, the remainder of the piece which had been wetted by the showers was strewn with unbreakable lumps of clay. This acre and a half Moore began to drill late in the evening, just as I was starting home. The rest I told him to leave for the present and to return the drill to Ditchingham early to-morrow.

February 4.—To-day is much colder, with occasional storms of snow and hail driven by a high nor'-west wind. As I write, for the first time during the present winter the lawn is white, although the weather is not bad enough to stop the thrashing. The steamer began to work at the All Hallows Farm on the little stack of barley from No. 38, the five-and-a-half-acre piece of glebe land. Now it is that we see what a drought, such as we experienced last year, means upon these light lands, for this barley is not yielding more than four coomb an acre. Next the wheat from the All Hallows six-acre, No. 29, was dealt with. This is a good piece of stiffish land, so here the tale was different. Notwithstanding that the corn suffered a great deal from the attacks of sparrows, it cast about ten coomb an acre—a result which in so poor a wheat year may be considered satisfactory. When these stacks were finished the machine moved to the Home Farm (smashing a gate in the process) and began to thrash the oats and beans from the nine-acre pit field, No. 23. These are pedigree black oats, which we are now trying for the first time. The return seems to be good considering the year, about sixteen coomb an acre, I think. The beans also are thrashing out well, about eleven coomb to the acre.

It is curious to look at the steamer and listen to its hungry swelling hum as it devours sheaf after sheaf of corn, and to compare it with the style of thrashing that I can remember when I was a boy. Now the straw is tossed automatically to the elevator, or to the pitchforks of those who are stacking it ; the husk is shaken out and rejected, grit and stones are caught and cast away, and the pure grain is sorted into three or four classes in accordance with the size and quality of the kernels, all by the ingenious mechanism of a not very complicated machine. In the old days the thrashing was done by an instrument like a large windlass, with four or six horses attached to the spokes and a man seated on a little stool in the centre armed with a long whip to keep them up to their work as they walked round and round. The actual machinery that did the thrashing was hidden inside a barn, and I cannot recall sufficient of its details to describe it. I do, however, remember seeing the flail used from time to time, the last occasion being not more than fifteen years ago. From a flail to a modern steam-thrasher is a long stride, and the time and labour saved by the latter are almost incalculable. Yet I believe that farming paid better in the days of flails and reaping hooks than it does now in those of steamers and self-binders.

In walking round the farm this afternoon I noticed that the rooks are playing havoc on the three acres of mixed grain which we drilled a few days ago for sheep food on No. 24. They are congregated there literally by scores, and if you shout at them to frighten them away, they satisfy themselves by retiring to some trees near at hand and awaiting your departure to renew their operations. The beans attract them most, and their method of reducing these into possession is to walk down the lines of the drill until (as I suppose) they smell a bean underneath. Then they bore down with their strong beaks and extract it, leaving a neat little hole to show that they have been there. Maize they love even better than beans; indeed, it is difficult to keep them off a field sown with that crop. Hood promises to set up some mawkins to fright them, but the mawkin nowadays is a poor creature compared with what he used to be, and it is a wonder that any experienced rook consents to be scared by him. Thirty years or so ago he was really a work of art, with a hat, a coat, a stick, and sometimes a painted face, ferocious enough to frighten a little boy in the twilight, let alone a bird. Now a rag or two and a jumble-sale cloth cap are considered sufficient, backed up generally by the argument, which may prove more effective, of a dead rook tied up by the leg to a stick.

In the course of my walk I came across sheep's-parsley in bloom and, in sheltered places, honeysuckle and the arum-like plants which we call 'lords and ladies' in full leaf.

February 6.—Yesterday we had heavy snowstorms with intervals of sunshine, which left the ground quite deep in thawing snow. The ox of which I have already spoken has turned sick again, so, as he is a big brute, with a good deal of meat on his bones, Hood came to the conclusion, and I agreed with him, that rather than run any further risk we had better sell him for whatever he would fetch.   Accordingly the butcher from Bungay was sent for, and after some bargaining offered 12*l.* for him as he stood, that is 1*l.* less than he cost some months ago.   So that ox went away, taking his inefficient third stomach with him, if indeed it is his third stomach that is to blame, which I doubt; and very glad we were to see the last of him.   Before he departed Mr. Little made a drawing of him as he stood in a place by himself, a melancholy and rather dangerous-looking object, gloomy-eyed and hump-backed, from time to time producing a strange grating noise by grinding his teeth together.   My own belief is that the animal has some obstruction fixed in his liver, perhaps a bit of stick or glass which he has picked up in his travels from market to market.   However, we shall hear all about it in a day or two.

In the afternoon, having studied the theory of ploughing, Mr. Little and I proceeded to put it into practice on All Hallows six-acres, No. 29, which was being thwarted for root.   Ploughing, I can assure the reader, is one of those things that look a great deal easier than they are, like the writing of romances, which is supposed by the uninstructed to be a facile art.   The observer, standing at a gate to watch a man with a pair of horses strolling up and down a field for hours on end, if inexperienced, is apt to conclude that beyond the physical endurance involved the difficulties are small.   Let him take the pair of horses, however, and follow this pastoral pursuit for, say, forty minutes, and he will come away with a greatly increased respect for Mr. Hodge.

To begin with, the setting out of a field to plough in accordance with the kind of work selected as suitable to the purpose for which it is being cultivated, is by no means an easy matter.   (If anyone doubts this statement, let him consult Stephens's diagrams, and try to work them out.)   Nor is it easy to keep a perfectly straight line, or, by pressing too much or too little on the plough handles, not to cause undesirable variations of depth in the furrow.   But all this is simplicity itself compared to what happens when you reach the end of the field and are called upon to turn round. Even if you have mastered the mystic word, or rather noise—it sounds like *wo-is-sh Dlun* (Dlun represents the name of the mare, which afterwards you ascertain to be ' Darling ')—the Open Sesame, at the sound of which, and at nothing else, the horses will turn at all— the probability is that you bring them about too sharply, throwing the plough on to its side and yourself into the ditch. Or perhaps you wheel them round too widely, with the result that you find yourself a yard or two beyond the spot where you purposed to begin the new furrow, vaguely wondering how you are going to drag a heavy plough and two very solid horses back into position.

The end of it is that, having in vain endeavoured to take the half-sarcastic counsel offered to you by Mr. Hodge, who at last feels himself your superior, as, if all the truth were known, very likely he is in more than ploughing, you wipe your perspiring brow and present him with the handles and a shilling. These things, and others, I observed happening to my companion yesterday afternoon. For my own part, whether by good luck or good management modesty forbids me to say, with the exception of a few *contretemps* unworthy of notice, I got on exceedingly well.

The intelligence evinced by farm horses at ploughing, and indeed all other work—if only you are master of the language which they understand—always strikes me as astonishing. The carriage and riding horse is generally very much of a fool and misbehaves himself, or gets frightened, or runs away upon most convenient occasions. How different it is with his humble farm-yard cousin, who, through heat or cold, sun or snow, plods on hour after hour at his appointed task, never stepping aside or drawing a false line, always obedient to the voice of his driver, and, provided he is fairly fed and rested, always ready for his work the long year through. I often wonder whether, taken as a class, the common plough horse is really more intelligent than the aristocrat of the stable, or whether it is simply that the latter has, as a rule, so little to do and so much to eat that he seldom comes to understand the responsibilities of life. On the whole, however, I am inclined to believe that countless generations of semi-intelligent labour, that is, labour in which the animal takes what seems to be a thinking part, have really given it more brain and power of reflection than belong to the class of horses used only occasionally, and, for the most part, for the purposes of pleasure.

To-day, Sunday, there were showers of snow and sleet in the morning, though after church the sun came out. In the afternoon it was dull again, with a strong west wind ; but the moon-rise to-night was one of the most lovely that I have seen for a long time. In front of where I stood, on the top of Hollow Hill, lay a stretch of bare plough, bordered by a little belt of plantation. Above these trees the moon, full, bright, and round, appeared in a perfectly clear sky, turning the tree-tops and the cold purple plough silver with her light.

February 10.—For the last three days all the available carts have been at work carting litter out of the yards. The weather has been bright and colder, with slight frosts at night, which have done much good. The manure, I may explain, is hauled on to a heap in the field for which it is intended, where it heats. After about fourteen days it can be turned so that the bottom of the heap becomes the top, and to do this properly is part of the mystery of farming. Then it heats again, after which, shortened and sweetened, it is fit to go upon the earth. This heating kills all seeds of docks or other rubbish that may have been brought in with the hay or straw ; also it breaks up and decomposes the fibre of the straw, so that the mixture becomes more readily incorporated with the soil. Summer muck, however, being much shorter owing to its containing less straw, is often carted straight on to the land without being 'haled' or heaped. The manure this year should be of good quality, as so little rain has fallen to wash the yards and spoil it. Before another winter comes round I hope to have most of it safe under cover of iron-roofed sheds.

To-day is Bungay market, and Hood sold about fifty-six coomb of wheat grown on the All Hallows land at 18*s*. 3*d*. the coomb of 18 stone, or 36*s*. 6*d*. the quarter. This is sixpence less than he was offered last week ; but the markets for corn are so dreadfully uncertain, and so much at the mercy of American ' corners ' and speculators in ' futures,' that it seems best to take it, as, for aught we know, by next sale day wheat may be down two or three shillings a quarter. Of course, on the other hand, it may be up, especially as it is said that there is really a shortage in the world's supply. But this it is not safe to count on.

February 11.—To-day is dull and mild, with a very high glass. I hear that the sick ox, which was sold to the butcher, after its decease was found to be suffering, not from its third stomach, as the veterinary thought, nor from liver, as I thought, but from its brain, on which it had an abscess. When it was being driven away, the animal suddenly rolled over, though afterwards it picked itself up, and managed to get along in a lop-sided fashion. On dissection, the abscess was found to have burst recently, probably when it fell. No doubt it was caused in the first instance by a heavy blow over the eye. This may have been received on board ship, or more probably it was inflicted by a drover's stick. The poor creature must have suffered greatly ; indeed, it is wonderful that it did not either die or go mad. Here is another caution against buying these store cattle, of which it is impossible to know the past history.

This afternoon I went to Bedingham, where I found the draining nearly finished, and Moore in sad straits to find bushes for the end of it. He has begun to plough this field, No. 18, that is to be planted with swedes and kohl rabi. First of all he runs the plough along the side of each drain, turning a spit of soil on to the loose lumps of earth with which it is roughly filled in. Then he sets to work in the ordinary fashion ; although a newly drained field never looks quite neat after the first ploughing, owing to the clods of bottom clay with which it is sprinkled, the bits of stick and other débris, and the parti-coloured lines that show where the trenches have been cut. The land at Bedingham looked drier to-day than I ever remember seeing it at this time of year.

February 19.—There has been little to record during the past week. The weather has been dull with a good deal of wind, which rose to a strong westerly gale on the 16th, and on the whole mild. We have been carting a quantity of manure from the various yards, also delivering the wheat which was sold upon the 12th after it had been cleaned, or dressed as we call it, in the winnowing machine. On the 17th we ploughed the Ape field, No. 27 (I wonder how it got that name; perhaps because a monkey escaped on it in some past age). This field is to be sown with barley, but as the soil has gone down tight, it was thought advisable to give it a second ploughing. The three ploughs finished it to-day and began re-ploughing No. 25, opposite, also for barley.

A day or two ago the principal hotel in Bungay, called the King's Head, together with another inn in Bridge Street, was put up for public auction. I think that they are the last 'free' houses in the town; that is, houses the occupiers of which are entitled to sell any beer that they or their customers may prefer. All the other houses, and their name is legion, are 'tied' houses; in other words, they have been purchased by various firms of brewers, and are forced to sell the beer made by their owner exclusively, whether it be good, bad, or indifferent.[1] To my mind, speaking as the chairman of a bench of magistrates, who has now had a good many years of experience in matters connected with the licensing of public houses, this 'tied' house system is a crying evil. In practice it constitutes a monopoly of the worst sort. The license granted by the magistrates is nothing more or less than

---

[1] In some parts of England, I am told, the brewers oblige their nominees in tied houses to purchase through them groceries and other goods besides the drink they retail. This is an arrangement from which the firm supplying the articles sucks no small advantage, but I have not heard that it is in force in these counties.

an endowment, which, whatever may be the letter of the law, in fact, as opposed to theory, the bench has little power to refuse. Indeed, any such arbitrary act would be denounced and agitated against as an attempt to offer violence to that god of the English, the Rights of Property, unless it chanced that the management of the house had been reported upon adversely by the police and the license endorsed by the local bench.

When this happens—and it does not often happen, since for their own sakes the brewers are very careful whom they put in —it is the occupier who is dismissed ; the house abides.   On such occasions the brewer's agent appears, apologises for the trouble, and announces that the tenant has received notice or been got rid of, whereon the bench has practically no option but to admit any new nominee who can produce decent testimonials.   The great value of such an endowment, even in the case of a quiet country town like Bungay, is shown by the fact that not many years ago the local branch of the Oddfellows purchased the King's Head for about 1,800*l.*, whereas at the recent auction it was sold for over 6,500*l.*, although I believe that the lease of the present tenant of the inn has some years to run, during which time he cannot be forced to sell any particular brand of beer or spirits.

I confess I am unable to understand the advantages of this system, that enables people with long purses to force the public to buy any yellow-coloured liquor which they choose to honour with the name of beer, although, in truth, in some instances it is, I believe, scarcely more than a chemical compound manufactured from I know not what.   The only explanation is that, being the wealthiest men and a magnificently organised power in this land, the brewers are careful to stop any legislation which can possibly cut into their great profits.

As a further safeguard, most of them have made their businesses into public companies, in which they retain the controlling interest, thereby converting tens of thousands of small shareholders into their partners and enthusiastic supporters.   How vast and dangerous is their strength is well shown by the disaster that overtook the Liberal party when it made a platform plank of Local Option. Looking at this scheme from a practical and not a political point of view, I think, however, that it deserved to fail, because, as it seems to me, it would foster the very thing which I consider such an evil—the indirect endowment of public-houses. It is not to be expected that any town in England would vote for the closing of all drinking places within its limits, as sometimes happens in America, nor will most people consider it desirable that this should be done. Therefore it is probable that what might happen is that a certain proportion of the houses would be penalised by a popular vote, while the value of others which escaped would be enormously enhanced. Nobody can be more convinced than I am that there are far too many public-houses ; in Bungay, for instance—I think that I once reckoned in the course of a disputed licensing case—there is a liquor shop of one kind or another for every 100 of the total population. Yet as the people love to have it so, it seems impossible to escape the evil. Now, to make matters worse, the houses, or rather the licenses, have been bought up by the brewers and turned into a close monopoly.

Under these circumstances, I suggest that as the first appears to be beyond remedy, the second ill, at any rate, might be combated by empowering the magistrates to grant a license to sell liquors under strict police supervision to any and every respectable man who chooses to apply for it. The effect of this would be that the brewers could not buy up an unlimited number of licenses ; that the holders of licenses would be at liberty to supply sound liquor, which in some instances, at any rate, is not now the case, and that, as I believe, for the most part, the number of liquor shops would not, in fact, be increased, since in the majority of towns and villages there are already as many as can possibly earn a livelihood.

I have no doubt that many objections can be urged against such a plan, but at least this may be said in its favour, that it would tend to foster the sale of honest beer made from malt and hops.[1] People who study the subject have told me that almost as much drunkenness is occasioned by the deleterious quality as by the amount of drink consumed. At least, as it is difficult to imagine a worse state of affairs than that which exists at present, any reasonable remedy is worthy of consideration, even if it takes the shape of free trade in beer or of State control of its manufacture and distribution. At this contemplative stage, however, the matter is likely to rest, for the brewers have the British public by the throat, and, while their money commands so vast an influence, after the experience of the Liberals at the last election, no Government is likely to enter on the crusade of forcing them to loose their grip.

I am very glad to hear from the Duke of Norfolk that it is he who has purchased the King's Head, not that his Grace is connected with brewing or desires to turn that ancient hostelry into a tied house, but for quite another reason. At the back of the King's Head, and standing in its grounds, are the ruins of Bungay Castle, of which I have spoken in the first chapter of this book— once the home of the Bigods, the predecessors of the Dukes of Norfolk. These ruins a good many years ago were, I believe, sold by the present Duke, who had never seen them, under some misapprehension as to their nature and extent. After various vicissitudes they were purchased by the Oddfellows for, I think,

[1] Since writing this passage I have been informed that a scheme of a similar nature has been tried in Liverpool and failed. Even if this be so, it does not follow that regulations which have proved unsuitable to the needs of a huge city might not answer well in country towns and villages, where the circumstances are totally different.

(Owing to the publication of the above note in the course of the appearance of this work in serial form I have received a considerable amount of correspondence from magistrates and other gentlemen connected with Liverpool, protesting that the famous licensing system was by no means a failure.

I must say that a study of the pamphlets and letters that have been forwarded to me leads me to much the same conclusion, and I think it a matter for great regret that experiments of this character have not been given a fuller and a fairer trial. *April* 1899. H. R. H.)

200*l*., and turned into the pleasure grounds of the inn. Now the Duke has had to give over 6,000*l*. to recover the home of his ancestors, but doubtless he will be able to recoup himself for the most of this outlay by re-selling the hotel. Indeed, should the brewers' mania for the acquisition of tied houses continue, I dare say that were he to keep the property in hand for a year or two he might make a handsome profit on the transaction.

February 21.—Winter has come at last, for the thermometer shows that there were ten degrees of frost during the night. One of my best cows, Miss Pegotty by name, calved last night, or rather tried to calve, with the result that when Hood went into the cowhouse this morning he found the calf dead and the cow not far off it. I think that the calf was the largest which I ever saw, and that the trouble was undoubtedly occasioned by nobody being with the cow This sounds like carelessness, but in fact it is not always so. All mammals seem to prefer to produce their young at night, although in the case of cattle this rule has many exceptions. Therefore, when a cow is overdue, and shows the usual signs of calving, the cowkeeper has sometimes to sit up night by night to watch her, until at last he is almost worn out. In the present case, for instance, I believe that Miss Pegotty has been expected to calve for the last fortnight, and that Hood and his brother have watched her during all that time. Last night, however, the signs of immediate calving vanished, and Hood, on whom the watching had devolved for several nights, thought that he was quite safe in taking a rest, with the result stated above.

It will be a terrible business if we lose Miss Pegotty as well as her calf, for she is one of our most prolific and reliable cows. She has been dosed with a pint of whisky in gruel, but is quite unable to get on to her legs. The farrier has come to visit her, but does not recommend that she should be slung, as he thinks that the pressure of the slings might upset her inside, which indeed occurred to me as probable. I may explain that the slinging was suggested because it is feared that if she lies much longer she will get set fast with stiffness, and never find her feet again.

As I returned from the farmyard after visiting Miss Pegotty, I noticed one of the cocks in a dreadful condition. Its comb was nearly torn off, it seemed to be almost blind, and its neck ran red with blood. On inquiring the cause I discovered that not war with its own species was to blame for these gory wounds, but rather the malevolent behaviour of a certain turkey hen. This hen, for some reason best known to itself, has a grudge against that particular cock, and attacks it upon every occasion. The cock stands up to it as well as he can, but weight will tell, and that of this morning went near to proving his last fray. Indeed, I doubt whether he would survive another. Turkeys, so far as my observation goes, are singularly cruel and overbearing in their habits. Not long ago, in the little meadow on the All Hallows Farm, I found a cock lying on the ground, still alive, but absolutely pulled to pieces. Walking round him, and now and again inflicting a scientific and meditative peck upon some open wound, was the old gobbler, who no doubt had previously reduced him to this sad condition.

Decidedly to-day was unlucky for fowls, for the two terrier dogs, Di and Dan, hunted and slew one of them in the shrubbery. They were caught in the act and received their just reward. Afterwards the hen, a very large one, was lashed to the younger dog, Dan, its legs being bound about his neck, and its head fastened under his stomach. For a while the dog sat looking the picture of dejection, his sharp nose poking out between its tail feathers; but I think his grief arose from the sense that he was an object of ridicule rather than from remorse for his crime. At any rate, as he could not gnaw the corpse off, or even walk away with it, after a while he turned it into a mattress, and spent the rest of the afternoon slumbering on the top of it, to all appearance utterly undisturbed in conscience. (Note.—No more dead hens have been found, but since then Dan has killed a duck.)

February 22.—Last night there were twelve degrees of frost,

but the ground remains soft enough to allow of one plough work
ing on some light land, the rest of the horses being employed in
carting manure.   The cow, Miss Pegotty, is still unable to find the
use of her hind legs, but in some extraordinary and unexplained
way she has dragged and rolled herself the length of the cow-house,
and through the open door into the hovel.   Here she lies with
sacks over her, shivering violently from time to time, and stretching out her head upon the straw in rather an alarming fashion.
Her eyes, however, seem bright and healthy, also she can eat.
Mustard is being rubbed upon her loins with the object of
stimulating the muscles.

It is a curious day for the end of February : very clear, cold,
and still, the sky heavy as though with snow, except when the sun
breaks out, as it does from time to time.   Standing at the gate of
one of the new pastures behind the house, I was struck by the
quiet and peacefulness of the scene.   On the back lawn, at some
distance from me, the lambs were at play, their bleats sounding
loud in the stillness, while the green of the pasture was dotted here
and there with feeding ewes, that looked extraordinarily white
against the grey skyline.   Near to me, and in the same field,
grazed the two colts, till one of them, discovering my presence,
ceased to nibble at the short brown grass and advanced gingerly,
as though to inquire my business.   Presently, having satisfied his
curiosity, he wandered off again to join his companion.

Notwithstanding that the air was almost at freezing-point, the
thrushes and blackbirds were singing in the little plantations round
the house, though not with so full a voice as they sang a fortnight
since ; while from the tall hedgerow to my left came from time to
time the insolent crow of a cock-pheasant, rejoicing perhaps that
he had, and that his companions had not, escaped the guns.   Presently a rustle caught my ear, and in the ground-ivy on the bank a
yard or so away I perceived two little field-mice sporting together,
the rustle being caused by the stir of the dead leaves and sere
grasses as they moved among them.   While I watched, one of
these mice climbed up the stem of a maple bush in the fence, and

began to nibble at the bark. Perhaps it was collecting materials for its nest, though of this I am not sure, as I do not know when these little creatures begin to mate. The rabbits, at any rate, are already breeding freely, for I have seen some half-grown young ones in the wood on the Bath Hills; indeed, I believe that in mild seasons they continue to multiply all through the winter. As I turned to go home, frightening away the mice by my movement, the Bungay church clock struck, and although it is a mile and a quarter distant, in that clear still air it sounded close at hand.

The labourers' rate of wages on this farm is now 13s. a week and harvest money. The milkman, however, who receives no harvest money, gets a cottage free instead. The man employed about the plantations and on odd jobs is paid 12s., and an old fellow, who has been working as a stop-gap for the last six months, 11s. only. I wish that there were any reasonable prospect of wages increasing, but this seems impossible until farming can be made to pay again. Under the present state of affairs, even at to-day's prices the labour bill frequently devours all the profits.

To-day Hood sold a pair of the little red-poll bullocks, two-year-old things, to the butcher. There was a disagreement as to price, Hood asking 19l. apiece, and the butcher offering 17l. Finally, it was agreed that we should be paid by dead weight at the rate of 7s. a stone, which at present is the top figure for prime beef in this neighbourhood. The butcher, I understand, lays the weight of the animals at forty-five stone each, while Hood estimates them at fifty.

This evening I went to support a neighbour who is standing for the County Council in this division. As a rule there is now little interest shown in these counties in elections to the Council, but, as it chances, in this parish there lives a gentleman of advanced views, a pedlar by profession, who, with a courage which does him credit in the face of an ever-increasing lack of support, fights the seat at each election, the more light heartedly perhaps as I believe that the expenses of the contest are put upon the rates. It cannot be said that a meeting of this sort is otherwise than rather dreary, as it is impossible for the most eloquent speaker to become impassioned and absorbing on the subject of main or parish roads. Before I made my speech, however, as nobody seemed to have anything to ask, I put the candidate a question, and was glad to elicit from him the information that he would support a bye-law forcing all wheeled vehicles, as well as bicycles, to carry lighted lamps after dark. This is a regulation that would add greatly to the comfort and safety of the roads, especially near towns on a market-night.

There is no doubt that the County Councils have proved a great success and very useful to the community; but in our part of the world it is not always easy to find men to stand for them. Thus, at Bungay, the other day, I am told that there was considerable difficulty owing to the lack of a candidate, which was only got over by persuading the present excellent and worthy member to allow himself to be re-elected somewhat against his will.

But if the interest in County Councils is waning, to judge from this village and others that I know of, that in Parish Councils is practically dead. In the beginning there was a great excitement about them—I never remember seeing so many men in the Ditchingham schoolroom together as on the occasion of the election after the passing of the Act; but now it is a very different story. For the first two years I was chairman of our Parish Council, but I cannot say that we accomplished anything exciting. There was a good deal of talk about allotments, and applications were put in for a great number of acres of ground —forty I believe; but in the end the *bona fide* demand was satisfied by my offering a four-acre field to the Council, the third that I let in allotments. Also the parish charities were a burning question; but the matter was referred to the Commissioners, with the result that we are very much where we were before, excepting only that the charities have decreased in amount owing to the fall in the value of land. What excited most argument, however, was, I think, the question of a safe, which it was proposed to buy at a cost of 17*l* I pointed out that, speaking *prima facie*, and with a mind open to correction, it seemed useless to spend 17*l.* of the parish money upon a safe when we had few or no documents to put in it. But although the Council as a body admitted that there was some force in this argument, it was not held to be conclusive, since, urged the opposition, there might at some future time be documents, and that then a safe would be greatly missed. The matter came up again and again ; indeed, I am not sure that it was settled when, at last, I resigned the chairmanship. I did not again stand for the Parish Council, as it seemed to me that the amount of time spent in discussion was disproportionate to the results achieved. Possibly, however, we are an extra argumentative set in Ditchingham, and in other parishes it may be different.

February 25.—I have been ill for the last few days and unable to go about the farm, but this afternoon I managed to get out for a little to see the drilling, until I chanced to meet the doctor, who sent me home. On the 23rd we drilled the oats on the top of the fourteen-acre on Baker's, No. 42, and on the 24th on the two pieces of glebe, Nos. 39 and 40. Here they went in but fairly well, for, after it has been ploughed for some weeks, this land, being so gravelly, has a tendency to set hard and impede the action of the drill.

The two bullocks which I mentioned as having been sold on the 22nd turned the scale when cleaned at $47\frac{1}{2}$ stone each, that is, exactly midway between the estimates of the seller and buyer. This is instructive, as it suggests that a man's perfectly honest prejudice in his own favour amounts to about five per cent.—at least where cattle are concerned. It was supposed by both parties that one of these little bullocks weighed three stone more than the other. In fact, however, the difference was only three pounds, which shows how easily the best and most experienced judges may be deceived in their estimates of the weight of live stock.

Miss Pegotty, I am thankful to say, found her legs a day or two back, and is now making a good recovery. Had it gone otherwise it would have been a sad loss.

To-day the Ape field, No. 27, was drilled with barley, which went in beautifully. When I crawled away in company with the doctor the drill had just moved into the four-acres opposite, No. 25, but I do not know if it finished there to-night.

February 28.—On the 26th we drilled the three-and-a-half acres on All Hallows, No. 33, with barley. The cultivator, that is a heavy instrument with hook-shaped teeth, was put through it in the morning dragged by three horses, after which it was cross-harrowed. Thus it took all day to drill this little field and harrow the seed in.

Yesterday, Sunday, was squally and cold, with rain in the morning, and to-day there is a nor'-west gale with intervals of sunshine. We have dragged the nine-acre on All Hallows, No. 36, with the cultivator and drilled about half of it, the barley going in so well that I think it will puzzle the rooks to find it beneath the fine mould. This morning I was marking the trees that have to come out from the Bath Hills. We are so busy that it is hard to find time for tree-cutting this year; but as the Lodge has been let to a tenant for a term from next September, I am anxious to get them out and have done with it in order to avoid disturbance beyond the house during his occupation, as everything felled on that portion of the Vineyard Hills must be carted down the drive. Also, we need the timber for the iron-roofed sheds which I hope to put up over the various yards. It would be very bad economy to buy oak and deal when we have stuff that ' wants to come out ' which will serve our turn.

I know of nothing in life that needs more discretion than the marking of trees, unless it be an attempt to patch up a family quarrel. I am supposing, of course, that the trees are being cut more with a view to the advantage of the survivors and of the plantation generally than for simple profit. One may have the very best intentions, and have studied the tree or trees from all standpoints and at every season of the year in order to decide which shall go and which shall stay, and then, after all, find that a mistake has been made. Also the error, if it be one, is so utterly irredeemable, for no ordinary person can hope to live long enough to repair it.

It is extraordinary, however, to see what growth trees will make during the span of a single life. Thus on the lawn of this house stand many good-sized timbers, elm, oak, beech, lime, and walnut. With the exception of the walnuts, which are ancient, every tree of them was planted within the memory of a relative, now just eighty years of age, who was living in this house at the time. Indeed, the man who actually set them was shoeing horses until, having been much hurt by a kick, he took to his bed and died not very long ago. It is not given to many to see oaks planted, cut down as good timber, seasoned, made into bookcases, windowframes, and shutters, and set up to furnish the room from which in childhood they watched the gardener setting them. Yet this has happened to the relative in question ; moreover, it is now some ten years since the trees were felled.

It should be added that there is something in this soil which is extraordinarily well suited to the needs of hardwood timber, which flourishes here exceedingly. This is shown by the fact that in Websdill Wood, at Bedingham, which is also a clay soil, though stiffer, the oaks, that seem to have been planted for many generations, are for the most part no larger than those upon this lawn. At any rate, old men at Bedingham have told me that they have not been able to notice any change in them since they were boys. The timber of the trees also goes to corroborate this statement, as when we steam-sawed a parcel of them a few years ago, I noticed that the wood seemed as hard as iron, and that there was practically no ' sap,' that is, soft outer wood, which is useless for most purposes.

Altogether I think that I marked about fifty trees this morning, small for the most part and of every variety. Some of these I find, by the healed-up scars upon them, I have already marked in past years and then spared. Indeed, it is evident that in several instances I have done this twice, but the day of doom has come at last. The trees upon these Bath Hills have been very much neglected in past times ; if someone had thinned them judiciously fifty years ago they would be much better specimens than they are at present. As it is, the younger stands have been allowed to crowd each other, and even to destroy and distort the few old-established timbers by cutting off the air from their lower boughs and causing them to die.

I find, however, that there are two schools as regards the treatment of timber. The first, in which are included eight women out of ten, love to see trees of all sorts huddled up together as close as nature will allow them to exist—long, lank boles, with tufts of foliage on the top of them, and below a few dead or dying branches. He who ventures to suggest that it would be a good thing to let a little air into a thicket of this sort is generally received with indignation, and probably hears it stated afterwards : 'Oh, yes, So-and-so wants to cut down every tree he sees !' As a rule, indeed, such a plantation is too far gone to be touched with the object of improving the beauty of the specimens ; also it is rather dangerous to let in the wind among these long-shanked fellows, for then more are apt to go than you wish to part with. I understand, also, that to grow timber in this fashion is the most profitable method of forestry ; at least, I have observed very large woods managed thus in France and Germany, where I believe they understand such things. But for beauty, surely there is nothing to equal trees as they are grown in a ordinary English covert, where they receive attention when the fell is cut, once in every seven years, and any which are not wanted are turned into profit.

On the lawn in front of this house stand four single trees, two beeches and two limes, which have never been crowded or deformed by the too close company of their kind. To my fancy those four trees are better worth looking at than all the dozens which surround them; indeed, their proportions are a pleasure to contemplate at every time of year. But about trees, as in other things, opinions vary.

This afternoon I had a discussion with Hood as to what should be done with the lambs. He is of opinion—and on the whole I agree with him—that it will be best to sell them all out and buy in some black-faced ewes in the autumn. I very much doubt whether it would pay to keep on these cross-bred 'gimmel' lambs and make ewes of them, as I think that they would lack size. So they will have to go, poor little things, and the Southdown ewes with them. I think that I shall keep to Southdown rams, however, as I am sure that the cross gives quality to the mutton.

MARCH

March 1.—To-day we finished getting in the barley on the All Hallows nine-acres, No. 36. The last of it was drilled in a drizzling rain and under a threatening sky. While the barley was being sown the cultivator got to work upon the eight-acres on Baker's, No. 41, preparing the seed bed ; but so soon as the drill was at liberty a sharp storm of hail and rain came down, making this stiff land too sticky for us to attempt to deal with it. In the afternoon we took refuge in the ordinary bad-weather occupation of carting manure. No. 41 was under root last year, and had been dosed with 'artificial,' as is customary when a crop is being grown which must be taken at a valuation by the landlord or next tenant. In walking over the field I observed little grey patches of this manure still lying undissolved in the soil, a curious illustration of the persistent character of the drought that has prevailed since it was scattered up to the present time, which has prevented the stuff from melting away and becoming assimilated with the earth.

March 2.—Winter seems to have set in at last, for this morning we have storms of snow and sleet, and can do nothing upon the land except cart from the yards.

Here I am obliged practically to suspend my diary, as I spent the remainder of March in London. From the farming point of view this is no great loss, however, as throughout the month, to judge by the notes that Mrs. Hood has kindly kept for me, the weather was so bitter and generally bad that vegetation made but little progress. Still, the work on the farm went on, barley being drilled whenever the state of the land would allow of it, varied with ploughing and manure carting when it would not. The remainder of the ewes lambed satisfactorily, and we made an average of something over sixty pounds of butter per week. Towards the end of the month, also, we began to chain-harrow the pastures, and this, with the ordinary routine of root carting into the sheds, and stone carting on to the roads in satisfaction of a small contract with the surveyors, makes up a not very interesting record.

March 31.—I returned home yesterday to find the country in very much the same state as I left it nearly a month ago. During this month the weather seems to have been persistently cold. For the first three weeks it was dry. Then came a great three-days' nor'-east gale with a heavy fall of snow— here we had six inches on the level—followed by a cold rain which filled up the dykes and ponds, and not before it was needed. At one house in this neighbourhood the drought had made it necessary to cart water from the lake, and in the villages beyond Bungay known as 'the Parishes,' where the inhabitants depend mainly on shallow ponds for their supply, they were in great straits for water ; indeed, a famine of it was feared. However, this risk is done with for the present ; indeed, the floods have been out on the marshes.

The snow still lies in the holls, and the meadows are more rusty-faced than when I went away. In the sown fields it is difficult to see any change, though the oats drilled for sheep's food have pricked through, and the wheat has perhaps grown a little. The barley does not stir as yet, and Hood has already begun to shake his head over its prospects. He believes that its early seeding (of which I was an advocate) will prove of no advantage, although it went in so well, alleging as his reason that much of the grain will perish in the ground. I, on the other hand, believe that the fate of the crop will depend not upon its early seeding, but upon the weather we experience during the next three months. Barley in our parts will not stand continuous wet and cold, it turns yellow, and the sample is injured for malting purposes.

The sheep have done fairly well ; the forty-nine ewes, one of which, if not ghast—that is, barren—has not yet lambed, having produced sixty-one lambs without accident to themselves or their offspring. We reckon one and a half a very good fall of lambs, but one and a quarter, which is about our proportion, is by no means to be despised. Of course it means that there are not quite so many doubles as there might be; but where the farmer looks to sell his lambs fat to the butcher within a month or two of Easter, doubles have their disadvantages, as then it must be a strong ewe that can cause them to meet the butcher's eye as he would wish to see them. The flock is being penned at night on the three-acre, No. 11, with a view to improving the bottom of this young pasture, which has grown somewhat thin. In the daytime they run out on one or other of the meadows, where root is thrown to them, and every night they are shut in a new fold on the three-acre and receive a ration of corn, hay, and beet.

One of the ploughmen, Fairhead, is harrowing the pastures with the two-horse patent chain drag. This is a new instrument which I have bought this year, and, though it looks light, a very effective one, being so contrived that every part of it pulling against the other part causes an equal strain to come upon each tooth or cutter. These teeth are solid triangular wedges of steel, which bite into the moss and tear it up. Either face of this harrow can be used for dragging purposes, but one of them cuts a good deal more deeply than the other.

All my three mares here have proved to be in foal, also the old one at Bedingham. This is rather too much of a good thing, as while they are attending to their domestic duties we may be rather short of horses. I did not think that the ancient dame at Bedingham would produce any more foals, nor should I have greatly grieved if she had taken the same view of the matter. I am tired of her Roman-nosed, long-legged offspring, which, although they are good animals enough, feed them as you will, steadily decline to grow fat. The worst of breeding horses is that, if a colt is unhandsome or has a blemish which would prevent its fetching full value on the market, his owner finds himself doomed to its company for the rest of its natural life. The good animals are sold to make a better show in the balance-sheet, the bad ones remain at home.

APRIL

April 1.—Last night there was a frost, but except for a shower in the afternoon the day has been fine. The meadow harrowing goes on, one plough is at work, and the remaining men are spreading muck for root on All Hallows, No. 29. This is done by throwing the manure between the baulks, which are then split back over it by a plough. I went to see the oxen at Baker's, or rather the eight survivors of them. One or other of these unlucky beasts has been continually ill since I was away, mostly from 'blowing.' My own opinion is that, having been starved for years, they cannot resist the temptation of gorging themselves with good food whenever they get the chance. However, their various ailments notwithstanding, they are without doubt very much improved in personal appearance, less hungry-looking and slab-sided, with better coats.

At Bedingham this afternoon I found the first sown field of barley, No. 5, and the oats on No. 13, coming up strongly, but the pease upon the same piece are backward. If anything, the winter beans, No. 14, are too close, and in spite of various horse-hoeings tufts of the self-sown barley are still showing among them. The wheats are looking very well, but two of the three pieces are so thick that it has been necessary to thin them by dragging out some of the plants with the harrow. The third piece, No. 9, which it may be remembered was a clover layer last year, is thinner, but I think that there is a sufficient plant. Moore was employed in dragging the meadows, but as we have no patent grass-scarifiers here the work has to be done by an ordinary harrow into which stout bushes of white-thorn are twisted. A very good instrument for brushing pastures, where there is little or no moss to be dealt with, can be made by twining thorns into the bars of an ordinary lift-gate, weighting it with a log, and using it as a drag.

April 5.—Last Saturday, the 2nd, we had another frost, followed by a fine day. Sunday was cold and cloudy ; Monday also cold with sunshine and a high wind, west and nor'-west ; to-day also cold, wind east to south, with intervals of sunshine. The work is the same as that of last week : grass harrowing, manure-spreading, and baulk-splitting, not very interesting operations, any of them, but absolutely necessary. Compared with other and rougher countries, it is curious to note the ceaseless nature of the work needful to the carrying on of an English farm. Although it is the fashion among people who know nothing about him to hold up the English agriculturist as the commonest of fools, he has brought cultivation to such a pitch of science that every day demands its appropriate and necessary labour, without which all would be spoilt. Yet the pity of it is that, notwithstanding the care, knowledge, and intelligence which are put into the working of the land, under present conditions it can scarcely be made to pay. The machinery works, the mill goes round ; the labourers, those who are left of them, earn their wage, such as it is, and the beast his provender ; the goodman rises early and rests late, taking thought for the day and the morrow, but when at Michaelmas he balances his books there is no return, and lo ! the bailiff is glaring through the gates. Although there have been gleams of hope during the past year, in our parts the ancient industry of agriculture is nearly moribund, and if the land, or the poorer and therefore the more considerable portion of it, is farmed fairly, it is in many instances being worked at a loss, or at any rate without a living profit.

The reader may say that this is impossible, that no one would carry on the business under these conditions ; yet it is still carried on, very often from sheer force of habit, or because those who practise it have nothing else to which to turn. The small men only too often keep up the game till beggary overtakes them, when they adjourn to the workhouse or live upon the charity of their friends. The larger farmers struggle forward from Michaelmas to Michaelmas, and at last take refuge in a cottage, or, if they are fortunate, find a position as steward upon some estate. The landlords with farms upon their hands work them with capital borrowed at high interest from the bank, till they can let them upon any terms to any sort of tenant. Unless they have private means to draw on, or are able to earn money, into their end it is best not to inquire ; they sink and sink until they vanish beneath the surface of the great sea of English society, and their ancient homes and accustomed place are filled by the successful speculator or the South African millionaire.

This is the result of Free Trade, which if up to the present it has brought a flush of prosperity to the people as a whole, has taken away the living of those classes that exist by the land, at any rate in our Eastern Counties. When that principle was introduced ruin to agriculture was foretold, but at first, owing to a variety of circums ances, it did not fall. Yet disaster was only postponed ; now it has come, and whether the land and those who live on it will survive is more than I or anyone else can say. The truth is that the matter is no longer of pressing interest to the British nation. The British nation lives by trade and fills itself with the cheap food products of foreign countries ; the fruit of the fields around its cities is of little weight to it one way or the other. If all England went out of cultivation to-morrow, I doubt whether it would make any material difference to the consumer—the necessaries of life would still pour in from abroad. What would happen if a state of affairs should arise under which corn and other food could not be freely imported is another matter. When it does arise, no doubt the town-bred British Public, and the Governments which live to do what they conceive to be the will of that public, will give their earnest attention to the problem, perhaps too late. Meanwhile, all is doubtless as it should be, and, as there is not the slightest prospect of redress, we poor farmers must bow our heads to the inevitable, and, while hoping for a turn of Fortune's wheel, make the best of things as we find them and be thankful.

Yet, with becoming humility, I would venture to ask a question of those who understand these matters.

A., an English farmer, grows a quarter of barley which pays rent to the landlord (part of which the landlord hands over to the Government in the form of taxes), rates to the parish, tithe to the parson, and land-tax to the State. This quarter of barley he offers for sale on Bungay market. B., an Argentine or other foreign farmer, grows a quarter of barley and also offers it for sale on Bungay market, to compete against that offered by A. This quarter of barley has paid no rent to a British landlord, no rates to a British parish, no tithe to a British parson, no tax to the British Government. Also, in practice, it has the benefit of preferential rates on British railways, and is carted to the market over roads towards the cost of which it has not subscribed, as A.'s quarter is called upon to do.

In what sense, then, is the trade which takes place in these two competing quarters of barley Free Trade? That it is free as air in the case of the Argentine quarter I understand. I should go further, and call it bounty-fed; but surely in the case of the English quarter it is most unfree, and indeed much fettered by the burden of rent, rates, tithe, and taxes, which have been exacted upon it for the local and imperial benefit. To make the trade equal, just, and free in fact as well as in name, before it appears on Bungay market, ought not the Argentine quarter to contribute to our local and imperial exchequers an exact equivalent of the amount paid by the British quarter? Why should the Englishman bear all these burdens and the foreigner who seeks the advantage of our markets be rid of them? In the case of whisky I understand the principle to be that imported spirits should pay an approximately equal tax to that exacted upon those manufactured in this country. Why, then, should not this rule—if it is the rule—be applied to other things besides whisky; the barley from which it is distilled, for instance?

This afternoon we were engaged in harrowing the young pease and beans to kill the redweed, as poppies are called here. One might think that the result of dragging iron spikes over the tender plants of these crops would be to destroy an enormous number of them, but in practice this is not the case. Indeed, it is quite rare to see a seedling broken off. I suppose the explanation to be that if the tooth of the harrow hits it, the young shoot, being pliable, bends to one side and allows the instrument to pass. With twitchgrass and redweed the case is different—they catch on the spikes and are dragged out of the soil. In harrowing the beans on Baker's, No. 43, we discovered that a baulk had been missed by the drill, which was sent for at once to sow it. Owing to the cold weather and the backward state of the crop, I do not think that there will be much difference when harvest time comes, although the crop has nine weeks' start of the seeds sown upon this particular baulk. To the observer it seems curious that this accident should not happen more often than it does, since, with two sets of harrows going before and behind them, it is very easy for the men with the drill to make an error and imagine that a baulk which has been harrowed is one which they have just drilled. A faint blush of yellowish green—I can describe it in no other way—is beginning to spread itself over the brown surface of the field as the myriad tiny spears of the sprouting oats and barley rise from their long sleep in the winter earth. As yet, however, the progress of vegetation is very slow, owing to the persistent cold of the nights.

April 7.—Yesterday, which was cold again, with a high sou'-west wind, we were ploughing the two acres of land in the middle of the Thwaite field, No. 28, where we propose to sow carrots. For this crop the plough is set as deep as it will travel, since carrots love to have well-stirred soil for their roots to work in. Also they like light soil, and some people hold that it is wise not to give them too much manure. I know that the carrots which we grew last year upon the All Hallows field, No. 33, which was heavily manured with Bungay compost, came very coarse and 'fangy, although the beet upon the same field were splendid. Of course, this may have been owing to the drought, but a tenant of mine showed me some beautiful roots, long, straight, and clean, that he had grown on light unmanured land. We have been dragging this Thwaite field vigorously to get the twitch out of it, which upon this soil is a fearsome and persistent weed. I wonder how many tumbril-loads of twitch I have burnt upon the Thwaite field since I began its cultivation? And still the smoke of those fires goes up!

The back lawn is being rolled also. It has been fed for either two or three years, and is now to be set for hay. This pasture has indeed a different face on it to that which it wore when I took it in hand some eight or nine years ago. Then it was waterlogged and mossy; moreover, the tenant, I believe, had mown it for nine years in succession, which of course he had no business to do. Since then it has been pipe-drained at a cost of 5*l.* per acre, dressed with basic slag, sown with trefoil seed, three pounds to the acre, and heavily grazed, with the result that it is now as good a pasture as any in the parish. I am always grateful to that back lawn, since it was owing to a difference of opinion with my late tenant concerning it that I took to farming, which, if as yet it has not enriched me, has at least taught me many things about the ways of Nature that seem good for a man to know.

To-day is, in fact, the first of spring, whatever the calendar may say to the contrary, the air being many degrees warmer notwithstanding the high sou'-west wind. It is perfectly astonishing to see the difference caused by only twenty-four hours of warmth and sunshine. Fields that were brown, or only just tinged with green, are now almost verdant; the tulips have begun to blow, and the primroses to appear in yellow clusters of tight buds and star-like blooms. When, amidst the long succession of vile samples that make up the English climate during the months of March, April, and May, we do chance to 'happen on'—as they say here—a perfect day, how perfect it is! How glad it makes us also; worries that seemed heavy enough before become suddenly lighter, and, like the opening flowers, prospects which were of the gloomiest take the rainbow hues of hope.

It is curious how extraordinarily susceptible some of us are to the influences of weather, and even to those of the different seasons. I do not think that these affect the dwellers in towns so much, for, their existence being more artificial, the ties which bind them to Nature are loosened ; but with folk who live in the country and study it, it is otherwise. Every impulse of the seasons throbs through them, and month by month, even when they are unconscious of it, their minds reflect something of the tone and colour of the pageant of the passing day. After all, why should it not be so, seeing that our bodies are built up of the products of the earth, and that in them are to be found many, if not all, of the elements that go to make the worlds, or at any rate our world, and every fruit and thing it bears ? The wonder is not that we are so much in tune with Nature's laws and phases, but that we can ever escape or quell their mastery. This is where the brain and the will of man come in.

To-day Fairhead is harrowing on the nine-acre marsh, No. 19. The bottom of this marsh grows thick as tow, and it is hard work for the two big mares to drag the new patent harrow through it, especially as they are both of them very near to foaling. One might think that under these circumstances such toiling was injurious to them, but, on the contrary, it seems that the more exercise they have right up to their time the better, provided that it is steady in its nature, and not of a kind which is likely to wring or jerk them, such as shaft work while carting heavy loads. Harrowing or ploughing they can do as well as ever, though, of course, they are a little slow in their movements, and especially at the turns. By the way, Fairhead tells me that we very nearly lost one of the two, the mare Scot, last night. About ten o'clock he went up to the Buildings to see if she was all right, and found her 'cast' upon her side in such a position that, owing to her state and size, she could not find her feet again, but was lying with her legs in the air, kicking. Had he not chanced to discover her, there is no doubt that by the morning she would have been dead from fright and exhaustion. As it happened, however, by the help of another man and a rope he was able to get her up with no worse hurt than a little hair rubbed off her eyebrow.

April 8 (*Good Friday*).—This afternoon I went to Beding-ham. As I leaned my bicycle against a post of the pond fence, I noticed that the shallow edge of the water was simply full of frogs (some of them dead) and spawn. This pond sup-plies drinking-water for the farm, and certainly it might occur to the uninitiated that a plentiful flavour of frog and occasional globules of spawn would not improve its quality or wholesome-ness. As a matter of fact, however, many of the people about here absolutely prefer pond to well water—not superior pond water such as that at Bedingham, which comes from a deep, recently cleaned moat, and is filtered in a gravel drain, but thick stuff from any little roadside pit-hole. Nor is this water as a rule in any way unwholesome—at any rate, to those who are accustomed to drink the stuff. Frogs and ducks and countless long-legged insects evidently do not disagree with man. Of course, if a pond becomes infected with any disease-bacillus it is another matter; for instance, a year or two ago there was an outbreak of diphtheria in ' the Parishes ' from this cause. But the same danger exists in the case of wells; indeed, I would rather have to deal with an infected pond than an infected well, as in the first the source of the mischief is more likely to be noticed and easier to remedy. Also I believe, though I have no scientific authority for the state-ment, that infected water which is exposed to the air and sunlight is much less likely to be virulent than that which is shut up in the darkness of a well.

While I am on this subject I will say that, so far as my observation goes, the system of water-supply in villages appears to be abominable, and is, indeed, a question which should be taken in hand by Parliament or the County Councils. So long as it is left to small communities, and, for that matter, sometimes to large ones also, to choose between a good and bad water-supply, in five cases out of six they will select whichever is cheapest. This, I maintain, they have no right to do ; a person visiting a town or village ought to be able to drink a glass of water with the absolute certainty that it is pure, and that he is not running the risk of bringing about his own interment within three weeks. He would be a bold man, however, who dared to travel from village to village in East Anglia and swallow whatever water was put before him. Indeed, as recent events show us, even in some of our towns he might find cause to rue his rashness.

What I suggest, although it may not be practicable everywhere, is that, in the case of villages at any rate, the problem could be solved at no great cost. An artesian or some other suitable kind of boring might be made to tap the water at a depth where it was not possible that it should be contaminated, whence it could be lifted by means of an ordinary windmill into tanks large enough to hold a supply of drinking-water sufficient for the needs of the population during any period of aërial calm that was likely to be experienced. The only essentials are that the tanks must be of ample size, and that the windmill should be powerful enough to pump even in a light draught of air ; then, if its site were properly chosen, I do not believe that it would often stand still for more than twenty-four hours at a spell.

The bullock which I am keeping at Bedingham with a view of showing it is not coming up to expectations. His fore-quarters are splendid, but he falls off behind. He has a box made expressly for him in the barn, but I believe that he is lonely and pines there ; at any rate, he does not take his food so well as he did.

It is a half-holiday, as is usual on Good Fridays and Christmas Days, though the agricultural labourer keeps few others ; therefore I found no one working on the farm. The land looks very well— indeed, I never saw it in better condition—and, except for the rolling, the beet fields are ready to drill. The mare, however, one of the pair of horses which are left here, is so old and heavy in foal that she cannot do much, so I have arranged with Moore to send over another horse with the drill to help to sow the beet to-morrow.

April 11.—On Saturday—that is the day before yesterday—we had good showers of rain. Whitrup harrowed the wheat on Baker's, No. 42, to drag out some of the small weeds which swarm upon the surface of the land. This wheat, which was rather thin in places, has improved greatly in strength and colour since it received a special compound dressing of artificial manure last month.

Yesterday, Easter Sunday, came stormy, with sudden and very violent tempests of rain and wind. In the course of my usual Sunday afternoon's walk round the farm I noticed what great progress everything has made during the last few days. Fields that were bare and brown are now clothed in green. I hear from Fairhead, who took over the horse and drill to Bedingham on Saturday, that they only succeeded in getting in two acres of beet. More, if not all of it, could have been drilled, but the land was unrolled, and after a few showers this soil becomes too sticky to admit of that operation. It is necessary to pass the roller over the baulks in order to flatten their crests and break the clods into mould before the drill goes down them; but if this clay is at all sticky it clings like wax and clogs the roller. Thus it often happens that although such a small volume of wet has fallen that drilling would be perfectly practicable, because the sharp coulters of the machine cut through the top crust and drop the seed in the dry soil beneath, yet, to the disappointment of the farmer, who knows not when he will again find his fields in suitable condition, it has to be given up because the roller cannot be used upon the land.

To-day I went down to the Bath Hills to watch the tree-cutting, which is getting on well under the charge of the woodman Reeve and an assistant. This timber-felling, where the trees are at all crowded, is an operation that requires great skill and judgment. The first thing the woodman must do is to decide in which direction the trunk is to fall and the exact spot of ground whereon he desires to lay it. Very possibly the state of the wind, if it is at all high, will make it difficult to do this with the requisite nicety, and in such case that tree must be left till another day.

If, however, there is no wind, or the set of it seems right, he places his ladder against the trunk, and, climbing as high as he can go, so that there may be a better pull and purchase at the moment of the fall, ties his line about the tree. Then he goes to a distance and makes the other end of the line, which is about thirty yards long, fast to the bole of a second tree, if one should stand conveniently to his purpose. Should there be no tree near of sufficient strength to bear the strain, then at the critical moment the line must be held by men—that is, if its use is considered necessary. The object of this rope, I may state, is to make it sure that in spite of other precautions the tree will not fall in a direction different to that intended, thereby causing damage, or possibly hurt, to the woodcutters ; for should it begin to fall thus perversely, the slack comes out of the rope, which, growing taut and rigid as a bar of iron when it takes the strain, swings the dead weight of the trunk round and brings it to the earth near to the place where it is desired that it should lie. That is, it does these things if the rope be strong enough. There is nothing more dangerous in wood-cutting than a weak or frayed rope, which is apt to fly apart at the moment of stress. When the line is successfully fastened and pulled as tight as one or two men can draw it, it is probably considered desirable—though this, of course, depends upon the character of the 'top'—to saw off such of the branches as can be reached with ease and safety, especially those upon that side to which the tree must fall, that otherwise would be splintered and spoiled.

Then the actual felling begins. This there are two ways of doing—one the careless and slovenly chopping off of the tree above the level of the ground, the other its scientific 'rooting.' In rooting a timber, the soil is first removed from about the foot of the bole with any suitable instrument till the great roots are discovered branching this way and that. Then the woodmen begin upon these with their mattocks, which sink with a dull thud into the soft and sappy fibre, first cutting those of them that are upon the rope side. When all which can be conveniently reached are severed, leaving only those that go straight down, and in the case of oaks and some other trees the great tap-root which pierces far into the earth beneath, they begin upon the bole, cutting it with hundreds of strokes, none of them delivered with very great force, and to the eye of the careless observer apparently aimed at random, which ends in shaping it to the form of a pear, the stalk of the pear being represented by the tap-root and the portion of timber that still remains above.

I remember a curious incident connected with the tap-root of an oak. This oak, a good tree of perhaps two hundred years' growth, was being felled in Bradenham Wood, in this county, when the woodmen called attention to something peculiar on the tap-root. On clearing it of soil, we found that the object was a horse-shoe of ancient make. Obviously in the beginning an acorn must have fallen into the hollow of this cast shoe, and as it grew through the slow generations the root filled up the circle, carrying it down into the earth in the process of its increase, till at length we found wood and iron thus strangely wedded. That tap-root with the shoe about it is now, or used to be, a paper-weight in the vestibule at Bradenham Hall.

It is curious to notice the changes in the colour of the wood as its separate layers are cut through. First there is the pink hue of the bark and the membrane beneath it, then comes the white of the outer wood, which in the case of oak we call 'sap,' and lastly the dark-coloured heart of oak. When the cutting has gone so deep that the shape of the bole approaches to that of a peg-top, the woodmen go to the end of the rope and pull upon it. Probably the tree makes no sign, but, with the exception of an occasional slight quiver as though of fear, which causes the twigs to tremble to their tips, stands as proud and upright as it has stood for the last century or more. Thereupon one of the men remarks to his mate that 'she wants a chip or two off the hinder side,' and then comes another five minutes of quiet and scientific chopping, followed by a return to the end of the rope. At about the third tug the observer will notice the topmost twigs of the timber bend themselves with a sudden curve, not unlike that of the top joint of a rod when a trout first takes the fly. At the next pull the curve is more sudden, and deeper. Now the great tree begins to groan and rock, and its boughs, rushing to and fro, to flog the air in wide sweeps, but still with a desperate tenacity the thin neck of wood and the remaining rope of root keep it from falling.

'She's a-coming,' says the head woodman ; 'now, togither, lad, togither.' Two more pulls and the doomed tree swings so far that it cannot recover its upright position. For a moment it hangs trembling, as though making obeisance to its murderers ; then— a swift rush, a sound of wood rending and of tough roots flying apart with a noise like that of pistol shots, and down it tumbles to the earth with a thunderous rattling crash that echoes through the wood and dies far away upon the breast of the quiet river.

It is done, and a change has come over the landscape ; the space that for generations has been filled with leafy branches is now white and empty air. I know of no more melancholy sight— indeed, to this day I detest seeing a tree felled ; it always reminds me of the sudden and violent death of a man. I fancy it must be the age of timbers that inspires us with this respect and sympathy, which we do not feel for a sapling or a flower.

While I was on the hills this morning an oak was felled that from its girth and general appearance I should say had been growing for at least a century. The curious thing about this tree was that when we were cutting it down we discovered that in the beginning it had sprung from the stump of another oak which stood there before it, and had in its day been felled by long-dead woodmen. Unskilful or careless hands they were also, for, as that portion of the stub which was incorporated and overgrown by the bole of the present tree showed, they had not 'rooted' their timber, but hacked it off level with the ground. Perhaps, however, they did this in order to cause it to throw up a bush of undergrowth. At least that is what must have happened, and afterwards, on the occasions of successive cuttings of the fell, gradually the growths were thinned out to a single sapling, which, spared from decade to decade, went on until at last it became a timber.

What interests me in this tree is that I had no idea a stub oak —that is to say, an oak growing upon roots which have done duty for a predecessor—would increase to such a size. I knew that it is quite possible and a common practice to re-grow blue-gums in this fashion, the child tree becoming as large and as vigorous as its parent, but that the oak would succeed even to a moderate extent under such treatment was new to me.

The ways of trees, however, are often very curious. Thus, last autumn, when shooting on the Ditchingham Hall estate, I saw with regret that a great bough had been torn off a famous beech which grows there. Going to examine it, I found that the first fracture was of ancient standing, but that to support and nurture itself the injured bough had put out roots from its torn surface, some of them as much as an inch in diameter, which were feeding on the leaf mould and decayed wood collected in a fork below the break. I have frequently seen. this kind of aerial root emission in the case of tropical trees, especially in the *tierra caliente* of Mexico, but never before in trees of English growth ; although it is common enough to find one seedling tree flourishing upon another of a different variety, sometimes indeed growing to a respectable size.

To-day we have been harrowing the three-acre new pasture, No. 11, and sowing on it a good coat of clover seed saved from that which I grew at Bedingham last year. This is the process : Fairhead, with the new steel chain-drag set to cut its deepest, harrows the pasture crossways, to scatter as evenly as possible the ' tether ' left by the sheep, which, it will be remembered, have been penned upon this field, and to disturb any moss that may remain after their treading. Even this harrowing requires care, since the triangular knobs of steel are apt to be clogged with bits of stick and rubbish, and occasionally must be cleared by lifting, or now and again by turning, the chain fabric. Before the harrow walks Buck with a basket full of seed strapped on his breast. He goes to and fro across the meadow scattering the clover seed with which it is to be refreshed, about a peck and a half of it to the acre. The method is very neat and pretty. Grasping handfuls of seed first with the right and then with the left hand, by alternate motions of his arms he casts them in a fine shower so that each handful is spread evenly over a certain space of ground in front of him. Watching him, it is easy to see that his farming education began before the day of drills. I doubt whether a man of the present generation could perform this task with half his nicety, as I understand that the necessary evenness of spread depends upon the exact force of the swing of the arm and the loosening in its proper order of the grip of each finger upon the seed. When the pasture has been harrowed transversely it is again harrowed lengthwise, thereby burying the seed. After this it only remains to roll it and leave the issue to the kindly influences of Spring.

Last night we had a tragedy. The sheep, having finished No. 11, were penned upon a little stretch of grass (not more than an acre in extent) that is separated from it by a fence which it is proposed to remove, laying drainage pipes in the ditch and filling it up, so soon as we can find time for the task. I must explain that among the movable hurdles, which are of iron and mounted upon wheels, is what is known as a lamb-hurdle—that is, an ingenious contrivance fitted with rollers set horizontally, too narrow to admit of the passage of ewes, but large enough to allow the lambs to pass in and out of the fold, as they do not grow well if kept constantly confined with their mothers. Doubtless some of these wandered out in the darkness, and while they were thus away from the ewes, that could not go to protect them—as they will do with great courage if free—were attacked by a dog or dogs. The ravening brute, or brutes, seized one of the lambs—the finest that I have—and murdered it. In the morning it was found lying in the holl, its throat torn completely out and half the head eaten, a dreadful and a piteous sight.

Another lamb was also badly bitten in the leg, but managed to escape back into the fold. Both of these had been sold to the butcher for twenty-nine shillings each, on the understanding that he was to take them when it suited him ; but as they had not been delivered, of course I am liable for the loss.

The discovery of what had happened filled Hood and myself with consternation, not so much on account of the actual damage as from fear of what might come. It is well known that when once a dog takes to this dreadful practice of lamb-killing he will often travel great distances, and show the most extraordinary cunning, in order to gratify his appetite. I believe it to be hopeless to attempt to break any brute that has acquired this habit ; for him there is only one cure, a rope, and Tusser, who farmed in this country, was of the same opinion three hundred years ago, *vide* his ' March Husbandry ' :

> Of mastiffs and mongrels that many we see,
> A number of thousands too many there be.
> Watch therefore in Lent, to thy sheep go and look,
> For dogs will have victuals by hook or by crook.

Such hounds, however, hunt only in the dark ; they know better than to work their crimes in the light of day ; therefore it is generally difficult, if not impossible, to identify them. To-night we have arranged to set a watch of men armed with guns, one to be relieved by the other at midnight ; but, even if the dog should not catch their wind and take warning, as there is no moon I very much doubt whether they will be able to see him.

Worse however than the ravening dog even is the wandering stag that has baffled the pack and is outlying in the woods. Such animals seek the company of in-lamb ewes at night, to sport with them as I suppose. But the ewes do not appreciate the game ; perhaps sheep are superstitious, and in their innocent minds the visitor's great horns, that tail, those cloven hoofs, all point to one conclusion. At any rate, round and round the fold they tear in terror, and when the lambs are born they come deformed and with twisted heads. Twice in this neighbourhood have I heard of great loss of lambs from this cause, once quite recently, where, as I was told, nearly half of the total number perished. Little wonder, then, that shepherds fear the visit of a lonely stag.

To-day being Easter Monday, the annual Vestry Meeting was held in the church at seven in the evening. It has now been my lot, as people's churchwarden of this parish, to attend a great number of these Easter-Monday Vestries. The similarity between the proceedings in different years is really remarkable, although once I remember, when there was some question of accounts which excited popular interest, the place was crowded. The average attendance, however, runs from six to nine, including the clergyman, the churchwardens, the clerk, and the organ-blower, which cannot be called excessive out of a population of about eleven hundred. The fact is that, although they are far more truly democratic than the Parish Council, since in them every parishioner can say his say and exercise his rights of voting, such as they may be, nobody takes the slightest interest in vestry meetings, or the trouble to walk a yard to be present at them.

The procedure is simple. When a quorum is present in the exceedingly cold vestry, which is lit by one of the dazzling church lamps, the Rector takes the chair and reads the minutes of the last year's meeting. Then, the church accounts having been produced, and the normal deficit sighed over, some gentleman present, in earnest tones, proposes the re-election of the people's churchwarden. Another gentleman seconds it, and the people's churchwarden, duly re-elected, responds with an emotion befitting the occasion, wondering in his heart how much he will be expected to advance on account of the church coals during the coming winter. Then the Rector nominates his churchwarden, who is also re-elected, and after a long and rather desultory conversation, generally about insurance or lightning conductors, that meeting is gathered to its fathers.

April 12.—Hood, who has been suffering from a cold upon his chest, is this morning absolutely set fast with lumbago, so that he can scarcely stir hand or foot, the result of neglecting his first ailment. Luckily he has a most worthy and capable wife, for he is not a man who takes care of himself.

Our watch for the dog last night proved unavailing. Just as the darkness was finally closing in, Fairhead declares that he saw it—a long, dark-coloured animal, which came through the iron gates of the right-of-way, and advanced towards the fold. On winding him, however, for it could not have seen him where he stood in the doorway of the shepherd's hut, it turned and fled, thereby showing how guilty was its conscience. Unfortunately, at the time he had not the gun with him, and the dog put in no further appearance that night, or, if he did, it was too dark to see him.

Towards daybreak the mare Scot foaled, a 'fine upstanding foal,' as they say here. This morning I found Fairhead rolling the new pasture, No. 10, in the heavy rain. One of the oldest and quietest horses on the farm was dragging the wooden roller, but when it saw me advancing upon it beneath an umbrella it took fright, and nearly precipitated itself and the roller into the ditch. Sensible as they are, farm-horses draw the line at umbrellas, to which they are unaccustomed. When he had finished the rolling, I went with Fairhead to see the foal. Undoing the door of the box, he entered it, still wearing his wet military greatcoat; whereupon the mare, although he called out at her, laid back her ears and drew up her lips. Indeed, she looked very nasty, and I thought that she meant to attack him, an opinion which Fairhead shared, for he got out of the box as quickly as he could. Remarking that he had never known her behave like this before, he tried to re-enter, with the same result. Then the solution of the mystery struck him.

'She don't know me in this here coat,' he said, 'and can't smell me through it'; and, pulling it off, he went into the box boldly. The mare thrust out her head and sniffed, then she literally seemed 'to smile all over,' as the Americans say, and made no further attempt to interfere with him, even when he caught hold of the foal and dragged it on to its legs. Two or three years ago a change of the stockman's clothes resulted in a tragedy in this neighbourhood. My friend Mr. Henry Smith, the squire of Ellingham, had a bailiff named Bensely. Also he had a very savage bull. This bull was turned out on a marsh, where it could injure no one, but Bensely, unhappily for himself, went to look at it after church or chapel, dressed in his Sunday best. The bull did not know its attendant in this attire, and attacked him so that the poor man was found dead in a dyke. His actual death, however, was, I believe, due not to his injuries, but to terror acting on a diseased heart.

New-born Pride, our oldest, and once our best, cow—she is about twenty—also calved last night, for the animals seem to be taking the opportunity of Hood's indisposition to hurry their offspring into the world at as inconvenient a time as possible. I am glad to say that her calf is a heifer, the second only out of all the number that she has given us. She is so old that probably she will be sold out before she calves again, so I want to keep as much of her stock as possible, for she is a magnificent stamp of cow, long and broad and low, possessing that size which many red-polls lack. Her other heifer calf is now a member of the herd, with a calf of her own, and promises very well.

To-day, as I was walking by, I noticed great flocks of sparrows and starlings on the three-acre pasture. Doubtless they are busy devouring as much of the clover seed sown yesterday as they can find, but I hope that enough will escape them to serve our purpose.

April 13.—This has been a sad day for the lambs, for on it they have made their first acquaintance with the terrors of existence under our present dire carnivorous system, wanting which, by the way, they would never have lived at all. About breakfast time all the flock, sheep and lambs together, were driven into the All Hallows barn, and the farrier arrived in a cart as per appointment. Half the barn was hurdled off, and behind the hurdles the mob of them stood wondering. Then, with the assistance of various boys who always assemble upon such an occasion, very much as in Africa I have seen the vultures, led by instinct, gather together round wounded game, the ewes and those of the lambs upon which, as the fattest and finest, the butcher had already set his seal, amidst a frantic baa-ing and confusion, were one by one ejected through a hurdle hinged by means of a rope and stood ajar. Out they rushed, all of them knocking their shins against the weather-board of the door, and leaving behind them the little mob of doomed lambkins. Then the veterinary, who, should he ever peruse these lines, will, I trust, not be offended if I describe him as a peculiarly skilful and benevolent-looking young gentleman, said in a soft and sympathetic voice, 'Small ones first, please.'

So a 'small one' was procured by an eager youth and presented to the surgeon with its ears drooped and its tail pointing to the skies, which tail he felt in a contemplative and almost dreamy fashion, as though he were sampling a piece of cloth. Still in the same mild voice, he asked for the 'large knife, please,' and it was handed to him, a formidable-looking weapon. Next there was a single swift and adroit motion of the arm and off flew about six inches of tail. This was the beginning of a perfect saturnalia of tail-cutting and other operations, at which, as the sight was not agreeable, I did not long assist.

About a couple of hours later, however, the whole flock reappeared on the back lawn ; but now—those that were marked for the butcher and rejoiced prematurely excepted—there was little of their playful skip left in the unfortunate lambs. They lay about in knots or singly, for they were too stiff to walk, but I noticed that some of them nibbled such grass as they could reach. I hope that they may soon recover, though, myself, I believe that all this cutting about has been put off too late. However, the season has been so cold that it was not considered advisable to attempt it before.

On the farm we have been baulk-splitting, manure-carting, layer-rolling, and ploughing.

April 14.—My fears were not without foundation. Last night the sheep were shut up in the barn to protect them from the cold after the operation, and also from the power of the Bath Hills dog. This morning one of the lambs—of course the finest—was found bled to death. Later in the day they were turned out upon the front lawn, when I noticed that many of the poor things went very lame.

As, although dull, it was not actually raining, we drilled between three and four acres of beet on All Hallows, No. 29, a portion of this field, that nearest the fence, being reserved for swedes and white turnips. The land was rather sticky, but on the whole the seed went in well.

The process of root drilling is different from that of sowing corn. First a roll drawn by one horse is passed over the land, covering four baulks at each journey. Then comes the root drill, also drawn by one horse and fitted with three coulters only, each of which pierces the centre of a baulk. Another roll passed over the baulks after the drill has done its work completes the operation. We make it a practice to mix a little cabbage seed with that of the beet. Formerly we used to grow the cabbage by itself, but experience has shown us that if sown amongst the beet the 'fly' and other destructive insects seem much more likely to overlook it. During the last year or two, by following this system, we have raised a quantity of splendid cabbages, which are cut as occasion requires, either before the beet is drawn or after it, and thrown to the cattle on the pastures when the grass becomes too sparse and innutritious to support them. This cow-cabbage, by the way, which has an enormous white heart, is, if properly boiled, quite suitable for table purposes—much better, indeed, than many of the obnoxious vegetables, to my mind, known to gardeners as winter greens.' I tried it several times last winter and found it excellent.

To-day I saw the first swallow ; it looked very cold, and certainly does not make a summer.

April 15.—This morning some rain fell, after which the weather became fine and springlike, causing everything to grow so fast that one can almost see the increase. To-day we are plough- ing and manure-carting on to the eleven-acre at Baker's, No. 44, which is being prepared for mangolds and swedes. The clover layer on half of the All Hallows ten-acre, No. 37, is getting quite thick and high. The wheat on Baker's, No. 42, is also improving very much, as the dressing of artificial manure continues to tell upon it. It is, however, full of docks, which is not greatly to be wondered at, seeing that the ploughman, Whitrup, tells me that my predecessor as tenant of this land, except at haysel and harvest, employed only three men on the 150 acres that he farmed, a force which would not leave any spare hands for dock pulling. I think that the most frequent cause of the ruin of tenant-farmers is their wild attempt to work twice as much land as they have capital to stock. It can end only one way, for the land will not grow two crops. Sooner or later the weeds get the mastery, and then—the bank forecloses.

Fairhead is engaged in harrowing the pastures on either side of the Lodge drive which runs beneath the shelter of the Vineyard Hills. The grass here, at least under the slope, is somewhat coarse, owing to the damp and occasional floods from the river, but affords useful feed because, lying so warm, it springs early. It is however, very difficult to cut with the mowing-machine on account of the little stones thrown up by the moles, which frequent this place in great numbers. Let the driver of the machine take what care he will, these stones are apt to get into the teeth of the knife and jag or break them.

Though he is still a sorry spectacle, Hood's lumbago is a little better ; but one of the ewes, I fancy the mother of the lamb that died, is queer, and two more lambs are very ill. Most of these poor creatures are so stiff that when once they lie down they do not seem to care to get up again. Thus, as they neglect to run to their mothers to suck, naturally they lose strength, till at length in the worst instances they sink beyond recovery and die. The veterinary has inspected them, but can only shake his head and say that although every possible care had been taken, as was indeed the case, undoubtedly the cutting about was done when the lambs were too old. I quite agree with him ; but it is only another instance of how, in trying to escape one danger, we may fall into a worse. Another year, be it hot or cold, off go the lambs' tails before they have seen out three weeks.

The cattle at Baker's seem to have got over their ailments for the present, and are growing into fine beasts, as they ought, considering the amounts of corn, cake, and root that vanish down their capacious gullets. The beet clamps, indeed, are melting very fast ; at the beginning of winter it looked as though it would be impossible for any number of cattle which we could keep to devour the contents of those scores of yards of hales before the summer came again. Now it is clear that this was a mistake, for we have many mouths to feed, considering the size of the place, most of which get hungrier as they grow. It is difficult for us to imagine what our forefathers did before root culture was introduced. I suppose that they never attempted to fat beef in winter, but were content to keep it in store condition by the help of hay. I think it was my friend, Mr. John Cordy Jeaffreson, who told me that in his father's time in Suffolk the meat for the winter's consumption of a house was always salted down from the beasts killed in autumn, which had grown fat on the summer pastures.

To-day I heard the first nightingale on Hollow Hill. Ever since I have known this place, and, as I am told, for generations before I knew it, nightingales have frequented that spot. A little plantation grows in what was no doubt an ancient clay or marl pit, through which the Norwich road now runs, and here two couples of these sweet-tongued birds build year by year. It is a very public place, but they do not mind that in the least; indeed if you stand in the road they will often sit and trill within a few feet of your head, as though they knew that you appreciated their music and that they were singing to you. I should have thought, however, that the boys who break in and steal their eggs would have frightened them away; but fortunately the nests of nightingales are very difficult to find, so possibly they escape.

April 20.—There is not much to record since last Friday. On Saturday we had a heavy shower in the evening, and two more lambs died from the effects of the cutting. Sunday was a lovely day, and another lamb died. While I was in church on that morning an incident occurred which shows how varied are the duties of a country magistrate.

As I chance to be one of the justices nominated to exercise the powers conferred by the Lunacy Acts, I am brought a good deal into contact with the insanity of this district, which, by the way, seems to be greatly on the increase and to occur chiefly among women. About breakfast-time on Sunday morning I was requested by an overseer to attend in a neighbouring village to satisfy myself by personal examination as to the madness of a certain pauper lunatic before she was removed to the asylum. This I promised to do, fixing the hour of two o'clock. In the middle of the service, however, on returning from the lectern after reading one of the Lessons, I found a young man by my pew with a note, on which was written, 'Lunatic waiting for you at church gate. Sir, please come and examine.'

Accordingly, as I judged that the case must have become urgent, I went to investigate the condition of the poor woman's mind by means of a *tête-à-tête* with her in a fly at the gate of the churchyard. Having satisfied myself as to her insanity, I signed the orders necessary for her removal to the asylum, and reappeared in church before the conclusion of the Litany. It seems that it was not considered advisable that the patient should remain longer out of proper control; so, as she could not be removed without a magistrate's order, I was followed to the church.

On Monday the second lamb that the dog bit—by the way, that brute has not troubled us again—died of mortification, so that up to the present our total loss is six. Yesterday there was a cold east wind, which, however, was favourable for the beet drilling and harrowing. To-day I went to Norwich to open a great missionary bazaar in the Agricultural Hall, where the attendance was surprisingly large. Many of the exhibits were very interesting indeed, especially the models of Eastern houses and of Jerusalem as it existed in the time of our Lord. There was also a first-class collection of African fetishes, jujus, and miscellaneous assorted gods, some of the holiest being represented by cowrie-shells fashioned to the shape of a cone. I wonder if there is any connection between this and the cone that was always a feature in the Phœnician worship. But that subject is too large to go into here. I wish that someone would write an adequate book upon superstition and its effects, as distinguished from and opposed to revealed religion and its effects. This curse of the world, civilised or savage, deserves a worthy chronicler. Walking round the exhibits in the Agricultural Hall to-day, it was borne in to my mind that superstition in all its hideous phases is perhaps the most concrete and tangible form in which the Evil One manifests himself upon earth, and I think that those who have mixed much with native races will not disagree with me. Here is an instance of its working, which has just come to my notice.

Not long ago two Matabeles were tried at Bulawayo for the murder of their grandson, an infant of two. Poison having failed, the boy was held beneath the water and drowned. The crime was admitted, but the defence raised was that the child had *cut its top teeth first*. Such children being unlucky and the cause of ill-luck to others, it was customary to kill them, and a 'witch doctor' on being consulted had ordered that this one should be put to death!

Well, only a century or so since we did things almost as bad in England, and I am told that to-day, in London, societies exist composed of educated men who devote themselves to the practice of a black art of the mediæval 'Ingoldsby Legends' pattern, such as aims at calling injury and doom upon obnoxious persons by the fashioning of images of wax into which the instructed thrust pins fortified with appropriate curses and invocations.

Indeed, if one may judge from the records of coroners' inquests which appear in the papers, all this mischievous mystery-mongering is on the increase. Thus I have a paper before me, from which it seems that the victim, a middle-aged woman, was frightened into committing suicide by a fortune-teller who prophesied troubles to her. I remember also seeing a report a while ago which stated that the deceased, a young girl, killed herself because she had been told by some seer that she was under the influence of the planet Saturn, a malevolent orb, which would certainly bring evil upon her. In this instance also the prophecy achieved its own fulfilment, and some astrologer or palmist walks the world to-day with that woman's blood upon his head. In short, in such matters, humanity, its vast advances notwithstanding, reverts continually to the primitive type, and the myths of ancient Chaldæa and mediæval Europe still find votaries in modern London and New York. It would almost appear as though man, civilised or savage, must cling to something beyond the natural—or at least as though those of the strongest mental fibre only can stand quite alone and self-reliant. Take away the convictions of religion from the average human being, and no fetish seems too gross for him to welcome—none so degraded that he cannot build to it an altar. Thus the individual whose mind rejects the conception of a patient and purposeful God as mere childish vapouring may be quite ready to believe that his fate and future are plotted out for him by planets whereof the attributes and influences are fabled from names bestowed upon them by the fancy of the ancients ; or even, like some poor savage, be prepared to find the promise of prosperity or sorrow in the appearance of a magpie, and, with a faith as full as it is piteous, to augur death among its inmates from the blooming in the house of a flower that has been announced ill-omened.

This was the second day of the Bungay Races, but I was only in time for the last three events. About provincial race-meetings there are many opinions, and my own, as a non-racing man, is rather against them. To begin with, they encourage gambling; and as a person who has lost hard-earned money in various sporting ventures, though not on horses, my attitude towards gambling is, theoretically at any rate, severe. Apart from joking, there is no doubt that betting does an immense amount of mischief—let those who doubt it walk down the Strand and watch the news-boys on the afternoon of any race-meeting—especially to novices who are so unfortunate as to be successful in their first essay. All who enter upon this field should pray for failure. I remember a story that my late father used to tell me of how when he was a boy he went to the Bath racecourse, and there lost a guinea, which his father had given him, either to a gentleman who manipulated a thimble and three peas, or to a bookmaker—I forget which—and of how, then and there, he made up his mind that it would be the last coin of his which was ever risked in this fashion. Many a man who had won a guinea would have a different tale to tell.

If these meetings encouraged the breeding of good horses, and if the prizes were in the main confined to the owners of animals bred in the district, their desirability, to my mind, would be easier to argue; but, in fact, I believe that this is not the case. The racers that appear on these local courses are for the most part second or third class platers which travel from meeting to meeting with their attendant crowd of professional jockeys and white-hatted bookmakers. Against these very experienced persons the astute and horsey gents of the neighbourhood, grooms who have saved a little money and what not, pit themselves, and as a rule come off second best. Indeed, as the late Mr. Barney Barnato is reported to have said of the 'sound business man' who thought that he could see through and profit by the financial machinations of the 'Magnates' of the Kaffir Market—'a snowflake in hell fire would have a better chance.' Also, as my own experience shows me, sometimes these 'clever ones' get drunk and lose their situations.

On the other hand, it is urged that race-meetings bring money to a neighbourhood, and afford innocent enjoyment to many country people who make a holiday of the occasion. Without doubt there is much to be said for this view of the case, and I am bound to add, from my experience as a magistrate, that singularly little trouble has arisen at the local races. The worst case which I can remember was that of some welchers who were brought before us on the charge of having defrauded a number of people of their money, one of whom escaped, while his companion, a very smartly dressed gentleman, was convicted and sent to jail for a month. Perhaps the best comment on the undecided state of my mind as to these festivities is that I subscribe a modest sum towards them.

April 23.—Thursday, the 21st, was cold but bright. On the farm we were horse-hoeing beans. This is an operation that to the inexperienced looks terribly destructive, especially in the case of winter beans, which by now are tall. However carefully the horse may march down the rows, or with whatever skill the hoer may manage his instrument, many of the stalks are cut by its sharp knives and utterly destroyed. At first sight this seems a wanton and a cruel waste, but in fact it is not so. To begin with, those that are sacrificed most likely have sprung outside the exact line, and are therefore encroaching upon the air and space required by their neighbours. Also, even if a mistake is made occasionally, and some are so unfortunate as to be annihilated although occupying their right and lawful place, still, if the 'plant' be a fair one, a little hole here and there does it no harm, since down it the sunlight percolates to the survivors. Any such losses are amply compensated for by the destruction of thousands of weeds and by the stirring of the soil about the roots of the crop. Also we rolled beet-land and dragged out twitch-grass on that portion of the Thwaite field, No. 28, which is to be drilled with carrots.   Of this pestilent stuff there seems to be no end; I suppose that the soil of the field is particularly well suited to its growth.   Already this year we have burnt a great quantity, and still there is more to be destroyed.

Several of the lambs are still sick and stiff, but I do not think that any more will die.   Hood and I counted them by opening the back lawn gate a little way and allowing the flock to rush through, which it did eagerly, imagining that there was something fresh to eat on the other side.   There are now fifty-two lambs left, the balance, with the exception of a few that the butcher has taken, having deceased.

Yesterday, Friday, was dull and cold with a north-east wind. We drilled the beet on Baker's (half of No. 44), using the Tankard variety, which on the whole we have found about the best for this land, and among it some cabbage as usual.   Also we rolled pease, beans, and barley, to press the earth about their roots and discomfort some of the grubs and insects at work beneath.   As in the case of the harrowing about which I have spoken, it seems extraordinary that the passing of a heavy roller over young pease and beans should not crush or greatly injure them.   Yet this is not the case—they bow their heads to the roll and for a while look a little depressed, but on the following day they are as upright and smiling as ever.   One cart was employed carrying root to the sheds ; it is astonishing what an amount of time and labour is taken up in this needful operation when there are many cattle to be fed and the hales in some instances lie at a distance from the buildings.

The sheep have taken to scouring, though whether owing to the grass being lush after the wet, or to their eating it while the night frosts are still upon it, I do not know.   As a remedy we are folding them on the Buildings-meadow, No. 6, and giving them some dry food in the shape of corn and hay to eat at night.   This will do the field, which is one of my young pastures, great good, and, I hope, cure the sheep of their ailment.   I notice that now, when they have had a bite at the new grass, the ewes will not eat the beet half as greedily as they did. Formerly they used to gobble every bit of them with the exception of a dirty little piece of that portion of the rind which lay undermost ; now it is common to see the root messed about and half of it left uneaten.

By the way, the beet which we drilled yesterday were, I think, our last. Certainly we have no reason to complain of the way they have gone in this year ; I only trust that they will come up as well.

In the evening the nightingales were singing most beautifully upon the Vineyard Hills, their favourite haunt.

This morning I received a lithographed form telling me that the Unionist member for South Norfolk had resigned, and that my presence was requested at Norwich at 11.30 to assist in the selection of a candidate to fight the seat. As to reach Norwich by 11.30 I should have had only a few minutes to change my clothes, get breakfast, and catch the train, it was not possible for me to attend the meeting. This, however, will not matter much, as no doubt the candidate is already fixed upon by the responsible people at Norwich who are managing the election, for had it been otherwise a longer notice would have been given. I confess, however, that in these democratic days I think it is best that a candidate should be chosen by a general gathering of the party, and after he has laid his views before them in a formal speech. That was what happened when, some years ago, I contested a seat in this county in the agricultural interest, and I am sorry that the precedent has not been adhered to in the present case, although very possibly there were good reasons for its neglect. If all the leading members of a party have attended, or are afforded a reasonable chance of attending, such a meeting, having been personally consulted, they will work harder and with more enthusiasm for the candidate who happens to be chosen.

Putting this question aside, it seems to me that the party has hit upon a most unfortunate moment to accept the resignation of the late member, as the baker tells me that, owing to the war between Spain and America, and the cornering of wheat by Yankee speculators, flour has already risen threepence a stone. This the agricultural labourer, who very often is not logical, will be pretty sure to score up against the Government, and by way of protest vote for any one who opposes them.

Wheat has risen over four shillings, and, for the first time since I know not when, stands at more than forty shillings the quarter, a price at which it will pay to grow. This, however, will not benefit farmers much, seeing that in these parts most of them have long ago sold every grain. Indeed, the majority of the small men are in such chronic want of money that, in order to pay their labourers, they are forced to rush their corn on to the market immediately after harvest, no matter what may be the condition of the trade. Most of mine has gone also, but I believe that here and at Bedingham I have a hundred coomb—that is fifty quarters—left. We must get it thrashed as soon as possible, for I have no faith in the permanence of a boom in wheat, and quite expect that it will come down as fast as it went up, although perhaps not to the level which it reached a few years back.

I think it was in 1894 that we were offered only eighteen shillings or a pound a quarter for good wheat. As it was ridiculous to sell at this price, I fed the pigs on it, and the following year put but ten acres under corn for the sake of the straw. Free Trade may, as many declare, be a boon sent straight from Heaven, but I cannot help thinking that there is something wrong in a state of affairs which forces farmers to accept twenty-two or twenty three shillings for wheat that cost them about thirty to grow. Perhaps, however, this is due to my stupid agricultural way of looking at the question.

Peachey is ploughing up the strip of land where the beet-hales stood on the All Hallows nine-acre, No. 36, the last of these beet having been carted into the shed. This space will be sown with barley like the rest of the field, and though it will come in later and be a different sample, the crop can always be used as food for pigs or pheasants. Afterwards he began to re-plough the glebe-piece, No. 38, on that side of the dyke which is reserved for swedes, the remainder being kept for potatoes.

It is very cold with a piercing wind to-day, and the night frosts continue.

April 24.—To-day, Sunday, is also very cold, with east wind and occasional bursts of sunshine. On my way to church I saw a little whirlwind—Roger's Blast is the local name—tear across the field and strike the road in front of us, lifting dust, bits of sticks, and dead leaves high into the air, where they twisted round and round in the form of a cone till the blast, which though small was violent, passed on and left them. I have often seen these miniature cyclones in Africa, but, so far as I recollect, very seldom in England, and I never yet met any one who could explain exactly what they are. When they do occur here the labourers say that they portend fine weather.

This afternoon I went to Bedingham, and as a rather feeble bell was still tolling when I approached the church, I leant my bicycle against a gravestone and entered. Altogether there were about twenty people present in the ancient but somewhat dilapidated building, of which the most uncommon feature is the beautiful carved rood-screen that, from slots still existing in the masonry, seems once to have filled the arch. Indeed, now that I think of it, I remember the daughter of a former rector telling me some years ago that in past days—I believe within her own memory, though of this I am not certain—some of the carved work of this screen was pulled down and used for fuel. The church is divided into two almost equal parts by the screen, the chancel being much larger than is usual, doubtless because in past generations it was used for the accommodation of the monks, who had a private door at one side of it communicating with the priory.

About this fane, with its stonework stained by the dust and damp of centuries, its mouldering monuments and marbles, its worn benches and rough brick pavement, beneath which lie the bones of those who like myself once held lands in Bedingham and sat to worship in its sanctuary, there is an atmosphere—a very presence of the past—which impresses me more and comes closer to the tangible than that of any other church I know. Perhaps it is the half-forsaken appearance of the place, or the dull light of the April afternoon, or the solemn echo of the rector's voice as he reads the prayers, or all of them together, that have this peculiar power of reviving that which sleeps, and almost of making visible that which has vanished. But that which sleeps may awake, and that which has vanished may appear. It is not necessary to be superstitious—indeed there is no superstition in the belief, or perhaps in the vagary, that here are present the spirits of the dead pressing round us in the place once familiar to their feet, watching us with their quiet eyes which have looked on peace, and waiting to welcome us to the number of their company.

At least this is certain—our old English churches bind together the generations who passed beneath their doors in life, and in death sleep about their walls, with a tie that is not the less strong because it can scarcely be defined in words.

After church I walked over the farm. The old mare, who looks very spare and aged, has now produced a rather thin foal, whose presence seems to surprise and annoy her, for from time to time she turns her ancient head and contemplates it with a hollow and inquiring eye. We have, therefore, but one effective horse left upon the place at present, by the help of which Moore got in the kohl-rabi yesterday on part of the new-drained field, No. 18. First the horse rolled the land, then he went into the drill and drilled it, ending up a useful day's work by returning to the roller and rolling it again. On No. 21 I found the grass sown for per-manent pasture just pricking through among the barley, thousands of tiny green and yellow spears, with here and there an unfamiliar seedling, doubtless of chicory or burnet, or one of the other tap-rooted herbs that have been sown among the grasses. The beans grow well as usual, but are again being hoed to get rid of the shed barley springing among them. The wheats also flourish, but the barleys look somewhat stunted and yellow. In walking across the meadows I found a purple orchis, the first that I have seen this year.

April 25.—To-day we have been setting potatoes on part of the glebe five-acre, No. 38. Mr. Robert Simpson, who is my agent, came over here this morning with the pleasing intelligence that the repairs upon a little farm belonging to this estate at Rumburgh, which produces a rental of about 25*l.*, will cost not less than 95*l.*, or about four years' rent. It has been the same story ever since I have had to do with this property, until at times I wonder how there can possibly be anything left to repair. Of course, the explanation is that in the old days farmers were not so particular about buildings ; indeed, they 'made out' with sheds and hovels that tenants at the present time would not even look at. But then, thirty years ago the land was valuable, and a farmer did not throw up his holding merely because the landlord refused to execute extensive and costly repairs to the buildings on it, for he knew that it might be a long while before he could get another to his mind. Now the position has changed entirely, and just when he can least afford to bear the outlay, the owner of the soil must at any cost atone for the neglect of his predecessors, or lose such tenants as remain to him.

In walking through the Bath Hills plantation this evening I observed that my plan of enclosing the hillside with barbed wire is already beginning to bear fruit. I can never remember seeing or hearing so many birds about the place. In addition to all the commoner kinds, I observed a yellowish bird with the shape and general appearance of a hawfinch, with which I am quite unfamiliar ; also green woodpeckers, hawks, nightjars (I think), jays, and many others.

April 26.—Three of the horses have gone to-day to drag waggons loaded with furniture for the house at Kessingland, but

Whitrup is ploughing with the two in-foal mares in the eleven-acre on Baker's, No. 44, while the mare that has foaled is rolling barley, and the old horse has been fetching root into the sheds.

I went this morning to look at the young cow which has just calved. Her mother was one of the Shotley lot, of which I bought six or seven at the sale some years ago. I remember that I gave 27*l.* for her, because she was so beautiful to look at, but shortly after she produced her calf (bred by a Shotley bull) she turned out such a hopeless kicker that we were obliged to fat and sell her to the butcher. Her daughter is now making a fine cow, and yesterday produced a calf, I think her second. Like her mother, she is rather wild—at least, she did not at all appreciate my appearance upon the scene ; indeed, I found it necessary to retire quickly. Old New-born Pride knows better than to make a fuss ; her calf is small but very pretty, and, perhaps from force of long-continued habit, the production of it does not seem to have affected her in any way whatsoever. I hear that after I left Bedingham, the day before yesterday, the best colt there, a very fine young animal, managed to hurt his shoulder, probably by dashing himself against a gatepost. The farrier is of opinion that he will be bad for about three months, and I trust that we may get off so well. A year or two ago I had a foal which injured its shoulder so badly that in the end we were obliged to kill it, a very grievous loss.

The wind still holds exceeding bitter, and owing to the night frosts there is but little growth. A beech-tree—one of several that stand upon the garden lawn of this house—has, however, come into leaf. During all the many years that I have known this place, whatever the season, that tree has never failed to be the first to unfold its foliage, something in its constitution making it of an earlier habit than its fellows. The hawthorns also have dressed themselves in tender green, and down by the Bath Hills I noticed an oak almost bursting its buds, while those of the ash at its side were still asleep in their hard sheaths of winter black. Although it was quite hot here under the hill, where the east wind never comes, many of the beeches also have made no start at all. The butterflies, however, know that spring is at hand, for already I have seen peacocks, large sulphurs, and two specimens of the scarce great tortoiseshell. To-day also I heard the cuckoo for the first time this year.

April 27.—Last night there came a fine and welcome shower, for the country was parching in the harsh cold wind, followed this morning by a blessed change in the weather to the conditions of an English spring, as it is fondly imagined by poets and persons living in the Colonies. The birds seem to appreciate this unexpected improvement, for they are all singing madly, especially on the Vineyard Hills.

To-day we have thrashed out our last little stack of wheat, which produced about twenty-five coomb of grain, and—notwithstanding that it was built upon vermin-proof iron supports—a large quantity of mice. By the way, I wonder how mice in a stack of this sort, which they cannot well leave, manage for water. Of course, when rain falls, they can climb to the thatch and drink, but sometimes there are long periods without any rain, and what do they do then, feeding, as they must, upon the dryest of dry foods? Unless they are able to live without moisture, which seems improbable, I cannot imagine a solution of the problem.[1] The wheat which we thrashed at Bedingham yesterday proved disappointing so far as quantity is concerned, as we got about twenty coomb less than we expected. In this neighbourhood, however, it is the almost universal experience of farmers that last season was a very bad one for wheat. It is a grain which can stand, and even enjoys, drought, but in 1897 it seems to have had too much of it.

April 28.—This morning there was a soft and gentle rain, which stopped about an hour after midday. The election excitement is beginning. The Conservative candidate is my friend,

---

[1] A correspondent suggests that dew is the solution.

Mr. Sancroft Holmes, and I cannot think of any one who, if elected, would make a better member, as he is a gentleman who for many years has had a large experience as an owner and a farmer of land, and who has given his time to serving the county in various capacities as a magistrate, county councillor, a chairman of the assessment committee, and in other offices. I am, however, by no means certain that all this will go in his favour with the voters.

Two of his agents have been here this morning to arrange about meetings, and, as one of them said to me, the best qualification for a Conservative or Unionist candidate is that he should have no record whatsoever in the county. Indeed, if he chances to reside in the agricultural division which he contests, the more colourless his character the better. Public services will not help him, for the public servant makes enemies ; the only fame and qualities that are likely to be of service to him are a reputation for wealth and an open purse. If he is a magistrate, every bad character who has ever been committed before a Bench, together with that character's friends, will work and vote against him, and the vote of a bad character is just as valuable as that of the veriest saint. If he is a farmer, he is naturally held to be an enemy of the labouring race ; if he is a landlord, then the hoary but inextinguishable and effective lie that he has been heard to say that nine shillings a week is enough for any labouring man is sure to be circulated to his detriment. Also it will be said that he makes a custom of turning off his hands to starve during winter, and that he has dismissed men for expressing sympathy with political opinions of which he does not approve.

In saying this I speak of what I know, for in the course of a contested election I have suffered from all these fictions, which, as I believe, by a small majority finally turned the day against me, with a picturesque addition which I was told proved very effective, namely, that I had been known to murder quite a considerable number of black women. In short, in an Eastern Counties agricultural division, I incline to the view that the ordinary 'carpet-bagger,' on whichever side he may be standing, has a better chance of suc-

cess than any local man, however suitable, who does not happen to
be a brewer. It may seem almost incredible to the intelligent
dwellers in cities who are not acquainted with our more remote
country districts that this should be the case, but so it is.

I do not know if the labourers in their heart of hearts accept
all these falsehoods, but I am sure that a large proportion wish
to accept them. In many cases they are ignorant and prejudiced ;
also, not unnaturally, they are embittered by the humble nature of
their lot and the pitiful smallness of their wage. Then come the
agitator and the gentleman from London, who tell them that this
condition of affairs is brought about by the parson and the squire,
and especially by the individual who is seeking to represent them
in Parliament, and his friends. That it is caused by the dreadful
depression in agriculture, which makes it impossible for their wages
to rise to the level of town rates, they steadily neglect to explain.

To all these fierce prejudices money is too frequently the only
answer. Very often the rich man standing for a rural division
fortifies his cause by a deliberate pauperising of the constituency ;
and in this case, unless he is confronted by an opponent with
equal or greater means, he will probably be returned. In one Eastern
Counties division two giants of wealth opposed each other at
a recent election, turning it between them into a very land of
Canaan ; for so fast did the milk, honey, blankets, and other good
things flow that, thus said rumour, cottages in that happy country
commanded a handsome premium, like London houses in the
season. But one candidate was rather richer than the other, and
he won. Lately also we have learned, through the press, that a
financial Star benefited the constituency he hoped to represent to
the tune of 14,000*l.* per annum distributed in doles. How does
such generosity differ from the commonest corruption ?

Even the candidate of humbler means is exposed to what can
only be described as a system of blackmail. From the moment
it becomes known that he proposes to stand every village club
and institution within the borders of the constituency makes its
request upon him for subscriptions. I say its request, but prac-

tically it is a command, since he can well guess what will be the result if he declines or is unable to pay.

From this state of affairs it would appear that our election system, which purports to be pure, is in reality tainted, since, although votes can no longer be bought openly, they are, in fact, bought, and largely, under cover of social and charitable subscriptions ; further, that unless he is young, ambitious, wealthy, and not too squeamish, the man is rash who allows himself to be put up to fight a seat in an agricultural division in our parts of England. That this is becoming widely recognised is shown by the growing difficulty of obtaining suitable candidates on the Unionist side who reside or have any considerable stake in their own divisions. Among the other party, the candidates are in most instances gentlemen quite unconnected with the district; though why this should be so I do not know, seeing that in these counties it is by no means difficult for any one of sufficient means and a humble modicum of ability to contest and win a seat in the Radical interest. Indeed, given the money—plenty of it—and the ability may be dispensed with, let the candidate's party badge be red or blue. Why should we wonder ? A people to whom wealth is an object of such heartfelt homage can scarcely object to the wide dominion of King Cash. The hypothesis may be denied, but if we do not serve Mammon, or money, which is the same thing, how does it chance that we so much admire those who contrive suddenly to acquire it in great heaps ? Although there may be exceptions, an especially successful speculator, in drinkshops for instance, would not in general be sought out simply for the charm of his conversation or the graces of his mind, but set him in a palace in Park Lane with the appropriate accessories, and how delightful he becomes !

Again, there arise people whom the financial Press speaks of respectfully as Magnates. Sometimes the observer knows their past. He knows by what means Mr. Magnate's fortune has been created : how the market was 'beared,' that is depressed, and hundreds ruined or impoverished that he might buy in cheap; how it was 'bulled,' that is inflated, and hundreds more ruined or impoverished that he might sell out dear; how, also, the worthless vendor's shares in the unpayable mine, obtained, perhaps, for nothing, became the property of the stockholders in Mr. Magnate's companies at 4*l.* each. (Who can possibly have sold them? Not Mr. Magnate; they were never even in his name.) He knows, too, how Mr. Tradesman, shrewd, industrious person, reaped those mighty millions out of the misery of the sweating (and sweated) toilers with whom he ploughs his plenteous field, scourging them to his half-paid tasks with the bitter lash of want; or, mayhap, far-seeing Merchant Prince, gathering up his honey by the simpler expedients of sharp practice. Butter! Margarine?—In fact there is small difference—Foreign meat sold as British? Why not? Really it is a better article Table Delicacies? Well, a mere trade description implying no guarantee; and, my dear sir, these are just the little foresights and economies which, when at last the books come to balance, make the difference between a simple living, such as any old-fashioned, fossil-headed shopkeeper may expect, and a fortune worth the winning. Also if the business is to be floated as a company large profits must be shown or the public won't apply. And so forth.

The rest is easy. Shall that excellent champagne stay uncorked, those glittering halls untrodden? Why, don't you know every guest will receive as a cloak-ticket a numbered pin or bracelet of that raw red gold set in diamonds? What do you say about, yes—red as 'the blood of righteous Abel'? 'Murdered by his brother!' Well, of course, sometimes people have to do funny things out in those places. Who was Abel? His partner?—a Jew I suppose. I dare say he wasn't righteous; I dare say that he had treated him badly. Oh! you mean the old Bible story. How silly you are; what has that to do with Mr. Magnate and the way he got his money? Anyhow, it is no affair of mine, and I shall accept—there!

And so the Duchess goes, and the Lord Mayor goes, and everybody goes, and are paid in bracelets or otherwise, and next morning —is it not written in the book of all the papers? Then comes the sequel: the social success and the public banquet in the City; the advertised subscriptions and the Knighthood; the thumping party cheques, and perchance, with good luck, the Peerage. Thus another constellation blazes in the fetid firmament of lucre, and longer grows the roll of its aristocracy.

Worship him, the Right Honourable the Lord Mountmagnate of Mountmagnate, the finest of our new nobility, and understand that money is a defence indeed. Listen to his glad continual song, the pæan he puts up to Heaven as he treads his fallen fellow-travellers into the mire of the universal Way, rejoicing over them with the joy of harvest and as men rejoice when they divide the spoil. Bow the knee you honest, outworn workers, whose antlike toil built up his millions; you, too, who are sodden-witted with his adulterated drink; you also whose shares he captured in the panic upon the day of the False Cable; and, above all, you whose child was poisoned by his preserved fruits or milk or fishes. Praise him on his palm-hung, marbled balcony, and then back to your 'bus, if you can pay the fare, and home to wonder why benighted foreign nations think the English hypocritical, and whether a graduated income-tax would after all be so monstrously unjust. For the world, especially the British world, is to the rich and the good things thereof. Therefore grow rich—as best you can. At the least, thus by precept and example preacheth the triumphant Lord Mountmagnate of Mountmagnate and his peers.

The gentleman who is opposing Mr. Holmes is Mr. Soames, who contested Ipswich at the last election. I understand that he has never been in this division before, and has no property here. Whatever happens, this will, I think, tell in his favour. There is no doubt that, looking at the matter from the point of view of a Unionist, the time is peculiarly ill-chosen to contest the seat, as, outside of any personal considerations, the rise in the price of bread and the widespread dissatisfaction with the Chinese policy of the Government, which will affect the intelligent class of out-voters adversely, are sure to tell against our candidate. Further, the reduction of the duty on tobacco, that has just been announced by the Chancellor of the Exchequer, has, I think, done more harm than good, at any rate in this neighbourhood. The ordinary smoker does not care whether he pays a few pence more or less for his pound of tobacco, while the working man will be charged exactly the same for his 'screw,' and many thinking electors are angry because they see a million a year gone for ever from the revenue of the country (for once remitted these taxes cannot be replaced), while the heavily burdened payer of income-tax wins no relief.

Also the country clergy are in many instances exasperated, believing as they do that a portion of this million would have been better expended in relieving them of some of their double burden of rates than in enlarging the profits of the dealers in tobacco. They point out that for years they have been the steady sup porters of the Conservatives, whom on many occasions they have done much to return to power, and think it very hard, when there is money to spend, that they should be neglected in the hour of their need. Of course I am aware that some hold that the clergy have no grievance, and should not object to pay the double charges, inasmuch as their income is not professional in the ordinary sense of the word, since, nominally at any rate, it is fixed, and does not depend upon continuous and constantly renewed exertion, like that of a doctor or a writer. Doubtless there is something to be said for this view of the case, with which, however, for my part I do not agree.

To-day at Bungay market Hood actually refused forty-eight shillings a quarter for my wheat, as he is standing out for fifty shillings. Forty-eight shillings a quarter! It sounds like a beautiful dream in the ears of the poverty-stricken farmer—if a dream can sound. But a lively recollection of the recent history of the corn trade makes me think that such dreams are 'too bright to last.' I cannot forget how in 1894 and 1895 we were selling wheat at about twenty-two shillings a quarter. The present rise strikes me as too sudden and too violent to continue, for it is bred of scarcity, scare, and speculators, but chiefly, perhaps, of speculators. If only wheat would keep at about forty-two shillings the quarter, arable farming could be made to give a reasonable return, and everybody must be benefited, not excluding the agricultural labourer. But of this I fear that there is little hope, since the moment there is any moderate profit to be got out of the article, hundreds of thousands more acres will go down in corn all over the world, and especially in Argentina, where they have the advantage of paying their labour in silver and notes at face or nominal value, and being paid for their produce in gold at real value, netting I know not how much per cent. by the transaction. Then grain would be poured into this country as before, and the unfortunate farmer will find that his gleam of hope was delusive, and that he must continue to submit to the grinding and one-sided system of competition which has brought disaster to him and to all dependent upon British land.[1]

Yet the unexpected may happen, and these fears may prove to be unfounded, as I hope devoutly will be the case. For instance, some future Governments of Great Britain may come to the conclusion that in view of possible contingencies it is worth while to keep a larger quantity of land under wheat. I do not mean that they would reimpose the corn duties; which is improbable unless the agricultural labourer should become convinced that such a step would be to his advantage; or, as a last resource, the country should insist on it in order to keep the rural population upon the land. But I do mean that possibly it might be wise and politic for the State to give a moderate bounty to the growers of wheat, payable for so long, or whenever the market price of that cereal fell below thirty shillings a quarter. Certain good arguments can be advanced in favour of such a course, but I will only instance one of them—that it is worth while to make an effort to preserve the sturdy class of man who has been concerned with the cultivation of the land as a yeoman or tenant farmer, and to check the continual and progressive drifting of the agricultural labourer from the villages that bred him into the maw of the great cities,

---

In illustration of the advantages enjoyed by the foreign over the British farmer the reader is referred to Appendix II.

whence for the most part he does not return. 'The inevitable issues of Free Trade which must be faced in all their logical completeness,' and such phrases, sound very fine and conclusive in the mouths of platform speakers, but to the minds of many people it is a question whether doctrines cannot be driven too far, and whether it is worth while to sacrifice classes which from the beginning of its history have been the pith and marrow of England to a blind and narrow spirit of fiscal and political consistency.

Whatever may be the theoretical rights and wrongs of this Free Trade, certainly to some of us it does seem a matter of regret and danger that the system should have dealt so fatal and sweeping a blow to agriculture and to all connected with the land. It is curious to reflect also that a tax so small that the consumer would scarcely feel it, a tax which might merely clip a tithe from the swollen profits of some thousands of middlemen, besides largely benefiting the Exchequer, would suffice, in most cases, to nullify these very substantial evils. Yet such salvation is, and is likely to remain, impossible, not because it might work a practical hardship, but for the simple reason that it would offend against a modern law of the Medes and Persians and excite bitter prejudice among the electorate. So there the case stands ; alone amidst the peoples of the earth we have set this King Stork to rule over us, and—we must feed him. At present he is engaged chiefly in depleting and digesting the rural interests. When he has finished with them ; when the strike system has become perfected ; when, too, in another score of years America and Germany, and possibly India, Japan and the Colonies, have really found their feet as producing manufacturers, and gone into serious competition with the British towns and their trades, as already they are threatening to do—then, perhaps, we shall hear another frog begin to scream in those remorseless mandibles.

To show how extraordinarily the price of the different kinds of grain may vary in the course of a century, I will here copy out the contents of a tablet which is let into the front of a house belonging to this estate in Bungay.

PRICES OF GRAIN PER COOMB, APRIL 3, 1800

	£	s.	d.
Wheat	3	2	0
Barley	1	15	0
Malt	1	18	0
Pease	2	10	0
Beans	1	10	0
Oats	1	4	0
Hay, per cwt.	0	7	6
Straw	0	3	6

From this table it appears that at Bungay market in 1800 wheat was 6*l.* 4*s.* the quarter, barley was 3*l.* 10*s.* the quarter, and oats were 2*l.* 8*s.* To go to the other extreme of the scale, I find that, according to the average 'Gazette' prices in the year 1895, wheat was 1*l.* 3*s.* 1*d.* a quarter, barley was 1*l.* 1*s.* 11*d.* a quarter, and oats were 14*s.* 6*d.* a quarter. But these figures do not show all the difference, since it is to be presumed that in the year 1800 gold was scarcer and the purchasing power of money greater than is the case to-day.

In walking along one of the roads this afternoon I noticed that the boys, or more probably the hobbledehoys, have again been breaking down the little hawthorns left to grow in the hedgerows. Ever since I began to farm I have been endeavouring to rear up shoots at regular intervals in the hedges, so that in time they might make fine may-trees. Fifty or sixty years ago an old man in this parish known as Rough Jimmy, a very curious character, in trimming a fence belonging to the Hall estate which borders the Church lane, left certain shoots in this fashion, with the result that in June the entire roadway is splendid in trees white with haw-thorn bloom, although unfortunately the strangling ivy has choked one or two of them.

A generation hence I hope that owing to my efforts such a spectacle will be more common in this village, though chiefly, I fear, in the field hedges and by the side of private paths. Along the main road many of the young trees do not survive, since when they get to a noticeable size the gilded youth of Ditchingham and Bungay batter them down with sticks, or slash them through with knives. It is a sight that moves me to indignation. Two of the fields where these trees were growing nicely I have since let in allotments, and now I am sorry to see that the thrifty husbandmen who hire them have trimmed the saplings to the shape of round bushes, partly perhaps from a sense of neatness, but more, as I believe, because they think that the white-thorns as they increase will cast some shadow on their land.

Picturesque as they may be, there is no doubt that forest trees in hedgerows, and especially elms, are very mischievous in this respect, as any one who has observed the effect of a line of them upon a growing crop can testify. With the single exception of grass, where the shade they give to cattle in summer and the protection from winds in winter amply compensate for the depreciation in quality of the herbage within reach of their drip and shadow, there is no crop that does not suffer much from the influence of hedgerow timber. Oak does the least damage, and elms and ash do the most, because their roots run so fleet that for many yards round about each tree sucks the goodness from the soil. Beech—that lady of the forest—as I think, of all timbers the most feminine in appearance, is also the most poisonous, since the drip from it seems to have the effect of destroying under-growth of whatever nature. Owing perhaps to its spreading nature, or to the poor quality of the wood, this tree, however, is never planted in fences, at any rate in our neighbourhood.

This morning I inspected the sheep, and found that they are not yet really recovered from their recent misfortunes. Some of the lambs seem still weakly and half-crippled, while several of the ewes are suffering from dreadful colds, which necessitate their being caught and the clearing out of their nostrils. It is a ridiculous but pathetic sight to see an old ewe having her nose sympa-thetically wiped by Hood armed with a wisp of rough clover hay.

April 30.—Yesterday was fine and warm, and the horses were employed in ploughing and in carting home the faggots which have been cut upon the Bath Hills.

To-day there is a gale from the sou'-west. In the morning the farrier came to perform a rather serious operation upon two yearling colts. Within five minutes of its conclusion I saw one of them eating hay, and Fairhead told me that the other commenced to feed so soon as it had struggled on to its legs. This strikes me as an instructive commentary upon the often argued point as to whether or no animals feel pain as intensely as human beings. It must be remembered that in their case anæsthetics are not employed, and I conclude, therefore, that the answer to the question is—in diplomatic phrase—in the negative. Even after having a double tooth out or a finger-nail removed, no man—at least no white man—could sit down and enjoy an immediate lunch. I have, however, known cases of Zulus sitting apparently unconcerned while boiling water from a kettle was poured into an open wound ; but I believe that this is not because they are insensible to pain, but owing to the natural heroism of their characters, which forbids them to show any outward sign of suffering. Also I have known native women perform feats under trying domestic circumstances which, if narrated, would appear almost incredible. To what this hardiness is owing I am not in a position to say ; the question is one for medical men.

It is, however, satisfactory to be able to conclude that dumb animals do not suffer in the same proportion as more highly organised and nervous creatures ; for, otherwise, between birth and the butcher in many instances they would be called upon to endure more than it is pleasant to contemplate.

On the farm the faggot-carting and ploughing are going on, but I have not seen much of them, as to-day has been one of political excitement. Having received an urgent note from a friend and neighbour informing me that he was to take the chair to-night at a meeting in support of Mr. Holmes in his own parish, and requesting my assistance, I struggled gallantly against the gale on a bicycle to his house to tell him that I had already promised to speak elsewhere. As this intelligence seemed to disappoint him, I added that it was a matter of complete indifference to me where I spoke, and that if only he would undertake to arrange matters with the authorities in Norwich, I should be delighted to support him to the best of my poor ability. On hearing afterwards that this was done, I started about 7.30 (one of the delights of political meetings is that you very seldom get any dinner), and, having driven to the appointed school-house, sent my cart to be stabled at the Hall, a mile and a half away. Presently arrived my friend, and we stood for a while talking amid the small but excited crowd which on these occasions always gathers round the doors. Soon, however, I was aroused by an indignant voice exclaiming, ' Why are you here, sir? Why ain't you at D——?' and turned to find myself confronted by the agent with whom without doubt I had arranged to appear at D—— on this very day and hour. I explained humbly that it was not my fault, whereon there arose what may be called a slight altercation.

You must go to D——,' said the justly indignant agent; 'there is no one to speak there; the meeting will come to an end if you don't before ever the candidate gets round. What's the use of my making arrangements when you gentlemen go and upset them?'

Again, though with a certain sense of guilt, I protested that whoever's fault this unhappy state of affairs might be, it was not mine, adding further that as I had sent my trap away I had now no means of getting to D——.

'Means!' he replied wrathfully, at the same time proffering me a very low bicycle without a lamp (it was growing pitch dark, and I am somewhat long in the leg); 'jump on this and be off at once.'

'What!' I urged, 'ride a strange bicycle in the dark and in this coat?'

'Oh, never mind the coat,' he answered; 'take it off.'

Then I struck, alleging with perfect truth that every ounce of zeal which I possessed for the success of the D—— meeting was not sufficient to urge me to this adventure, complimentary as might be his anxiety for my presence. Ultimately, to cut a long story short, we compromised, and I found a friendly farmer to drive me in his gig to the Hall, where my horse was put up, whence in due course I made my way to D——. On entering the schoolroom, which was well filled, I found an unfortunate friend, the only speaker present except the chairman, addressing the meeting. I say unfortunate, because clearly he had been thus engaged for about three-quarters of an hour. As I came in he cast a despairing glance towards the door, and his face became suffused with smiles.

'Gentlemen,' he said in joyous tones, 'I will detain you no longer, since here is my friend, and yours,' &c., &c., &c.

'For Heaven's sake, keep it up,' I whispered back, 'until I have had time to look through the candidates' addresses,' and, responding like a hero, he kept it up.

Then I began. Believing that the candidate would not be able to arrive for at least another hour, and as there was no one else to speak, I laid my plans accordingly ; that is to say, I adopted the clerical method of oratory.

Taking each clause of Mr. Holmes's address as a text, I preached upon it to the most enormous length : at what length may be guessed when I state that I had only waded through three paragraphs before the candidate really did arrive. By that time I was callous ; indeed, I believe that, if necessary, I could have gone on for another two hours, since, when I had come to the end of the address of Mr. Holmes, there was that of his opponent, Mr. Soames, to fall back upon ; after which I might have perorated.

I doubt whether to any one with an eye to humour there are many things more amusing than a rural election meeting. For instance, there is the ecstatic gentleman who, on these occasions, is generally to be found standing outside the door, and murmuring at intervals, his red face turned to the heavens as though he were addressing the stars, ''olmes for ever ! 'olmes for ever ! A Norfolk man for Norfolk.' Then with a sudden welling-up of enthusiasm, and fixing his eye upon the planet Jupiter, 'Vote for 'olmes, old feller, and you won't do wrong ! I say vote for 'olmes !'

For true and earnest political enthusiasm, however, I think he is surpassed by the intelligent elector who becomes so moved at the speaker's eloquence that he punctuates his impassioned periods with ' Ah, that's true. You've got it this time, sir '; or ' Let 'em have it, the varmints '; or, ' Don't you be afraid, we'll see to that.' With skill and care such a listener can be worked up by an orator of experience till he becomes a fairly effective imitation of the Greek Chorus. What is more, he is of considerable assistance at a village meeting, since generally he is something of a reader and a thinker, and represents a section of local opinion.

Such things as accounts of political meetings of this character sound trivial enough when set down in black and white, but to my mind they have their interest, and perhaps those who read of them a century or two hence, when everything is totally changed, will be of the same opinion. How valuable to us are those scraps of local information as to life and manners in past ages that chance to have survived to the present day ! How eagerly do we search through registers, or court rolls, or what not, to find anything of human interest, anything that gives us an insight into the actual life of times bygone, for, alas ! the endless processions of names and dates tell but little. Why is Pepys so priceless an author if it is not because, among other things, he sets down what he saw from day to day, portraying with his pen the life about him, as Hogarth portrayed it with his pencil, if in a more genial spirit ?

Nowadays the novel is almost everything. If a matter is to be read of, it must be spiced and tricked out with romance. But, rightly or wrongly, I imagine that the generations to come will study our facts rather than our fiction. It may be replied that if they have a mind this way they can turn to the daily press of the age whereof they wish to learn, but I think that the vastness of such a task will appal the boldest. Doubtless commentators and literary précis-writers will spring up who will boil down the events of each past period for the benefit of their contemporaries, but, at the best, all such narratives must lack the personal quality which alone can make them entertaining. They will be to the future very much what the church registers of three centuries ago are to us to-day—a mine for the curious to dig in and nothing more.

MAY

May 1.—By common and time-consecrated repute the first of May is the beginning of summer, and, unless tradition lies, as seems probable, at that date our forefathers used to picnic in the open and dance about poles wreathed with flowers, although it must be remembered that under the Old Style their May-day fell two weeks later than our own. They would scarcely do it now, for nine May-days, or, for the matter of that, nine Mays out of ten are distinguished by abominable and frigid weather, though primroses and, where they grow wild, daffodils are plentiful enough. As for the may itself, it rarely appears in any quantity until the end of the month.

To-day we are ploughing and carting stones off the light glebe land for the roads. I suppose that for hundreds of years the farmers of this land have taken from it an annual crop of stones, and still, season by season, more appear. Where do they all come from, and why do they continue to work up to the top without appreciably lowering the level of the land? No doubt geologists can explain this phenomenon, but to an ordinary ignoramus like myself it is a mystery. Indeed, the existence on much the same level and in close proximity of stretches of soil sandy in nature and full of flint, and other stretches stiff at top with a substratum of dense blue clay, seems difficult to understand. I suppose that it has to do with the laying bare of various strata in far past ages by the action of floods or of the ocean.

To-day, also, we have carted twenty-five coomb of beans, sold at 15*s.* 6*d.* a coomb, an advance of two shillings on last year's price. These beans have to be placed at Loddon, six miles away, which is practically a day's journey for a man and horses. Here the practice is that the seller must deliver to the purchaser unless he despatches the stuff by train under special arrangement, in which case he delivers at the station. To-day, too, the brown mare produced her foal in safety.

May 3.—This morning Hood sold twenty-five coomb (twelve and a half quarters) of wheat at *forty-nine shillings a quarter*, so it seems that he was justified in refusing forty-eight shillings last week. It is a curious advance upon the prices of recent years. I wonder what would happen in this country in the event of a really earnest and prolonged war between, let us say, Great Britain opposed to France and Russia, which probably would entail subsidiary wars in every quarter of the world. There is no great bulk of wheat kept in England, as it is a commodity apt to deteriorate in warehouses unless very carefully and scientifically managed, and Governments seem to set their faces against any system of national granaries, for reasons which are sufficiently obvious and familiar to the student of Roman history. Pharaoh, who was an autocrat living in a dry climate, with the assistance of an exceptionally able and honest minister, was in a position to manage such granaries satisfactorily, but I greatly doubt if this would be so in the case of any given set of party politicians in power and with the fear of an election before their eyes. As no such stores do or are likely to exist, the possibilities in the event of war are somewhat terrifying. Even if our fleet should prove strong enough to keep the seas perfectly open against a combination of foreign Powers, which, in the opinion of many experts, such as Lord Charles Beresford, seems doubtful, what fleets could control the ingenious machinations of the foreign speculator in grain? And if, owing to a variety of causes, corn went to a hundred shillings a quarter, what would be the result in a country full of some millions of independent (and hungry) voters? On that black sheet of the future it is not difficult to imagine three words, ominous as those of the writing on the wall.

They are:

Peace with Dishonour.

Peace, not because the ancient strength of England is broken, but because its citizens are wrath with hunger and have the power to make their rage felt in high places. *Absit omen!* may I be wrong; at least may I not live to see the day. Still, the most ardent lover of democracy will admit that our present system has its dangers, especially in a narrow land where the production of food-stuffs, and notably of corn, is in practice discouraged.

In America the case is different. Were America cut off from any intercourse with the outside world for a long period of time it could still produce enough food to feed itself.

It is curious to notice the change caused in the aspect of the country by the recent rains and mild weather; the growth of the grass and the bursting of the leaves are almost visible. To-day on the Bath Hills I saw a sure sign that the winter is over and past—a grass-snake basking in the sun. He was a fine fellow, over two feet long I should say, and when, resisting the first instinctive impulse to kill him, which is natural to anyone who, like myself, has lived in a land of poisonous snakes, I contented myself with stirring him up with my spud, he retreated up hill till he was tired, then, having apparently no hole to go to, turned round and hissed at me with open mouth and flickering tongue. Indeed, had he been a cobra instead of a poor painted worm he could not have looked more ferocious. I thought of holding out my hand to see if he would strike at it with some hereditary recollection of past æons, when his forefathers were poisonous, but coming to the conclusion that it would be better to persuade some one else to try this experiment, since I might possibly have made a mistake as to the breed, I refrained and went away.

Writing of cobras reminds me of an incident which is perhaps worth recording although I have little business to introduce it here.

Once, many years ago, I was riding in search of small game upon the veld in the Transvaal when a hare jumped up before me. Halting the horse, I shot at it from the saddle, and with the second barrel broke one of its hind legs and injured the other. Springing from my horse, and without reloading the gun, I ran to catch it, but as it could still travel faster than I did, I saw with chagrin that it would reach a hole for which it was heading (in Africa these hares go to ground if pressed) before I was able to overtake it. Presently it came to the hole, but, instead of bolting down it, sat quite still upon the hither side. Thinking that the animal was expiring, I crept up cautiously and stretched out my hand to seize it. The next instant I received one of the sharpest shocks that I can remember to have experienced, for, on the other side of the hole, within about four feet of my face, like some child of an evil magic, there rose up suddenly the hugest cobra ('ringhals' I think the Boers call it) that I have ever seen. The reptile, which appeared to me to be about six feet long, stood upon his coiled tail and, puffing out his horrible and deadly hood, flickered his tongue and spat upon me. There was no reason why he should not have struck me also. since for the moment I seemed paralysed and did not move. Recovering myself, I sprang backwards and began to search in my pocket for a cartridge to load my gun, whereon the great snake sinking down again, with a single swift movement vanished into the hole, which was between it and me.

Now, as the 'ringhals' had gone, I thought that at any rate I might as well secure the hare, which all this while, petrified with terror, had been crouched by the top of the hole. So once again I leant towards the creature. It heard me and tried to run away, but evidently was too weak. Then it looked first back at me and next at the burrow down which the snake had vanished, and, seeming to decide finally that the mercies of a cobra are greater than the mercies of man, it uttered a scream and followed the reptile into the hole. I stood by and listened. Presently from under the earth came the sound of a rush and a scuffle, followed by another pitiful scream. Then all was still.

The butcher at Bungay has offered Hood 80*l.* for four of the Irish bullocks at Baker's, which he has refused, as he is of opinion that they are worth 85*l*. In the end it was agreed that the offer should stand open till Friday, so as to give both parties an opportunity of thinking it over.

May 4.—To-day the weather is squally with heavy showers of rain. In the Home Barn I found the curious village character known as Rough Jimmy, a weird-looking and picturesque old man, with a strongly marked countenance and flying locks of iron-grey hair, seated on a sack by the open door and employed in splitting broaches to be used for thatching stacks. This is the process of broach-splitting : First the hazel or ash rod is measured by another to a length of about three feet, at which it is chopped upon a block. Next the edge of the bill is set across the end and tapped gently so that it enters the wood. Then it is levered sideways and twisted with the hand until, if there are not too many knots, the rod splits neatly in half. This process is repeated with the severed halves, so that each rod makes four broaches, while the trimmed off ends are used for firing. In bygone years Rough Jimmy was the most expert woodman in the parish, but now he can only do such jobs as this. Peering up from the seat on the sack, for he is half blind, the old fellow said :

' A lowerin' time, squire ; a rare lååring time. There'll be a hay crop now. Rainy May, plenty of hay.'

After this we had a conversation. He told me that he remembered flour at five shillings a stone, and the time when his father sold his wheat at two guineas a coomb, 'and could have sold a thousand coomb if he had had it.'

Asking me about the war, he said : ' Poor Spain, she's chosen a rum place to fight with, she hev—Amurica. All the best of the earth go there, they du—English, Scotch, and that like. I've got a son in South Africa, I hev, though I haven't seen him for many yèèrs, and never sh'an't no more. He gets on won'erful well, he du. Began as a mason working on a bridge, and is his own master now, so I onderstand, with lots of land, cattle, black men, and bacca plants.'

Here, I thought to myself as I walked away, is a fine instance of the contrast between the old country and the new, and of the good fortune of those who are bold enough to break their ties and seek their fate in the Colonies. The father, bent with years, roughly clad and half blind, seated on my barn-floor splitting broaches for a few pence, or, as I have seen him again and again, standing all day in the wild December weather at the corner of a covert to prevent the pheasants from breaking out, and the son who is in South Africa with plenty of 'land, cattle, black men, and bacca plants.'

I do not gather, however, that distance makes the heart more filial. I imagine that letters are few and far between, and but little of the produce of the black men and the bacca plants flows into the old man's pocket.

We are cursed with an egg-eating turkey. As I was sitting at lunch I observed a turkey-hen running about the lawn with what I took to be a frog in its beak, which it was making violent efforts to swallow. On investigation I found that it was not a frog but an egg. It seems that this unnatural creature lays eggs with unusually thin shells, and having chanced to crush one by sitting on it, was tempted, and found it uncommonly good to eat. From that day she began to devour every egg she laid, but being conscious of her guilt, she first carries them to a distance, where she thinks that she will not be observed. That is why she appeared upon the lawn, which at luncheon-time, when the gardeners are at dinner, is a secluded spot suitable for the commission of crime. She did not know that justice lurked behind the dining-room windows, and that after judgment comes execution.

In to-day's *Times* I see that a deputation waited upon Mr. Chaplin, the President of the Local Government Board, to urge, amongst other things, the prohibition of the artificial colouring of margarine to resemble or imitate butter, and the prohibition of the mixing of margarine and butter for sale. From Mr. Chaplin they got uncommonly cold comfort. He told them that he had 'heard the arguments of the other side,' and that if this fraudulent

colouring—for the object of the colouring is fraud—were pro-
hibited, it was urged that it would 'practically destroy the trade.'
He intimated in addition that whatever might be the rights of
the matter, the Government had no time to deal with it.

It is impossible to comment upon these strange statements
better or more clearly than does the *Times* in an admirable leading article. Therefore, with proper acknowledgments, I take the
liberty to quote a few lines from that article.

'Is it not rather hard on the man who wants to get butter
that he should have to eat margarine, because the man who wants
margarine will not eat it unless it is made to look like butter?
If either of the two trades is to suffer injury, is it to be the trade
which wishes to sell butter under the name of butter, or the trade
which—to please its customers—wishes to sell margarine made to
look as like butter as possible?'

Yes, and is it not rather hard on the unfortunate British
farmer, who, like myself, makes honest butter out of cream and
nothing else, that he should have to compete with an article
cunningly coloured to resemble it, but compounded of beef
stearine, arachis oil, and pork fat? Is it not also rather hard that
such an answer should be given to an influential deputation by a
Minister supposed to sympathise with the distresses of farmers?
Of course everybody understands that, like so many other things,
this is a question of policy, and that it is supposed more support
would be lost by a measure which interfered with the town trade in
margarine than might be gained by securing a fair market to the
country farmer, and to the consumer that if he asks for butter and
pays for butter he should get butter. Well, this is the kind of thing
that we agriculturists have to fight against, but I doubt whether
Mr. Chaplin's answer will gain many votes for Mr. Holmes at
the pending South Norfolk election.

May 6.—Yesterday opened fine, but in the afternoon it came
on to pour, which, as there was a confirmation in the church of
this parish for the first time for many years, proved very incon-

venient. Hood sold the remainder of my wheat—about sixty coomb—at forty-nine shillings the quarter. It has been a little higher, and will very likely be higher again, but in such a tricky and artificial market as that which exists for corn I think it best to take what I can get and be thankful.

To-day we are baulking up the swede land and gilling trees from the Bath Hills. Certainly a timber gill is a wonderfully well-designed though a very simple implement. It is worked thus. First the gill, which is a kind of very high-wheeled cart, made to carry its load beneath the axle instead of above it, is run over the tree to be removed. Then the horse, which drags it by means of chains fastened to hooks at the end of shafts, or sometimes to a pole resembling that which in Africa we call a dissel-boom, is taken off, and the shafts are thrust backwards till they stand pointing to the sky. Next the chains are made fast round the bole of the tree and drawn up taut to the arched and ironed timber axle. Then, if the load be moderate, one, or if heavy, two men, with the help of the leverage afforded by the length of the shafts, drag them down, and the great tree swings up from the ground. Or should it be too weighty for their efforts, the aid of a horse is called in. Next, the load having been arranged so that it balances, the hooks are slipped through the eye, and away walks the horse, dragging after him a baulk of timber that in many cases one would have believed to be quite beyond his strength.

To-day I was obliged to do some canvassing, a task which I particularly detest. I think that it is hateful to ask anybody for anything, votes not excluded, more especially if the asker chances to be in a position of authority or advantage towards the person asked. It is this wholesale begging, and all the humbug attendant on it, that makes standing for Parliament so peculiarly arduous an undertaking. I cannot conceive why, with our present enlarged electorate, personal canvassing is allowed to remain legal, except it be from the idea that the party which proposed or carried its abolition would suffer at the polls, as the institution is believed to be popular—among the canvassed. Surely the facts of the case could be brought sufficiently home to the minds of the electors from either point of view by means of public meetings and posted literature. But this is a counsel of perfection which I suppose nobody now breathing will live to see put into practice, for the same reason that he is not likely to see an effort made to reduce election expenses, so that it will be possible for poor men of ability to stand for Parliament. It may be doubted whether the leaders of either of the great parties in the House wish to welcome 'poor men of ability' within its doors, for such people are too apt to think for themselves and develop individual opinions. Probably they prefer rich men who will follow the flag wherever it may lead, and ask no questions.

I began my efforts with Rough Jimmy, employing the usual 'Norfolk man for Norfolk' argument, &c. He listened in silence, which was disconcerting, then said, with an innocent air, and turning on me his one questioning eye, in which I thought that I could catch a twinkle :

'Well, squire, for well-nigh sixty year I've been trying to make up my mind which is the best party, and I'm danged if I can do it yet. But do yow kepp on a talking and p'raps I shall find out.'

I have a shrewd suspicion as to which way Rough Jimmy will vote. I am convinced that his principles are what might be called progressive. If a voter's views are very pronounced one way or another, generally it is best for the party which would like to mark him as its own to leave him undisturbed, for then there is always a good chance that he will not take the trouble to vote, whereas once he is brought to the poll the result is sure. One of the best and most trusted men in my employ is a stout Radical, and I have adopted these tactics with him. It is curious to any-one who mixes with the labouring classes, and perhaps, to some extent, enjoys their sympathy and confidence, to notice—if the crust of timidity and suspicion can be pierced and their real views ascertained—how marked is the dividing line of opinion among them. Some are by nature Conservative, and others by nature Radical, and in those cases where political conviction really exists

I do not think that the arguments of an angel from heaven would suffice to change them. Indeed, it seems to me that throughout every class of English society, from the highest to the lowest, the cleavage of political opinion is vertical, not lateral, and that in this happy state of affairs, so different from that which prevails in some other lands, lies our great guarantee of safety against violent changes and revolution.

A neighbour of mine tells me to-day that an entire field full of his beans have failed to appear above the ground. Those responsible for the sowing of the beans allege that his pheasants (he preserves) have scratched them up and eaten them. He, on the contrary, is of opinion that the beans were allowed to heat upon the stack and that their germinating power was thus destroyed. I know not who is right, but incline to the latter view, as pheasants, however mischievous—and they are very mischievous—would scarcely have removed every bean with such singular regularity.

May 7.—Spring is slow in coming this year. To-day is again sunless with a cold north-east wind. The young mangolds are beginning to look very yellow from lack of warmth, and so are the little grass-seedlings sown down for permanent pasture. Warm nights are needed now, and we get none. On the farm we are going on with our routine : timber-gilling, swede-baulking, and manure-carting.

By hiding behind a bush this morning—for they seem to have a great dislike of being watched—I saw a most curious form of courtship in progress between a cock and a hen turkey. They stood back to back at a little distance from each other, and then, after various deliberate preparations, began waltzing round in a circle, keeping their outspread tails pointing to each other. It reminded me of a figure in one of the square dances where the lady and gentleman walk round one another back to back.

All the bullocks at Baker's have now been sold to the butcher by weight at a price of 7*s.* a stone. Let us say that works out at 160*l.* for the eight of them, plus 14*l.* 10*s.* for the two which went wrong, or in all at 174*l.* 10*s.* On this estimate they will, I fear, still show a loss. Speaking roughly, they have eaten about 30*l.* worth of corn and cake, in addition to great quantities of root, hay and straw.

Writing on a later date I turn back to this page of my diary dealing with the subject of these bullocks, since it seems the best place in which to interpolate the final accounts now available after the decease of the last of them.

Here they are :

CREDIT				DEBIT			
Sold							
	£	s.	d.		£	s.	d.
1 Bullock (sick) . .	2	10	0	10 Irish bullocks bought	130	10	0
1 ,, ,, .	12	0	0	Hay and root by valua-			
4 Bullocks by weight .	76	8	0	tion . . .	65	0	0
4 ,, ,, .	79	9	6	Corn bought . .	22	10	0
				Grinding corn . .	1	15	0
				1 ton of cake . .	5	10	0
				2 coombs linseed . .	2	2	0
	170	7	6		227	7	0

From this interesting account it would appear that in return for the pleasure of housing, feeding, and caring for that choice lot of imported cattle I am out of pocket to the tune of 56*l.* 19*s.* 6*d.*, plus whatever bill the veterinary may think it just and right to present for his attendance upon them. They were the most voracious animals that ever I had to do with, and I believe the estimate for root, &c., which they ate to be absolutely correct ; further, it will be observed that nothing has been set down for labour, because we reckon that the manure they leave in the yard pays for the labour. Also they were the most unhealthy, for, notwithstanding every care, one or other of them was continually ailing, and I hear that the last which has been killed, although he weighed fairly well, was discovered to be suffering from long-standing disease of the liver.

It may be urged that I was very unlucky with two of these animals, but even on the supposition that they had fetched 40*l.* instead of 14*l.* 10*s.*, which would have brought up the total proceeds of the ten to 195*l.* 17*s.* 6*d.*, I should still have lost about 33*l.* net on the transaction. It is obvious that at this rate store-cattle cannot be made to pay. Of course there is an explanation—that if there chances to be a plentiful root-crop, as was the case last year, such animals rise in price. But the value of meat does not rise, for whenever it reaches a certain figure, unremunerative for the most part to the British grazier, dead meat pours in by the thousand tons from abroad and swamps the market ; or, which is worse, foreign cattle are imported by the drove, slaughtered at the port of debarkation, and sold to the consumer as best British beef.

The moral is that it does not pay to buy these lean and full-grown seaborne cattle for winter fatting. I have never done so before, and should not have committed the mistake last autumn had it not been for the accident of my finding myself unexpectedly with fifty acres more land and a large quantity of roots upon my hands. Far wiser is it to rear every calf that the cows drop, or, if more stock is necessary, to buy young home-bred things in the local market, and in our expressive Norfolk language to 'wriggle' them along till they grow into saleable beef. The food that such young creatures eat, most of it even in winter being picked up on the pastures, makes by comparison a small show in the farm bill, and yet by degrees they grow into value. The market cattle, on the contrary, have to be fed off the best, and plenty of it, if meat is to be put upon their great slab sides in sufficient quantity to render them acceptable to the butcher. And here, a sadder and a wiser man, I bid farewell to those ten unprofitable Irish bullocks.

Butter is dreadfully low in price just now, eightpence or nine-pence in Bungay market. My arrangement with my customers is that I receive a penny a pound more than the local market price. It will, I think, be admitted that this is not too much when it is remembered that my butter is made from the cream of pedigree cattle with the help of a separator, is never touched by the hand, and in summer is stored in a refrigerator with ice. Without disparagement to the produce of the district I may explain that it does *not* receive these advantages. But at eightpence per pound, plus one penny, I cannot make butter pay—indeed it costs more than this to manufacture.

If, instead of producing an average of about sixty pounds a week, I could turn out, let us say, two hundred, things would be better, for then I might enter into a contract at a more remunerative figure in London or some other large market. But with the amount of land that I farm this is just what I cannot do, since to undertake to deliver a certain quantity weekly, and then, owing to an unexpected failure with the cows or the prevalence of drought, to be unable to supply it, would prove embarrassing. Therefore I have to be content with local custom. Of this I have plenty ; indeed, could I supply twice the weight, I believe that I should have no difficulty in disposing of my stuff. Only if the market falls in the neighbourhood, buyers not unnaturally expect to get the benefit of the drop, and so it comes about that the producers must at certain seasons of the year deliver at a loss. The explanation of this, as of all our other troubles, is to be found in the vast importations of Danish and other inferior butters made up in co-operative creameries from cows fed on practically unlimited pastures. These butters can be retailed at a price with which we English farmers are unable to compete. What processes they go through before they appear upon the British breakfast table I know not, but if all accounts are true, and we have seen plenty of them lately in the newspapers, especially with reference to Scandinavian products, they seem to be sufficiently disagreeable.

A few years ago I travelled in Brittany, and observed the peasant farms there, whence, as I understand, much butter is collected, to be sorted into grades and worked up by dealers for the British market. The result of my studies was that for my own part I should prefer not to eat the butter gathered from those farms. But provided that the article is pleasant to the eye, agreeable to the taste, and cheap, our public cares nothing for the cleanliness or otherwise of its place of origin. Cheapness, and nothing but cheapness, is what they consider. Were it rank poison—which I believe it sometimes is—they would still eat it, provided it was cheap. What matters it to them that an ancient and festering midden heap stands before the door of the dairy, or that the water with which the vessels are washed is practically a concentrated sewage fluid, or that the butter itself is treated with boracic acid, fusel oil, and any other half-poisonous chemical that, forbidden upon the Continent, may be freely used to 'bring up' foodstuffs for the benefit of the British customer?

Nor is it only with the foreign butter that we have to compete; there remains the margarine which, as the deputation reminded Mr. Chaplin, is coloured to imitate it, and, thanks to such colouring, very frequently sold as butter by the ingenious British trader.

A few years ago I had the advantage of going over a large margarine factory on the Continent. In the course of conversation with the proprietors, I mentioned that I had been informed that persons in Great Britain who purported to supply the public with the best of butter were among their largest customers, and asked them if they felt at liberty to tell me whether or no this were the truth. After a little hesitation they replied that it was quite true, and changed the subject.

This margarine factory was a fearful and wonderful place. There were the barrels of fat extracted from American cattle or other animals—a great deal of the success in the manufacture depends upon a fine taste in fat; indeed, I gathered that the buyer will never do well unless he is gifted with the true *flair* in this important matter. Then there were the steam churns, for the best qualities of margarine are mixed with a proportion of genuine butter; and with these other machines innumerable. What chiefly remains upon my mind, however, is a vision of the subject-matter of the stuff, great lumps of oily nastiness large as men's heads, that bobbed up and down in cauldrons of seething yellow grease. If their ultimate consumers could have seen them at this stage I think they would have given up 'butter' for a week or two. Yet after those lumps had gone through all the necessary processes and refinements, the results were quite pleasing to behold—there lay the 'butter' in shining heaps, some of it yellow, some white, with every variety of intermediate shade, for different countries consume different colours ; indeed, it is not uncommon to find that one town in England will not look at the brand which pleases another town.   Moreover, it has to be packed in accordance with its place of destination, in oak tubs for one country, in baskets for another, and so forth.

Much edified, my friend, with whom I had inspected the factory, and I took our departure.   After we had walked for a while through the streets of the city, I was obliged to call his attention to the fact that his boots appeared to smell exceedingly disagreeable.   He retaliated with the remark that he had noticed the same phenomenon about my own, but had been prevented by politeness from mentioning the fact.   This led to investigation, and the discovery that the evil odour arose from the essence of margarine in which we had been walking.   Many days went by before those boots were again fit to wear, which shows the vitality and nourishing nature of the substances wherewith they had been impregnated.   By the way, I am able to reassure consumers of this article of commerce, who, I suppose, must include the majority of the inhabitants of these islands, that in one respect it has been libelled.   Shortly before my visit statements were extensively published in the Press to the effect that margarine is largely composed of oils and greases evaporated from the mud of the Thames below London, and other rivers that run through great cities.   I asked the proprietors of the factory if there was any truth in this allegation, and they replied that it was quite untrue. Margarine, it would seem, is practically the fat of animals flavoured to taste, and coloured in such a manner as to deceive an imaginative public into the belief that it is eating butter.   Also it is very remunerative to manufacture.   I have a friend who, having lost money in farming, invested in a margarine factory.   It has paid him twenty per cent. ever since !

But it is not only in the matter of butter that the public is deceived.   A while ago, to my astonishment, I saw in the papers that a trading corporation in which I chance to hold one or two shares, or their employés, had been prosecuted and fined for selling foreign hams as home-grown. Accordingly I addressed the following letter to the secretary :

'Sir,—I beg to enclose a cutting from to-day's *Times*, from which it would seem that —— have been heavily fined in a London police court for selling foreign hams, &c., as Irish, Wiltshire, and York.

'As (1) a shareholder, (2) a customer of several years' standing, (3) a British farmer and a producer of hams and bacon, and (4) a person who when in London has, unfortunately for himself, purchased and consumed pig-products at ——, I wish to ask what explanation your directors have to give of the circumstances set out in the enclosed cutting and in reports in other issues of the *Times* ?'

To this epistle I received an answer requesting me kindly to suspend my judgment pending an inquiry, which the directors intended to hold directly after the holidays. Accordingly I suspended it, and in due course the directors, having held their inquiry, issued a circular to the shareholders which, in my humble opinion, was an unconvincing document. After reading it, indeed, my judgment still remains suspended. There may be a satisfactory explanation of the peculiar proceedings detailed in the police court, although I have not seen one, therefore it would be unfair to take it off its peg at present.

[1] But leaving aside this particular case, it is, I fear, beyond

---

[1] Here, by way of example, are a couple of instances cut from the *Times* and *Globe* respectively on consecutive days in April 1899. I may mention that in past years when in London I have, I believe, myself purchased articles of food from this English Farmers' Association under the impression that I was supporting British industries :

'At West London there was a batch of summonses, taken out at the instance of the Butter Association, against shopkeepers for selling adulterated butter, and Mr. Rose, the magistrate, who heard them, took the opportunity of stating that the fines would be gradually increased until the *maximum* prescribed by the Act of Parliament was reached. In nearly all the cases the excuse was that a mistake was made in serving margarine instead of pure butter.

question that some traders hold it to matter little if the British
public be deceived, and the British farmer defrauded by the sale
as his produce of goods which he never grew, so long as the end
of all trade—a heavy dividend—is satisfactorily achieved.

I heard a good story to-day about the Radical candidate. It
is said that at one of his meetings a farmer in the audience, producing a swede out of one pocket and a mangold wurzel from the
other, offered them to the candidate, and asked him politely to
give them a name, whereon he gave the wrong name. Although
it was told circumstantially enough, I do not believe this story,
first, because it is an old one, which, if far more harmless, is used
against the Radical from a distance in very much the same way
that the famous 'nine bob a week' fiction is used against the local
Conservative ; and secondly, because I doubt any farmer having
the courage to try the experiment, since, if his would-be victim by
good luck or good judgment should give the right answer, it
would be long before that practical joker heard the last of his jest.
The tale, however, is interesting, because in a humorous form it
raises the entire question as to what sort of man best represents a
county division. The obvious answer appears to be—one who
lives in the country and is acquainted with its pursuits. But this
is by no means the view taken by many constituencies, who seem
to think that the less their member knows of them and they know
of him, the better

In the first case the defendant pleaded "Guilty," and said a mistake was
made. Mr. Ricketts said the article contained 84 per cent. of fat other than
butter. Mr. Rose remarked that the small fines hitherto imposed had not had
the effect of stopping the practice, and it was quite time to increase them. He
fined the defendant 8*l.* with 25*s.* costs.'

'ENGLISH MEAT !

' At Guildhall, yesterday, the English Farmers' Association (Limited), who
professed to supply the public direct with English meat of the finest quality,
so as " to save the consumer the large profits made by butchers," were fined,
including costs, 44*l.* 4*s.* on two charges of selling New Zealand or Australian
mutton as Welsh. It was stated that no English farmers were connected with
the defendant association.'

My own opinion is that it does not much matter. These London candidates (I will not use the term 'carpet-baggers,' because I consider it offensive) come down to stand for a county division, not because they have any particular interest in it, but because they desire to be members of Parliament ; and the county division returns them, not because it has any particular love for or interest in them, but because they are pledged to vote in a way which is pleasing to the majority of the electors. Sometimes such candidates turn out well, and make a mark in the House ; indeed, they have even been known to do good service to their constituencies ; but in eight cases out of ten, once they are elected no man hears of them more ; they vanish into the great crowd of Parliamentary nobodies, and for good or ill there is, politically speaking, an end of them.

This evening I went for a walk on the Bath Hills. The water meadows beneath them are now singularly beautiful, the green grass being tinged with the purple of the cuckoo-flower, varied by flashes of gold where the king-cups grow, that become brighter and richer along the edges of the dykes. Also I found a patch of the wild purple orchis flourishing quite under the shadow of the trees, in the fell indeed. As might be expected in that situation, they were very pale in colour, but being exceedingly conspicuous, as are most of the orchid tribe, tropical or European, they caught my eye at once. This orchid, like all its relations, is very fastidious as to its habitat. My observation of it goes to show that although it flourishes in certain old meadows, generally with a very heavy soil, it does best where it is partially, but not alto-gether, overshadowed by trees, and on a stiff clay. Some years ago I dug up several clumps of these plants, and set them out again in this garden, imitating the conditions in which I found them as regards soil and situation as nearly as was possible. They have come up every spring and bloomed after a fashion, but I cannot say that the experiment was successful. I have also tried transplanting the bee-orchid, of which, although it is very rare in these parts, a few roots grow, or used to grow, in a certain marshy spot at the foot of the Vineyard Hills. Now I wish that I had left them alone, for although I took every care, even to removing a large sod of their native soil and wiring them round, from that day to this they have never shown a single leaf.

By the way, the finest specimens of purple orchis that I have ever seen grow in Websdill Wood, on my farm at Bedingham.

May 8.—To-day, Sunday, is dull and rather cold, with occa sional showers of light rain, and none of the sunshine which is now so badly needed. When I was writing of snakes a few days back I did not guess that I should so soon be a witness of their dangerous properties even in this country. To-day I heard, however, that a son of a neighbour of mine, aged twelve, had actually been bitten by a viper, and went to the village where he lives to inquire after him, and to find out the facts of the case. This was what happened, as I had it from the lips of his mother.

On the previous day she and two of her sons were bird-nesting in a neighbouring wood, when the boy Dick, who it appears has a most unwholesome admiration for reptiles, suddenly called out, ' Here's a beauty ! Look, mother, he has bitten me ; let's take him home.'

Accordingly she looked, to see Dick holding a wriggling viper in his hand, although at the time she did not know that it was a viper. As she had lived in India, however, she called to him to throw it down, and then, very pluckily, trod on it until she killed it, the reptile striking savagely at her boot the while, although, fortunately for her, it was unable to pierce the leather.

Then, carrying the dead snake with them, the three of them started homeward till, a few minutes afterwards, the other boy said, 'Look, Dick is turning white,' immediately after which he fell to the ground almost insensible.

At this moment it chanced that a keeper arrived, for the party had been inadvertently trespassing in a preserve from which he had come to warn them, and by his help the swooning lad was carried to his home nearly a mile away, his mother running on to get brandy and telegraph for the doctor.

As soon as Dick arrived he was dosed heavily with brandy and ammonia; also, as I forgot to say, by his mother's direction, immediately after being bitten he had sucked the wound, which was between two fingers of the left hand. Further, he was walked, or rather dragged up and down, till at length he became utterly exhausted, and, to the terrible alarm of his parents, his throat began to close up so that he could no longer swallow.

Owing to various mischances nearly three hours went by before a doctor came. On his arrival he at once put the boy to bed, for it appears that a great mistake had been made in walking him about, which only served to consume his strength. By now poor Dick was almost *in extremis*; but the doctor, a man of resource, applied a succession of strong mustard plasters to the heart, and thus kept it going until the vital forces overcame the immediate effects of the poison. Had it not been for this treatment I understand that he would have died.

To-day, when I saw the patient in bed, his arm and hand were swollen to the size of those of a large man, and very hot to the touch, while the skin was tense, shining, and red in colour. The face also was red and flushed, but I am glad to say that Dick is now believed to be out of any danger.

Vipers are rare in this county; I never remember seeing but one of them, though they are said to be plentiful in the wood where my little friend was bitten. It is uncommon for them to strike human beings, for they are retiring in their habits; but even the most peaceably minded adder resents being pounced upon and picked up. It appears also that at this time of the year, when these reptiles have just emerged from their long winter sleep, the poison in their fangs is unusually virulent; moreover, it is their breeding season, during which they are supposed to be most deadly.

The last authenticated case of viper-poisoning in this neighbourhood occurred about forty years ago, when a schoolboy, who was, I think, attended by the father of Dr. Crowfoot, of Beccles, was bitten, but recovered.　My friend, Dr. Lyne Stivens, tells me also of a dreadful case which was seen by his father, a doctor in the neighbourhood of Chester.　In this instance a woman went with her eighteen-month-old baby into a wood to gather sticks, and laid it down asleep while she sought them.　Her movements disturbed an adder which, hurrying away to seek a hiding-place, crawled down the mouth of the child and choked it. He says that this horrible case made a great sensation at the time.

May 10.—Yesterday the weather was dull and raw, with a sou'-west wind.　On the farm we were doing odd jobs and split- ting the baulks for swedes upon the glebe-land.　Also the corn which we sold the other day was carted from Bedingham to Loddon, where we contracted to deliver it.　To-day I was walking round Baker's, and find that the docks, which with the other weeds will, for this season at any rate, as I fear, make the farm a *damnosa hereditas* to me, are simply countless.　Many of them also are marsh docks, a peculiarly virulent variety, with fanged roots, that break when one attempts to draw them, which have been brought up with the lowland hay and carted on to the land in the manure. The wheat on No. 42 is looking rather yellow, but I think it is because at this season its roots are beginning to pass down into the subsoil.　The roots of wheat penetrate, I believe, many feet through the earth, and when they first leave the cultivated stratum the top is apt to show a yellow tinge.　At Bedingham, whither I went this afternoon, the wheat continues to look magnificent, but the barley is rather thin and yellow, owing to the prolonged cold and damp.　Barley at Bedingham only does well in a hot, dry year.

The young red-poll steers and heifers, which are grazing in Websdill Wood, set to work to hunt the two terrier dogs that accompanied me, chasing them round and round the great field, till at length the dogs, growing tired and frightened, either hid in a ditch or bolted straight away for the open country.　At any rate they vanished, and I was obliged to come home without them. Spotting the grass in this oak-shaded pasture I found many splendid specimens of purple orchids (*Orchis latifolia*); indeed, in half an hour I gathered as large a bunch as I could bind round with my handkerchief.

Among them I discovered one pure white bloom, which shows that the tendency among orchids to produce an occasional albino is not confined to the tropical varieties. These albino sports in the case of lælias, cattleyas, &c., command great prices among the wealthier members of the orchid-loving fraternity, but I fear that they would not give me much for a pure white latifolia. Notwithstanding the rain, which fell with unpleasant persistence, I have not spent an hour so happily for many weeks as that I passed this afternoon gathering those stately purple blooms which stood up here and there in the green grass under the canopy of oaks now bursting into leaf. Perhaps this was because the scene and its surroundings afforded a pleasing contrast to the political turmoil which overshadows us to-day. Bedingham and politics are things incongruous and far apart ; indeed, it is difficult to connect this old-world place, on which the shadow of the past seems to brood visibly, with anything violent and modern.

Notwithstanding the industrious cleaning to which the fields here have been subjected during the recent dry years, I find that there are hundreds of little docks growing among the pease where last season not one was to be seen. The labourer, Cooke, who is employed in pulling them declares that seed which has lain buried for long periods of time is brought to the surface with each ploughing to germinate whenever the conditions are favourable. I imagine that this theory is correct, as under certain conditions the vitality of seed can be prolonged almost indefinitely ; witness the instances of the appearance of charlock after deep ploughings upon heavy land and of wheat found in mummy cases, which has, I believe, been known to grow from seeds thousands of years old. I have myself seen grain in Egypt taken from the wrappings of mummies that had every appearance of being sound enough to plant. Another proof of the vitality of seed prolonged over great periods of time is to be found in the fact that where railway cuttings or other deep trenches are made, flowers and herbage sometimes appear upon the earth thrown out of them different in character from those native to the district. Also I have heard, though of this I have no personal experience, that if dense forest is burnt down in Borneo and some other tropical countries, the growth which comes up is absolutely distinct from that which has been destroyed, which suggests that the seeds producing it were shed before the primæval forest came into being.

To my mind, if no satisfactory explanation of the marvel is forthcoming, this is the strangest example of the three, since it is more wonderful that germs should retain life in the damp heat of a tropical forest than in the intense dryness of an Egyptian sepulchre, or when sealed up beneath many feet of stiff clay.

May 11.—Last evening I took the chair at a political meeting in this village, which was well attended and went off satisfactorily. When we were about two-thirds through it the candidate arrived from some distant place, looking very tired. Remembering my own sensations when it came to the point of addressing a third or fourth meeting in the course of a single day, my heart went out to him in sympathy. The man who in middle life abandons the quiet of his home to tear round and round a large extent of country at considerable expense in the hope of winning the privilege of paying a great many subscriptions and sitting up very late at night for more than half the year does, indeed, deserve the gratitude of those whom he represents, or tries to represent. It is little to be wondered at that, in our part of England at any rate, local gentlemen suited to the task and willing to undertake it are growing rarer every day, the distinction of seeking parliamentary honours being left more and more to pushing barristers, who look upon them as part of the routine of their profession, or to strangers with axes of their own to grind.

Our meeting was very orderly ; there was not even any

'boo-ing,' though I heard a little of this the other night at Broome. Mr. Holmes tells me, indeed, that there has been no violence and very little interruption at any of his meetings, so it seems that our division is more civilised than are some places in East Norfolk. But although it is interesting enough in its own melancholy and discreditable fashion, and indeed instructive, that is a subject upon which I do not wish to enter in these peaceful pages.

May 12.—Yesterday we had another strong sou'-west gale, varied with storms of hail and rain, which were not, however, violent enough to interfere with the baulk-splitting and timber-gilling. Last night, in obedience to urgent telegrams, I had to drive six miles to another meeting. To my mind, looked at from the point of view of any political advantage, it was the very worst sort of meeting, for the room was not much more than half filled with steady-going supporters of the Unionist cause, who have probably voted the same way ever since they had a vote, and will continue to do so until voting ceases to interest them. Speaking to such an audience in a great half-empty hall is, moreover, about as depressing a performance as would be the making of harangues to rows of high-class mummies in a Theban tomb. Not that I wish to disparage the audience, which was of a most intelligent character, but it was impossible for the would-be-orator not to feel that there sat among them no man whom he could hope to convert, for the simple reason that their minds were already made up, and that they were brought there by a sense of duty only. From without came very different sounds, for the other side were holding an open-air gathering, and with shouts of enthusiasm chairing their candidate about the green. The difference was the old difference between the party of defence and the party of attack, but to me those shouts were ominous of the result of the poll to-day, especially as I hear that the publicans have in many instances turned against Mr. Holmes, partly because at one time or other he advocated temperance principles, and partly on account of some question which has to do with rates.

This morning I went to record my vote at the polling-station at Broome, where everything seemed very quiet, and then on to the bench. Here the greater part of our business consisted of School Board prosecutions, to my mind the most troublesome and perplexing form of case with which a magistrate is called upon to deal. Of course, as I have had to explain many and many a time during recent years, the law is perfectly clear. If a child under a certain age is irregular in its attendance at school, except for some very good reason, such as sickness, of which a doctor's certificate must be produced, its parents are liable to be fined five shillings, which fine can be recovered by distress.

Such is the plain law, but the enforcing of it is by no means as plain. Magistrates are frequently blamed—for the most part by doctrinaire enthusiasts or persons who have little practical acquaintance with the conditions under which the poor live—because they are not more severe upon this class of offence. Yet in many instances the circumstances brought before them are so piteous that they feel it would be nothing short of wicked to add to the misery of the persons concerned by a fine to be levied on such belongings as they still possess. Sometimes the husband is a drunkard, and the mother keeps the child at home to mind the little ones while she goes out to work in the fields to find bread to put into the mouths of all of them. Sometimes she is sick— very likely being confined of the twelfth or thirteenth baby—and an elder girl who has not yet passed her appointed standards is forced to take her place for the time being ; and so on, with variations.

For instance, to-day one woman, a widow with a large family, who burst out weeping in the box, told us a tale of her utter penury, and of how she was sometimes obliged to detain the child on whose account she had been summoned at home to look after her small brothers and sisters while she went out to work. Another woman drew from under her apron a pair of boots, or rather the remains of what was once a pair of boots, for they were all holes, and asked the bench how in this cold, wet weather she could be expected to send a delicate girl to walk a mile through the mud in such foot-gear, which was all she had.

There are many cases of this nature, but of course there are still more of utterly shiftless parents who will submit to be summoned and fined again and again rather than take the trouble to get their children to school. Also there exists an aggravating class who, when any of their family fall sick, wait till a summons is taken out against them to appear in court and explain the cause of absence, of course without corroboration in the shape of a doctor's certificate. These people are so numerous that on this bench we have found it necessary to make a rule that they shall be fined, however ill the child may have been, unless they can bring medical evidence (which costs them nothing) to that effect.

Since writing the above, a month or more ago, I have read the remarks of Sir J. Gorst, the Vice-President of the Committee of Council on Education, made on the occasion of the discussion of the Education Vote in Committee.

I see that he quotes, apparently with approval, the report of Mr. Currie, in which Mr. Currie states 'that the farmer and the squire are no friends of elementary education,' &c. Here I take the liberty to join issue with Sir John Gorst and Mr. Currie. The farmer and the squire, at any rate in this part of the world, desire to see the children educated, but it is true that occasionally they find a difficulty in the enforcing of the draconian regulations enacted to that end. It is also true that certain of the more old-fashioned and conservative among them, while acknowledging the necessity and advantages of education in these days of hurry and progress, sometimes wonder whether the increased bitterness of competition that learning naturally brings about, and the inducing of so many thousands of young men to forsake the rural occupations which contented their forefathers, in order to put on a black coat and to struggle to obtain a place, however ill-paid, in a city office, do in fact conduce to the happiness in life of those immediately concerned.

Moreover, in the opinion of many of us benighted farmers and squires, the plan under which the young are taught in rural districts is wrong fundamentally, being indeed a plan devised by dwellers in cities for the advantage and use of cities. What we seek is a system whereby boys and girls will be instructed in those arts and things which are likely to be serviceable to tillers of the soil and their helpmeets. We desire and ask for a course of education intended to make the pursuit of agriculture payable and attractive to those who are born to follow it, in the place of teaching which, either with or without design, does, in effect, turn their thoughts and feet from the country to the town.

Sir J. Gorst tells us that in that educational Utopia, the Upper Engadine, where the distances are great, the climate is inclement, and the difficulties of getting to school are enormous, such a thing as the unnecessary absence of a child is almost unknown, because of the very heavy and progressive fines which in that event are inflicted upon its parents. If I follow his meaning rightly, he seems to suggest that the regulations of the Upper Engadine might with advantage be introduced into England, together with the progressive fines, which apparently, after three days' absence, would amount to about ten shillings, and after a week to I know not how much.

Well, they may be a patient folk in the Upper Engadine, but the public would never stand it here. Indeed, many will think that such fines would be monstrous in this country, where the goods of numbers of the people prosecuted do not amount to a total value of five pounds.

May 13.—To-day the wages of all labourers on the farm were raised 1*s.* a week—'heigh'ned' is the local term. This improvement in the value of labour is consequent on the rise in the price of corn. Probably corn will be down again after harvest, and wages with it.

May 31.—After polling on the 12th I came here to Kessingland, where I have a house upon the edge of the cliff which was once a Coastguard station, and before that, as I understand, a famous resort of smugglers, who used to hide their unlawful treasures in the neighbouring wells.

As with the best will in the world I cannot follow the details of a farm fifteen miles away, my journal for the next fortnight or so must be somewhat scant. Here my farming is confined to trying to make the grass grow upon an acre and a half of land alongside of the house, which I wish to turn into a 'pightle' or paddock. Having cleaned this soil, I sent a man and horses over from Ditchingham on March 23, to sow it with oats and small seed and to dress it with artificial manure. As a matter of fact I find that I should not have attempted these operations for another month, as in this exposed situation the bitter winds of spring, rushing across the ocean, cut and perish the young grasses if they appear too soon. The result is that the expense of the permanent grass seed is, I fear, for the most part wasted. On that side of the pightle which is more or less protected by the house both grass and oats have come up well, helped, no doubt, by the fact that this was garden ground; but further away they are scanty, and will, I think, have to be re-sown. What are not scanty, although every bit of the land has been forked over, are thistles and young poppies.

On the day after we came here I heard the result of our election. My fears were more than justified, for Mr. Holmes, whose predecessor had a majority of 800, was defeated by a majority of over 1,300, and this by a gentleman quite strange to the county. Under all the circumstances, if an angel had appeared as the Unionist candidate for South Norfolk, I do not think that he would have been returned, but it must be admitted that the amount of the adverse vote is absolutely overwhelming. I understand that this vast total is attributed to no small extent to the action of the publicans, who consider that they have some grievance about their assessments, and therefore wreaked it on Mr. Holmes, the Chairman of the Assessment Committee. Of course, if there is anything in the complaint, which I do not believe, the whole committee is responsible, and not Mr. Holmes alone.

On turning back to that page of my diary which deals with the beginning of this contest, I see I expressed an opinion that a local man is at a great disadvantage when standing as a candidate, and the result of this fight certainly confirms me in that view. Next time, if I have anything to do with the matter, I shall certainly suggest that unless some gentleman connected with the brewing interest is available, a rich man from London should be asked to contest the constituency, for choice a successful financier. His record, good, bad, or indifferent, would not matter in the least ; what seems to injure a man is that he should have spent an honourable existence amongst those whom he seeks to represent, and during many years have laboured according to his lights and opportunities for the best interests of all about him. Then he may look to be rewarded by an adverse majority of thirteen hundred votes.

On the 26th I went over to Ditchingham, and found that the weather has been as cold and unseasonable there as it is here by the sea. The crops are backward, owing to the complete absence of sunshine, which everything needs sorely. The trees, however, are coming into full leaf, except the ashes, of which the buds are still black. On the 20th there was a tremendous thunderstorm, with a perfect flood of rain, both of which we had at Kessingland also, and very curious it seemed in such cold weather. The may is only beginning to show in the hedges ; indeed, never do I remember summer so slow in coming. On the farm and at Bedingham we have been drilling swedes and white turnips, and the two remaining mares have produced their foals without accident.

One of the little home-bred steers has been sold to the butcher at the top price which beef commands in our market—7s. a stone. Its dead weight proved to be fifty-one stone, which for an animal little over two years old, that has not been in any way forced, I consider very satisfactory. Two cows have also been sold, one

for 14*l*. and the other for 11*l*.   The latter of these was old
New-born Pride, the mother of the herd and once the best animal
in it.   It goes to my heart to have parted with her, and I am glad
that I was away and knew nothing of it, for I understand that she
was bought for butcher's meat, and by now doubtless has been
killed and eaten.   In farming, unfortunately, there is no room for
sentiment ; if an animal ceases to be profitable it must go for the
best price that it will fetch, though when one has been accustomed
to it for many years this seems hard.   Exit New-born Pride in
the twentieth year of her age.   I wonder how long a healthy cow
would last if well cared for and fed?   Nobody seems to know,
because nobody has ever tried, but I imagine that it would live
for thirty-five or forty years.   'New-born' was only in late middle-
life.   Old age still stretched before her.   Had she been placed in
a home for superannuated cows I believe that she would have
flourished well into the next century.   It is possible, indeed, that
if we had kept her she might have produced several more calves,
perhaps four or five ; but after a certain period of life the milk
of cows becomes thin and almost worthless, also their calves
are small.   Therefore they have to go.

On the same day, the 16th, ten lambs were sold at 30*s*.
each ; a fair price, as the trade in lambs is not brisk this year.

We are now making about 67 lb. of butter a week, which is
fetching tenpence and elevenpence a pound.

To-day the weather is still very cold and dull, and since nine
o'clock I think that at one time and another the wind has blown
from every point of the compass , while after sunset a violent storm
of rain came up out of a sky of extraordinary and vivid blackness.
I never remember a month of such wretched weather as we have
experienced this May, which has not brought us a single breath
of summer.   I have not kept any record of the readings of the
thermometer, but, if I may judge by my own sensations, I think
that the temperature of May has been colder and more miserable
than was that of last December.

This afternoon I walked up the beach to a beautiful spot

called Benacre Broad, about three miles away. Here is a large stretch of reed-fringed water embraced by trees as by great green arms, which gradually grow thinner and cease where they project from the shelter of the land and are exposed to the fury of the easterly gales that break upon them laden with salt spray lifted from the sea. Between the Broad and the ocean lie sand-dunes clothed with coarse grass and tenanted by rabbits, and for the populous coast of Suffolk the view from these, with the peaceful wood-encircled lake upon one side and the limitless waste of water on the other, is extraordinarily wild and lonely.

One of the charms of these Broads lies in the number of rare birds that still breed about them. As we walked across the sand-dunes this afternoon I saw two tiny creatures running swiftly in the grass. Going to the spot we could not find them, till presently they started up beneath our very feet, and on being captured proved to be recently hatched peewits, lovely little things, with long legs and large eyes, that, young as they were, had learned to hide themselves in such a fashion as to be almost indistinguishable from the sand in which they crouched.

All this while the old mother peewit was watching us, and now, in great excitement, she came circling and calling about our heads. Letting her chicks run we stood still, whereupon she went through every possible manœuvre to draw us away from the patch of gorse in which they had taken refuge. I noticed, however, that although she settled within a few yards of us, but always in an opposite direction to that where the little ones lay hid, she did not pretend to be wounded, and flop along the ground as though her wing or leg were broken, as I have frequently seen plover do in Africa. This habit seems to suggest a knowledge on their part that man wishes to capture them for his own evil purposes. In the case of partridges, which also feign to be hurt under similar circumstances, one can understand this knowledge, since they have been hunted for many generations; but in the wild parts of South Africa, where they have scarcely been disturbed from the beginning of time— for the natives rarely interfere with such small game—so intimate an acquaintance with the unfriendly designs of men strikes me as very strange.

Near the edge of the mere I put up two birds that were quite unfamiliar to me. They rose from the ground, and seemed to resemble a nightjar in shape and flight. Also there were more fowl flying about, with which I am unacquainted, in appearance like a large snipe, but having white fringed wings. Evidently they were nesting amongst the rushes, whence came the sound of ducks and other birds moving to and fro.

Of late years there has been a great outcry about the closing of some of the Norfolk Broads to the public, and the claim advanced by their owners to exclusive sporting rights upon them. Doubtless in some cases it has seemed a hard thing that people should be prevented from doing what they have done for years without active interference on the part of the proprietor. But, on the other hand, it must be remembered that it is only recently the rush of tourists to the Norfolk Broads has begun. It is one thing to allow a few local fishermen or gunners to catch pike or bag an occasional wild fowl, and quite another to have hundreds of people whipping the waters or shooting at every living thing, not excluding the tame ducks and swans. For my part I am glad that the owners have succeeded in many instances, though at the cost of some odium, in keeping the Broads quiet, and especially the smaller ones like Benacre, because if they had failed in this most of the rare birds would be driven away from Norfolk, where they will now remain to be a joy to all lovers of Nature and wild things.

These remarks, I admit, however, should scarcely lie in my mouth when speaking of Benacre, since on our return towards the beach, after rambling round the foot of the mere, we found ourselves confronted with sundry placards breathing vengeance upon trespassers, warnings, it would seem, which we had contemptuously ignored. Should these lines ever come under the notice of the tenant of that beautiful place, I trust that he will accept my apologies, and for this once ' let me off with a caution.'

I do not know many sayings connected with May.　One of the few, however,

> Ere May be out
> Cast not a clout,

has been peculiarly applicable this year.　In a paper on the saws and proverbs of Norfolk, by Mr. Gillett, I find another, that I never heard before, but which doubtless is true enough for the ailing and weakly in our climate :

> March will sarch ye ;
> 　April will try ;
> May will tell ye
> 　Whether ye'll live or die.

Indeed, to my mind, the cold of the bitter and uncertain month of May is the most trying of all the English year, perhaps because it comes at the end of our long and tedious winter, when the systems of most people are more or less run down.　The best-known proverb for this month, however, is,

> If the oak is out before the ash,
> Then you'll only get a splash ;
> But if the ash is before the oak,
> Then you will surely have a soak.

This year the oak has been much before the ash.

JUNE

June 2.—Yesterday proved about the fiercest first of June that I remember, for the weather was cold, with a gale of wind blowing from the west, and occasional squalls of violent rain. The night also was very bitter. Riding from Kessingland home on a bicycle in the teeth of the wind I found most excellent exercise.

This morning I walked round the farm. Notwithstanding the unseasonable weather, the grass grows thick and strong, but then grass does not mind cold ; drought is its great enemy. I do not think that I ever saw more beautiful turf than is to be found in the sheltered parts of Iceland ; where the hay also is good, although it does not grow high, and on account of the hummocks raised by the action of frost must be laboriously cut with a sickle. Yet in Iceland—or at any rate in some parts of it—the subsoil remains frozen for the greater part of the year. I remember once, towards the end of the month of June, digging on the site of Bergsthorsknoll, which eight hundred years or so ago was the home of Njäl, the hero of the saga of that name (in my opinion one of the greatest books that ever was written), to seek for proof of the legend of the burning of the hall by Flosi.

This I found readily enough, for, at a depth of about two feet beneath the surface, we came upon the hard earthen floor of the hall, still, to all appearance, sprinkled with a fine layer of black sand, which, if I remember right, the saga tells us was strewn upon it by the hands of Bergthora and her household nearly nine hundred years ago ; and among the crumbling fragments of the fire-blackened timbers of the roof, lumps of greasy matter, sup-

posed by the chemists who have analysed them to be the residue
of the whey that the women threw upon the flames. Breaking
through the floor, and but a little below it, although it was
midsummer, we found the ground still hard with frost, which,
perchance, was last thawed upon the day of the great burning.
Yet the grass grows and the flowers spring in Iceland !

The wheats are looking strong, and keep their colour, but
the barleys, for the most part, have an unwholesome yellow tinge,
especially upon heavy lands. Indeed, everything is very backward, for even now the ash trees are not fully out, and the hawthorns are but breaking into bloom. The beet plant has suffered
much from the sunless cold, and is still very small. Weeds, however, flourish like the wicked, particularly on Baker's land, where
the men are engaged in hoeing in a perfect sea of them. This
wet weather is most unfavourable for the work, for weeds are
gifted with a wonderful vitality, and when the soil is damp, to cut
them out is frequently but to transplant them from the ridges to
the furrows. Still, it must be done, or they would smother the poor
little beet ; and afterwards, when they are rooting in the furrows
and congratulating themselves upon having survived the violence
of man, the horse-hoe will come along and put them to sleep.

On the Thwaite field, No. 28, the swedes are beginning to prick
through on the ridges—delicate little two-leaved seedlings, with
the ' fly ' and all their other troubles before them. To-day the
sheep were to have been clipped, but the shearers did not put in
an appearance, which, considering the state of the weather, is
perhaps fortunate.

It is curious to walk from the uplands down the Vineyard Hills
and to note the difference in the state of vegetation beneath their
shelter. There the trees are in full leaf and looking lovely, the
chestnuts being covered with their stately spires of bloom, and the
scented hawthorns almost hidden in white flower. The garden of
the Lodge also is much more forward than that of this house, and
one can linger there without shivering.

This afternoon I went to Bedingham, and was caught in a

violent thunder-shower for my pains. The young red-polls—they are eleven—are running in the new pastures, Nos. 15 and 16, during the day, and in the wood at night. As at Ditchingham, the barleys show yellow, though No. 5, which was sown first, and has received a dressing of artificial manure, looks much the best; while the wheats, that in most seasons love this heavy land, keep their colour, and are growing tall and strong. If we get little else, at least this year there should be plenty of straw, which now-adays is often almost as valuable as the grain. The beans seem a splendid crop, as they have done from the first, and are in flower. Two of the little beasts that are fattening in the hovel—I do not think that they number much more than twenty months— have been sold for 14*l.* apiece, while their elder brother, Royal Duke, the ox that I kept to show, has much improved in appear-ance. This I attribute to his having been removed from the barn—where he lived alone, pining for lack of companionship— and placed in a shed with another animal. Since the change he has eaten much better, and his quarters, which were always a little slack, are beginning to fill out, although at present they cannot compare with his fore part, which is really magnificent.

June 4.—The night before last there was another frost, of the kind that is known here as 'water' frost, the ground being white with it early in the morning. Of such is the summer in England.

Yesterday we were ploughing in the manure for the swedes on the top of No. 24, the Bungay-fork field, and hoeing in the All Hallows field, No. 29, and on Baker's.

The trees have all been gilled from the Bath Hills into the stackyard, where Hindle, the captain of the steam engine, and his two mates are engaged in getting them ready for the steam saw by sawing off the butts, cutting the timber into suitable lengths, and chopping away excrescences upon one side of them, so that they may 'ride' easily upon the iron table. As the turn of each tree comes, Hindle makes up his mind into what kind of stuff it will cut to the best advantage. This requires a good deal of judgment and experience, especially in the case of a rather scrappy lot of thinnings, which includes every class of wood, such as we have to saw this year. One or two of the best oaks are set aside to rip into three-inch planks, and others to be converted into the backs and ledges of gates, while the tops and butts make gate- or rail-posts. What we chiefly need this year, however, are long posts to carry the galvanised iron roofs of the sheds which I hope to cover over, so most of the oaks are to be devoted to this purpose. The inferior woods, such as elm and beech, cut into very good bed- or wall-plates, rafters, and scantlings; indeed, if kept dry under cover, they will last for two generations. Limes, again, may be sawn into boards to be used for inside work in sheds, while all the refuse that can be put to no other use is sliced into blocks for firewood. I forgot to mention that the ash, which is our most valuable timber, is ripped into three-inch stuff and then laid aside under shelter to season, with little pieces of wood between the planks to keep them apart and allow the air to circulate. Ash is the best wood in the world, or at any rate in England, for use in the frames of agricultural implements, the shafts of carts, or for any purpose where toughness and pliability—'twig' is the local term—are needed.

To-day we have been baulk-splitting, cutting out thistles, and shearing the sheep This latter is done by a gang of shearers, four in number, who travel with a pony and cart from farm to farm, clipping the sheep at a charge that averages about threepence a fleece. The operation is carried out thus: first the ewes—for of course the lambs are not clipped—are penned in one-half of the All Hallows barn, their offspring remaining outside, where they make a fearful din, auguring the very worst from this separation. A boy—the invariable boy who always appears upon these occasions—steals in delightedly to catch a ewe. As soon as they see him the whole flock rush about madly, as though they were executing a particularly confused set of kitchen lancers; but when once he has gripped one of them, after a few struggles she more or less resigns herself, and without any great resistance is half led, half dragged through the open hurdle to the malevolent-looking person who, like one of the Roman Fates, is waiting for her with the shears. He seizes her, and with an adroit and practised movement causes her to sit upon her tail, in which position most ewes look extraordinarily foolish. Now she struggles no more, nor does she make any noise; indeed, in watching the operations this morning I was put very forcibly in mind of the prophetic verse in Isaiah: 'As a sheep before her shearers is dumb.'

The operator begins his task in the region of the belly, working gradually round towards the back until it is necessary to turn the animal on to her side, when he ties the fore and hind leg together with a thin cord. In the case of old and experienced ewes I am sure that they understand what is happening to them, as they look quite contented and struggle little—indeed, the shearers say that this is so. The moment that the thing is done—which seems to prove it—they spring up with blitheness, and, rushing from the barn, begin to bite hungrily at the grass outside.

It is funny to watch the behaviour of the lambs that are waiting without. One by one they approach the escaped ewe, till at last its own offspring finds her. It takes a lamb a while, however, to convince itself that this strange, naked-looking creature is in truth its dear mamma; indeed, not until it has smelt her all round, and, thankful to find that something is left, knelt down, and with an air of relief helped itself to refreshment, does conviction conquer doubt. The ewes often seem to resent these suspicions; probably their tempers, having been tried to breaking-point, will bear no further strain.

The shearers who make up these travelling gangs are very intelligent men, moving as they do from place to place, seeing much and knowing everybody. Also, as might be expected from the nature of their trade, they are capital gossips. I asked one of them if a certain person who owns a great flock of sheep was a good farmer.

'Oh, he puts it in and takes it out,' answered the old gentleman enigmatically.

'No, partner,' interrupted another man, 'he dew take plenty out for sure, but I never did hear that he put nawthing in,' thereby in a sentence summing up the character which report gives to this tiller of the soil.

The average weight of a ewe's fleece is from four to five pounds ; but I believe that the fleeces of hoggets, that is, year-old sheep which have never been shorn before, sometimes weigh as heavy as fifteen pounds.

While I was leaning this afternoon over one of the pit-field gates (No. 25) I was much struck by the curious contrasts of the lights and colours. The order of Nature seemed to be reversed ; the light lay upon the land, the sky was dark. The air was very still and heavy, and in the sou'-western heaven a dense thunder-cloud brooded like the shadow of advancing night. Against this lowering sky the red sheep-rack made a patch of brilliant colour, while Peachy and his horses baulk-splitting beyond it were out-lined with singular clearness upon a vivid green background of sprouting oaks and the long line of hedgerow elms. All round, indeed, appeared different shades of green, strangely varied and distinct in the low lights flung through the pall of overhanging thunder-cloud. Thus, to the left appeared the bright green of the sheep's-feed and the grey-green of the bordering land, where, although it has been fed, the corn is springing again at the roots, and contrasted with the yellowish green of the barley in the immediate foreground ; while beyond this, in the middle distance, another patch of colour was furnished by the faded pink of the double roller standing with its shafts pointing to the sky. Among this barley two labourers, an old and a young man, waded slowly side by side, cutting thistles with their hooked spuds. Thus they went like dream figures silently through the silent corn, never speaking, and only halting now and again to file their spuds, till at length they came to the foot of the field, and having thrown the bunches of docks gathered in their left hands upon its fence to wither in the sun, turned, as though at a word of com-mand, and once more began their search up the long slopes of green.

As I stood quite still watching them, two larks that had been fighting at a distance came twisting through the air, and passed so close to me that their flapping wings almost touched my head. Not more than an inch or so above the barley also skimmed a pair of swallows hawking after flies, their little bodies shining like flakes of tempered steel as they flashed by me. It was curious to see how, without any apparent movement of the wings, they glided in a curve from the level of the corn over the round top of the root hale to the left, down the open end of which the yellow mangold are rolled into a slanting golden heap. And all along the hedgerow the little may trees that I have grown stood out like bouquets of white bloom, while from the copse of Hollow Hill beyond rose the song of the nightingale, sounding loud and sweet in that heavy silence.

A little higher up the hill is the bean field, No. 26, just now full of bloom, that gives out what I think one of the sweetest of perfumes. A person standing near these beans on such a day becomes aware of a humming noise, which, on examination, he will find to be caused by bees passing from flower to flower. There seemed to be several bees to each stalk, and how many tens of thousands of stalks stand in a six-acre field I should not care to calculate. Where do all the bees come from, I wonder? I and a few others have some hives, but bees are not largely kept in the village. Yet in that close alone their number must be almost countless.

I walked back over the root field, No. 23, that which we dosed with Bungay refuse, the excellent and invigorating qualities of which are evident just now in a magnificent crop of the most flourishing weeds. The beet here, as elsewhere, are very small, owing to the coolness of the season. Also I fear that the birds have done them a good deal of damage, for this field lies so quiet and secluded that they can work mischief without fear of disturbance. Needless to say they—especially the sparrows—take full advantage of their opportunities, although I daresay that there are still enough mangolds left for a plant.

June 6.—Yesterday was warm and beautiful, a very oasis in
the desert of this year's cold and gloom. This morning also was
warm, but the afternoon weather has been diversified with thunder
and heavy showers of rain and hail, that do much injury to the
young beet by splitting up and spoiling them.

I have been watching the swallows laying the foundations of
their nest in the porch of the house. I did not think that they
would build here this year, as the nests had been knocked down
by workmen, and I imagined that the smell of recent paint would
not be to their taste. They have come back, however, and commenced the work by plastering two little heaps of mud at a distance of about two inches, which are gradually brought together
into an arch designed to bear the weight of the nest. It makes
one wonder where they learned architecture.

These swallows are very curious birds. For so long as I
have known this house four or five pairs of them have built
about it, and always in the same places. Once, when the house
was let, the tenant would not suffer them in the porch because of
the dirt they made ; but so soon as he was gone they returned, although it is difficult to imagine a more inconvenient spot, as they
are constantly disturbed by those passing out and in. The
puzzling thing is that their number never seems to vary, which
inclines me to think that in order to live in comfort they require
a certain area of ground over which to hawk. What I should like
to know, however, is whether they are always the same swallows
that return spring after spring. This, I think, can scarcely be the
case, since, even if they live a great deal longer than we suppose,
they must die sometime a natural death or meet with accidents.
Yet year after year they arrive, two by two, in the accustomed
spots, never more and never less of them, and that these are
very frequently the same birds I am convinced by observation,
since, in the early spring, I have often watched the pair in the porch.
This porch, until the month of May, is protected by glass doors,
which are removed for the summer. When the swallows come
one may see them dipping and twittering outside these doors,

evidently very indignant because they are cut off from their lawful and accustomed habitation. If the doors are set open they will fly in once or twice and look round, after which, very likely, there is nothing more to be seen of them for about a month, when they commence to nest.

This morning I walked round by Baker's, where we are engaged in a desperate struggle with the millions of weeds springing among the beet, and indeed everywhere. By the side of the beans also are little hales of docks, pulled from among them, and I daresay that more are left than have been taken. If 'one year's weed means seven years' seed,' how many years' seed will be furnished by seven years' weed? That is approximately the problem which we have to work out on Baker's. The carrots on the Thwaite field, No. 28, are pricking through nicely, but it is difficult to horse-hoe them as yet, owing to the extreme fineness of the seedlings, which makes a mistake with the knives easy, as the hoer cannot always see where the lines run. Some people sow a few white turnips with the carrot seed, as these, being large-leaved and growing rapidly among the tiny carrots, are a guide to the hoeman and to the lad leading the horse. We did so last year, but I believe that this season we have put in some parsnips instead.

Hood has visited Loddon market to-day for the first time since I have been farming. He says that it is a good market, especially for pigs, which is strange, as it lacks a railway. Our market at Bungay seems to be going from bad to worse: there are few sellers and hardly any buyers; indeed, farmers no longer send their stock there. They blame the auctioneer, whether rightly or wrongly I do not know; but I think it very possible that the slow death by atrophy of this market is due to natural decay consequent on long-continued agricultural depression. The owner of the Corn-hall told me the other day that he lets the merchants' stands where they do business on Thursdays for, I think, about one-third only of the rent received by his father. This fact alone is eloquent of the disaster that has overtaken us all.

Hood sold the wool at Loddon at eighteen shillings the tod, or two stone. This is a very poor price, less by half a crown than we got last year, and that was low enough. Wool, it is explained, is 'down.' There is no profit in it at such prices.

The gast ewe has paid for the neglect of her maternal duties by being sold to the butcher for 2*l.*—a very fair price. This evening I found Hood bargaining with a young man who wanted to buy a lot of five half-grown pigs. We have to be rid of them because they are already fat, owing to the quantity of milk which they get here at the Home Farm. As the ill time for pork is at hand it would probably not pay to kill them or even to send them to London, and they are too large and fleshy to stand till after harvest. The scene at the sale was amusing in a small way. The purchaser had arrived in a cart, in which a young woman was seated, and stood by the horse's head. Opposite to him, awaiting offers and watching his customer's face, as a good seller ought to do, was Hood.

Young man (excitedly) : ' 6*l.* 10*s.* ? '

Hood (staring at him stonily like an aggrieved sphinx) : ' *No.* '

Young man turns his cart round, then, thinking better of it, comes forward to make another offer. ' 6*l.* 15*s.* ? '

Hood (loftily) : ' You'd best go home. I've told you seven's the lowest.'

Young man rushes to horse's head, and in his indignation drags it forward so violently that the unsuspecting young woman on the seat nearly falls backwards out of the cart. Then once more reason comes to his aid and he returns.

Here I left the pair confabulating. When I passed that way again, ten minutes afterwards, Hood informed me that he had parted with the pigs for 7*l.*, 'all but half-a-crown,' which, he added, was, in his opinion, a good deal more than their value. But that was a *post factum* view. Pigs, like books, have their fate. These were a lucky lot. There were eleven of them in the family, of which five were sold a good while back at 1*l.* apiece. Five more have gone to-day for 6*l.* 17*s.* 6*d.* the parcel, and one, valued at

1*l.*, remains at the Lodge, where it is kept in solitude, a dirty and depressed-looking animal, to consume the cabbage stalks out of the garden. Their food, exclusive of the separated milk, is estimated to have cost 3*l.*, which leaves the net return from the litter at 9*l.* 17*s.* 6*d.* If horn and corn showed so fine a profit, farming would be a better business than it is. Pigs chance to be a good market just now, though a little while ago they were not worth breeding. They have fluctuated thus in value several times since I began to farm; when they are dear the supply rushes in from abroad, and everybody breeds them, until they become a drug. When they are cheap, on the other hand, the foreigner ceases to export, and farmers give up breeding them as unprofitable, with the result that scarcity ensues, to be followed in turn by a plethora.

June 7.—To-day I have been watching chaff being cut with the machine, which is driven by one of the horses, who walks round and round with a melancholy air. For some years we had trouble because we could find no stone or other material that would stand the constant wear of the animal's feet, till at length we hit upon the idea of sinking the butts of the oaks which were cut down at Bedingham in a circle for it to walk on. This was some winters ago, but as yet these butts show no appreciable damage; indeed, I fancy that they will last a good deal longer than any of us who set them there. The chaff we are now cutting is two-thirds of vetches from No. 21 field, where there is a very heavy crop of them, and about one-third of hay. This mixture the young cattle in the yards and the other things eat greedily so long as it is fresh, after which they turn from it, so it is well not to cut up too much at a time.

The steam-sawing has begun. It is a fascinating sight to see the circular saw eat into the trees as they are pushed against it on the smooth iron table. Some people complain that this system of cutting is more wasteful than the old plan of two sawyers in a pit, and no doubt the saw itself is thicker and makes more dust. On the other hand, however, bits of timber can be cut with the steam-saw that, on account of the awkwardness of their size or shape, the most skilful sawyers in the world could not deal with; moreover, the saving of time and labour is something enormous. There is a common idea that any labourer can cut timber with a steam-saw, but this is not the case. Doubtless anyone can cut it after a fashion, but to make the most of the stuff and avoid spoiling any requires judgment, eye, and experience.

In the timber room of the Horse-buildings, Robson, the labouring carpenter, is engaged in mending the wheels of an old pony-cart. Now, to make a wheel, or even to set some spokes in it, is a thing that looks easy, but, as a matter of fact, it demands much skill and practice; indeed to do it properly is something of a gift. This particular wheelwright is only a hedge carpenter, without even a shop of his own, but he has the reputation of being able to 'set' a wheel better than anyone about here, and certainly his work is always very sound and good.

Wheat is now down to forty-seven shillings a quarter, after having been up to fifty-five a week or two ago. These fluctuations show how artificial was the violent rise in price and what an uncertain crop is corn in these days. Before the year is out it may once more be selling at twenty-five shillings.

This evening I saw five curlew passing over the Bath Hills and travelling sou'-west. These are the first curlew that I have ever seen in this neighbourhood, though some months ago I heard one calling. By the way, when shooting at Earsham last winter I saw four wild swans flying about the river, and a beautiful sight they were. But these lovely birds look best of all floating like foam on the black breast of some mountain-circled tarn in Iceland.

June 8.—To-day we have been horse- and hand-hoeing on the All Hallows field, No. 29, where, although I believed the land to be clean, plenty of weeds have put in an appearance, for last season's drought and this season's rain have brought them up with a vengeance. When I pointed them out, Buck, who is by nature a *laudator temporis acti*, remarked sarcastically that there was a new kind of farming nowadays to what he was accustomed to when he was young, ' farming with the hoe instead of with the plough,' and that was what made the weeds. What he meant was that in the old days a root-field would receive three or four ploughings in addition to the necessary baulkings. Doubtless this was very good for it, but in our time we can scarcely afford to put so much labour into the land, which will not pay the price. This field, for instance, has been only twice ploughed, then baulked and split back (two baulkings are supposed to equal one ploughing). As it is, root is the most expensive of all crops to grow, because of the amount of labour that must be expended between the preparation of the land and the ultimate ' haling' of the crop—often an uncertain one—to say nothing of the value of the necessary manure. But although our ancestors did well enough without it after their own fashion, if we had no beet and swedes our farming would, I suppose, come to an end. Root culture is, after all, quite a modern thing ; I believe that it only began in the time of Arthur Young, about a hundred years ago.[1]

On my way to field No. 22 I passed the piece of beans, No. 26. On the other side of the Holly Lodge drive is another field of beans that does not belong to me. These beans the farmer sowed in the spring, whereas mine were got in last autumn, and it is extraordinary to see the difference between them to-day, the latter being almost twice the height of my neighbour's. This goes to confirm the local prejudice in favour of autumn-sown over spring-drilled beans ; but I must try to follow the fate of the two crops till they reach the barn-door, which will put the matter to the test. So far this season has not been favourable to the setting of beans.

The beet on No. 22 are sown on the flat, and not on baulks. Whitrup, with the assistance of a boy, who leads the horse, is

---

[1] In the *General Dictionary of Husbandry*, published by Messrs. Longman about ninety years since, I find that there is no entry under the heads of Beet, Swedes, or Mangolds. Turnips, however, are fully treated of ; but it is mentioned that their culture is of quite recent date.

hoeing them with the flat-work hoe, which has two knives in the centre and one projecting on either side.

There are four 'ringes,' or rows of plants, to a 'stetch,' that is separated from the next stetch by a furrow, and the hoe covers two ringes and a furrow, or a whole stetch in the double journey. The two centre knives clean the middle ringe completely, while one side knife cuts that portion of the furrow which was left untouched on the last journey and the other does half the outer ringe, which, on the hoe being turned at the end of the field, is completed by what was the furrow-knife. This sounds rather intricate, but in truth it is simple. I am afraid, however, that it is not possible to make the agricultural process of flat-hoeing quite clear to the reader without the help of diagrams.

At Bedingham this afternoon I found the colt with the injured shoulder in a fair way to recovery. It would have been a pity had it been otherwise, for he is bred from my best mare, and likely to make a fine animal. The farrier thinks that his shoulder-blade was cracked; if so, I suppose that it has mended up. I have never heard of Röntgen rays being applied to horses, but if the animals are valuable it might be worth while to try them in order to locate such injuries.

Many years ago, in Africa, I owned a horse of great beauty. It was a powerful creature, with an arched neck, small head, very fine legs, and round hoofs, not unlike the fancy horses pictured by Vandyke and other early artists. Its long mane and tail also were snow-white and crimped, while its colour varied from a dark cream in winter to a black roan in summer. This animal I was so unfortunate as to lose through the carelessness of a native servant. Ultimately it was found about fifty miles away, and pounded in a kraal with stone walls six feet high. This wall it tried to jump, and, indeed, did jump, but in the effort cracked its shoulder-blade, like the colt at Bedingham, and was returned to me dead lame. A gentleman who had always admired it very much offered me twenty pounds' for it, taking the chance of its recovery, which sum I accepted. Six months or so afterwards I was astonished to see the late Colonel Weatherley riding off at the head of his troop to the Zulu war upon this very horse. Afterwards he was killed from its back at Inhlobane ; but the horse escaped, for my friend Sir Melmoth Osborn [1] told me that many years later he recognised it in the possession of a native chief in Zululand, of which country he was then Governor. It has nothing to do with farming, but 1 hope that I may be forgiven if I mention a sad incident connected with that disastrous day. With Colonel Weatherley was his young son, whose name, if I remember right, was Rupert, a delicate lad of about fifteen. He was killed by his father's side, who was assegaied, indeed, in attempting to defend him. Ignorant of the dreadful slaughter that had taken place upon the mountain, another volunteer corps, which had been recruited in the Transvaal, approached the camp, and among them an elder son of Colonel Weatherley's, who had been my clerk when I was master of the Transvaal High Court. This corps meeting a number of saddled and bridled runaway horses, young Weatherley caught one of them, a good-looking pony, and rode it into camp. It proved to be the animal on which his brother had just been killed.

Last year field No. 21, by Websdill Wood, was under root, and, the summer being so dry and favourable, I certainly thought that we had exterminated every weed in it. Now it is laid down for permanent pasture sown with the barley crop, and, although the men have been through it with their spuds, to my disgust I perceive a number of thistles and some coltsfoot springing among the corn. Truly, of weeds there is no end. You think that you are rid of them, but deep down in the soil their roots or germs survive, to appear again the next wet season. The kohl rabi are coming up on the new-drained field, No. 18, though not with quite so thick a plant as I should like to see. Moore has been horse-hoeing them, but as they are sown on the flat the job is

---

[1] I grieve to state that I must now say 'my late friend,' as a few days ago Sir Melmoth's death was reported at Durban, in Natal.

June 15, 1899.   H. R. H.

almost as difficult as it was in the case of the carrots here, and for the same reason. I walked through the eight-acre pasture, No. 11, which is set for hay and promises a good crop, and in doing so came across two large rings of extraordinarily rich grass where grow many toadstools. I cannot understand why the grass in these fairy-rings, as they are called, should be so much more lush than that about it, or why the toadstools should spring in such a perfect circle.

Last night we had a great trouble with the swallows in the porch. As I opened the door to see out some friends who had been dining here, one of the swallows, attracted by the light of the lamp, flew from the nest straight into the house and up the well of the staircase, where it began to flutter about in a piteous fashion. Fearing lest it should burn itself or break its wings, I extinguished the lamps and set the windows open, believing that in the quiet of the early morning it would find its way out. When I got up, about seven o'clock, however, there was the poor little thing still perched upon a buffalo horn. In vain did I make the most desperate endeavours to coax it out of the house; it would only flutter round the ceiling or knock itself against the top of the window, until I thought that it must die of exhaustion. After a while I fetched a landing-net and tried to capture it, but it was too quick for me. At last, just as, wearied out, I was thinking of abandoning the business in despair, much to my relief an accidental dip took it through the open window. When I came down to breakfast I found it sitting very dazed on the railings opposite the house. Meanwhile the mate, untroubled by the absence of its partner, had been diligently building at their nest, and as, after the terrifying experiences of its night out, it could not, or would not, assist in that domestic duty, the other flew to it on the railings, and sat there, twittering and scolding, till it plucked up courage to skim away and secure a light breakfast of flies. By the afternoon it had recovered so completely that, in watching them at work, I could not tell which of the pair was the captive of the night before.

This incident suggests that the intelligence of swallows, great as it seems in many ways, must be curiously limited. Of course, however well accustomed to the place it was, any bird might make the mistake of flying into the house when suddenly awakened and bewildered by a bright light ; but it is strange that, although it was left in peace for three or four hours in the early morning, it should not have been able to escape through the open window. When it is in the porch it knows the difference between air and glass perfectly, for the upper part of the hall-door is of glass, and it never makes the mistake of flying against it. Also, it must have seen the staircase window standing open on many occasions ; and yet I believe, had it not been for my exertions, that the unhappy little thing would have starved to death before it was able to find its way through it, just because this window opens in its lower half and not up against the ceiling.

The result of this experience is that the swallows remain masters of the situation, and anyone coming into or leaving the house after nightfall has to do so by the garden door.

June 9.—To-day at the Bench we tried one of the egg-stealing cases which are always plentiful at this time of year. The defendant, a 'marine dealer,' was accused of sending a box of 251 partridge eggs ('twenty dozen smalls, eleven reds,' *i.e.* French partridge, according to his own invoice found in the box) to another 'marine dealer' in a neighbouring town. This second gentleman, by the way, was recently fined 31*l.* 10*s.*, being 1*s.* an egg, for 630 stolen eggs. The case against the defendant to-day was clear, and he also was fined a shilling an egg and costs, with the alternative of two months in prison.

I know it is commonly said that magistrates are severe upon this class of case, and very ready to convict upon slight evidence. This is not at all my experience. On the contrary, the fact that most of them are sportsmen tends to make them very careful, and I have on several occasions seen poaching cases dismissed when the evidence would have been thought sufficient to ensure conviction in most classes of offences. It is extraordinary what an amount of false sentiment is wasted in certain quarters upon poachers, who, for the most part, are very cowardly villains, recruited from among the worst characters in the neighbourhood. When some friends and I hired the shooting at Bradenham, one of our keepers, a very fine young fellow named Holman, interrupted a gang of poachers engaged in killing pheasants at night. He was unarmed, and they were armed, and the end of it was that one of them fired a gun straight at him, the contents of which he only escaped by throwing himself behind the trunk of a small tree. The man was identified, and tried at the Assizes, but as it was only 'a night poaching case,' a sentence of six months was thought to be sufficient punishment for this vigorous attempt at murder.

Not a year goes by without keepers, who are merely doing the duty for which they are paid, being murdered or beaten to a pulp by these bands of thieving rascals, who are out, not for sport, but for gain. Yet bad as is the night-poaching business, the trade of the egg-stealer is perhaps even more despicable, since, as I told the defendant to-day, not only was he himself breaking the law, he was causing many others to break it also. It is not to be supposed that these large lots of eggs are found and thieved by one man ; on the contrary, a system of 'feeders' is necessary to their collection. A rascal of the stamp of our friend the 'marine dealer' is in touch with various bad characters in the villages round about, who suborn labourers to find the nests in the course of their daily toil, and when they are full to bring away the eggs at night. These in due course reach the hands of the middleman, who pays for them at a certain tariff, and passes them on to some honest merchant who does a larger business. Ultimately they find their way, either through game-dealers or by the agency of a not too scrupulous head-keeper, into the possession of the tenants of great shootings who are anxious that their bags should be big in due season, and try to increase their stock of partridges by buying eggs, not knowing, of course, that they have been stolen, very frequently from their neighbours' land, and sometimes from their own.

The King's Head Hotel, Bungay, was sold again to-day without the ruins, which the Duke of Norfolk keeps in his own hands. This time it fetched 5,250*l.*, as against the former price of 6,800*l.* It would appear, therefore, that the Duke must write off a loss of at least 1,050*l.*, since, sentiment and historical associations, which do not fetch much in Bungay, apart, it would be impossible to value the site of the old castle at more than 500*l.* To anyone who has it, however, it is worth while spending a thousand or so to save the feudal towers of his ancestors from the hands of the speculator in villas and licensed premises.

I visited this afternoon the sheep on field No. 24, just about the time when they were waiting to be let into the new pen. While I was yet a great way off they saw me, and, mistaking me for Hood, raised a tremendous baa-ing, but when I came up to them and they found out their error, they seemed much depressed. Presently Hood arrived, and the baa-ing re-commenced. Now the hurdles, on the other side of which they had stood for hours, suffering all the tortures of Tantalus, were withdrawn. Heavens! how they rushed through the gap, grabbing at the green stuff as they ran, and knocking each other aside in their efforts to secure the juiciest tufts. The best dispositioned sheep, alas! are not altruistic in their views. They fell upon that patch of corn like locusts; indeed, anyone unaccustomed to their greed would have imagined that they were starving, although in fact their condition is excellent. They are allowed three of these folds a day, and clean off every scrap on them down to the thistles.

The price of lambs is poor. Now, in June, I cannot get twenty-eight shillings apiece for them, whereas two months ago, at Easter, they fetched twenty-nine. The reason of the fall is the coldness of the weather; at least the butchers declare that in an inclement summer like the present the public has no fancy for light meat such as lamb, but prefers to buy beef and mutton.

To-night another very heavy thunder rain is falling, which is curious after so cold a day. This weather is most discouraging to the farmer, as with such continual surface wet it is almost impossible to clean the land, for so many of the weeds take fresh root wherever the hoe has left them.

June 10.—Last night's rain was very heavy indeed; this morning all the ditches are full, and I expect that by to-morrow the floods will be out on the common. To-day the weather is clearing a little, but, notwithstanding the high glass, it remains unsettled; indeed, this year the glass seems a very uncertain guide. As the men cannot stand upon the land, which is as soft as mud, we are carting manure from the yards, and taking the opportunity to drag up some of the docks on the long marsh. This is a job that never seems to get itself done, as there is always something more pressing on hand; also docks can only be pulled while the land is very soft, and when the marsh is being fed. Even then the dragging out of these fangy, deep-rooted weeds is a backbreaking task, of which three hours at a stretch is enough for any man.

In a former chapter of this book I inveighed against the pervading dock, asking what useful part it can possibly perform in the economy of nature. Many—very many—kind correspondents have since written to enlighten me on the point, and from them I learn that what I have always considered a pest is, it appears, a plant of extraordinary value.[1] To begin with, there are eleven varieties of dock, if not more; various grubs and caterpillars feed upon them, and they have medicinal properties. But their main use is the discovery of that excellent institution the Colonial College in Suffolk, who have found out that one British variety of dock produces four times as much tannin as does oak bark, which tannin is believed to be perfectly suitable to trade purposes.

---

[1] One of these letters is worthy of preservation. It begins, ' I notice in the *East Anglian Daily Times* that you would like to know what good Docks can be put to. *What will you give me if I tell you?* ' Oh, careful and most provident correspondent, you deserve to prosper in this huckstering world. Another epistle suggests that docks might be destroyed by dropping quicksilver upon them, or that I ' might try inoculation on the Pasteur system ' !

though this is a point that cannot be finally decided for about
a year.   If the tannin is good, behold a new industry !   But any
land will grow docks—plant them once, and a dozen crops might
be taken in succession.   Will not this fact be apt to bring down
the price of tannin to a point at which it would barely pay to
extract ?

June 12.—Yesterday the land was still too wet to work on,
but the morning proved fine and breezy.   While attending the
funeral of an old friend, Mrs. Scudamore, the widow of the Rev.
W. E. Scudamore, the author of 'Notitia Eucharistica,' a most
learned man, and for many years the loved and respected rector
of this parish, I noticed two hawks hovering near the cemetery.
So clear and blue was the sky that, although they were soaring
high in heaven, I could almost see each feather of their wings.
I trust that they are going to build in the tower of the church
again, as they did for several years in succession, but for aught I
know this may be another pair.   Hawks do not last long in
Norfolk, as the gamekeepers wage a perpetual war against them.
To my mind they are the most beautiful of all birds, if the most
relentless.   Also they seem to be ubiquitous.   I never remember
travelling in any part of the world where I did not find a
hawk, or his big brother, the eagle.   In Iceland you see them,
splendid solemn fellows, sitting in silence on desolate crags, among
which the ravens croak incessantly ; in Egypt they sail from pylon
to pylon, and the Nile tourist pots them perched on the empty
granite shrine of Horus, of whom for thousands of years they were
worshipped as the incarnate symbol.   But I think that South
Africa is *par excellence* the land of hawks, where I fancy they
migrate from place to place in search of food.   At least I can
remember riding into a forest grove in the Transvaal where they
were gathered by the hundred, every tree being brown with them,
and it is impossible to suppose that one district could support so
many for more than a few days.

Mrs. Scudamore, who was buried yesterday, when she was

already a woman in middle life performed a feat which is worthy of record. Over a period of years she lay for hours at a time upon her back in a cradle slung to the roof of the chancel in Ditchingham Church, every inch of which she painted by hand. Already her labours are almost forgotten, although the result of them remains, and I am glad that she has found her last resting-place almost in the shadow of the fane she beautified.

To-day, Sunday, is very cold again, with a thermometer refusing to rise much above fifty. In the afternoon I walked to see how the young pheasants were getting on, and found that many of them have perished owing to the cold and wet, which Tommy, the keeper's son, tells me have made them liable to a fatal disease in the eyes. He says also that they have been greatly troubled by the hawks, of which he and his father have shot several. One, he informed me with pride, he killed himself while it was in the act of flying away with a young pheasant. Strangely enough, the shot passed through the hawk's head without injuring the chick in its talons, which is now running about with the rest of the brood.

One of the worst sides of game-preserving is that it renders the destruction of so much other life a necessity. For this many are apt to blame the keepers; but such critics should re-member that, like the rest of us, the gamekeeper is a man with his bread to earn, and that if he does not 'show his birds' in due season, he is very probably requested to earn it elsewhere. It is therefore in accordance with the rules of logic that he should be severe on hawks and every other living thing which he considers unfriendly to the well-being of pheasants, partridges, and hares. For my own part I think that he is a little indis-criminate, but wherever there is a doubt he prefers to be on the right side, and gives it in favour of the game. Thus, I do not believe that owls work any considerable harm to game, yet once when I advanced this view to a keeper in my employ, he gave me a striking instance to the contrary. He told me, and I always found him a very truthful man, that once he watched an owl settle on a coop in which was a hen with a brood of young pheasants, and beat the top of the coop with its wings, until the noise frightened the chicks that were nestling beneath their foster-mother's feathers, causing them to run out through the bars to seek shelter in the grass. This of course was the opportunity of that wise owl, and one of which he did not fail to avail himself. It was also the opportunity of the keeper.

Whilst walking past the pond in the farm lane my attention was attracted by a curious chirruping noise. On peeping down I saw a pretty and an interesting sight, for among the reeds and rushes a clutch of tiny moor-hens were swimming to and fro, little balls of black fluff with beaks red as the best sealing wax. Of the old birds I could see nothing ; doubtless at my approach they had run from the pond and hidden in the hay, leaving the young ones to take their chance.

It is curious that these waterfowl should build thus in a little lane-side pond, when within a quarter of a mile of them flows the river Waveney. Perhaps they prefer ponds to rivers because the former do not overflow the banks and perhaps flood their nests.

There is a great deal of water out on the common this evening, more than there was yesterday. With us the second day of the floods is generally worse than the first, as the water collected from thousands of ditches and drain-pipes along the whole length of the valley of the Waveney takes some time to come down.

June 14.—Yesterday was very cold, and to-day is still colder. The stove has been re-lighted to warm the house, and all are wrapped up in their thickest winter clothes. There is no gleam of sun, but day by day the north-easterly gale rages on us beneath an ashen sky. I wish that we all lived in Cyprus, that island of the blest. Of all the many places I have visited in the world, there are but two to which I wish to return—Iceland and Cyprus. Perhaps, however, I should add Egypt to the list.

For the last few days I have noticed that all the swallows, martins, and sand-martins are vanished away. This morning I found out where they go to, for in front of the Lodge, under the shelter of the Vineyard Hills, they were skimming to and fro by scores, waiting doubtless until the nor'-easter has blown itself out. Those of them which are breeding about this house put in an occasional appearance to see that their nests are safe, sit for a little while shivering on the railings, and then fly off again. Not the oldest man upon the place can recollect so cold a June, and certainly there has been nothing so consistently bitter and sunless within my own experience.

To-day we are cutting out beet on All Hallows field, No. 29, and Home Farm field, No. 22. The steam-saw also is still going merrily, while Robson, the jobbing carpenter, is 'making a preparation' to begin the shed over the unenclosed portion of the cow-yard. It seems a tremendous task for one man to undertake by himself, but once the materials are delivered for him, by the help of a rope and pulley and some stout iron bolts, with time he will do it all, and in such a fashion that, unless someone pulls it down, his work will be standing sixty years hence.

June 15.—The north-easterly gale is still blowing over a shivering world. As the ploughman Peachey says, it is more like after Michaelmas than four months before it, except that we rarely get it so cold between Michaelmas and Christmas as it is to-day. The actual temperature, however, does not go below forty-five in the daytime. I fear that all hopes of a good corn harvest must be abandoned, as the grain will not set well in such weather. According to present appearances, also, the roots will be small and backward.

To-day the sheep were dipped as a preventive of fly, for the bluebottle, to which most smells seem but as perfume, cannot bear the odour of the poisonous stuff wherein their fleeces are soaked. The process is rather curious : first the flock, as is usual on these great domestic occasions, are penned in the barn. Here two men seize the sheep one by one and plunge them legs upwards into a

V-shaped tub half full of unpleasant-looking fluid. Now, indeed, the long-suffering sheep thinks that the end of all things is at hand. Its legs kick convulsively, its anxious ugly head projects from the yellow flood, while in the subdued light of the barn its eyes turn green with fright as it utters a succession of gurgling groans and baas. Next, if it be a ewe, so soon as the liquid has got a good bite of the skin she is lifted from the tub and set free, the roller on the edge of it preventing her from hurting herself, however fiercely she may struggle. If, on the contrary, it is a lamb which has longer wool, it is laid upon the strainer, which, furnished with bars, is made of the cover of the bath and supported by a rest, where all superfluous fluid is squeezed from its fleece to run back into the tub. Then it is hoisted over the roller and departs into the field, looking exactly as though it had developed a violent attack of jaundice.

This afternoon, as I was working in my study, I noticed how great is the number of birds that haunt the lawn this year, perhaps because I have succeeded in persuading the domestic powers to dispense with some of their numerous retinue of cats. On the middle of the lawn is an old thrush busily engaged in feeding an apoplectic-looking member of its family, which hops after it in a most comical fashion, and takes down worms quite regardless of size or number. Indeed, the mother thrush is kept at it without pause. Again and again she sets her heels into the ground and pulls at a great worm, which slowly stretches out like an india-rubber band until it breaks in two or comes up bodily. But the old bird is never allowed to refresh itself with a delicate morsel, for its offspring comes behind and pecks at it until, with an angry little sound, it thrusts the juicy captive down its insatiable maw. These proceedings appear greatly to incite the indignation of the porch swallows, who have come up from below the hill to look after their nest. Perhaps, as they live on insects themselves, they do not like people who eat worms. At any rate, with loud twitterings they swoop again and again at the pair, missing their heads each time by not more than the eighth of an inch. These demonstrations, however, do not in the least disturb the old thrush, which goes on worming without even taking the trouble to look up.

Presently a squirrel arrives, and with an increased energy the swallows transfer their attentions to him, possibly under the impression that he is a cat or a weasel. The squirrel, not having the nerve of the thrush, bolts as hard as he can go, and takes refuge in a yew fence, where he vanishes. Next, a bullfinch comes and, perching on the stalk of a flowering weed that bends beneath his weight, picks off the buds one by one with the most astonishing rapidity, and, to all appearance, for sheer mischief. It is easy to see why gardeners dislike these birds so much. After the bullfinch appear a pair of water-wagtails, that for many years have nested near the garden door, and progress across the lawn with quick little runs, of which the objective is, I presume, a fly. On the gravel path two sparrows are fighting violently, and in the beech tree beyond a wood-pigeon coos till its mate comes sailing majestically through the air to settle at its side. But the list is almost endless, so here I will close the count.

To-day I heard that the clergyman in a parish where I have property has become involved in a controversy over the body of a parishioner. The case, as reported in the paper, is that my friend the clergyman refused to read the Burial Service over the deceased parishioner, on the ground that his conduct while in life had been notoriously immoral. Ultimately, I believe, this office was performed by a Nonconformist minister. I have no doubt, from what I know of the able and earnest clergyman in question, that according to the facts he was right in his decision. Yet the precedent seems dangerous. Supposing, however, that I am wrong on this point, ought not the deceased to have a fair trial? The ancient Egyptians, a people whose wisdom had mellowed through thousands of years of experience, formed an especially con-stituted court to try such cases. The dead man had his advocate, and Set, or the Devil, had his advocate, and, until the ordeal became a mere religious form, the thing was thrashed out before a competent jury. But here there are no advocates and no jury;

the clergyman apparently is both accuser and judge; for, even if he refers to his bishop, the statement of the case must necessarily be *ex parte*. Yet the verdict which he is empowered to give carries a very severe penalty—nothing less, indeed, than that a man's body should be refused Christian burial. Were that man still living, if such a verdict chanced to be given against him unjustly, one can imagine no injury that would entitle him to heavier damages. Yet this formidable power—for it is formidable, both in its spiritual aspects and in the effect that may be produced upon the minds and interests of survivors, to say nothing of the memory and repute of the deceased—is left in the hands of an individual, who might conceivably—though perhaps this rarely happens—be so prejudiced as to be incapable of forming a just and liberal opinion.

A century or so ago our forefathers condemned suicides to be buried at four cross-roads with a stake driven through their breasts, yet there must have been cases where such treatment was hard upon suicides. We have abandoned that practice, but apparently a single clergyman can still pass what—leaving out the stake and the cross-roads—is a similar sentence of excommunication from the company of the Christian dead.

Needless to say, I am not venturing to criticise the conduct of ministers who have the assurance of their convictions and put them into practice, for if a matter is left to their decision they must decide. Most people, however, would rather be rid of such a responsibility. Once I knew a clergyman who boldly excommunicated a parishioner, of whose conduct he disapproved, with bell, book, and candle, quite in the high old fashion. I admired his courage very much, but others, including his bishop, took a different view. Yet the case of the living man is better than that of the dead, for the one can bring an action and the other cannot.

It is pointed out in the newspaper that on January 21 the minimum temperature was 50·8°, and on June 14, 48·4°. What a commentary upon our climate.

June 17.—Yesterday, which was as cold as usual, we finished the steam-sawing. All the pile of rough timbers has been transformed into heaps of sawn stuff of every size and character. I think that there will be enough material for the framework of all the three sheds, in addition to the ash, oak posts, planks, rails, some gate stuff and waste for winter firing.

To-day the wind has veered to the sou'-west, and we have actually seen the sun, though not for long. The cutting of the layer on All Hallows field, No. 37, has begun. It is a thick lush crop, which looks as if it would weigh at least a ton and a quarter per acre on the stack, and perhaps more, but I should not think that the quality can be very good, owing to the lack of sunshine. The tall ripe grasses, over which the swallows skim, looked very beautiful rippling in the rare sunlight. It is the fashion to say that machinery is ugly, but that is not my own opinion. Certainly, while I stood in the hayfield and watched the cutter coming up the slope of the hill towards me, the two great horses putting out their strength as they breasted the rise, and the driver seated behind them alert, watchful, his hand on the lever and his eyes upon the knives, I did not think the sight ugly. Indeed, the picture struck me as fine ; although, perhaps, it owed something to its frame, for here, without being striking, the view has great charm. Beyond the crest of the rise the land slopes down gently to the meadow where the streamlet runs. Then it rises again, and the eye, travelling up the wide fields, rests upon the dark mass of Tindale Wood, and to the right is caught by the naked rafters of a ruined barn.

On my way back I stopped by the All Hallows pond to watch the familiar scene of a hen half crazy with the spectacle of the ducklings she had reared taking to the water. This caused me to reflect that it must be the fact of incubation which in these birds gives rise to the feeling of maternal love. Otherwise, why should a hen be so fond of little ducks whose aspect, as they arise out of the egg, must shock and terrify her, aware as she is that at no period of her own career did she ever look like that? Yet she knows them all by sight or by smell, and looks after them to the best of her ability, although, with the selfishness of the young, they decline to abandon a single habit in deference to her prejudices. I have heard a story of an unfortunate hen—I will not vouch for the truth of it—under whom some mischievous person placed a fine variety of eggs—a duck or two, some guinea-fowls, chickens, pheasants, and partridges. In due course they hatched out, but at the end of a week that hen was found dead, presumably of worry and nerve exhaustion.

On the road I met a pedlar, who produced for my inspection some nice Egyptian or Cyprian tear-bottles, one or two of them very iridescent. Also he had a finely proportioned small silver church paten stamped with a fleur-de-lis only, for it was made before hall-marks came in; I think that the date of it was 1581. From this pedlar I have from time to time purchased some of the best things in my small collection, notably a little bronze, which I believe to be one of the very few extant portraits of the great Egyptian queen, Taia. (I possess her golden ring, taken from her corpse.) On this bronze the crown is made of a perfect circle of *uraei*.

This afternoon, whilst walking on the Bath Hills, I noticed two pairs of swifts wheeling far above me, on wings so motionless that they might have been not living birds, but crescents of bright jet travelling the sky. I have often seen them here in bygone years, but have never yet been able to discover where they build. Generally, though not here, these birds rear their young in church towers. I suppose that these particular pairs nest at a distance, but visit this spot to hawk for the insects that haunt the slope. After all, a ten or twenty mile journey home would not be much to a swift.

The common beneath me looked unusually rich and lovely in the afternoon lights to-day, as they glowed upon the gorse, which is just bursting into yellow bloom, and on the red roofs of Bungay town beyond.

As I studied the scene, with the winding river and the rich pasture land dotted by scores of cattle and horses, it reminded me much of some that I have seen in Holland ; indeed, I think that in it an old Dutch artist would have found many opportunities.

June 19.—Yesterday the morning was fine and warm, but in the afternoon rain fell. We finished cutting the layer on All Hallows, No. 37, and began the trefoil on Baker's, No. 45. Also we drilled white turnips upon the strip left for them among the beet and swedes on Baker's, No. 44. Peachey has been at work all day with three horses, 'cultivating' a portion of the land on No. 24, where the mixed food has been fed off by the sheep, in order to drag out the twitch grass with which it has become infested. The implement employed is wooden-framed, and set with a number of curved prongs of steel that tear up the soil as they pass through it, drawing the grass and rubbish to the surface. To-day, to make the teeth sink deeper, it was weighted with an iron harrow laid atop. The land has been gone over three times, first transversely, then longitudinally, and again transversely, so I think that most of the grass must have been destroyed. As soon as it is a little dry it will be raked into heaps and burnt.

This afternoon, after attending church at Bedingham, Mr. Morgan, the vicar, kindly fetched the registers, and we looked through them. They begin in 1555, the year, I believe, of the Marian persecutions, and are kept in the usual form, baptisms, marriages and burials being entered in one book. I imagine that in those early days the usual practice was for the clergyman to make rough notes of these events in a commonplace book, which at any convenient time were entered up into the register by a travelling clerk, who wrote what was considered a good hand, and did such work for a fee—at least in several of the registers hereabouts I have observed what seems to be the same handwriting appearing contemporaneously. Most students of registers will have noticed that the entries of burials in early days seem to be much more numerous than those either of baptisms or marriages. Thus at Bedingham in the year 1558 it would appear that there was but one baptism, as against twelve burials—a comparative rate which must soon have extinguished the population. I suppose that the reason of this discrepancy is that whereas everybody in due course came to be buried, there being no other reasonable and decent way of disposing of a corpse, everybody did not come either to be baptised or married.

Here are a few extracts taken from these registers; quaint enough some of them. It will be observed that all of these are entries made during the incumbency of a single clergyman, Mr. Joseph Parsons, M.A., who was instituted in 1725.

Baptisms

'1737. John, son of George Smyth, Esq: of Topcroft Hall, the inhabitants thereof paying a pension annually of thirteen and fourpence to the vicar by ancient custom.

'1739. Elizabeth, baseborn daughter of Mary Fulcher, by oath laid to Will Smith Junr.

'1740. Cornelius, base son of Anne Hickleton, Tho : Smith of the Priory the supposed father.

'1743. George, son, base-born of Mary Fulcher. A sad one !' (Here it is evident that when called upon to make this second entry anent the peccant Mary Fulcher, the feelings of the worthy Mr. Parsons got the better of him. His note, 'A sad one !' refers, I imagine, not to the infant, but to Mary's character.)

Marriages

'1741. James Alderson, Sarah Tower both of this parish, single. did penance for ante-nuptial co-habitation.' [1]

Burials

'1742. Susannah Gowing, single woman aged 79. A miserable object, Thro' a fall in the Fire while an Infant, but always inoffensive, and always pitied.

[1] This is not the word used in the register, nor is the penance stated.

' 1742.   Richard Faired aged 78. poor but Chearful-Hearted and working to the last, extreme moderate in his desires but gratefull : now admitted we Hope to a Riches and Fulness, not prepared for the supine and lazy, the Ambitious and proud, unprofitable Spenders, or penurious Retainers of Superfluous wealth.' (What splendid but unimpeachable phrases!   Have we not all of us at some time been *unprofitable Spenders*, and are we not all acquainted with *penurious Retainers of Superfluous wealth ?*)

' 1747.   Charles Brown, a quiet, inoffensive, regular, and well disposed man, taken off sudenly, as we hope to peace, from evil which threatened.

' 1757.   John Lamb a Travailer drowned on The Holmes.' (Query. Does ' travailer' here mean a worker or a traveller ? And where were The Holmes ?)

' 1757.   Martha Chipperfield, reputed wife of Eras. Jerry.

' 1759.   Robert Plummer, Schoolmaster, a Steady Churchman and inoffensive neighbour, Indulgent to his Wife, well-affected towards his Minister; to the poor tender and Compassionate: To youth a painstaking Instructor, buried with regret.' (Note. This shows that a hundred and fifty years ago even such a small village as Bedingham had its schoolmaster.)

' 1765.   William Stone, eldest son of the late William Stone Esq, a hopeful youth.

' John Gunds for many years churchwarden, A friendly and peaceable Neighbour.'

The following notes appear at the end of the first register-book : ' There was collected in Beddingham in July 1659 towards the recovery of the Losse at Soulbay in suffering they sustained by fire the summe of three pounds and four shillings which was paid by appointment by James King, churchwarden to Mr. Walters, Chief Constable.'   (Soulbay, or Solebay, is an old name for Southwold in Suffolk, a town which gathered importance after Dunwich was destroyed by the sea.   It is still famous for its soles. The entry shows incidentally the terrible risks that were run from fire in towns built largely of wood, many of the houses of which were doubtless thatched. As I mentioned in my first chapter, Bungay was once entirely destroyed by such a fire, and from the above entry it seems that Southwold suffered in the same way.)

This is the next note : 'Collected in the parish of Bedingham August the 5th 1665 towards the relief of the poor of Great Yarmouth and of other parts of ye diocese being in affliction of a grievous plague, ye suṁe of one pound which accordingly was paid unto ye bishop.'

It will be noticed that the amount subscribed is the smallest recorded in any of these entries of collections. Perhaps the reason of this was that Bedingham itself suffered from the plague, though, if so, no record of it remains. Certainly it was at Bungay, for the pest-house stood upon the common, and it is said that the dead were buried in a pit-hole now sacred to a golf-green. I suppose that this entry was made by the Rev. William Copping, or Coping. Probably it was one of his last, since a monument in the church informs us that he died at the early age of twenty-seven, and '*hinc migravit ad aureolam coelestem* 4 *Junij* 1666.' Perhaps the plague took him off, as chanced to so many of the clergy in Norfolk. (*Vide* the researches of Dr. Jessopp on the Black Death.)

The next note, made, I suppose, by John Lathom, since Mr. Copping had been four months dead, is : 'Collected in ye parish of Bedingham October 10 (being ye fast for ye fire of London) towards ye relief of ye poor sufferers by ye fire ye suṁ of two pounds three shillings and fourpence paid to Mr. Augustus Cullien by order from ye Bishop.'

It would appear from this and the former entry that the collections for the plague and the fire of London were made throughout the diocese by the request or command of the bishop. This I hope to verify by searching other registers.

The next note which I shall quote is as follows—I suppose that it was made by John Brown, who was vicar in 1680, John Lathom having departed, whether to another parish or *ad aureolam coelestem* I know not : 'Collected in ye parish of Bedingham January ye 16th

1680 towards ye redemption of ye captives in Algiers ye sum of two pounds seven shillings.'

Here also is an entry which shows that the good folk of Bedingham lived long, although not quite so long as those in the neighbouring parish of Denton : ' In Bedingham there have been but 2 Vicars in the space of 94 years, William Cowper collated in 1680 died April 2. 1725 age 70 years held the living 45 years. Joseph Parsons collated in 1725 died July 1774 held the living 49 years.'

In the register-book of Denton, in Norfolk, where I have a small farm, Mr. Rogerson, rector of the parish, remarked that his predecessor was instituted into the living in 1595, and died in 1659. Mr. Rogerson was instituted in 1659, and died in 1715 : so that his predecessor was sixty-four years rector, and he himself fifty-six years ; two only in the space of 120 years !

This is a remarkable record, but I can almost match it by one that came within my own experience. The Rev. Mr. Edwards, the rector of Ashill, near Bradenham, who was a friend of my family for some generations, filled that cure, I think, for about seventy-five years. If I remember right, he told me that he had baptised, married and buried, nearly three generations of the inhabitants of Ashill. He was, I believe, within a month or two of a hundred years of age when he died, about fifteen years ago, from a chill contracted while recording his vote at a contested election.

Before leaving the subject of the Bedingham registers I must copy a last extract from them, a curious one enough to find in such a place. Here it is : 'John Francis, the Vicar of this parish underwent October 25th : 1780 an operation for the stone, when two, weighing an ounce and a half, were extracted by that very eminent surgeon, Mr. William Donne of Norwich, for which Mr. Francis paid him seventy [1] pounds. Mr. Francis is now perfectly recovered, for which great mercy he daily returns his most sincere and unfeigned thanks to the Divine Author of his Being, the Father, the Son and the Holy Ghost.

[1] It is possible that this word is ' twenty,' though it appears to read 'seventy.' Even in the former event the sum is large for the time.

'His affliction under this severe trial was greatly lessened through the affectionate tenderness and care of Elizabeth his well beloved wife, the generous kindeness which was shown him by his dear relations [here follows a long list of the names of relations and friends] to each of whom he esteems himself most highly indebted and begs them to accept his very sincere acknowledgments.' Aug. 7, 1781.

The largeness of the fee paid, which at the present value of money would represent a considerable sum, shows how serious was the operation which Mr. Francis underwent. That it could be carried out at all without the aid of anæsthetics seems little short of a marvel ; but he was not wrong when he said that his recovery was complete, as I find that he did not die till the year 1794. Doubtless the list of friends, to whom he returns thanks, between them contributed the money for the surgeon's fee. Under his name in the register-book one of his successors has written, ' He was a pious, good and learned man.' Few could wish for a better epitaph, even although it should chance to be seen by living eyes but once or twice in a century.

This evening I received a pleasing note from the manager of a very large estate in our neighbourhood. It was to the effect that a terrier dog with my name on the collar had been found in company with another terrier dog, owner unknown, doing its wicked best to tear the throat out of a ewe in the park. The wretched little animal, which up to the present had never killed anything larger than a harmless hen or a domesticated duck, has been lost for two days—now I know why. To-morrow he goes to town in charge of a friend, who, greatly daring, has offered to take him. If Dan tries to kill more sheep it shall be in St. James's and not in Flixton Park.

June 22.—On returning from London to-day I find that the clover-hay is still lying out on All Hallows field, No. 37. Just as preparations were being made to cart this morning down came the usual thunder-shower, so all the men had to go hoeing in Baker's root. The beet seem to have improved much owing to the warmer temperature of the last few days, but I think that the weather is still far from settled.

To-night there was a very beautiful evening sky, broken here and there by heavy heaps of cloud floating in a depth of the intensest blue. One of these resembled a huge mountain in size and shape, and on that side of it where struck the light of the sinking sun, thrown upwards in fan-like rays from behind another plumed and hearse-like bank of clouds, the appearance was as though this aërial peak were piled with snowdrifts in enormous masses, hanging high above each other like avalanches about to fall, and fringed, all of them, with many coloured fires. The air also was unusually quiet, so quiet that to the listener standing on the crest of the Vineyard Hills every sound from Bungay, such as those of the tolling bells, or of baying dogs, and even the song of quite distant birds, floated to his ear with extraordinary distinctness, while far away towards the horizon the thunder boomed from time to time like the deep notes of a Dead March swelling from some vast organ in the heavens to celebrate a demon's obsequies.

June 23.—To-day was bench-day, but there was no business except that of affiliation orders. In one of the cases the man, who had brought a young girl, a servant in his parents' house, into trouble, kept her from informing her mother of the facts by threatening—so she swore, and it was not contradicted—that if she did he 'would cut her throat.' After this sequel I wonder with what feelings that couple regard each other to-day. Some experience as a barrister in the Probate Court, and more of the cases which come before magistrates, makes me wonder at the hardihood of those who suggest that 'naturalism' of the French school should be attempted in English fiction. If the naturalism is to be real—and half the truth is but of little value—such matters as I have instanced, together with the details of mental disease and of moral obliquities, must be reported faithfully. Nature in these aspects should be set out as she is. This, at any rate among English-speaking peoples, is, I suppose, impossible at present; indeed, I think that I could furnish a few rural incidents, which some might be inclined to reject as beyond belief, that would cause even the intrepid author of 'La Terre' to hesitate. Yet they have been proved in court by satisfactory evidence, including that of the freely offered testimony of the individuals concerned.

Here is a terrible example of what may happen to people for want of a kicking-strap. Yesterday the ostler of the King's Head Hotel, a very worthy and careful man, attended with a brougham to drive a bride, the daughter of a farmer, to church. So soon as he had started with the bride and her parents, the horse, an animal hitherto supposed to be inoffensive, commenced kicking furiously. So high did it kick that it struck the driver on the *forehead*, cutting it to the bone and knocking him nearly senseless. He fell from the box and, catching his leg between the wheel and the body of the brougham, broke it in two places. Even then, however, he did not leave go of the reins, but clung to them so tenaciously that the horse was pulled over on to its side, the bride and her parents escaping unhurt, while the driver was removed to Ditchingham Hospital. It is hoped that he will recover; but at his age the case is serious. The mare is supposed to have been stung by a wasp or hornet; certainly, when I examined her to-day, I saw a lump upon her stomach that seemed to have been caused by a sting. Moral: Always use a kicking-strap.

June 25.—Yesterday was wretched, cold and dull, with occasional rain-storms and a strong sou'-west wind. To-day is even worse. In the morning a cloudy sky and wind, and in the afternoon came violent rains diversified by thunder and lightning. Before dinner-time the men were working in the hay on Baker's; but after it had all been aired by the tosser, and just as they were beginning to get it on to the cock, down fell the rain again, so that the only progress which this hay has made is towards decomposi·

tion. After dinner the men went to work cutting out the beet on Baker's, No. 44, a slow job indeed owing to the furious growth of weeds, which, even when hoed out, do not die in such weather as this, but very frequently root again in the furrows.

This morning I walked through some of the land that I let in allotments, as I wished to see what crops are most grown by the holders. I found that potatoes are chiefly in favour, while next to them comes beet. Wherever the plant of these has failed for a yard or so, or even less, the husbandmen sow a pinch of swede seed, which in due course they thin out to one or two roots as may be required. But little market-garden stuff is grown, as for this there is practically no market. So I have learned by experience, as the man in charge of the Lodge garden, which is one of the best in this neighbourhood, has been instructed to sell the produce that is not wanted. He tells me that with the exception of potatoes, which come on early in this sheltered spot, he can get no price for anything, asparagus not excepted. Clearly it would be cheaper to buy vegetables than to keep up a garden.

I went also to look at the seven young purchased home-breds, and two of my own in-calf red-poll heifers that are running on the dry marsh, No. 18. They are doing well, all of them, and the heifers, which are the progeny of two of my best cows, seem really beautiful animals. It is curious to notice the difference between these high-bred things and the seven steers. They also are red and polled; indeed I think that a bull from my herd was their father or grandfather, for I sold him as a young thing to the farmer who bred them; but their coats are many degrees lighter in colour, their limbs less fine, and generally they lack the unmistakable signs of breeding.

There is a thick crop of grass on the low marsh, No. 19, but it seems to be very wet at bottom, owing, doubtless, to the recent floods. Moreover, the docks are legion. Ever since I have had this marsh in hand it has been cut annually for hay, which makes it almost impossible for men to go on it in suitable—by which must be understood wet—weather to draw the docks. Also, up to the present we never seem to have had time to tackle this troublesome and laborious task. Being one of those things that *can* stand over, it is always left to stand over. At the best, to get these marshes quite clear of docks would, I fear, be practically impossible, for as fast as they are destroyed the flood water deposits a fresh supply of seed.

June 28.—Sunday the 26th was heavy and dull, with storms of rain in the morning, while yesterday was dreadfully cold, wet, and tempestuous. We finished cutting out the beet at Baker's as best we could, although it was difficult for the men to stand in the slop, and the showers fell so heavily that from time to time they were obliged to take shelter. The rest of the hands were engaged in carting the manure from Baker's and heaping it on the layer, No. 45, where it will stand till the time comes to spread it in autumn. It looks curious to see a compost heap among the mown hay, but we are anxious to empty the yard preparatory to the building of the shed that is to cover it in ; also there is little else for the labourers to do in such weather.

To-day is again very cold and damp, with a piercing northerly wind, but in the afternoon the sun shone intermittently till about five o'clock, when a dense blue haze, that looked like the approach of thunder-rain, spread itself over earth and sky, though no rain followed. All the men were at work in the hay, some of them engaged in turning and re-making cocks on No. 37, the All Hallows layer. It is high time that these were attended to, for the bottoms of them (which now become the tops), that have been lying all this while upon the wet ground, are beginning literally to stink. Everybody else who is available is down in Baker's field, No 45, trying to get the layer, which for a long while has been steadily and daily drenched, heaped into cocks. This is the process :

First the men go down the lines of stuff with forks, turning them and throwing to one side any particularly wet lumps ; then, after the hay has been thus treated and lain a while to dry, comes the horse-tosser, breaking up the wisps and airing them. Next follows the horse-rake, which rakes it into lines, the man seated on the machine from time to time freeing the roll of hay from the hollow of the rake by means of a lever at his side, which lifts all the prongs simultaneously, to be dropped again immediately the line is cleared. Lastly, so soon as it is dry enough, come other men with forks and build it into cocks of convenient size.

I notice that the wheat is beginning to come into bloom, for on what will be the sheath of each grain appear odd little worm shaped anthers or flowers, or what in our ignorance most of us believe to be flowers. Now it is that we require dry, warm, and quiet weather, for unless they have this while they are blooming the wheats do not often cast well. After our recent experiences, however, to hope for hot and sunny days seems Utopian.

June 29.—The improbable has happened ; to-day is fine and warm—our first taste of summer. We have been carting hay from the All Hallows layer as fast as we can, and I am glad to say that by night we had secured most of the cut. In the All Hallows beet, No. 29, Mrs. Fairhead, the wife of one of my horsemen, is engaged in singling the mangolds, that is, in drawing out all superfluous plants, leaving those that are to go on for crop at a distance of from a foot to eighteen inches apart. I think that this is about the only field labour in which women are now employed in our parts, unless it be occasionally as pickers of stones. I believe that fifty years ago they worked much more upon the land, and this seems to be borne out by old prints of agricultural occupations. Thus, in Stephens's 'Book of the Farm' four women and one man are represented as engaged in winnowing corn, the man acting as driver, and the women as riddlers and feeders. Again, in measuring up corn, four women appear as against one man, the man doing the measuring and the women all the hard work. Also, in a representation of the feeding of an old-fashioned thrashing machine, women workers are carrying sheaves from the mow to the mouth of the machine.

It is indeed a happy thing that females should no longer be

expected to undertake this heavy labour, for which they are un-suited by nature. It may be answered that women work in the fields in other parts of the world; among the African tribes, for instance, or, to come nearer home, in Normandy and Brittany. I have often seen the Zulu and Basuto women at their toil, which chiefly consists of hoeing, but I cannot say that it ever impressed me as being of a character likely to do them harm. Natives are very kind to their female folk and children, and for the most part would not overwork them. The horrors that we read of in the police-court reports, or, let us say, in the monthly journal of the Society for the Prevention of Cruelty to Children, are unknown, and would, indeed, be impossible, among those sections of the Bantu people with whom I have mixed. It is in Christian monogamous Britain that the enlightened and educated citizen beats the last breath out of his wife with a poker, or devises fiendish tortures for the bodies of his little children; the poor misguided black man shrinks from such things.

Perhaps the native women know that at the worst they have nothing more than a scolding to expect, or perhaps the pressure of competition has not yet overtaken them; at any rate, they always seemed to me to lighten their work with the pleasures of gossip, and, should any excuse arise, to be quite ready to postpone it for a while. How different it is in France, where one may see women, prematurely old and haggard, struggling up some hill bearing on their backs a great basket filled with filthy manure, or even playing the parts of animals to drag an implement through the soil. Let us be thankful that the day of such things has gone by in England.

I do not mean to imply, however, that even singling beet is child's play, for, until one gets used to it, I cannot imagine any more back-breaking task, especially in a hot sun. Still, it is a means of earning a few shillings, of which some of the older school of labourers' wives, whose children are off their hands—for the young women will do nothing—are glad to avail themselves; moreover, it is healthful, and does them no physical harm.

There is a belief here that mangold will not bear, or at the least will never thrive after, transplanting. To satisfy myself about the matter I collected some good plants that had been singled out by Mrs. Fairhead without injury to their roots, and with my spud dibbled them into a blank space on a baulk near the gate where the sparrows have destroyed the seedlings. As the land is wet they will have a good chance, and I shall be able to watch what happens to them.

The barley is now in full ear, but it is still rather yellow in colour.

June 30.—To-day has been dull and showery, with a thick close air in the afternoon. As the hay cannot be stirred in such weather, the men have been employed hoeing and on other jobs about the farm. Fairhead has been at work cutting the new pasture, No. 5, which was laid down with last year's crop of barley. Notwithstanding the drought of 1897, the seeds took well, making an excellent bottom, which, I think, has been somewhat improved by running the ewes on it for a little while before it was shut down for hay. The crop of grass is heavy, with a great deal of clover in it, but much 'laid' by the winds and rains. This makes it necessary to exercise great care in the cutting, as the machine can only be driven against the grain of the grass, that is, in the contrary direction to which it is laid ; otherwise, it merely shears off the tops of the stuff, leaving the bulk of it upon the ground. To cut a field thus means that the mower cannot be worked for more than half the round, as the knife must be lifted and put out of gear for all that part of the journey when the horses are walking in the direction in which the grass is laid. Mowing with a machine is very simple work if the crop stands stiff and upright, for then it is only necessary to drive the horses round and round in an ever lessening circle until all is down. But if, as is frequently the case, the grass is flattened by wind and rain, it requires thought and skill to cut it to the best advantage.

At Bedingham this afternoon I found the wheats in full bloom and looking very tall and strong. Of the barley, that on No. 5 seems by far the best; indeed, by comparison with it the other two fields are yellow and stunted, owing to the long-continued cold and wet. No. 5, it may be remembered, was the piece first sown, having been drilled on February 1, a very early date for this heavy land. Hood was somewhat opposed to this rash venture, but I was in favour of it, as all the best authorities seem to agree that if only the land is in proper order, the earlier barley is got in, the better the chance of a good cast and sample. It must be borne in mind, however, that this field has received a dressing of crushed-bone manure, whereas the other two have had none, to which, and not to the early drilling, its superior appearance may be due.

The kohl-rabi and the beet look fairly well, though both these crops require dry weather and sun. The swedes, on the other hand, which share the newly drained field, No. 18, with the kohl-rabi, are a total failure, for that dreadful insect, 'fly,' has taken them off so completely that to-day we have re-drilled the land with white turnip. The fly, I hear, has been very destructive this season in the neighbourhood of Bedingham; but, oddly enough, at Ditchingham we have been little troubled with it—indeed, I never remember a better plant of swedes upon this land. I hope also that we are fairly safe from its ravages, as the belief here is that it does not do much harm after the longest day, which is now a week behind us.

The red-poll ox that I think of showing has improved considerably, especially in the hind quarters; but the iron-roofed shed under which he lives is hot, notwithstanding the hedgeside rubbish that has been thrown on to the roof to break the force of the sun, and cattle never make good progress when they are heated and teased by flies. To remedy this I have told Moore to get the carpenter to cut out two or three feet of boarding at the back of the shed, and to make a sliding shutter to close over the opening when needful.

I never knew a place so fertile in wild orchids as is Websdill Wood. To-day I found quantities of a new variety, *Orchis maculata*, which have appeared now that the *Orchis latifolia* has done its blooming. These *maculatas*, which have spotted leaves, although not so richly coloured as the *latifolia*, are still very beautiful and attractive flowers. The wood seems to be full of nesting partridges. In walking about it to pick the orchids I put a sitting bird off her nest, wherein lay thirteen lovely eggs. Also I started two other couples of birds, which, by their curious behaviour, showed me that their young were hidden somewhere in the grass. They flew a few yards, then settled again, and ran about in an agitated fashion, apparently with the design of persuading me to try to catch them and leave the neighbourhood of their chicks, of which, search as I would, I could see no trace. As I walked away I heard the corn-crake calling loudly in the fields about the wood, and looked for it, but it is very difficult to fix the exact spot from which the sound comes ; indeed I have never yet succeeded in the attempt. The corncrake is a skilled ventriloquist.

JULY

July 1.—Half the year has now gone by. So far it has been a somewhat curious season, that is when considered from the farming point of view. It opened with mild and beautiful weather, followed by a cold stormy spring and a wet and bitter early summer, with a general prevalence of northerly and north-easterly winds. The strange thing is, under the circumstances, that the crops should look so well as they do. Hay, which does not require much warmth, is everywhere a heavy 'cut,' though doubtless more sun would have improved the quality. Wheats are tall and strong, but it remains to be seen how they will fill. Barleys look only moderate, but with fine warm weather may yet be a good sample. Oats seem rather short in the straw, and I doubt whether they will give anything like the return expected from this crop if it is to pay, namely, almost double the yield per acre that can be credited to wheat. Beet are about a three-quarter plant, but backward ; they are sun lovers, and we have had no sun. Swedes are a very full plant in this village. Beans stand tall in the·stalk, but the cold seems to have prevented them from podding satisfactorily, so that I fear they will give but a light yield per acre ; indeed, contrary to general experience, spring beans appear to be better than autumn sown. Pease, on the other hand, look well with us. All nature is now crying aloud for warmth and sunshine, and upon the character of the weather during the coming month to a very large extent will depend the amount and quality of the year's increase. Wretched as it has been so far, I prefer it (speaking as a farmer) to the scorching suns and rainless days of recent summer seasons.

To-day is dull and rather cold, but as the rain has held off we are carting hay. That from the All Hallows layer, No. 37, having been in cock, has taken no great harm, but the stuff from Baker's, No. 45, is much damaged, and will, I think, need to pass through the chaffing machine before it comes to the manger. We are still cutting on No. 5 with the machine, but owing to the grass being so laid and twisted it is a tedious and difficult business. This morning Robson, Hood, and I had a great confabulation as to the roofing in of the cattle-yard at Baker's. The span is very wide, namely, twenty-eight feet, and we came to the conclusion that two rows of oak posts will be necessary for the support of the roof. Galvanised iron is not heavy in itself, but the strain comes in winter, when it may chance to be covered with six or eight inches of snow, weighing, I suppose, a good many tons. This shed will remain my property, since I am putting it up as a tenant's fixture, and at the end of my tenancy it must either be taken over at a valuation by the landlord or sold for what the materials will fetch.

July 6.—On the night of the 1st we had torrents of rain, which stopped the haymaking and set all hands carting and hoeing. Truly this year Candlemas has been as good as its word.

On Sunday I went to afternoon service at Woodton, which is quite close to Bedingham, the two churches being not more than a thousand yards apart as the crow flies. Indeed, Bedingham seems to have been the 'mother' church of Woodton, and it is several times mentioned in the registers that certain leading inhabitants of the latter place and of Topcroft received the Sacraments there. I believe also that in old days two chapels existed in Bedingham church dedicated to Woodton and to Topcroft, by which I understand that they were set apart for the use of the dwellers in those villages. Woodton church is a small but very curious and ancient building, standing quite away from the village, but near to the site of the Hall, which was pulled down, so says tradition, by an owner who lived some miles away, and who feared that after his death his wife would return to live at Woodton, the old home which she preferred. At least it is gone, and there remain of it now but the well, part of the stables, used as a keeper's cottage, the crumbling walls of the ancient garden, and a tangled woodland still known as the Lady's Walk. Alas, poor Lady, you cannot be more forgotten and dilapidated than is your earthly home to-day!

The tower of the church (I speak entirely from local information and without guarantee, being myself ignorant on the point) is what is called a 'Thane's tower,' that is a tower such as, according to tradition, Thanes alone were allowed to build. The peculiarity of Thanes' towers seems to be that, like this at Woodton, they have four little windows in them looking to the cardinal points of the compass. Possibly the Thanes sat behind them and watched for their enemies, or possibly they were put to some other purpose; at any rate, after the Thanes and their *régime* were done with, the Normans finished the tower in a different style of flint work. The font, which is square in shape, with carved panels and supported on moulded pillars, is pure Norman. For more than two hundred years it was supposed to be quite plain stonework, till, in a happy hour, Miss Long, the daughter of the present rector, chanced to examine it, and found that it had been bricked or plastered up, doubtless to avoid the destructive zeal of the infamous William Dowsing or one of his associates.

Dowsing was appointed 'visitor' to the Suffolk churches by the Earl of Manchester in 1643, and raged through them terribly, destroying whatever beautiful thing could be found, whether it were carving, or statuary, or pictured glass, or paintings, upon the plea that they were popish and superstitious. Indeed, this pious wrecker and ruffian kept a journal of his performances, which is sorry reading for us to-day; but still more sorry is it to see where his hammer has been at work, as, for instance, on the lovely fane of Blythborough, in Suffolk. From church to church this Vandal rushed, wrecking as he went; it is recorded, indeed, that he ruined eleven of them in one day. Whether he himself came into Norfolk I am not certain, but if he did not his fellows and subordinates did, for here at Ditchingham they have broken off the heads of the sculptured saints at the foot of the tower and defaced the sacred emblems of the Bleeding Heart surrounded by a crown of thorns. Little wonder that the poor clergymen of that generation took fright, and in some instances, if time was given them, plastered up the fonts and hid such of their treasures as were portable. For the most part, when they were able to do this, the carved work escaped, as the iconoclasts were in too great a hurry and had too much congenial sacrilege on hand to search for anything that was not plainly visible.

In Woodton church there still exists a great part of the staircase which led to the niche whence, in pre-Reformation days, the Host was elevated in the presence of the congregation. The place can yet be seen also where the rood beam was built into the wall, and the local tradition is that the rector was in the habit of preaching from the centre of that beam. This legend I decline to believe, since, having with some difficulty scrambled up the little stairway and inspected the site, I am convinced that no elderly clergyman could have crawled along a ten-inch baulk and spoken from the centre of it, standing at a considerable elevation above the floor of the church. Had he attempted it, vacancies in the cure of souls at Woodton would have been frequent; indeed, I doubt whether any preacher accustomed to emphasise his points with appropriate action would have survived a month.

On the exterior of several of the windows of this church are little sculptures of an exceptionally refined and charming character representing the coiffed heads of nuns or queens. In the chancel also is a very beautiful and quite perfect monument of alabaster, for, having been wisely placed high up in the wall, it is out of reach of easy ravage by boys and Puritans. This statue is erected to the memory of Anne, wife of Robert Suckling, daughter of Sir Thomas Wodehouse of Kimberly and Dame Blanche, daughter of the Lord Carey, Baron of Hunsdon (query, Hunstanton).[1] The face of the

---

[1] A correspondent writing from Florida, U.S.A., informs me that this conjecture is inaccurate. It seems that Sir Henry Cary, K.G., was created

kneeling figure is turned towards the east, and, because of its position in the deep niche, I doubt if anyone has seen it quite clearly since it was placed there generations ago, unless it be those who from time to time have had the curiosity to examine it by aid of a ladder.

A few pages back I stated my belief that the registers in this neighbourhood were written up at the beginning by a clerk who travelled from church to church. Here, at Woodton, oddly enough, I have discovered his name, for he has scribbled it in unmistakable writing upon the fly-leaf of the first register. It was Spendlove ; probably the brother or son of a rector of Woodton of that name.

After the year 1730 printed forms of register-books began to be issued, in which, as they do to-day, the brides and bridegrooms signed their names, or, rather, made their marks, for not one in a score of them could write. In that day they very seldom used the ✕ which is now the common token of illiterates. Such marks as these, ⌐ , or ⌂, were the favourite signs, especially among the women. It is pathetic to look at the long succession of these little marks, made every one of them with a trembling hand, and to reflect that they are all that remain, absolutely the only record, of those forgotten brides who generations since bent one by one over this shabby, faded book. They have departed so completely that even those in whose bodies their blood runs do not so much as know that they existed, and these wavering signs, which no one ever sees, made by them in the supreme moment of their lives, are all that is left to show that once they breathed this very air, walked these fields, and passed beneath this ancient porch to baptism, to bridal, and to burial.

I never heard of labouring people, or even of the farmer class, taking the trouble to consult a register ; but were they to do so, most of them could establish their pedigrees, at any rate for the

in 1559 Baron Hunsdon of Hunsdon, co. Hertfordshire, and that this Dame Blanche was daughter to Sir John Carey, third Baron Hunsdon, whose second husband was Sir Thomas Wodehouse, who died 1658.

last three hundred and fifty years, with much more certainty than many of their betters. It is probable, however, village morality being what it is, that in the majority of cases a descent during such a period of time would not always have been such as is recognised by law. It would include a proportion of bars sinister.

Here are a couple of curious epitaphs from Woodton church :— On a stone, under the symbol of a skull and cross-bones and an hour-glass with wings rising from it, is cut :

> My breath is stopt,
> My glass is run,
> My life is cropt,
> And I have done.

The second is from a brass :

> In Wootton porch among these stones
> I craved leave to lay my bones
> Erasmus Stanhow inter^d is heere
> The 1 October the 78 year.

This is confirmed by the registers, which state that ' Erasmus Stanhaw of St. Margarite in Suffolk was buried heere Oct ye 1st 1678.'

In the register-box was a torn piece of paper which proved to be an interesting memento of the time when, in order to give encouragement to the wool trade, every corpse must by law be wrapped in a woollen shroud. Here is a copy of it :

'Elizabeth Wirr made oath 19th Jan. 1756 that the Body of Anne Squire Deceased and Buried in the Church of Wotton, was not wrapt, or Bound up with any material, But Sheeps wool only and that the Coffin was not lined or Faced with any thing but Sheeps Wool only.

'Sworn before me Francis Johnson Vicar of Brook.

'In Presence of   ANNE CHURCH
            MARY LINCOLN '

I forgot to say that the hall at Woodton which was pulled down is reported to have been practically a replica of that in this parish, having been built by the same architect. I do not refer to the old Ditchingham Hall, where lived the early Bedingfelds and, I suppose, the Bozards before them, but to the new house built about one hundred and eighty years ago.

To me it is a perfect mystery whence came all the wealth that enabled so many families which had never been remarkable for riches to build or re-build large houses in and about the Georgian era. In this district alone there exist a number of them which, even when labour and materials were cheaper than they are to-day, must still have cost great sums, to say nothing of the considerable income required to keep them up. In times when so many horses were necessary and so much wine and other liquor was consumed housekeeping cannot have been cheap in a large establishment, whatever may have been the price of meat and milk.

Yesterday we were carting hay from the new pasture, No. 5 ; it is an excellent crop and of good quality ; but to-day the weather is so threatening that we are afraid to open the cocks. We have finished cutting the three-acre, No. 11. This was the first pasture that I laid down, the land being about the worst I have on the farm. So lately as last year, indeed, doubts were expressed as to whether the grasses would stand, and therefore I am the more delighted to see it throw up so splendid a crop of hay. The grass is so thick and fine that the machine can scarcely toss it, as the hay winds up 'like a cart-rope,' or rather like the bonds that are used in thatching stacks. All of this I attribute to the sheep, which were penned here at the beginning of the year. Indeed, their beneficent effect upon the pasture is proved by one little circumstance. I think that on an earlier page I mentioned that for some cause, which I forget, a certain corner of this field was left unfolded. Also, it happened that in one small fold the sheep lay for two full nights. I have remembered these spots and watched the results. They are that on the double fold the crop is even heavier than elsewhere, whereas in the corner which was unmanured, except by the lambs which ran over it, its proportionate bulk is less by quite a half than that of the rest of the field. The same thing is observable on the little piece of old pasture next to the three-acre. Here the sheep were penned for one night and then taken away because a dog from Bungay came and harried the lambs. On the spot where they lay that one night there is certainly half as much grass again as elsewhere, and this although the meadow was heavily fed last year. Certainly my belief in the value of sheeping pastures, and especially those of them which are young and only half established, seems so far to be justified by the results. That of sheep, however, is, I believe, among the hottest of manures, and if applied in quantity to light land often causes it to burn, that is to scald and turn brown in hot weather. With clay lands such as those under discussion it is a different matter.

We have also been cutting the new pasture, No. 10, which was, I think, the third piece that I laid down. This has not been sheeped, so the crop is nothing like that on No. 11, although on the whole a good one. By much the heaviest cut is down a breadth of it opposite the first gate, and this again is to be accounted for by the action of manure, for true indeed is the old farming saying, ' Muck is the mother of money.' Of course all the field has been heavily fed by cows, but cows do not improve land in anything like the same ratio as sheep, or cake-fed stock, or, I believe, even horses, for the reason that the goodness of what they eat goes for the most part into their milk. Lying as it does near to the cattle-sheds, it has been our custom, whenever the trimmings from the roots accumulate inconveniently, to cart them into this field and scatter them there. As, however, it takes a great many root trimmings to fill even one cart, of course all the field does not get the benefit of the dose, and thus it happens that the hay is so much thicker on the belt which has thus been dressed.

During the last day or two Peachey has been ploughing and harrowing that portion of the vetch field, No. 21, which has been fed off by the sheep. Our original idea was to green-soil (that is feed off a growing crop upon) the whole of this little field, and afterwards to plant it with Indian corn, as we did with great success in the case of some other land last year. Owing to the heaviness of the vetch crop, however, this has proved impracticable, so we are leaving more than half of it to stand for seed, which always comes in useful and saves the expense of buying. Notwithstanding the wet, that part which has been fed is extraordinarily hard, and even after being harrowed and rolled is quite unfit to be sown until a good rain falls. No other stock tread land so close as sheep, especially in wet weather, as their sharp little feet press and re-press every inch of it a score of times, till it becomes of the consistency of a green brick, or that variety of building material, now rarely used, which we know in this county as clay lump.

All the ewes have now gone to Bedingham to run in Websdill Wood until the remaining lambs are thoroughly weaned. In a fortnight's time or so the Southdown ewes will return from Bedingham, when they and the lambs will be fatted together for the butcher, a fate which the blackface ewes escape, as we are holding them for breeding another year.

At Bedingham this afternoon I found them carting hay from the two-and-a-half-acre new pasture, No. 10, which was laid down last year. It is a very good crop. No. 19, by the wood, has also been cut—a capital crop. The farming reader may remember that this was the first field laid down at Bedingham, that in which the deep-rooted seeds were sown according to Mr. Elliott's receipt, and it is for this reason that I watch it with peculiar interest. Up to the present the plan has certainly answered admirably, and, so far as I can judge, the field, which, beyond feeding and a partial dressing of mud, has received no manure, looks like making a really sound pasture on land out of which I was told that pasture could not be created. The herbs, and especially the chicory, it is true, throw up stout and somewhat unsightly stalks, which even now are rather tough to cut ; but these, while young, are perfectly edible, and make no great show in the withering hay.

Here at Bedingham the haysel is conducted in the old fashion, for we have no cutting machine and no horse-tosser. This is the routine. The men, three of them, mow till breakfast-time, or perhaps till dinner, then, if the weather is fine, they turn the hay cut two days or so before, and, if necessary, cock it, in the afternoon carting such of the stuff as may be ready. It is a somewhat slow process, but while the 'make' is good it answers well enough. There is no doubt, however, that even in a small holding farmers who possess modern machines have a great advantage over their poorer neighbours. Without them the time of the entire force on the farm is occupied with the hay and other absolutely necessary tasks, such as the feeding of the stock. With them a man can generally be spared to attend to other matters which, at this time of the year, are apt to press ; for instance, horse-hoeing, cutting out, or singling in the root fields, where, as always, the weeds grow apace.

I find that there are disadvantages in planting kohl-rabi near a wood, as it appears to be a plant for which pigeons show a very particular affection ; at any rate, they have devoured a great number of the leaves. It is said that 'mawkins,' or scarecrows, have no terrors for these bold bad birds, and as labourers for the most part have neither the skill nor the time to go a-shooting, the 'dows' work their will unmolested.

This evening I was a witness of a singular and expensive exhibition of temper on the part of a young pony which I have bred, the progeny of, I think, a little Russian mare and a high-stepping hackney cob. This animal has been broken, and for a few weeks driven regularly, though I fear not far enough. To-night the groom put it in the cart with the assistance of another man, but instead of starting as usual, the pony reared up four or five times straight on end ; so high, indeed, that I feared he would fall backwards. Finding that he could do nothing in this fashion, after a peculiarly perpendicular rear the wicked little beast, whilst still in the air, deliberately doubled his front legs under him and hurled himself down on to the ground, which he did not even touch with his fore feet. One of the men was bundled out of the cart, two considerable holes were made in the roadway, and the pony rose minus a vestige of hair on his knees. These are, moreover, considerably cut, thus taking, in all proba- bility, eight or ten pounds off his value, unless indeed he heals up better than can be expected. It is a vexatious business, but I am thankful that only the animal was hurt, and not the men. The moral is that no young horse should be driven without knee-caps, which, of course, on this unlucky occasion had been forgotten.

July 8.—Yesterday we were able to make good progress with the hay-carting, as the weather, though threatening, held out. There was a fine stormy sunset, and, viewed from the high land on the pit field, No. 23, the landscape looking towards Beccles was singularly impressive. So dense and dark was the thunder-cloud which hung above it that in its shadow the trees beneath looked massive and almost black, their aspect, at once gloomy and mysteri- ous, reminding me of sylvan scenes portrayed by Mr. Peppercorn in his impressive pictures. In a hedgerow in the middle distance also appeared a line of elder bushes, just now covered with masses of white bloom, and the effect of the light falling on these from beneath the edge of the cloud was most vivid and striking.

To-day I went up the ladder to examine the condition of the hayrick we are building in the Buildings stack-yard. Some of the stuff which we have carted on to it from No. 11 was decidedly 'dumpy,' that is, damp and heavy on the fork, a condition that arises from insufficient making. Indeed, the hay on this piece is so thick and fine that with the somewhat sunless weather which we have experienced it is difficult to get it dry. I expected to find the stack hot, and I was not disappointed, for under the tilt the steam was rising steadily, while the surface of the hay looked as though boiling water had been poured upon it. Indeed, when I thrust my arm into the stuff as far as it would go, the tem- perature was more than I could bear with comfort. Now it is a good thing, and even necessary, that hay should heat to a certain extent, for otherwise it would lack 'nose' and flavour, but once that limit is passed the results are apt to be serious; indeed, ricks thus overheated have been known to take fire by spontaneous combustion. For this particular stack Hood bethought him of an ingenious remedy. Sending down to No. 45 on Baker's, whence the trefoil hay had been carried, for a load of dry rakings, he built these into the rick, and then carried more meadow hay on to the top of them. The rakings, being so dry and difficult to compress, make it easy for the heat to escape and the cool air to enter into the body of the stack; in fact they introduce a ventilating course, the action of which will be assisted by the bitter north-east wind that is blowing to-day. Though I have never seen it made use of, I believe that straw is sometimes employed for this purpose of hay-rick ventilation.

I see in the *Times* to-day that the Committee which was appointed two years ago to consider the question of Old Age Pensions have made their report, which practically may be summed up in two words, *non possumus*. This, however, is not wonderful, as it seems that the terms of the reference precluded the Committee from using any scheme based on compulsion, and it is fairly evident to anyone who has considered the question that, to be generally effective and useful, an old age pension scheme *must* be based on compulsion. To exclude compulsion, therefore, from the possible methods under the consideration of the Committee was almost to ensure a negative result, and to doom that industrious body to plough the sand for two long years.

My own humble and private views upon the question of Old Age Pensions, which, if impracticable at present, are at least sincere, I have set out in the beginning of this book, so I need not allude to them again. What strikes me as strange, however, is that at the last General Election a great number of Unionist candidates preached this gospel with no uncertain voice, some because they believed in it, and some perhaps because they thought that it would pay. I remember that I did for one, and for the first reason. Indeed, the practice has continued up to the present time, for, unless I am mistaken, Old Age Pensions were mentioned on the Unionist placards in the South Norfolk election two months ago, and also in the candidate's address. Now, the candidates who made use of this war-cry were not, I think, informed that the heads of the party were out of sympathy with the movement, or, if in sympathy, believed it to be impossible. Had they received a hint to this effect, most of them would have dropped Old Age Pensions like a hot coal, while those who, with myself, are firm believers in the potential benefits of compulsory insurance, would have been careful to explain that we advocated it as an individual fad. As it is, if the matter is to stop here—and in the face of the Report of the Committee I suppose that it cannot go on—many a Unionist member will look a little foolish when the time for the next election comes. Indeed, I think it not unlikely that in the country districts seats will be lost over this question.[1]

In to-day's paper also is the report of the debate in the House of Lords on the second reading of the Benefices Bill, which most Churchmen hope may become law. But some Churchmen, of whom I am one, think that it does not go half far enough, since it is very difficult to see any moral difference between the sale of a next presentation and the sale of an advowson ; that is, of a right to perpetual presentation whenever a vacancy may arise.[2] I fear,

---

[1] Since the above passage was written a second Committee has been appointed. Will it result in anything? I doubt it. Except upon a basis of compulsory insurance, a problem with which no Government will attempt to deal at present, I believe the whole question of Old Age Pensions to be beyond the reach of practical politics.

[2] I ask respectfully whether advertisements such as I reprint below tend to advance the reputation of the Church of England? They refer to these counties, and are cut at hazard from recent issues of the *Times*, names only being omitted.

' MISCELLANEOUS

' Advowson, Suffolk, for sale, within four miles of —— town and railway station, branch of G.E.R. Commuted tithe, 883*l.* Twenty-nine acres of glebe. Present net income, 543*l.* Good rectory house and grounds, charmingly situated, with capital shooting and golf links in the neighbourhood. Incumbent

however, that there are many people who would differ violently from the opinions of Church of England progressives like myself, although often enough these are founded on long and careful observation of the working of the present system in country parishes and elsewhere. For my part, I think that the chief immediate need of the Church—and not less in villages than in towns—is discipline and uniformity of view and ritual, ends that can be obtained by putting greater power into the hands of the bishops, and still more by the readmission of the laity to what, as I believe, was their ancient right, some real and effective share in its government. At present they have none, for lay representatives are naught, and churchwardens but pew-openers writ large. It seems strange, for instance, that in a single parish, and under the authority of the same rector, services of a very different tone and character should be carried on in separate churches. And yet this happens. Surely the service and the ritual should not be left to the individual discretion of the clergyman ; surely they should be settled by the bishop, or by a council of bishops, which might act with the assistance and support of a council of the laity. Otherwise all is confusion, religion is brought into contempt, and, as I have amply experienced as a churchwarden, trouble and bitterness ensue.

A man may be a moderate High Churchman and not object to choral services and vestments, or even to incense which is symbolical, yet it may be anathema to that same man to see a clergyman kissing a book, or some portion of his elaborate attire. Another may overlook the kissing but will take grave offence at the prostrations of priests or attendants before the altar, or to being sprinkled with water, or to the leading of girls and young married women into the confessional. And so forth.

In religious as in other matters, *quot homines tot sententiæ*, but

in 68th year. Population (census 1891), 598. Voluntary Church School. For further particulars apply to ——

'Advowson, Suffolk. Life over 80. Gross 500*l*., net 300*l*. Pop. 500. Rail, $\frac{3}{4}$ mile. Beautiful rectory and grounds. For sale, half down, half on vacancy, without interest. " Safeguard against Simony," 2nd Edit., 13 stamps. ——, M.A., Cambridge.'

all these various opinions, when put in practice, do not, so far as my observation has gone—and recently we have had object-lessons in these counties—enhance the position or cement the unity of the Church—indeed, they furnish arguments to its critics and opportunity to its rivals. Imagine, for instance, the comments of the College of Cardinals upon reading a report of the police court proceedings against Mr. Kensit ! But while our present system prevails, while clergymen can defy their bishops, or bishops will not control their clergymen, while cures of souls are advertised and bought, while an incumbency is a material freehold as well as a spiritual charge, these questions must continue to arise, and Churchmen must continue to see, as a matter of property and not of fitness, men occupying positions for which they are not suited, with an almost absolute right to hold them until death. Also the spirit of mutiny will spread and deepen.

In the future, although it may be distant, I believe that all this will be changed ; priests will not be pitchforked into livings by the arbitrary decision of the owners of advowsons, which in practice often means by their own decision, but will be selected by proper authorities, in consultation may be with the representatives of the parishioners, for their qualities and nothing else. Also, perhaps, the revenues of the Church will be paid into a general fund and portioned out according to its local needs, to be supplemented, if needful, by the contributions of the laity.

I think that I know the other side of the question, as I have myself, for what at the time I considered to be good reasons, purchased a next presentation, and in due course presented to the living. But my view, right or wrong, is that the whole system is bad, and should be changed. I know the common answer is that if this were done the ' best class of men ' would not enter the Church. Some hold, on the other hand, that they would not be of the best class who were kept out thus—but rather, for the most part, men who seek the greatest possible pay in return for the least possible labour, and whose desire it is, by purchase or interest, to lay up for themselves treasure of those snug and easy livings which, in a more ideally managed institution, would be reserved as the resting-places of its aged and work-worn servants. Sundry sine-cures and abuses have vanished during the last few generations, yet the Church still finds faithful ministers, and many believe that the more she is purified the greater will be the opportunity of her true votaries—of those who serve her first for herself and afterwards for their own advantage. Amongst plentiful examples, the exist-ence of such noble and self-denying corporations as the Universi-ties Mission to Central Africa, whose devoted members, I am told, in most instances receive nothing but food, lodging and an allow-ance for clothes, proves that such men exist, and will come forward when the call for them arises. But the labourer is not grudged his hire—in the vast majority of cases I, for one, should like to see that hire considerably augmented—and doubtless these are counsels of perfection. Yet is it not towards such counsels, by many a thorny avenue of doubt, failure, and derision, that the spiritual nature of man, as expressed in faith and works, should and does make good its slow advance?

Of one thing I am almost certain—if the Church does not or cannot reform itself, ere long the laity will lose patience and take the matter into their own hands. Then perchance may come not reform but revolution.

July 9.—To-day is exceptionally cold and dull, with the usual strong north-east wind, and a temperature this evening on a south wall of about 50°. Even in this climate it strikes one as a little strange on the 9th of July to see people driving about the roads wrapped up in thick shawls and ulsters. I said some days ago that the farming position was becoming critical, and now for 'becoming' we must read 'become.' Suitable weather may yet save the situation, but if so it must be met with soon, as, if we do not have sunshine within a week, the corns will, I think, be poor.

July 12.—After Sunday the 10th, which was cold and dull with a nor'-east wind, the weather seems to have taken a turn,

as, notwithstanding the nipping breeze, yesterday was fine and sun-
shiny, an ideal haymaking day. We have carted the remainder
of the hay on Nos. 10 and 11, and cut a little more of the back
lawn, No. 7. I noticed that the stacks at All Hallows and at
Baker's are leaning a good deal ; indeed they have been supported
with props. Their bent seems to be towards the direction of the
prevailing winds—that is, to the north and east. This I cannot
understand, as they ought to lean the other way. The theory, I
believe, is that the wind blows the heat in the stack to the further
side, where the increased warmth, acting on the hay, causes it to
ferment and sink quicker than on the face that is left cool.
The practice on my farm this year, however, seems to be the other
way about. Possibly however, this is due to indifferent stacking.

To-day we began to cut the three-oak or ' Brittle ' meadow, No. 9,
so called because tradition says that a brickfield once existed in
this field, where, owing to its having been shut down so late, the
grass is somewhat thinner than elsewhere. Buck, by nature a
critic, is of opinion that the back lawn was cut too soon,
before the hay had got its proper growth ; a proceeding, he added,
'that minded him of killing a sucking pig.' I cannot say that I
altogether agree with him, for grass mown before it has attained
quite its full growth makes the best and most succulent hay;
also we must be getting on, or we shall have harvest upon us
before haysel is done and the roots are thinned out.

Whether it was cut too soon or not, the back lawn this year
has certainly borne a good crop of beautiful quality. That lawn
offers a busy and picturesque sight this afternoon. By the low
fence at the top end the mower is still at work, as, even when it
is hidden behind the trees, may be known by the sound of its
rattling hum. Near at hand, by the tennis-court, a boy leads the
horse-tosser, and it passes to and fro surrounded with a very halo
of whirling grass, through which the light shines as it floats and falls.
In another part of the field the horse-rake is dragging the hay
opened up previously from the cocks into long dull green lines,
down which come the waggon and cart to be laden, each in

its turn to roll off presently to the stack-yard, a labourer still seated atop of the towering load. There it is heaped and hidden in the bowels of the great stack, to be cut again in the dark days of winter as fragrant food for the cows, that munch it eagerly while they stand in the shelter of the shed and dream of the sweet spring grasses.

In my diary for April I think that I spoke of the difficulty our forefathers must have had in feeding their cattle in winter before the days of root culture. Since then, in 'The Five Hundred Points of Good Husbandry' of Thomas Tusser, who wrote in 1557, I find that straw and hay were eked out with the bare branches of trees. Here is the quotation :

> If frost do continue, this lesson doth well,
> For comfort of cattle the fuel to fell :
> From every tree the superfluous boughs,
> Now prune for thy neat, thereupon to go browse.

> In pruning and trimming all manner of trees,
> Reserve to each cattle their properly fees.
> If snow do continue, sheep hardly that fare,
> Crave mistle and ivy for them for to spare.

In those days the cattle and 'neat'—that is, horned oxen—must have looked forward to the coming of spring with considerable anxiety. This, indeed, is still the case in Africa, where it is not uncommon to see oxen that were fat as butter at the beginning of winter so thin and weak before the grass grows again that they are scarcely able to stand. Many indeed die of poverty.

July 14.—Yesterday we had some showers, which stopped the hay, but to-day is warm and rather dull, and we are carting again from the back lawn. At Bedingham they have not carted any more, but are cutting the far meadow, No. 11. Although the machine has its beauties, after a long course of it it is pretty to watch the mowers at work, and to hear the long *hu-ush* of the scythes as they sweep through the deep cool grass. I found Moore indignant because Hood, perhaps by way of chastening his

pride, had told him that he could 'chuck a sixpence' anywhere
into that field of grass and find it again—by which he meant to
convey that the crop was decidedly thin. 'If he'd been a-dragging
of a scythe through it all day long he wouldn't think it too thin,'
Moore added wrathfully. I consoled him by saying that I thought
the cut a very good one ; much better, indeed, than when we
mowed this field two years ago. I think it will come out at quite
a ton and a quarter an acre, if not more, as the grass here,
although not tall, is exceedingly thick at bottom.

The pigeons continue to do a great deal of mischief to the
kohl-rabi on the new drained field by the wood, No. 18. Moore
is going to borrow a gun from a neighbour and try to shoot
them on Sunday morning. Unless he catches them sitting I
do not think that any young 'dows' will be orphaned.

July 15.—St. Swithun's, and a beautiful day, with a rising
glass and a north to north-easterly wind. Clearly the Saint does
not intend to 'christen the apples' this year ; indeed, everybody
thinks that he is going to give us a long spell of fine weather.
There is an almost universal belief in St. Swithun in these parts,
and certainly, so far as my memory goes, it is justified. I hope it
may be so this year, as we sadly need a spell of summer weather.

We are considering the advisability of buying a reaper—an
expense that seems to be justified by our corn area. I have been
to Bungay this afternoon to look at a specimen which is highly
recommended, a very light but strong and serviceable machine of
American make. It is curious, by the way, that the Americans
should have won such a hold of the market in agricultural machinery. I suppose that there are English-made reapers, and as,
on the Christian principle of turning the other cheek to the smiter,
I prefer giving my support, insignificant as it may be, to home
industries, I should have been glad to buy one, but there do not
seem to be any on show at Bungay. If manufacturers wish to sell
their articles they must have local agents to push them. Farmers,
very naturally, have a great dislike to buying things through

advertisements only, or that are sent by some distant firm.   If they
buy at home, not only do they give their custom among their
own people, but also the local merchant who sells to them is more
or less responsible for the article sold, and will generally undertake
its repair.   The advantage of this can scarcely be over-estimated,
especially in the case of any sudden breakage while the machine is
in active use.

The price of this machine—that is a reaper only, not a binder—
is 26*l*., which seems a good deal of money for a farmer in these
times to expend on one article.   In certain seasons, however, it is
quite possible that it would pay its cost twice over, for when the
spell of fine weather is short the rapid work of a machine has an
enormous advantage over the slow toil of the labourer, even if the
labourer can be found, which nowadays is not always the case.
It is, however, a mistake to suppose that a reaper will cut corn in
every case and every season.   So long as the straw stands up
quite straight it will deal with it admirably, but if it is badly laid
and twisted about the machine often does more harm than good.
Nor is it safe to use it among very tall and thick beans if they are
in the least beaten down.   Here also we do not put a reaper into
barley, as the treading of the horses is too destructive to that delicate
grain ; moreover, the machine throws off the corn in sheaves or
bundles, which is not good for barley, that should be spread out
thin to dry as it leaves the scythe.

July 16.—To-day I experienced one of those disappointments
which are the natural lot of those who try to improve.   Some
years ago I planted willows round the edges of the dry marsh,
No. 18, and the low marsh, No. 19, setting them also on the
bank of the Waveney that borders those fields.   I went to much
trouble and some expense about these trees, enclosing them sepa-
rately for the most part by means of stout stakes, four of which
were sunk at the proper angle and at a distance from each other.
Round the stakes I fixed barbed wire, about five strands ⟨f it
to each sapling.   From the beginning I had bad luck with these

willows, for two years of drought coming after they had been set
caused most of them on the dry marsh to die. Some of those on
the low marsh, however, and all that were planted by the river
edge, thrived admirably. Only a week or two ago I noticed the
beautiful heads which they were making, several of them about
five feet through.

This morning I went to see what progress was being made
with the cutting of the low marsh, and on my way stopped
to look at the young cattle and in-calf heifers that are running on No 18, through which one must pass to reach No. 19.
All of them, looking very sleek and comfortable, were gathered
by the bank of the river, but as I approached to examine
them I noticed that the stems of the young willows had unac-
countably turned white. In another minute I discovered the
truth. These destructive animals had stripped them of every
inch of bark; had stripped them from the branches to the
ground. Close as the strands of wire were set, heedless of
pricks and cuts, they had thrust their heads between them, and
by patience and perseverance had contrived to peel off every
fragment of the sweet and succulent bark. I can scarcely describe
what I felt when I understood that the care of years had thus
been brought to nothing, for though the trees still looked green
and vigorous, I knew well that they must die. Returning home,
I reproached Hood with some warmth for not having informed
me of what was going on, and for his neglect in not taking steps to
stop it, only to discover that my wrath, if natural, was unjust. It
seems that so lately as the previous day the trees were quite
uninjured. Then, as ill luck would have it, some inquisitive
beast contrived to get a taste of one of them, and to communicate his delight to the others. In twenty-four hours they had
destroyed every willow.

The truth is that unless great expense is incurred to fence each
tree in such an impregnable fashion that nothing by any possibility can reach or force its way to it, it is absolutely useless to
plant where any animals are turned out to graze, since, through

idleness and curiosity, they will not rest till they have destroyed them. These particular trees might have survived to grow quite big, but sooner or later a horse or an ox would have got a taste of the bark, and then the end must have come. Plantations to succeed should be in places quite apart, where no four-legged creature can enter. Horse stock and donkeys are especially destructive in this respect, as they will gnaw any smooth-barked trees, even after these have attained the size of timbers. I know of nothing more melancholy than to see, as more than once I have seen, park-lands which have been carefully planted by some owner and subsequently let, in which the tenant has allowed the tree-rails to be broken down, and the beautiful growing chestnuts and beeches to be gnawed to death by colts and cattle.

These losses, however, vexatious as they may be, are trivial compared to those to which planters are exposed in other lands. Thus, in Cyprus, the forests upon thousands and thousands of acres have been destroyed by the ravages of that iniquitous animal, the goat. In South Africa—land of pests and plagues—it is the same story, for there, in addition to other dangers, grass-fires have to be guarded against. There are few things sadder to see than a fine plantation of red or blue gums, the result of the care and cultivation of years, withered up in a single night, probably through the neglect of some drunken man or Kaffir. Here is an extract from the recently issued report of an African company in which I am blessed with shares. It speaks for itself.

'The directors much regret to state that the tree-planting venture has, owing to local mismanagement, locusts, white ants, drought and frost, turned out a total failure. The whole cost to date stood in our books at 9,012*l.* 5*s.* 3*d.*, of which 7,012*l.* 5*s.* 3*d.* has been written off as a loss.'

After this it seems foolish to be vexed at the destruction of a few willows.

Willows, by the way, if of the proper sort, are now about the most valuable timber that can be grown in England. Not only do they meet with a ready sale for manufacture into cricket-bats, but of late years they have been in great demand for sawing into dust, which is, I understand, used in the making of wood powders.

July 18.—St. Swithun has not disappointed us. This is a splendid hay day, hot, with a high west wind. The cutter and tosser are busy on No. 19, but the grass there is not so thick or so good as it was last year. These marshes always do best in a dry season; but this has been wet enough to bring out the water over them, which, if it stands for more than a few hours, turns the foot of the grasses brown and rots them, so that in places they come coarse and scanty. The only herb that the floods do not affect are the docks, which grow here with frightful vigour, and have roots like carrots. The presence of so many hundreds of these poisonous weeds standing above the level of the grass like young and particularly flourishing trees, each of them laden with thousands upon thousands of ripening seeds, is to me a most distressing sight, but as yet we have found it quite impossible to attempt to get rid of them. Indeed, this can only be done if the marsh is fed, and ever since I have had it in hand it has been mown, when the docks are collected out of the hay into heaps and burnt. The other day I found a dock growing on a manure heap, whither it had been brought among the mud fyed out of a marsh dyke. That plant was over seven feet high. I also discovered that there exists a living creature that will eat docks, for in the root of one which I pulled up I found a white, fat, and most unwholesome-looking grub, which had gnawed a deep channel all down its length, without, however, in the slightest degree affecting its general health.

The hay off this marsh has a curious quality. Although in wet seasons it is coarse and reedy-looking, and therefore would fetch but a moderate price at market, even when it has been saved in bad condition, after being washed with floods and rain, stock will eat it in preference to the best upland hay. Hood tells me that he has frequently seen the cattle turn to it from any other sort of food, so I suppose that there must be among it some grass which gives it a flavour delightful to their taste.

As the corn ripens and the ground gets hard the sparrows are beginning to do much damage to the wheat, especially in fields that lie near the village. A tenant of mine, whom I met this morning, tells me that he is 'fairly crazed' with them, and that in one plot they have nearly stripped the ringes which are nearest the hedge. It is not so much what these vermin eat that does the mischief, as what they destroy. I believe that for every grain they swallow they throw down six. Also I hear great complaints of loss from rooks, which, being unable to find grubs and worms in the hard ground, devour whatever they can discover.

July 20.—Yesterday and to-day have been much colder, with the usual north-east wind; indeed, this evening the temperature is down to 50°. The glass also is rising and the ground already grows steely with drought. Three men—all that can be spared from the hay—are engaged in cutting out the swedes on Baker's, No. 34, a slow and arduous job owing to the hardness of the land. In order to get room for their hoes they work leaving a row untouched between each man, which is dealt with on the next journey down the lines. When, as is the case on Baker's, the land is poisoned with rubbish and there is a full plant of swedes, the cutting of them out is rather a delicate operation, as about a dozen plants are destroyed for every one that is left hanging limply by a mere filament of root, from which the hoe has dragged away the earth in clearing the surrounding weeds. It is astonishing that these little plants can pick themselves up again after such rough treatment; but return to the field in a week or so, especially if there has been a shower of rain, and you will find them standing stiff and straight and not a little improved by the thinning of the family. 'One man dead, another man's bread,' runs the old Boer saying. It applies to plants as well as to human beings.

I see in the paper to-day that the Government has given way suddenly on the Vaccination Bill, and that henceforth ' conscientious objection' on the part of parents is to entitle them to disregard the law and neglect the vaccination of their children. It appears, and this is my reason for talking about the matter here, that we magistrates are to decide whether the objection in each case is one of conscience or of mere prejudice and idleness ; that is to say, that we are to sift a man's mind and, without any evidence beyond his own statement, to decide whether he is speaking the truth. I maintain that the task is impossible, and one which should not be laid upon the shoulders of any judge. In practice, what will probably happen is that the chairman or clerk will ask the objecting parent if he or she is prepared to take an oath that his or her objection to the vaccination of the child is founded on conscientious scruples. The parent or guardian will reply that he is, and there will be an end of the matter.

These safeguards even, such as they are, will scarcely stand, for what official or Board of Guardians will go to the expense and worry of instituting prosecutions to which the answer is so easy and complete ? My belief is, that knowing this, but a small proportion of anti-vaccinationists will take the trouble even to apply for a certificate.[1] One may be certain, too, that henceforth

---

[1] This view seems to be borne out by returns recently issued by the Local Government Board. I take the following report from a newspaper :—

' This return shows that between the date of the passing of the Act and the 31st December, 1898, the number of certificates of conscientious objection received by the vaccinating officers was 203,413, and that the number of children to whom such certificates related was 230,147. It is explained that the number of unvaccinated children in England and Wales at the time of the passing of the Act in respect of whom certificates under Section 2 might have been applied for cannot be stated, but over 12,500,000 births were registered during the years 1885–98, and the total number of children, including all who died before vaccination, not reported as having been vaccinated may be taken at 3,235,000.'

It is not a pleasant thought that, allowing for the deaths, there are at the present moment something under three million unvaccinated young persons moving about amongst us.

the workings of conscience upon this matter will be marvellously quickened among certain classes. If the same test could be applied to the case of sending children to school, in six months the class-rooms would be half emptied by 'conscientious objections.' A false-hood is easily spoken, and such an Act seems to put a premium on the speaking of it. Among tens of thousands of the population, by consent of the State, vaccination, in my belief one of the greatest boons that the century has brought to mankind, will henceforth cease to exist. Never before, I imagine, at least in these enlightened days, has such sanction been given to the wretched theory that 'freedom' consists in giving a man the right to gratify his own whim, however mischievous, at the cost of society at large, and never before has the doctrine of the power of the parent over his offspring been pushed so far. In future an indolent, or a pre-judiced, or a 'conscience-stricken' father or guardian is to be licensed at will to expose children to the ravages of a fearful sickness and the risk of death, and, helpless though they are, it is by Act of Parliament decreed that no hand shall be held up to save them. Whatever the political advantages, this appears to be a heavy responsibility for a Government to bind upon its shoulders, especially, as I gather from the reports and the speeches, as together with 95 per cent. or more of those who constitute the present House of Commons, every member of the Committee is a firm believer in vaccination, and knows well what may happen to those who cease to vaccinate. O Liberty ! what things——

It seems a pity that the leaders of the anti-vaccination party, who, no doubt, are very honest in their faith, and therefore can scarcely be blamed for endeavouring to enforce it, cannot, as I have done, when a small-pox epidemic is raging travel in foreign parts where that prophylactic is unknown or little practised. I think that they would come back with their views much modified. At present they think little of the disease because they have scarcely seen it at its dreadful work. What they lack is imagination. Well, I have heard that Jenner prophesied that it would be so.

As I am discussing the subject, here is an object-lesson in

small-pox which I submit to the consideration of these crusaders. The tale reaches me from far Venezuela, and I believe the facts to be accurately stated, although I cannot guarantee the details, which I have no opportunity of verifying. In the course of a recent epidemic the small-pox struck the unvaccinated, or very slightly vaccinated, town of Valencia, whereof the population is estimated at 35,000. Out of this population, speaking roughly, 8,000 were treated at the small-pox hospitals, about 4,000 of whom died. These numbers, however, do not include those treated in private houses, who were many. Also everyone who could escape from the place did so, till at length it became as a city of the dead; so that the percentage of cases to population must have been much larger than the figures quoted above would suggest, especially as no precautionary measures were taken, at any rate before the outbreak. By this time the authorities at the capital, Caracas, had become alarmed, and set to work to do their best to enforce conpulsory vaccination of its inhabitants. In due course the plague fell upon that city also, which has a population estimated at 80,000, as against 35,000 at Valencia. Here, however, after the compulsory vaccination, the results were very different, for (not counting the cases treated in private houses, for which no figures are available) the patients numbered only about 400, a curious contrast to the 8,000 reported at Valencia. As the hygienic conditions of the two towns are said to be practically the same, these figures seem to be remarkable.[1]

I have been very much amused to-day watching the behaviour of a game-cock which, for dynastic reasons, has been separated from his harem and removed out of the Horse-yard Buildings to All

[1] It is right to add that in an article printed in a London journal of anti-vaccination views, to which the above passage provides a text, it is stated that according to a pamphlet published at Valencia by Pedro Izaquirre, the record in the epidemic of 1898 amounts to 5,221 cases, with 1,515 deaths at Valencia. I know not for certain which set of figures is actually or approximately correct; but on the lower basis even a percentage of about 29 per cent. seems sufficiently alarming.

June 1899.

Hallows Farm.   Last night he was carried off, and this morning Hood set him at liberty, whereon he departed towards home literally *ventre-à-terre*.   Apparently, however, he could not find his way there, for afterwards I discovered him in the Home Farm stackyard trying to attract to himself a hen of light and wandering mind.   This he did by scratching in the dust and making pretence that he had found something particularly nice to eat. I know that it was a pretence, for from where I stood I could see that there was nothing at all, although he pecked violently and pretended to swallow, calling all the while.   Finally the light-minded hen was attracted, and came up to see what could be got, although with doubts, for the lawful rooster, a Dorking, was watching these proceedings from a distance with a threatening and lurid eye.   Her disgust when she found that there was naught was very comic, and away she marched.   This evening I found that poor divorced cock roosting quite alone in the exact centre of a large hen-house, which the fowls do not use during summer, as they seem to prefer to sleep in the trees.   I suppose that sooner or later there will be a battle, but, oddly enough, the game-cock does not seem to seek the encounter.

To-day two of the little steers at Bedingham were sold to the butcher for 27*l.* the pair.   I estimate—'lay' is the local term— their weight when cleaned at about thirty-five stone, but I suppose that the butcher thinks that they will weigh more, as 7*s.* a stone is the average price for prime beef.   These young things—they are under two years old—make the best and most saleable beef, and perhaps for this reason he may be willing to give a little more for them.   The day of heavy three- and four-year-old cattle, at any rate in this neighbourhood, is gone by, and as a rule the price they bring does not compensate the grazier for the extra expense of their keep for so long a period of time.

July 21.—To-day Buck has been at work thatching the haystack in the Buildings stackyard, with the assistance of young Fairhead.

This is the process. A quantity of straw is placed in a heap and soaked with buckets of water to soften it ; otherwise it would not 'lie.' Buck, seated close by, draws from a bundle, which for the last few days has been 'tempering' in a pond, some of the broaches that Rough Jimmy split a few months ago. These he sharpens at either end, and then, holding the broach in both hands, wrings it in the centre to make it pliable. When the broaches are prepared, he and his assistant go to a heap of coarse hay which is handy. Here Fairhead fixes a wisp of the hay on to an instrument called a bond crank, that is, a bent iron with a hook at the end of it, and two hand pieces of elder wood, so arranged that by holding one in the left hand and turning the other with the right the hook revolves and twists the hay into a long grass rope or bond as it is deftly drawn from the heap by Buck. These bonds, when of sufficient length, Buck winds into a rough spool with a broach for the centre of it, much as a fishing line is wound on to a stick.

When enough of these spools are prepared he mounts the tall ladder that is laid against the stack, and Fairhead brings him a bundle of straw fastened with a rope, which bundle is secured to the side of the stack by means of broaches, whereon it rests. Dragging out handfuls of straw from the bundle, he lays these neatly on the slope, tucking them in where necessary and drawing them smooth with an instrument called a thatching comb. Then he takes one of the bond-spools and, loosing the end of it, lays the bond across the straw, fastening it in place by the doubled up broaches, which, in shape and purpose, resemble rough hairpins, driving them home into the stack by means of a thatching mallet. For this covering up of haystacks two lines of bonds are generally used, with others, which are arranged in a kind of dog-tooth pattern at the ends of the stack.

Buck and his assistant, beginning to work at this stack, which may contain eighteen or twenty tons of hay, after breakfast, had finished it by evening. For quick thatching, however, three hands are required : one to make ready the bonds, broaches, &c.,

one to carry the bundles of straw up the ladder, and one to lay and fasten them.

If, as in the present case, the hay is very dense and hard, the thatching takes a little more time, since then it is not easy to force the broaches home into the body of the stack.

July 23.—Yesterday I found Buck putting in a spare hour after he had finished with the cows, hoeing beet on All Hallows field, No. 29. Here the ground is so hard that in places the swelling bulbs of the beet have actually split the soil about them. Buck, who, as I have said before, is a critic, is of opinion that this hardness is chiefly caused by the land having been rolled for drilling when too wet. I think, however, that the drought has a good deal to do with it. I find that my half-dozen little beets, which I transplanted in this field, are looking green and flourishing, but I must admit that they are not so large as the beet which have not been transplanted.

About three in the afternoon a soft shower came on, which continued at intervals until 10 o'clock at night. Although it has stopped the hay-carting, this rain, light as it is, is most welcome, as the young swedes and white turnips are beginning to suffer much from drought, and the shorn pastures sadly need refreshment to start them into growth again. Unless we have some wet before harvest I fear that the aftermath and the second crop on the ollands will be but scanty.

To-day is stormy, but without rain. Whitrup has been at work with the flat hoe, cleaning the beet on No. 23. Going to the field after he left it, I found that this instrument had worked considerable havoc to the roots as well as to the weeds, for a great many beautiful beet were broken off and destroyed. Damage of this sort is difficult to avoid, especially if the ground is hard, as the leaves of the beet catch in the hoe and the roots are snapped in an instant. In this case it is wise to take the wrench and set the knives a little closer together, since it is better that a few weeds should escape than that good beet should be destroyed, especially in a year when the plant is not too thick.

After many doubts Hood and I have come to the decision that we had best buy the reaper. To this there are two alternatives: to do without a machine altogether and trust to the old-fashioned scythe, that is very slow where the extent of ground to be dealt with is considerable, especially in this uncertain climate, which may set in wet at any time. The other is to hire a machine, as we did once before. Now, the rent of a reaper would not be less than 5*l*., and it may be hazarded that the instrument would be of bad make and quality, as people do not buy good machines to let out to anybody who asks for them. Therefore, especially when the risks of breakage and consequent delay, which are many in the case of such a machine, are taken into consideration, it seems scarcely worth while to hire at a fifth of the price of a new instrument.

This year we propose to make our agreement with the men for the *harvest*. This means that, allowing an approximate area of twelve acres of corn crop per head to be cut, carried, stacked, and thatched, each man will receive about 7*l*. for the work. In fact it is piece work, and the sooner the hands are through with it and put their 7*l*. into their pockets, the sooner they will be able to get back to labour at their ordinary wage. It should be added that, in return for the use of the reaper, which, of course, saves time and lessens their toil considerably, they will be expected to undertake a certain amount of root cleaning when necessary. The alternative plan—a very bad one in my opinion, which we adopted last year—is that the men should be paid 7*l*. for the month. Under this system, if they finished the harvest under a month, they would have to return to their ordinary work for such days as remained without wage, their labour having been purchased for the full time. If, on the other hand, the harvest is prolonged beyond a month, they are expected to complete it at the ordinary rate of wage. Under these circumstances, as Mr. Hodge is human, it is scarcely to be expected that he will get on quite so quickly as he does when he is paid by the piece. Indeed, I believe that there are many instances upon record of things being so nicely timed that the harvest is finished on the evening of the last day of the appointed month.

At the farmhouse of a neighbour this afternoon I saw two little boys, who told me that they are the sons of a pastry-cook in the neighbourhood of the Edgware Road. They are two of about a dozen children which have been sent by some charity to be boarded out for a fortnight in the village at a price of 5*s.* a week per head. I can imagine no truer kindness than that of those good people who thus enable these poor city-bred children to enjoy a fortnight of pure country air, to the great benefit of their minds and bodies. I hope that this work may prosper and increase, as there is unlimited room for the accommodation of such children, and many respectable village women would be only too glad to take them in and feed them well for 5*s.* a week.

July 25.—This afternoon, in walking over the Thwaite field, No. 28, to look at the carrots and young swedes, which are suffering from drought, I saw a curious thing. Over the field, skimming here, there, and everywhere in the air, but within an area of a well defined circuit, were two or three hundreds of swallows and martins, all of them busy in the ceaseless consumption of some invisible insects. I suppose that the 'fly' was in the air, and that this was a 'rise' of swallows collected to take advantage of it. As they were hawking within so limited a space, it would seem to show that these myriads of tiny insects on which they feed pass from place to place in swarms.

July 31.—On Wednesday we began carting the hay from Baker's Marsh, No. 46. It is a very good crop, a ton and a half an acre, I should say. I believe that shutting this field down so late has, in fact, improved the turf, as it gave the fine grasses time to get up before they were overshadowed by the coarser-growing sorts. Before we began to cart some of the men were employed fixing the galvanized iron roofs on to two of the haystacks in the home yard. These roofs, although not ornamental (what, I wonder, would our forefathers have said had they been asked to cover their stacks with tin ?), are exceedingly useful. I bought them four or five years ago, in a season when, owing to the drought, we had literally no straw left with which to thatch, at a cost, if I remember rightly, of about 4*l.* 10*s.* each. Since then they have been in use every year, and the hay protected by them has invariably been found to be as sweet and good immediately under the iron as in any other part of the stack. The roofs themselves consist of an iron ridge with grooves, to which are hung the galvanized sheets. When the stack has sufficiently settled, these sheets are fastened to the hay by long corkscrew-shaped pins, which, if properly driven home, secure them against any wind, although in the course of years the iron is apt to get torn at the eyelet-holes and corners. One disadvantage of these roofs is that the stacks must be built to fit them, and another that they undoubtedly look ugly in a farmyard, although this fault might be mitigated by painting them straw-colour. This I have always intended to do, but as yet we have never found time to be æsthetic.

At Bedingham on Wednesday afternoon I found all the hay up, though a few loads of it were still standing upon the carts and waggons ready to top up the last stack when it settles. According to my measurements, which may be inaccurate, I think that we have thirty-four or thirty-five tons of excellent hay on the two Bedingham stacks, a good crop off a farm of a hundred acres on which no clover layer has been grown this season. But throughout the country the cut of grass is one of the largest that has been secured for many years, so hay will be cheap. Indeed, I doubt whether valuers will lay it at much more than 2*l.* the ton on the stack. This, however, will not hurt farmers who have any to spare, and can afford to save it. Hay, if re-thatched, will keep five or six years, and perhaps before that time has come and gone it may fetch nearer 7*l.* than 2*l.* the ton. Here, alas ! we have so many mouths to feed that even in plentiful seasons forage seems to melt away almost to the last stalk ; I doubt if at the present moment we have more than a truss or so of the crop of 1897 left upon the place.

Every farmer must be thankful that this, the first harvest of the year, has been secured in plenty, and, on the whole, in such good order. Here, at the beginning of haysel, we had one field of layer, No. 45, badly damaged by the wet, and more than half of the stuff on Baker's Marsh is still out, but all the rest is safe and snug in the ricks—and to the farmer's eye hay always looks best upon a stack. I think that here at Ditchingham, so nearly as I can estimate, we must have carried about a hundred tons.

On my way back from Bedingham I went to look at some yearling cattle belonging to a tradesman in Bungay, who has taken them over for a debt, and wishes to dispose of them at the price they were valued at to him, namely, 6*l.* 10*s.* each. About six of these I found to be fair-looking animals, not polled, but 'slug-horned,' that is, with horns about the size and shape of a large sausage. On the whole they are a coarse-bred lot, and I think that 6*l.* each would be plenty to pay for them; indeed, I do not know that they will suit us at all. Our difficulty here is to buy well-bred things. It would seem that anything with four legs and a tail is good enough for a Norfolk farmer to breed from. He will not understand that good blood means good beef, and, what is more, quickly grown beef.

The morning of the 28th was sunless, but we managed to draw up two loads of hay from Baker's Marsh. Just as the men were returning there with the carts after dinner, a slight shower came on, which stopped them, but they were able to get some of the made hay into cock. About half-past five it came on to rain in good earnest—a welcome sight indeed to farmers who have been watching the earth grow harder day by day, while the mangold remained almost at a standstill and the young swedes languished and turned blue and lousy. When the rain began to be heavy I walked round the farm, visiting some of the root-fields. I know of no more pleasant experience after a long period of drought than to stand in such a field watching the dry earth suck up the bounteous downpour, and the green things gather life and increase as they draw it into their tissues. What smell is there half so good as the smell of the soil new-washed by rain? People who only go out walking in fine weather miss much; the best times to walk, in my opinion, are in the snow, the wet, and the storm.

Friday the 29th was cold and overcast, with occasional light showers driven by a high north-east wind. On the farm we took advantage of the welcome wet to plough the headlands and drill maize on that part of the vetch field, No. 21, which was fed off with sheep. Of course it is late to sow this crop even for the only purpose to which we put it—green fodder; but the ground has been so hard that we have been unable to get it in before. If we have a warm August and September, however, which are surely due to us after so cold a summer, I hope that it will still furnish a good cut for the cows in autumn. There are few fodders that they like better than the stalks of this Indian corn after they have gone through the cutter. They are an excellent milk-producing food, and, as I have learned in Africa, horses will grow fat upon them.

Yesterday we were sowing mustard broadcast and drilling white turnips upon the headlands, which have been ploughed and harrowed to receive them. Even if they never grow very large, these headland white turnips make a welcome bite for the sheep in autumn, while the mustard is always useful, especially to give a flavour to chaff, or to be fed off by sheep.

At Bedingham I find that in one of the fields, No. 6, the wheat, which here is very tall and strong, is in places laid by the wind and rain. The white turnips which were drilled there when the swedes failed are a first-rate plant. Even if no more rain falls for another month or so I think that they should now make a crop, for this stiff Bedingham clay holds the moisture, and here the saying that 'drought never yet made dearth' is certainly true.

The reader may remember my entries about the swallows that build in the porch. After the adventures of one of them in this house at night they sat, and in due course produced one young bird only, which has now been reared to maturity and flown. Thinking that the coldness of the season had caused the remaining eggs to be unfertile, as chanced with all of them two years ago, I examined the nest in order to remove the rotten eggs, so that, if the birds wished, they could again make use of it. It was quite empty. The eggs had not been thrown out of the nest, for, if so, they would have lodged upon the board underneath it ; so it is clear either that the swallows have carried them right away, or that only one egg was laid. I believe the latter to be the explanation. Perhaps it was the hen bird which passed the night in the house. If so, would it not be possible that the shock given to its system by fright may have prevented it from producing more than one egg? Perhaps some naturalist can answer the question.

To-day is beautiful, by far the finest which we have yet experienced this summer. In the afternoon I rode over to Denton, a village some six miles away, where there is a small farm belonging to this property. The house on it is ancient, probably early Tudor ; indeed, some very beautiful oak panelling that I removed from it to this place can scarcely be later than that date. From the shape of the portion that is now standing I imagine it to be the remains of a larger building, of which parts have been pulled down as it fell into disrepair. Such fragments of houses are common about here ; indeed, there is one of them at my own gate which is so old that it had to be strapped up in 1613, as is proved by the 'anchors' let into the wall, whereof the faces fashion that date in wrought iron. I suppose that all these dwellings in the times of the Plantagenets and the Tudors were the homes of yeomen who owned or farmed from one to three hundred acres of land. Or, possibly, they were in many cases the farmhouses let with the holdings. That tenant farmers were common so early as 1560 we learn from Thomas Tusser's rhymes, for he talks of the taking over of farms at Michaelmas as a familiar thing :

> At Michaelmas lightly new farmer comes in,
> New Husbandry forceth him new to begin ;
> Old farmer still taking the time to him given,
> Makes August to last until Michaelmas even.
>
> .   .   .   .   .   .
>
> Good farm and well stored, good housing and dry,
> Good corn and good dairy, good market and nigh ;
> Good shepherd, good tillman, good Jack and good Jill,
> Make husband and huswife their coffers to fill.

Nor does the country—he farmed in Suffolk and at East Dereham, in Norfolk—seem to have been so lonely as might be imagined, for he talks of journeys to market, and of the visits of chapmen or dealers. Indeed, I believe that the enormous increase of the population in England has taken place in the towns only, and that the country was almost as thickly populated in the times of the Henrys as it is to-day. The size and number of the churches show it, as do the death entries in the earlier registers.

This ancient Denton farm has fitting tenants in the aged couple who occupy it. Their name is Skinner, and they are eighty, or over, both of them, but still hale and handsome; we discovered them sitting in the quaint porch of the house reading the Bible, as old folks should do on Sunday afternoon. They have been connected with this property, or in the service of its owners, all their lives; indeed, the old man's father was gardener to this house and died here, while so far back as fifty years ago he himself was steward to my father-in-law, Maior Margitson, managing for him the land which I now farm. When he dies, which I trust may not be for many years, there will vanish a fine specimen of the old stamp of tenant-farmer, of whom so few remain ; one who loved his land, and did not look upon the landlord as his natural enemy.

I walked over the farm with the old gentleman, and found it cultivated like a garden. I think that his beans and beet are quite the best that I have seen this year.

AUGUST

August 1.—To-day the weather has been lovely, which is fortunate, as the annual Primrose League fête of the Ditchingham Habitation was held in Ellingham Park. I think that there must have been quite two thousand people present, all of whom seemed to enjoy themselves very much wandering about on the green grass and under the beautiful trees. For amusements there were open-air theatricals, swing boats, cocoanut shies, and that most fascinating of sports, a shooting gallery, where the skilful may break glass balls and knock over tin animals, supplemented of course by a liberal tea and dancing in the evening. Then there were the speeches, which, in my opinion, are the least popular part of the entertainment, although, together with a fair proportion of the male sex, a large number of ladies and their offspring listened to them with rapt attention, and were, I trust, duly instructed upon Imperial matters. I forget who invented the Primrose League, but he was certainly a political genius, who had mastered the great fact that the majority of people detest unmitigated politics and love entertainments and threepenny teas, and that, of those who enjoy the entertainments and absorb the tea, a proportion, at any rate, will reward the party which provides them with their support. The affair was very well managed and a great success, but shouting patriotic sentiments from a waggon is tiring to the throat. At last year's festivity, however, I was much more arduously employed, for the advertised speaker having telegraphed suddenly to say that 'a toothache' prevented him from attending, I was called upon to fill his place. For me that meant three-quarters of an hour of unpremeditated and al-fresco oratory.

To-day we have finished carting the hay from Baker's Marsh, No. 46 ; also I sold two young red-poll heifers to a clergyman in this neighbourhood for 10*l.* apiece. Considering how they are bred it is not a high price, but of course more than they would fetch upon the market and more than they are worth to keep for fatting purposes. I am coming rapidly to the conclusion, however, that it is a mistake to consign so many of these pedigree animals to the butcher. They have some of the best blood in East Anglia in their veins, and ought to be worth more to sell for stock purposes, although, of course, it is hard for the small breeder like myself to compete with the large and well-advertised herds.

August 2.—To-day we are hoeing root upon the farm, of which there is a deal to be got through before harvest begins. On my way back from the root field I went to look at the pease on No. 37, and found them absolutely scarlet with red-weed or poppies, to which this land is very liable. If possible we propose to cut them a little green, so as to kill the thistles and poppies before they shed their seed abroad.

I inspected also the carrots on the Thwaite field, No. 28, to find that the rabbits are doing them much damage. These pestilent vermin, which are unusually numerous this year, for they bred all the winter through, come at night and bite out the crowns, an injury from which the plants never quite recover. Although many people have grumbled at it, certainly the Hares and Rabbits Bill has proved a most useful measure, that is, to those who avail themselves honestly of its provisions and do not make it an excuse for poaching. As I know from bitter experience, there is nothing more maddening to a farmer than to see his crops injured, or perhaps destroyed, by these mischievous brutes, which, if there should chance to be any coverts or sandy banks in the neighbourhood, it is almost impossible to keep under, however much one may shoot, snare, or trap. A single nest of them in a barley field will destroy the yield of quite a large area of the corn ; indeed, I am inclined to think that they do even more damage to growing corn than to root crops. Perhaps, however, they are most troublesome in the case of young trees, for, wire these in as one will, they manage to burrow beneath the fence and to kill the saplings by gnawing the sweet bark off their stems.

August 6.—Last Wednesday Hood went to Harleston market, which is a very good one, in the hope of picking up some young home-bred beasts at a moderate figure. This he did not succeed in doing, but he reports that fat cattle were selling as low as six shillings a stone. This is an utterly unremunerative price, caused by the plentiful root-crop of last year; but now the beet is done, and poor farmers have to empty their yards and take what they can get. Yesterday and the day before we were horse- and hand-hoeing the root, and to-day, which is dull with heavy showers of rain, we are carting house coal as well. To-day, also, we have finally arranged with the men for the forthcoming harvest.

It will be remembered that this can be done on two systems : namely, the hands can agree for a month, after which, should the in-gathering take longer, they must complete it at their ordinary wage ; or they can agree for 'the harvest,' receiving a lump sum, be it long or short. Under this arrangement, of course, it is to their interest to get through their task at the greatest possible rate of speed, since every day saved is a day upon which they can be earning wage over and above the stipulated sum. It is perfectly marvellous how hard men will labour under this system of piece-work. At Ditchingham this year we have about ninety-one acres of corn to be gathered by seven men, each man receiving 7*l.* 10*s.*, including the hiring shilling to be paid according to ancient custom. Query—Is this hiring shilling the origin of the queen's shilling formerly given to a recruit on his enlistment? For this the hands are to do all that is necessary, that is, to cut, to carry, to stack, to trim, &c., thatching alone excepted. It will be seen that the average area to each man is thirteen acres, which is two above what is usual. This is accounted for by the fact that I intend to purchase the reaper, which will be thrown into the harvest for the men to use wherever corn can be cut with it to advantage. Of course such a machine means an enormous saving of labour, but it cannot always be set to work, as it will not deal satisfactorily with laid and twisted corn.

At Bedingham we have thirty-five acres of corn to be dealt with by three men and one boy, each man receiving 7*l*., and the boy 2*l*. 10*s*. This allows ten acres for each man, and five acres for the boy. The hands, who do everything except thatch the stacks, also undertake to go once through the piece of white turnips on No. 18 with the hand-hoe. It will be observed that their rate of money is ten shillings less than the wage to be paid upon this farm, the reason being that, although they have no reaper to help them, the area to be dealt with by their labour is less.

Here at Ditchingham the cowman, Buck, and a boy stand out of the harvest and are paid no extra money, although Buck will have to undertake the thatching of the stacks. In compensation, however, for his receiving no harvest money he is given a cottage valued at 4*l*. a year rent free. In addition to his thatching he and Hood between them will have to manage the milking of the cows and to take care of the cattle.

Eleven is the average number of acres which an able-bodied man is supposed to be able to harvest. That is the extent arranged for with his labourers by a neighbouring farmer in this village. These men, however, are to receive 7*l*. 7*s*. each, and their bargain includes the thatching of the stacks. In this case there is no reaper to assist them, and the straw of his crops is supposed to be stouter than mine, an important item in reckoning up the amount of work to be done.

This afternoon I went to examine the reaper which I have purchased, that is being put together at the foundry in Bungay. It is an American machine, very light, but strong in make, and seems well fitted for our work.

In a greenhouse in this garden I have two tame toads, named Martha and Jane respectively. Also there is a tiny one called Babette, but she can hardly be counted, as she is so small and seldom on view. (Martha, there is reason to fear, has recently eaten Babette.)

These toads are strange and interesting creatures, differing much from each other in appearance and character. Martha is stout and dark-coloured, a bold-natured toad of friendly habit; Jane, on the other hand, is pale and thin, with a depressed air which suggests resignation born of long experience of circumstances over which she has no control. Some of this depression may be due to the fact that once, entering the greenhouse in the twilight, I trod upon her accidentally, a shock from which she seems never to have recovered, although, owing to the adaptive powers of toads, beyond a slight flattening she took no physical harm from an adventure which must have been painful. Indeed, I am not sure that of the two of us I did not suffer most, for I know of few things more upsetting than the feel of a fat toad beneath one's foot. Anyhow, since that day Jane has looked reproachful and never quite trusted me.

These toads I feed with lobworms, or sometimes with woodlice and centipedes taken from traps made of hollowed-out potatoes, which are set among the flowerpots to attract such creatures. In the latter case the insects must be thrown before the toad, which never seems to see them until they begin to run, although, its ears being quick, it can sometimes hear them as they move along the floor behind it.

When a toad catches sight of an insect its attitude of profound repose changes to one of extraordinary and alarming animation. Its swivel eyes seem to project and fix themselves upon the doomed creature off which it is about to lunch; its throat begins to palpitate with violence, and its general air betrays intense and concentrated interest. Presently, from contemplation it proceeds to action. By slow but purposeful movements of its crooked limbs it advances; pauses, and advances again, till at length it reaches a position which it considers convenient. Then, just as the centipede gains a sheltering pebble, a long pink flash seems to proceed from the head of the toad. That is its tongue.

Another instant and the pink thing has twisted itself round the insect and retired into the capacious mouth, and there, once more wrapped in deep peace and rest, sits the toad, its eyes turned in pious thankfulness to heaven, or, rather, to the roof of the greenhouse. The other day even I saw Martha take a woodlouse off her own head. Mistaking the nature of its foothold the insect had been so unfortunate as to run up her back, till, becoming aware of the tickling of its little feet, Martha guessed the unusual situation and acted on it with all the decision of the great.

If the observer wishes to see what my old head gardener calls 'the beauty of the thing,' woodlice and centipedes undoubtedly provide the best show; but for real grim earnest, for a perfect microcosm of the struggle for existence in which somebody has to go down, the spectacle of Martha meeting with a selected lobworm is to be recommended. In this instance she sees the thing at once, for it is long, active, and shiny (toads will not touch anything that is dead), and instantly clears for action. Creeping forward with a dreadful deliberation, she arches her neck over the worm, considering it with her beady eye. Then, as it begins to take refuge beneath the shingle—for worms seem to understand that toads are no friends to them—Martha pounces and grips it by the middle. Next comes a long strain, like that of a thrush dragging at a brandling in the garden, and after the strain, the struggle.

Heavens! what a fight it is! Magnify the size of the combatants by five hundred, and no man would dare to stay to look at it. The worm writhes and rolls; Martha, seated on her bulging haunches, beats its extremities with her front paws—cramming, pushing, gulping, and lo! gradually the worm seems to shorten. Shorter it grows, and shorter yet. It is vanishing into Martha's inside. And now nothing is left but a little pink tip projecting from the corner of her mouth, in appearance not unlike that of a lighted cigarette.

The tip vanishes, and you think that the tragedy is over. But no; presently there is a convulsion, followed by a resurrection as

frantic as it is futile.   Again the war is waged—this time more
feebly, and soon, once more shrouded in holy calm as in a
garment, Martha sits smiling at the roof of the greenhouse,
reflecting probably upon worms that she swallowed years before
anybody now living was born.   But as a matter of curiosity one
would like to know what is happening inside of her.   Clearly her
digestive fluids must be of the best.

I imagine that toads live a great while—at least that is the
impression among country people.   Old men will declare even
that they have known a certain toad all their lives ; but this
proves nothing, for some descendant may so exactly resemble its
ancestor as to deceive the most careful observer.[1]

[1] During the winter of 1898 Martha and Jane vanished and were no more
seen.   In February 1899, however, they reappeared from their hiding places
beneath the hot-water pipes and would sit for hours with their noses glued to
the zinc screens of the ventilators, and even against the cracks of the doors,
desiring doubtless now that the year had turned towards spring to escape into
the open to spawn.   Clearly lobworms and woodlice artificially supplied no
longer consoled them for captivity.   At length I took pity upon the poor
things, and on a certain mild damp day let them go.   Off they waddled
in haste, heading for the rose border, the bold Martha leading the way and
the pallid Jane with backbone painfully distinct following humbly at a
distance.   When I searched for them half an hour later they had departed,
probably beneath the soil.   Let us hope that in generations to be the recollection of their imprisonment in that shining mysterious place where towering
creatures provided them with worms in bewildering abundance will come to
be regarded by them as a pleasant episode in a somewhat monotonous career.

The further Manœuvres of Jane

June 2, 1899.

A marvel has come to pass—Jane has returned to captivity, plumper and
in better condition than she left it four months ago, but without doubt the
same pallid, patient, gentle-natured Jane.   It happened thus.   This very
morning, going to the door of the cool glasshouse, which is devoted to hardy
cypripediums and other moisture-loving plants, I found sitting on the stone sill
and staring hard at the cracks of the door none other than dear Jane.   Guessing
her wishes I opened it, and in she waddled, turned to the right as usual, and
at once established herself amongst the wet shingle.   Now what can have
brought this creature back in so strange a fashion ?   My own belief is that the

The sight of Martha wrestling with a very large worm always reminds me of a seldom-seen combat, which once it was my good fortune to behold, between a thresher (*Alopias vulpes*) or threshers— for I could not be sure whether there was one or more of them—and a large whale. What the exact connection in my mind may be I cannot say, for the creatures concerned are different indeed in size, but I fancy that it has to do with the ferocity of the efforts made in either case by the attacker and its victim. Never shall I forget that titanic scene. The huge ocean mammal lay floundering and blowing upon the surface of the sea, into whose depths from time to time he tried to sink; but whenever he began to 'sound' something always seemed to prevent him. Whether this failure was owing to the action of a swordfish working away at the whale underneath, in order to keep him on the top of the water while the thresher or threshers attended to business above, is more than I can say. I have been told, however, that these two creatures enter into partnership for this murderous purpose, with the result that, notwithstanding his size and strength, the whale attacked has about as much chance against them as has the log which lies between the top and bottom sawyers of escaping unsevered from the pit.

sudden change of the weather from unseasonable cold to summer heat has caused it to remember with pleasure the damp shaded greenhouse with its abounding worms, and to seek shelter there. But this presupposes memory, for instinct would not bring a creature back to a conservatory. And if toads have active memory of such sort?—but the problem is too deep for me. At any rate there is Jane—all have recognised her pale complexion, her widowed air. I am proud to add also that the sympathy between us, which I thought gone, is quite restored, for now Jane allows me to stroke her speckly head, and puffs herself out with pleasure at the touch of kindness which makes us kin. Her appetite, too, is excellent; she has just breakfasted off three woodlice (one large), two centipedes, and half a worm—and yet almost do I wish that I could persuade Jane to become a vegetarian. Another strange occurrence: a second half-grown toad has appeared in the same greenhouse, a weird, wild, fear-haunted creature, that won't sit still. Can this be Babette—the lost Babette, whose fate was hid in mystery—Babette whom we thought anthro- or Bufo-pophagically absorbed—escaped and adolescent? Who knows? But the bold Martha—where is She?

So there the agonised and stricken creature rolled, wallowing in a fringe of bloody foam, while continually the great butcher-fish leapt high into the air, as he fell striking Behemoth such a blow upon the head or back with his fearful tail that the sound of it echoed far across the quiet sea.

The last act of this tragedy of the deep was seen by no mortal eye, for ere the end came our ship had passed out of sight of it. But I think that it was near at hand, and that before we were hull down the cruel sea-foxes and the swordfish, with their retinue of sharks, were tearing the tongue and blubber in great lumps from the throat and belly of the dying whale.[1]

Truly nature is a savage thing, and the Natural law, of which St. Paul talks, an abomination. Here, by way of example, is a hedge-side instance of it. The other day, while walking on the road, I heard a sound of sharp, thin screams coming from the long grasses of the bank. Peeping among them I saw a cruel sight, for writhing there, in vain efforts to escape, was a half-grown frog, whilst gnawing and worrying at its legs and hinder parts I perceived a mole. Never before did I know that moles could be so active; for this one would let go, vanish amongst the tall grass stems, then glide up swiftly and recommence his savage attack, that caused the frog to cry out thus piteously in fear and pain. Frightening him away with my stick, I examined the frog, which now was lying exhausted on its back, its hind legs and stomach chewed to a red pulp, so that I think it can scarcely have recovered. Do moles, then, eat frogs, after the fashion of water-rats, or was this onslaught inspired by some individual hate?

Another instance: some years back I was standing on the Gibbet

---

[1] Since writing the above passage I have read in a book by Mr. Louis Becke, the chronicler of the Southern Seas, a thrilling account of a fight between a thresher and a whale, which took place off the coast of New South Wales. In this instance the thresher was assisted by two bulldog fish of the whale tribe, called *Orca gladiator*. Perhaps in the battle I saw *Orca gladiator* was at work also—if he frequents the West Coast of Africa. Certainly I saw fish leaping out of the water, and falling on to the back of the whale, which looked to me as though they weighed many tons.

Common at Bradenham, when I saw and heard a full-grown rabbit run by me and vanish into a dense clump of gorse, shrieking loudly, for no apparent reason. Astonished, I remained still to watch what happened, till presently, from half a minute to a minute afterwards, I caught sight of a white-bellied stoat gliding along the rabbit's spoor to hunt it down by scent. It vanished also into the gorse clump, and there the tragedy completed itself, to the accompaniment of more piercing screams. But when I first saw the rabbit it was crying out, not with pain, but with nervous apprehension. Instinct doubtless told it that it was doomed, and its screams were an appeal to the deaf heavens for mercy. It was the creature's evident foreknowledge of agony to come that made its fate so dreadful.

These are the mercies of Nature 'red in tooth and claw.' What wonder that the vegetarians and others preach and strive against her, although with as much chance of success as has the tortured lobworm between the jaws of Martha? In the infinite past, in the present, and in the future for so long as time shall endure, the law of our physical universe is a law of death made as terrible as possible to all that breathes by antecedent torment of the frame and the intelligence, for there seems to be no creature so humble that it cannot suffer fear and dread. Such being the heavy yoke of the Natural law, certainly the promised advent of the Spiritual is needed to redress the balance.

August 8.—Yesterday afternoon we had heavy rain, which set in at twelve o'clock and continued till sunset, but as it was Sunday this interfered with nothing. To-day also it has been raining since early morning—a real old-fashioned wet day, of which we have seen few for the last three or four years. Notwithstanding the weather, however, we have been hoeing the root on Baker's, which is a work we are most anxious to get done with before harvest.

Towards evening I walked to one of the root fields, in order to have the pleasure of seeing the much-needed rain fall upon it. How the turnips seemed to rejoice in the moisture as it pattered continually upon their green leaves, now flagging no longer, and ran in shining beads down to the neck of the bulbs, then over them to the droughty earth, that sucked up every precious drop of it as greedily as does a sponge parched by the sirocco! One could almost see their delight—thirsty children new satisfied could not look more glad.

Leaving the field, I walked down the Bungay road, on which thin pools of water glimmered like March ice; till presently I met a man in a cart who was looking for Hood. I asked him what was the matter, and he told me that the foal which had been running with its dam—the pony from Bedingham—on the long railway marsh, No. 20, was stretched upon its side dying. Asking my informant to find Hood, I pushed on to the marsh, and there I found the foal—a beautiful little black-pointed and muzzled thing of five months old—not dying, but stone dead. There it lay upon its side, its slender legs stretched out stiffly, its head quite motionless, not asleep—dead, dead—a glance showed it. Over it stood the mare, as still as though she had been cut in stone, her ears sloped back, but not with vice, her under lip projecting, the milk dripping from her distended udder, and in the large eyes and on the patient face a look of woe utter and pathetic. No human mother grieving over her first-born could have shown sorrow more visibly; yet this creature made no moan, and weep it could not. It knew that its offspring was dead; and to me, the watcher, it seemed to be trying to understand what this death meant, and why it caused such suffering.

Perhaps, however, this was fancy; perhaps horses do not know mental pain, and the impression I received was due partly to the surroundings of the scene. Above, the sky sullen and grey, dropping a thin and failing rain; below the sodden grass, in which water splashed beneath the foot; to the west the struggling and smoky sunset, whereof a red ray lit upon the surface of the long, reed-fringed dyke; and for background a few melancholy willows, round about which stretched the desolate expanse of marsh. Not a soul to be seen, not a sound to be heard save the

far-away note of a plover calling towards the common.   And there,
falling naturally into that sad scheme of colour, a key and answer
to the picture as it were, this live animal, with the milk trickling
from its udder, standing over the dead, itself as still as the dead.
Could it be painted as I saw it, that scene might serve as a
symbol of all loss, all sorrow, and all death.   And yet it was made
up of a mare standing over a dead foal in a wet pasture—nothing
more.

We had great difficulty, by the way, in driving the pony from
the body of the foal, to which it broke back continually through
the ring of those who were engaged in its capture.

Only once before in my life did I witness a pastoral scene that
left quite so strong a sense of desolation upon my mind.   It was
in the uplands of Natal, in the year of the Boer rebellion, when a
snowstorm, such as had never been known, swept the country,
killing thousands of horses and cattle.   I was travelling towards
the coast, walking with my companions behind the cart, so that
the mules might find it lighter to drag through the snowdrifts.
Presently we saw two waggons, that seemed to have a deserted
appearance, standing at a distance from the track, and went to
look at them.   What we found is not easy to forget !   There was
a space between the waggons, where their owners had tried to
make a shelter for the cattle by tying a tilt from one roof-tent
and dissel-boom to the other.   This had availed nothing against
the icy blast, however, for in the enclosure lay the oxen dead—a
confused and motley-coloured heap of them.   Or, rather, thirty
were dead.   One still moved in the heap, and one, the last
survivor, stood over them, his great horns swaying to and fro, as
little by little the unaccustomed cold froze into his heart.   At
the back of the nearest waggon, staring at the dead cattle and
wrapped round with sacks, sat a man and a woman, rude, unwashed
Boers.   We asked them if the snow had killed the oxen, and the
man answered '*Ja.*'

'They were all we had,' added the woman in an unemotional
voice.   'Now we are beggars.'

Then we ran on to overtake the cart, but at a little distance I turned back to look, and there was the living ox swaying over its dead yoke-fellows ; there the two Boers staring sullenly at the sight ; there the dismal-looking waggons on the vast and lonely veld, lifeless now beneath its winding-sheet of snow ; while over all, piercing the grey cloud, a fierce ray from the westering sun fell like some sudden and gigantic sword.

To-day I have received by the post two interesting documents. The first of them is a prospectus of Garton's, Limited. The work done by Messrs. R. & J. Garton in producing new breeds of cereals, grasses, and clovers is well known among agriculturists. Myself, I have never seen any of these corns or grasses, but, if the published accounts are correct, some of them must be remarkable.

In their prospectus Messrs. Garton claim that among the cereals they have created 'are composed a series from which new and valuable food elements can be obtained which it is impossible to obtain from the varieties now generally cultivated.' They do not, however, propose to offer the seed of this series for sale, as all its produce is to be retained by the company, when formed, for the manufacture of 'new and distinct food products for human consumption, for which patent rights will be applied for in due course.' On the feasibility of this scheme it is difficult to express any opinion. It may be remarked, however, that hitherto the existing cereals, wheat, barley, oats, &c., have amply satisfied the wants of man, although this does not prove that tribes of grain possessing still richer qualities cannot be evolved by human skill. Here is a question which only the future can decide, and one whereof the development will be watched with great interest by the world, though it may be doubted whether, should Messrs. Garton succeed in their tremendous aim of the creation of a new and superior food-stuff, any patent law would enable them to withhold the advantages of their discovery from the public. For the present, however, most people would be satisfied with the improvement of existing cereals, a task to which their skill seems to have been directed with admirable results. It is to be hoped that the company which they are forming will be as successful in the future as their firm seems to have been individually in the past. As I gather from the prospectus that the whole of the ordinary shares are to remain in their hands, and that they will continue to manage the venture, this does not seem an extravagant expectation.

The second document is a circular from that splendid society, the Royal Agricultural Benevolent Institution, addressed to me as churchwarden of this parish, and asking that the whole or part of the Harvest Thanksgiving collection should be devoted to the Society, which since the year 1860 has already distributed over 360,000*l.* among distressed agriculturists and their children. Appended to the circular are a few examples of agricultural misfortune. They are melancholy reading, but, like most people connected with the land, I could supplement them from my own experience by instances equally sad. The distresses of those who in this country try to win a living out of the products of the earth are a very favourite subject of jest among celebrated after-dinner speakers, and rarely fail to provoke a ready laugh from an audience which has just dined upon American flour, River Plate beef, Australian mutton, Russian fowls, French milk, Dutch margarine, and German beet-sugar. Heaven knows, however, that they are genuine enough, as the Agricultural Benevolent Institution will have no difficulty in proving to any who trouble to inquire into the matter.

August 9.—I forgot to state in my diary yesterday that the foal was supposed to have expired of chill resulting from exposure to wet and cold on the low railway marsh. This theory struck me as odd ; first, because I was told that the little creature had been seen playing round its dam not four hours before the end, and secondly, because it showed no outward and visible sign of having come to its death from any such couse. For these reasons I directed that a post-mortem examination should be made. This was done by the veterinary this morning, with the result that the animal is proved to have died from the effects of an irritant vegetable poison. The stomach, which I saw, is perfectly scarlet in colour, and spotted here and there with bright purple patches. That the working of this poison must have been very violent and sudden is proved by the fact that the inflammation does not descend into the passages beyond the stomach, and by the absence of all swelling. The suggestion of the veterinary is that the animal must have eaten the poisonous weed known as water hemlock, which it seems that foals will devour, although older animals reject it. As he informs us that the fee will only be ten shillings, we have agreed that the inflamed organ shall be sent to an expert to be scientifically examined. If there is any venomous herb growing in this marsh, it is desirable that we should know its nature.

August 10.—The wet weather continues, but we are able to plough and drill headlands with turnip seed. Hood and the veterinary have been searching the railway marsh, and have found a poisonous weed growing upon it which is known as fool's parsley, some plants of which seem to have been recently bitten. As no water-hemlock has been discovered—the administration of any drug being out of the question—it is supposed that this fool's parsley did the mischief. The odd thing is that all last year, and I think during previous seasons, foals were running on this marsh without taking the slightest injury from its herbage. This spring, however, the weather was wet, and it occurs to me as possible that damp favours the production of deadly weeds. At the same time it must be remembered that we have had wet springs before that of 1898.

August 12.—To-day arrived two Southdown rams and thirty-one black-faced ewes, which Mr. Robert Simpson had bought for me at the sale at Bury. The rams are aged, and one of them is rather shaky on his feet, from foot-rot in past seasons I suppose ; but I understand that their pedigree is distinguished, and as they only cost forty shillings apiece I cannot complain. The ewes, on the other hand, were bought at fifty-one shillings a head. This is twelve shillings apiece more than I gave two years ago for my present lot of black-faced ewes, which are very much better bred than these new additions to the flock. The fact is that black-faced Suffolk sheep have recently become more popular, with the result that their price has risen. Large sums are paid for the best of them ; thus I hear that a gentleman in the neighbourhood has just given fifty guineas for a ram of this breed.

To-day we are cutting the All Hallows pease, for it is our first of harvest, and, what is of good augury, very fine. These pease are a poor crop, partly from the coldness of the spring and partly because of the red-weed with which this land is infested. At Bedingham they begin harvest to-morrow. To-day Moore is horse-hoeing the white turnips which are drilled on No. 18, where the fly took off the swedes. Oddly enough, it did not touch the turnips, so there is a very good plant of them.

August 15.—Last Saturday, the 13th, we cut the pease on Baker's, which are a much better crop than those upon All Hallows, probably because this field was manured, part of it, with Bungay compost. Some authorities say, however, that pease do best without the stimulus of manure, but I suppose that this is only when the land is in good heart, which is not the case on Baker's. The weather, both on Saturday, Sunday, and to-day, has been lovely, and exceedingly hot. The barleys are now very white and 'dying' fast, too quickly, I fear, for the good of the sample. The wheat also has turned a rich golden yellow, and is not so much beaten down by the recent rains as might have been expected.

This morning we set the new reaper to work on the glebe fields of oats, Nos. 39 and 40, which are bearing a good crop for so scaldy a piece of land, owing doubtless to the wet of the early summer. Before the machine can be put in a pathway for it must be mown round the field with a scythe. Then the thing starts, drawn by two horses. It is beautiful to see it work, for it cuts wonderfully clean, the arms sweeping the bundles of corn from the platform in sheaves, ready for the binder. By a clever contrivance of the mechanism, which it is impossible to explain here, this act is not always performed by the same arm. The limb that at one revolution delivers the bundle from the table to the ground, at the next merely bends the straw over the knives, while another dips down to the platform and clears it.

Thus into these various and complex operations the strength of the horses is transformed and distributed to each of them in such proportion as is needful. Care, however, must be taken at the corners, where the reaper turns, or it will jam ; indeed, it is well for a man to round these off with a scythe. Some people yoke three horses to such machines, but I use only two, which are changed at noon, as half a day's work with a reaper behind them is quite enough for a pair of horses. I believe, by using six horses instead of four, under favourable circumstances, that twelve or thirteen acres can be 'knocked down,' but we are quite satisfied if we get through six or eight in a day's work. By the way, I see in the papers that a terrific accident has just happened with one of these machines. A pair of horses attached to it bolted, and in trying to stop them their owner was thrown to the ground and so cut about by the knives that he died.

August 18.—Yesterday we finished mowing the barley on the Ape field, No. 26, and that on the part of No. 23 opposite which was sown with this grain. I heard from Hood that two parties had expressed a willingness to take Bedingham if we could come to terms. I shall decline their offers with thanks, as, after the expense and labour of bringing this farm into condition, I do not care to run the risk of its ruin at the hands of a yearly tenant.

This morning there fell a very heavy dew—indeed, as I walked down to bathe in the Waveney, about half-past seven, everything was drenched with it, and the feel of the air was quite autumnal.

We have carted all the barley from the Ape field, after it has been but two days cut; which can only be done when no grass-seeds have been sown with the grain to make a hay crop in the second year. This used to be an invariable practice with us, but now that I have so much land down to permanent pasture, some of the barley stubbles are broken up for other crops ; thus beans will be drilled upon the Ape field this autumn. I should have added that the reason why the presence of layer prevents an early carting of barley is that, being green and succulent, it takes a while to dry, whereas the corn itself, which in this respect differs from wheat, and still more from oats, is as a rule practically sapless and dead when it is severed from the ground. A sample of this barley rubbed in the hand looks a little white to my eye ; but I hope that it will take more colour after 'sweating' for a few weeks on the stack, or rather in the home barn, where it has been stored till the day of thrashing.

About the end of last May, in the quiet of evening, when no gardeners were about, a pair of cuckoos might have been seen gliding with their curious dipping flight to and fro across the lawn-tennis court, as they flew uttering from time to time a broken and unusual note. Now we know what was their felonious intent, for on the lawn has recently appeared a young cuckoo being fed by two water-wagtails, with which I have been acquainted for many years. Heavens ! how those poor little birds must work to keep their fosterling supplied ! There the voracious, angry-looking creature sits, now in one place and now in another, his scarlet maw extended wide, and eats, and scolds, and scolds, and eats from dawn till dusk, and for aught I know to the contrary from dusk to dawn as well. After about a week of it one of the wagtails has either deceased from exhaustion or thrown up the contract—at any rate his mate is now alone and working double tides—for the cuckoo grows fast and is continually hungrier. Sometimes it perches in the boughs of a beech tree to be fed, and this afternoon I saw the wagtail actually seated upon its head there, and from that position thrusting insects down its insatiable throat.

August 19.—To-day I drove with my agent, Mr. Simpson, round some outlying farms belonging to this property. One of them is being farmed by two maiden ladies of an old-fashioned type. By 'old-fashioned,' however, I mean nothing disparaging, but that, instead of playing the piano and looking genteel in a silk dress and a sham diamond ring, these ladies bake and brew and cook, employing a managing man to see to the stock and field-work. They are types of a class that is fast vanishing from this county, and whom it is well to study while there is yet time. Moreover, they always seem to welcome their landlord when he chances to pass their way, and the land they till is in excellent condition.

The next farm we visited is that where the old gentleman lived who slept every night of his long life in the same room in which he was born, and died. Since his day, however, there has been another tenant here, and one of not a good stamp. He has departed, leaving the land in a very different condition from that in which he took it, and the place has been re-let to the present holder. The house, where his predecessor lived and died—a low, steep-roofed building, rather long for its size—is in fair order, but the state of the farm buildings is—or was—fearful. The old gentleman, who had known them from his childhood, did not care to see them interfered with, and the last man was not a person to be encouraged with repairs, but now these have to be faced. This year about 90*l.* is being spent on the barn, cowshed, and stable, and there remains a good deal more to be done in the future. When finished the buildings will be snug and convenient, being wood-clad with a brick footing; but the rent of the holding is now only 27*l.* 10*s.*, so that when even the present repairs are paid for no profit will come out of it for more than three years. At this rate it would take a landlord some time to develop into the plutocrat familiar to the mind of the rural agitator.

After inspecting these repairs we went on to a much larger farm—two hundred acres of land—which for some years past has been bringing in the magnificent revenue of 50*l.* a year minus

tithe (about 25*l.*) and repairs (a varying quantity).[1]   On the
pastures of this farm grow some very good oaks, and, remembering
a particularly grand tree in a certain meadow, I went to look at
it.   Presently it came in sight, but although the big bole was
there, somehow its appearance seemed to have changed.   Then I
saw the whole truth.   The lower limbs of the tree—great rungs
which had been perhaps one or two hundred years in growing—
had been mercilessly sawn off.   It was ruined.   Full of feelings
which it would be improper to express on paper, I proceeded to
another part of the farm where stood a second fine oak.   To be
brief, the same thing had happened—the lower boughs were
sawn off, and its shape and beauty, which had slowly matured
through centuries, were destroyed for ever.   Then I am afraid
that I lost my temper.   Calling the head man on the farm—the
tenant himself was not there—I spoke my mind to him, and asked
why this thing had been done, telling him with truth that however
little I might be able to afford it, I would rather have given a
year's rent of the farm than see those oaks thus mangled.   To all
this his only reply was that his master had told him to cut off
the limbs ; the fact being, I presume, that as in each case the trees
threw some shadow on the adjoining arable land, it was thought
profitable to thin them by removing the lower boughs, which
could be used as firewood.   I know another instance of the same
thing, where, on an estate belonging to a relation, the lower
branches of a whole line of oaks which stand by a footpath
were hacked off by the tenant without the owner even being
spoken to about the matter.   Five-and-twenty years ago such
an outrage could scarcely have happened, but now the tenant
is often master of the situation, and this is one way of showing
his independence.

I must add that since the above was written Mr. Simpson has
received a letter from the gentleman concerned in this tree-

[1] To show what has been the decrease in the value of agricultural land in
these counties, I may point out that in 1860 this farm brought in an annual
rent of 263*l.*

tragedy. He says that his man tells him that the trees he cut were damaged in a gale last March twelvemonth. It may be so, but in that event it is strange that the wind chanced to strike the lower and more sheltered boughs only; also that their removal had been put off for so long, and that the man did not mention these facts, but told me that he cut these rungs away by order of his master. However, they are gone, leaving the world poorer by two beautiful oaks, so there is an end of the case. I daresay that if they still stand, in another century or more the upper boughs will have thickened and they may look picturesque again; at any rate, I like to think so.

In driving through this heavy-land country I noticed two things : that the system of cleaning fields by summer fallowing them is more prevalent than with us, and that they use a good many 'maffies.' 'Maffie' is derived from hermaphrodite, and signifies a cart on to which, for the purpose of carting hay or corn, is affixed a contrivance like the fore-part of a waggon, so that in fact it is neither cart nor waggon. Hence the term. In all this stiff-soil district the corn crops seem to be heavy this year.

August 22.—Saturday the 20th was a fine, indeed a perfect, harvest day. The men were engaged in cutting the barley on the Thwaite field, No. 28, where there is a fair but not a heavy crop, with a bottom rather full of layer, as this portion of No. 28 is sown down for clover hay next year. The sight of the men, one following the other across the field in a jagged line as they cut down the ripe corn with wide sweeps of the scythe, made a fine picture of effort strenuous and combined. The place is pretty too, with the windmill in the background, and the heat-haze softened the scene, keeping it in tone and making it restful. One of the features of these mowings is the almost invariable presence of a man with a dog—someone in the village who is fond of a bit of sport. As the mowers approach the end of a stretch a bunny or two will bolt, and be swept up by the dog before it can win the shelter of the hedge. The rabbits thus obtained are,

I believe, divided among all concerned, upon some fixed system, but what it is I do not know.

Here is a story of a gentleman who knows about everything in the world except the art and practice of agriculture, who accompanied me to Bedingham yesterday. Scene : a beet field, and by the gate a patch of tiny white turnips recently drilled upon the site of the last year's root-clamp, or 'hale,' where swedes had been stored and earthed over.

'Why are these so much smaller than those?' asked my friend, pointing first to the patch of little turnips and next to the tall beet in contact with and surrounding them.

'Because of the hale,' I answered.

'Indeed!' he said, 'that is *most* interesting. Do you know, I had no idea that hailstorms were ever so strictly local and so limited in their destructive effect. Look, the line might have been cut with a knife.'

After all, though we laughed at it, his mistake was natural, for 'hale' and 'hail' are pronounced the same, and he had never heard the former term, which is, I think, peculiar to these parts.

Coming home through the orchard from church about eight o'clock last evening, I stayed a while in the Buildings stackyard, to watch a great white owl hawking silently in the twilight. By day and by night life seems to be a very solemn thing to an owl ; but perhaps—who knows?—he is really a merry bird. Presently, grey and ghostlike, he glided close to my head, for in the shadow of the tall paled gate I think that I was invisible to him. Then he turned, and rising to clear the haystack, saw, I suppose, a mouse running about upon the thatch. At any rate, he swooped, striking the roof of the stack with a heavy bump. But the mouse had been too quick for him, so, recovering himself, that owl departed in disgust, and a minute later I heard his melancholy note far away across the lawn.

This morning the machine was cutting wheat on the top portion of the pit-hole field, No. 23. Here the sparrows have done great damage ; indeed quite enough grain for a seeding is lying

on the land, picked from the ears and cast away by these mischievous little wretches.   In this field there was a mighty rabbit
hunt, for at the end of it lies the little Hollow Hill plantation, also
the old sand-pit in its midst is a great harbour for them.   Several
men and dogs appeared upon the scene, and as the area of standing
corn was narrowed to a little patch the rabbits began to bolt from
it freely.   To and fro ran the men, shouting, while the scared
coneys, after various vain efforts to hide themselves, made a
wild attempt to escape, the cur dogs leaping high into the air to
try to catch a glimpse of them as they scuttled through the fallen
corn.   With many turns and doubles they coursed the poor
bunnies, uttering short sharp yaps of excitement, and, gripping
them at last with their white teeth, shook and bit them till they
were dead.   In all about a score of rabbits were killed, but quite
as many more gained the shelter of the hedges and plantation.

In the afternoon the machine was moved to the All Hallows
wheat, No. 32.   On half of this field the corn is badly laid by the
recent wind and rain storms, while in the other half it stands
quite upright and unharmed.   The laid half, through which the
thistles and divers rubbish are growing freely, was, I remember,
drilled a fortnight before the upright half.   Last year this laid
portion produced a crop of vetches, and, as vetches are supposed
to exhaust the land, it received a good dressing of farmyard manure;
while the rest, that was under beans, among the stubble of which
some mustard had been sown, was only folded over with the sheep.
The results seem to suggest that it is a mistake to manure wheat
land too heavily, as it makes the straw rank and liable to go down
under wind and rain ; also that vetches are not after all a very
exhausting crop.

The weather to-day has been very sultry, and heavy rain must
have fallen within a few miles of us, as a thunderstorm growled and
muttered past in the direction of Loddon, but left us untouched.

A friend with whom I was talking this afternoon about the
poverty of those who follow the profession of agriculture, pointed
out that here and there are people who seem to thrive upon it.

This indeed is the case, for in our district I know of two men who a short time ago had little or nothing, but now are farming hundreds of acres of land. How, under the present circumstances of agriculture, they have managed to get their capital together is to me a mystery. I can only suppose that it has been done by shrewd and successful dealing, or possibly such men may be the representatives of others who are willing to entrust them with money. Otherwise, in these days of unprofitable prices, the gulf between a farm employing two horses and one of a thousand acres seems too wide for the most intelligent person to span in the course of a dozen years.

August 23.—To-day the men have been tying up wheat, which is left by the reaper in bundles ready to their hands, and carting pease from No. 37 into the All Hallows stackyard. First the pease, now brown and withered, are raked into lines, where they lie in lumps as they left the scythe, with sufficient space between the lines for a waggon to travel. Then they are loaded on to the waggon, a lump being lifted at each forkful.

While the carting was in progress I had an opportunity of watching a botfly, or horse-bee, at work. The insect buzzes about the horse, and continually touches it on such portions of its frame as lie within reach of the animal's tongue, for the most part on the inner side of the knees and upon the shoulders. At each touch of its tail there appears a little white egg, which is securely gummed to the extremity of one of the hairs of the horse's hide. How is the hair selected so surely and swiftly, and how is the egg thus fixed to it without fail? This egg the horse when licking himself transfers first to his mouth and thence to his stomach, where it affixes itself to the coats of the membrane, and in due course becomes a bot. In the following spring this bot, having completed its unsavoury development, and being now a maggoty and unpleasant looking object, passes from the stomach to the earth, where it lies until it is transformed into a fly exactly resembling that which buzzed around the horse last autumn. I succeeded in catching this particular fly, after I had seen it lay an enormous number of eggs. It is an insect greatly resembling a bee, with an arched tail, or egg-depositor, and very large and transparent eyes. Hood assured me that they live in nests like ordinary bees, but on this point I think that, for once in his life, Hood is mistaken.

To-day I received the report of the analyst on the stomach of the foal, which was sent to him to be examined. It is a negative document, for he can tell us nothing of the cause of death beyond that it was probably brought about by a violent vegetable poison, of which we were already convinced. What is not negative is his bill, which, instead of the ten shillings that I understood I should have to pay, amounts to three guineas, which sum, however, he has reduced to two guineas on the urgent representation of the veterinary who forwarded him the organ to be analysed. I daresay that the charge is fair and reasonable enough, although the investigations of the chemist leave us none the wiser. I wish to point out, however, that such fees are beyond the means of the farmer. The value of such a foal as I lost, when alive, may have been four guineas, and half that amount is too much to pay for abortive post-mortem researches on its stomach. If the Board of Agriculture, or the County Councils, could provide laboratories, where such inquiries might be carried out at really cheap rates, it would be a great boon to farmers.[1]

This evening the air was very close, and the gnats were extraordinarily active. Indeed, the sound of their humming reminded me much of that of the mosquitoes on some of the tropical rivers in Mexico or in the African fever districts. If watched, these

---

[1] I find, what I did not know at the time I wrote the above passage, that the Royal Agricultural Society, to which I belong, will undertake such investigations for its members at very reasonable rates. The cost of an examination of viscera for all vegetable poisons is 1*l.*, and the highest charge in the scale for more complicated operations is 2*l.* Charges for various other services, such as the treatment of sick animals, the inquiry into outbreaks of disease among stock, or the reporting on the purity of samples of seeds, &c., seem to be on the same moderate scale. It is a pity that so few farmers know where they can find such advantages.

gnats may be observed to form a pillar over a man's head, above which they rise and descend as the fancy takes them, or in accordance with aims and arrangements that we do not understand. It is, I think, this rise and fall of their multitudes that produces such very curious variations in the noise of the humming, which now sounds quite loud and angry, and now seems faint and far away.

August 27.—All this week we have been very busy with the ordinary routine of harvest work, which has gone on without interruption from the weather. On Wednesday the 24th we finished carting the All Hallows pease, and carried the Baker's pease into Baker's yard, in each case topping the sacks with oats. On Thursday morning, strangely enough, there was a slight frost, and the men engaged in mowing that portion of the wheat on the All Hallows field, No. 32, which is too laid to be cut by the machine were quite drenched by the dew. Afterwards we carted barley from the Thwaite field, which seems to be a fair sample, and a bulkier crop than I expected.

Yesterday was fine, though cloudy, with a dropping glass, but to-day the weather holds. I went to lunch with my friend and neighbour, Mr. Henry Smith of Ellingham, and looked over his farm, which is a large one, for he has about eight hundred acres in hand. There are points in favour of farming on a large scale ; for instance, Mr. Smith has his own steam-engine, and thus saves the cost of thrashing. Also, he is able to cut chaff and saw timber with economy and despatch. Mr. Smith is a believer in sheep, and owns two fine flocks of ewes, which are folded about the lands, thus saving the muck-cart many a journey. But with all these advantages, including those which cannot quite be estimated of his personal intelligence, experience, and supervision, he confided to me that, so far, he has not found farming an absolute Klondyke. More, he produced his books to prove it, and very clear they are, being kept upon a most excellent system. He has thrashed a little wheat, coming off some rather light, sheep-tethered land, and it runs out at ten coombs the acre ; a result with which he has every cause to be satisfied. I only hope that my own will do as well.

Near to the Hall in the park at Ellingham stands a great poplar tree, on which the lightning fell some weeks ago. In this instance the current behaved rather strangely, for, lighting on the extremity of a bough, it passed round and round it and the trunk, leaving grooves such as might have been cut by a carpenter, until it came to a strand of barbed wire, which was fastened to the bole by a staple. Tearing out this staple, it fled along the wire to an iron stanchion, down which it descended to the earth, burning the grass and taking all the rust off the stanchion as it went. Luckily, there was no living thing beneath the tree. A few years ago Mr. Smith was not so fortunate, for six or seven cattle that were grazing in the park, which seems to be a favourite playground for the lightning, were destroyed by a single flash. They were found with foam upon their mouths and their bodies bent into a bow, as though by tetanus or the effects of strychnine.

This is the third time in my life that I have known lightning to pass round and round trees or poles, cutting neat spiral grooves in their substance. In Ditchingham Park, however, about three years ago, it played a stranger trick, for in this instance the current travelled down the centre of an oak, and by the exercise of its gigantic force drove the heart of the tree through the outer wood and bark, where it appeared in numberless white splinters. Only once did I ever see anything resembling the result produced by that stroke. On an occasion when I was shipwrecked the vessel, of about 1,000 tons burden, hung upon a point of rock, with sixty-fathom water beneath her stern. Presently her back broke, throwing so fearful a strain on to the mast and rigging that something had to give. The shrouds would not part, for they were of steel wire, and the mast did not snap, because the pull upon it was vertical and from both sides. Therefore under the awful pressure the very fibre of the wood of which it was formed seemed to disintegrate, at any rate grey splinters forced from within outwards became visible all over its varnished surface, to which they gave a frosted appearance.

Owing, I suppose, to the proximity of the river bad thunderstorms very seldom visit this house, which perhaps is providential, for when long ago I was first acquainted with the place, I found that for years the severed end of the lightning conductor, that was broken in two by some accident, had dangled against the wall of the building about fifteen feet above the ground. Had a flash come down it?—but fortunately it never did! The story reminds me of one which I have been told of a local plumber, who volunteered to fit his church tower with a lightning conductor, and having brought the cable to ground, in order to make a tidy job of it fitted its end into a soda-water bottle, which he buried. In due course the lightning descended the rod, and on finding itself cut off from the earth by the non-conducting glass, fled up it again and through the church, to the disturbance of the congregation.

On one occasion, however, I remember a heavy storm here, that is as storms are judged in this country. A meeting was going on in the house, when suddenly the speaker was silenced by a vivid flash and a crashing peal of thunder. I was sure from a certain rending sound that something had been struck, and on going out after the rain had ceased I found that I was not mistaken. About one hundred yards from the garden stands an elm tree, down which the lightning had descended, leaving a broad white gash. Further investigations revealed a very badly scared farm boy. No wonder that he was frightened, for his escape had been marvellous. The lad, who was employed mowing down thistles on the back lawn, when it began to rain went to stand beneath this very tree, taking his scythe with him. The rain increasing in volume and the water beginning to drip on him through the leaves he determined to shelter in a little fowl-house which stood not more than ten paces away. As he entered the fowl-house the lightning struck the tree, passing into the ground at the very spot where he had been standing a few seconds before, and scattering fragments of bark and wood on to the tin roof of the hut. This was the same boy who, as I think I have mentioned, once lay for an hour under the bull's manger, while that animal, having first knocked him there, sniffed and pawed at his prostrate form. If he is not now a firm believer in a protecting Providence he must be of a singularly sceptical turn of mind.

But, after all, the tempests which we experience here compared to those of Africa are much as the floating models on the lake at the Earl's Court Exhibition would be to a fleet of ironclads in action. A friend once informed me that he was actually driven out of a certain district in East Africa by the frequency and fearful violence of the thunderstorms, which so affected his nerves that he could neither shoot nor sleep ; and personal experience proves to me that they can be bad further to the south. A gentleman whom I know told me that once he was riding along a road in Natal, at a little distance behind a waggon full of people. A thunderstorm came on, and after a vivid flash the waggon stopped. He rode up to it, and found that of its occupants, who had huddled together beneath the tilt to escape the rain, no less than seven were dead. I am glad to say that I have never seen anything so dreadful as this, although I have had some experiences of lightning. Once, accompanied by my wife and a woman servant, I drove a 'spider' at full gallop before an advancing storm. Reaching the inn we handed over the horses to some Kaffirs, and ran for shelter. As we entered the door the lightning struck in the courtyard, not more than a dozen yards behind us. The conduct of the maid—a middle-aged and determined woman—on this occasion was amusing. In her terror she lost her head and informed her mistress that she was 'no lady' because she remained calm ; under these circumstances a 'lady,' it appears, ought to have screamed and gone into hysterics.

On another occasion I was on duty in court at Pretoria, when there came such a fearful flash that everybody there, including the judge and myself, sprang to his feet. It transpired that the lightning had struck the next house and actually cut or shook a child out of its mother's arms, but, strange to say, without doing more than stupefy either mother or child. Here is a second instance of lightning producing stupefaction without doing physical harm. One night at Pretoria I was kept very late at my office attending to some official business. During the evening a thunderstorm passed over the town, but it cleared away by midnight, and I did not reach home before three o'clock in the morning. On entering the sitting-room, as he is a very abstemious man, I was astonished to see the friend with whom I lived hanging over the arm of an easy chair apparently quite intoxicated. I roused him, and muttering something he staggered off to bed. Next morning he told me that the last thing he remembered was sitting in the chair and seeing a bright flash of light. Afterwards, on going to inspect the hen-house which we were building at a distance of about fifteen paces from the cottage, we found several of the poles neatly grooved round by the lightning in the fashion of the tree at Ellingham. It must have been the shock and proximity of this flash which stupefied my friend, for I do not think that it entered the house.

In short, in Africa the lightning is a thing which even Ajax would scarce have ventured to defy. If the traveller is overtaken by a tempest on the open veld, the best thing that he can do is to get off his horse, or out of his cart, and lie down upon the ground. It was through neglect of this precaution that a gentleman whom I knew was killed, as he drove along the road in his spider. His name was Carter, and he kept an hotel in Pretoria. He had been educated at Eton, or one of the other large public schools, and I think that some tankards which he had won in the school sports stood upon a shelf in the bar or sitting-room of the hotel. If I remember rightly, the companion who was with Mr. Carter in the spider escaped. In the same way, while I was in Natal, a flash struck near a man and wife sleeping side by side. One was taken and the other left.

But of tales of the doings of lightning in South Africa there is no end, so with these samples I will leave the subject.

August 29.—Yesterday being Sunday I employed the afternoon in walking over the farm at Bedingham, in order to learn
how they were getting on with the harvest.   Generally I find
something at Bedingham that interests my bucolic mind, and
yesterday the discoveries were two : one satisfactory and the
other the reverse.   On the new pasture, No. 19, that is sown
with the deep-rooted herbs, the young cattle are grazing upon the
aftermath or eddish which has grown since the hay was carried.
I watched them, and was glad to see that whenever they came
to a plant of chicory they ate it with relish almost down to the
ground.   The second sight I saw was that of long streams of
thistle seeds being borne by a stiff breeze on to my land from
territories in the possession of neighbouring powers.   I believe
that it has been declared by competent courts of law that an
action lies against a neighbour whose fields produce an unreasonable crop of weeds to the detriment of other land which is
well farmed.   I never heard, however, of such a suit being
brought in East Anglia.   It seems to me that the damage would
be very difficult to prove.

To-day has been cold, and during the afternoon the threatening rain fell in showers.   About eleven o'clock the machine
stopped cutting the wheat on Baker's, where it works to perfection,
for the corn here is upstanding and not too thick, and we began
to cart the black oats from the glebe field, No. 40.   These we
secured, but the drizzle prevented us from carrying the white oats
from No. 39.   Oats are grain that must be carted quite dry, for
if damp they heat and spoil.   Wheat, on the other hand—especially if it stands on the stack for some months before thrashing—
may be carried when damp without injury to the corn.   Buck
tells me that he has carted wheat in a rain so heavy that he was
soaked to the skin, and that on being thrashed the grain was
found to have taken no harm.

This morning I was talking to the bricklayer who is rebuilding
one of the cottages on Baker's Farm for the owner, Mr. Carr.   He
gave me a brick, which he found built into the wall, which has

cut upon it, in antique figures, the date 1393. This brick, which is of our modern shape, weighs five pounds eleven ounces, or originally nearly six pounds, for some portions of it are broken away ; and I suppose, from their shape and character, that before the clay was set into the kiln to bake the figures were cut, in 1393, and not at any subsequent date. But the reader may judge for himself, for below is printed a reproduction of them.

It would seem, therefore, that so long as five hundred and five years ago housen stood at this spot, where meet four cross-roads and a path that is now a lane. Doubtless, however, these dwell-

ings have been several times rebuilt during that long period of time, although the mason tells me that, so far as he can judge, this particular brick seems never to have been disturbed since it was first set in place. Here is an example of the great antiquity of our country life in England. Doubtless, five centuries ago, as to-day, men lived in cottages at this very spot. Doubtless, as they do now, the four roads met there and the lane ran down to the marshes ; and the seed was sown and the crops were gathered on the field above as I gather them this very harvest-tide.

Oh ! if only the place could tell all its story, with the detail which would be necessary to make us understand it, what a story that would be! A humble tale, perhaps—a tale of little things and obscure lives, and yet how fascinating! When we consider bygone ages we are apt to dwell only upon the histories of distinguished individuals and the records of great and startling occurrences. Yet these do not really make up the past. Notable men are rare; there be very few in any age who can lift their heads and voices high enough above the raving crowd for the world to see and hear them, and great events occur only from time to time. But behind these Titans existed the dim multitudes of the people—those whose qualities and characters really fashioned the nation for good or ill; our forefathers, whose instincts and strivings built up the empire we inherit, in whom lay the weight and influence which brought about the revolutions of our history, and from whom were produced those strong characters that carried out their will and with whose names we are still familiar. But of all these forgotten humble hordes there remains nothing but our-selves, who, by the mysterious descent of blood, continue their existence, and such poor memorials as are inscribed by some long-dead hand upon this imperishable clay.

What a strange instinct it is, by the way, that prompts men to try to perpetuate some little token of their existence and individuality upon substances not likely to be destroyed, in the hope, I suppose, that in a far-off future age other men will unearth them and think such thoughts as I set down upon this sheet. Is it not, in fact, the feeble and half-unconscious striving or revolt against the oblivion which awaits us all—a weak but quite human desire for recollection in the unshaped future, for recognition of the fact that once beneath the same eternal sun they, the for-gotten ones, were born, suffered, worked, and died? In Egypt, among the wreck of buildings reared thousands of years ago, I have found such relics of those whose toil created them; in breaking up an old floor in these very rooms I have noted the name of the carpenter who laid it rudely scrawled upon a board. And see how the tendency continues. Myself, I remember writing my own name, the date, and a Latin inscription, with the record of my repairs, upon the back of an oak panel that is set into the hall of this house, thinking the while that, long after I am dust, it might prove of passing interest to some unborn creature who may chance to be present when at length the place falls into ruin, or is pulled down piecemeal.

Another curiosity about these cottages is that the two possess but one brick oven between them, which, for reasons too long to explain, was, I am convinced, common to both. What neighbours' quarrels, what small but very active bitternesses may not have arisen during the last few centuries over the use of that oven ! If some experience of such differences is any guide, these must have been many. Those who frequent a bench of magistrates will know them well.

These cottages, at their last reconstruction, which I should judge to have taken place a hundred and fifty or two hundred years ago, were largely built of stud-work framed on sapling boughs measuring about an inch and a half in diameter, and lashed to the roof beams with string. This string, of which I secured some pieces, is for the most part still fairly sound, and of a very strong and even make.

August 31.—Yesterday was fine, so the rain of the previous afternoon proved but a passing shower. We finished cutting, tying, and shocking the wheat on Baker's, and mowing that on All Hallows, which has proved a most troublesome and exhausting task, it being matted together by the weeds which have grown through it as it lay upon the ground.

To-day, the last of the month, is still fine. Truly we are enjoying a harvest to be thankful for. We have been carting the vetches from No. 21 and the white oats from the glebe land.

This evening, standing on a high ridge in the Pit field, I watched the rising of the harvest moon. She appeared in an absolutely cloudless sky, a huge and lambent ball, pale at first, but growing brighter with each passing minute, till her mountain ranges and valleys showed clearly upon the shining disc.

Looked at from my standpoint, there, on the top of Hollow Hill, the scene was singularly beautiful and solemn. Below me lay the village, backed by the windmill with its tall sails at rest, while to the left the wide and shadowed sweep of the Waveney valley stretched on and on until it lost itself in gloom. Little by little the dusk gathered, dimming and blotting out the less salient features of the landscape. Now I could no longer distinguish the boughs of the poplars, showing like a net hung against the sky, and now the poplars themselves had melted away. Then, as the sky darkened, like stars appearing, one by one the lights of the village began to glow, and the evening hush of Nature deepened into perfect silence, for at this season the birds have ceased to sing.

Very lovely were the colours while the twilight lingered. In front stood the golden sheaves of corn, contrasting sharply with the shining green of the mangold tops, beyond which stretched the expanse of stubble land, dead pale beneath the pallid sky, and on its borders a group of yellow stacks.

Soon, as I watched, the air grew chill and autumnal, with just a hint of frost in it, giving warning that it was time to go; which I was loth to do, for never can I remember, at any rate in these latitudes, seeing the moon look more grand and perfect than she did to-night. Doubtless, however, when beneath this ridge of ground whereon I stood lay a swamp tenanted by monstrous reptiles, she shone just as sweetly with no human eye to note her. When the deep sea rolled here, her broad rays broke upon its bosom; when from century to century the thick-ribbed ice ground and gripped this land, its glaciers gleamed blue in that soft light; and when man, having gathered his last harvest, has returned to the Lord of harvests, still that light, piercing the gulf of airless space, will flow upon this hillside, and creep down yonder valley, grown black and dead, and desolate.

The reflection is old and trite, but perhaps it is as well to remember from time to time what gnats we are—gnats humming in an autumn twilight, forgetful of the day behind us and without knowledge of the dawn to be.

SEPTEMBER

September 1.—To-day we held our Brewster's Sessions at Bungay when, as no complaints were made, all the licenses were renewed. According to the calculation of the superintendent of police there is in Bungay a licensed house to every 106 of the population, infants in arms included, and this without reckoning the wine-merchants or the establishments which trade in alcoholic liquors by virtue of what are known as 'grocers' licenses.' In the parishes of the district things are little better, for here there is a licensed house to every 207 of the population. It will be observed that in Bungay and its neighbourhood the toper need not go thirsty for lack of opportunity to quench his drought.

The superintendent also read his report for the year on the crime statistics of the district. I am glad to say that they show a marked and progressive diminution, owing chiefly, I believe, to the spread of education among the classes from which spring the majority of criminals. For instance, I can remember that when first I served upon this Bench we were often called upon to deal with charges of brutal assault, cases in which people had been got down and kicked or knocked about with heavy sticks, and so forth. Now we have but few of these offences, a fact that cannot be attributed solely to the measures which we took to put a stop to crimes against the person.

This afternoon I went to Bedingham, where the harvest is going on well. There remains, however, a good deal to be secured, including the beans, the oats, a little wheat, and one field of barley. The bottom in the last laid pasture, No. 21, on which the barley has now been cut, is looking really splendid. All the seeds seem to have taken, not excepting the chicory and other herbs, which appear everywhere among the grasses.

September 3.—The layer in the barley which we were cutting at Baker's yesterday on No. 41 is so thick that the straw, if well saved, will really be almost as good as hay. Take them all round, the crops are wonderfully heavy this year. There is so much of what the men call 'boolk' that the difficulty is to get them on to the stack.

To-day I went out shooting with a neighbour. The partridges seem to be rather scarce, and the sun was terribly hot. Never do I remember feeling the effects of heat and thirst in this country more than I did towards the close of our tramp this afternoon. In a day's September shooting the sportsman walks over a good many miles, especially if he happens to be the right- or left-hand gun. Partridge-shooting in a hot autumn is very different from partridge-driving or covert-shooting later in the year, when the gun merely moves from place to place and stands until the birds come over him. I am inclined to believe, also, that the advent of cycles (or is it perchance the advent of age?) makes people suffer more from the exertion of walking than they were wont to do. All the summer long one has been accustomed to roll from spot to spot upon a bicycle—I even use mine for going about the farm—so that when it comes to a long day's honest trudging, with many a fence to scramble through and no friendly wheel to help, one feels the change. It is certain that people who, before the invention of these Heaven-sent machines, were devoted to walking now walk no more, and I believe that soon it will be difficult to induce the children who are growing up to-day to put one foot before the other. The same thing may be noticed in countries where everybody rides. Thus, in Africa I have known men have their horses saddled in order to carry them a couple of hundred yards.

To-day we are busy getting up barley, and have finished building the wheat stack at All Hallows.

September 6.—Sunday was again very hot, but yesterday the sky became overcast, so we took the opportunity to push forward with the cutting of the beans on No. 26 and with the carting of those that are already down. Beans are things which it is very difficult to deal with in hot weather, as the sun causes the pods to open and the grain to shed out. When dead ripe, also, they are a strange-looking crop, especially if, as is the case with this field, they chance to have grown very tall. I recommend them to the attention of Mr. Horton, the artist, who, with strange success, uses natural objects in furtherance of a symbolical art that, to my mind, is full of grim and spiritual imagination, and to Mr. Sime, to whom the gift is given of portraying scenes connected with what the old Egyptians called the Underworld as surely man seldom did before him. Seen beneath a sullen sky, or in the light of an angry sunset, there is something forbidding about a large expanse of their black, ungainly stalks, dead, but still standing. The crop would be eminently appropriate to the infernal fields, which one might expect to approach through an avenue of shivering and melancholy blue gums, or of huge cedars hung with greybeard Spanish moss, such as the traveller may see in the home of the ill-fated Emperor Montezuma at Chapoltepec, in Mexico, and lurid 'nepenthe' plants.

To-day I heard by chance that in the course of the repairs of Mettingham church, in this neighbourhood, a skeleton had been discovered very peculiarly disposed. Knowing that such things are apt to be disturbed or quickly bricked up out of sight, I started at once to investigate the matter. Arriving at the church just as the workmen were leaving, I asked them if they knew where the bones lay, but they had no knowledge of any bones, and could only show me one or two ancient stone coffin lids. Then they departed and we began to search on our own account, but for a long while without results. At length my companion called to me that she had found them. On the south side of the church is an annexe or chapel, dating apparently from the fifteenth century, and in the wall of this annexe a recess, resembling the canopies that we see erected over tombs, but not more than fifteen inches deep. Whether it was ever larger of course I cannot say In this little recess is a stone slab about the width of an ordinary bench, out of the centre of which a V-shaped piece had been broken. On lifting this fragment a cavity appeared beneath, and in the cavity lay the skeleton of a man packed in a space of about three feet in length by one foot in width. Here the bones had been arranged in some past age and with great care, the skull being placed in the centre of the pile. Unless the outer wall has been altered it is obvious that the corpse cannot have been laid thus for burial, for even supposing that our ancestors were willing to suffer a decaying body to be packed away above the level of the ground in such a position that the gases arising from it must have percolated into the church—which is possible, for in those days people were not particular—it could not have been accommodated in so small a receptacle. There were no traces of any coffin. The remains are those of a large man of about fifty years of age, for the teeth seem somewhat worn, and his femurs show that he was old enough to suffer severely from the gout. Whose they can be and how they came here must, I fear, remain a matter for conjecture, though doubtless this is the skeleton of some important person who was buried a very long time ago, since it is quite yellow with age.

Are these perchance the bones of a Crusader or of a gentleman who was killed in the mediæval French wars, which were collected and sent home in a bag or box for interment in his native place? Some of them, especially the ribs, are frayed and knocked about at the ends, a fact which would go to support such a theory, for this damage might have occurred in the course of long travel. Or is it possible that here are the relics of a saint that once lay before the altar, but in the Reformation times were moved and hidden away in this hole to save them from desecration? It is a mystery, and a mystery it must remain, for the records throw no light upon its secret. Now the slab is cemented down, and if ever it should be lifted again hundreds of years hence, doubtless the grizzly remnants which it covers will once more excite the interest and wonder of the antiquaries of the future.

There was a great castle at Mettingham, whereof the gateway and some fragments of the keep still stand. It was founded by Sir John de Norwich, under a license granted by Edward III. in 1342. Later it became a monastery, and the keep was converted into a residence for the masters of Mettingham College, and afterwards, about 1750, into a farmhouse. Suckling quotes an entry from the register of Mettingham dating from the Commonwealth, when the custody of such documents appears to have been transferred to laymen. It is worth transcribing, showing, as it does what was the bucolic idea of a joke in the year 1653:

' *Mettingham Register Booke.*

' Wherein are written all the Marriages, Burths, and Burialls, according to the late Act of Parliament made the 22 day of September, 1653.

' Richard Stannard, of the same towne, in the Countie of Suff. Gent., approved by us, whose handes are here under subscribed accordinge to the choice of him made by the Inhabitants of the said Parish, to have the keeping of the Booke, and sworne to performe the Office of a Register accordinge to an Act of Parliament made in the yeare of our Lord God one thousand six hundred fifty and three.

SIMON SUCKBOYTLE	JUMPING JONES
NASTY NAN	BOUNTY BRIDG
JOHN GINGERBREAD	DICK DEVILL
HALFBRICKT MAN	

Inhabitants of Utopia.'

The reader will please observe the signatures.

The difference between the bulk of the crops this year and last year is extraordinary. So plentiful is the straw that, as

Peachey said to me to-day, 'Carting don't fare to be no manner of use.' To give one example : last year it took the produce of about twelve acres of land to fill the All Hallows barn with barley, whereas this year the crop from under seven acres is all that it will hold.

September 8.—Yesterday we were carting barley and wheat on Baker's, and on going over the field I came to the conclusion that we cannot finish harvest for another week, even if the weather holds. It was very hot and dry, and to-day is still hotter. The sun has a burning quality about it, owing, I suppose, to the thin parched atmosphere through which its rays penetrate—the kind of quality, I imagine, that gives people sunstroke. It is hard, however, to say what does produce sunstroke, for in Southern Africa, where the sun is very hot, I never heard of a case of it, and during all the years that I lived there I wore nothing except an ordinary cloth or felt hat, whereas for the last few days I have been glad to fill the crown of a Panama straw with cabbage leaves.

Here is a curious instance of the power of an English sun. In a Norfolk village with which I am acquainted lived a man, a retired soldier, who, when serving in India, had married a native woman, and brought her home to England. This woman, while working in the fields at harvest time, was struck by the sun and died. Certainly it seems strange that she, who had passed her youth beneath its most terrific rays, should have fallen a victim to them here in foggy Britain.

To-day we made an attempt to use the reaper to cut the barley on All Hallows field, No. 36. It proved a total failure, and had to be abandoned, for not only do the horses tread the corn a good deal, but the straw, being twisted and bowed, the knives snip off an enormous number of ears quite close to the grain. In walking round after the machine I picked up a quantity of these, which in all probability will be an utter loss, as the rake will not rake them and the fork will not lift them. To cut this barley with the reaper would mean the loss of at least two coomb an acre, but I am told that the machine does well enough where the straw stands up strong and straight.

Sir William Crookes, in his presidential address delivered yester-day to the British Association, draws a fearsome picture of coming wheat famines, which, if we had all of us a proper respect for science, ought to turn our—or rather our children's—hair grey, for I do not gather that the present generation need fear death from hunger. He tells us that 'a permanently higher price for wheat is, I fear, a calamity which must ere long be faced.' It is also a calamity which many farmers would face without dismay. He points out that in the United Kingdom we grow 25 per cent. and import 75 per cent. of the total amount of the wheat we consume annually, and asks, with good reason, how it is proposed to safeguard the country from starvation in the event of a hostile combination of European nations against us, or of any other accident preventing the arrival of our foreign food supply. His own address furnishes a possible answer, for from it it appears that 8,250,000 acres of land will grow all the corn our people require for food ; the total area of the United Kingdom being, I believe, about 70,000,000 acres. I suggest that the way to 'safeguard the country' is by means of a bounty, or in any other fashion, to make it profitable to farmers to put that 8,000,000 and odd acres under wheat, not an overwhelmingly large proportion out of the total acreage available. That it is prices and prices alone which have caused the wheat area to shrink so much in this kingdom I think I can prove.

In 1852—I quote from Mr. Henry Rew's pamphlet named 'The Agricultural Position of To-day'—the acreage under wheat in the United Kingdom was 4,058,731, and in 1885, 2,553,000, the population in the intervening period having increased by 8,500,000, while the wheat acerage during the same period declined by 1,500,000. But this is not all. According to the Agricultural Returns, the wheat area in the United Kingdom in 1897 had further decreased to 1,889,161 acres, whereas we shall be fairly safe in assuming that the population has increased by another

3,000,000. It appears, therefore, that we grow less than half of the wheat that we grew fifty years ago, although the number of mouths to eat it has multiplied enormously.

It will, I think, be admitted that this cumulative result is due purely to the fact that wheat production no longer pays.[1] If the nation wishes to be assured of a home supply sufficient to its needs, the remedy lies in its own hands. But while wheat comes in without let or hindrance and at very cheap rates from abroad it is not probable that the matter will be so much as taken into consideration. My own view, indeed, is that in face of the pitiful price commanded by this cereal and the rapid shrinkage of the supply of labour necessary to grow it, the cultivation of wheat should be abandoned wherever possible, and replaced by the cultivation of grass.

The question of our home stock, however, occupies but a fractional part of Sir William Crookes's address. Ranging from land to land, he surveys the wheat-producing capacity of them all, and comes to the distressing conclusion that very shortly it will be impossible for the world to produce the corn which it requires. This is a point upon which I cannot pretend to argue, especially with an eminent authority who has made a study of the subject.

But when it comes to the case of South Africa I may perhaps venture an opinion. Sir W. Crookes says, 'At the present time South Africa is an importer of wheat, and the regions suitable to cereals do not exceed a few million acres.' It is true that South Africa imports wheat, for the simple reason that the population there is too lazy to grow corn. I should say, however, that the land suitable to the production of cereals in this vast territory— and from Northern Rhodesia to the Cape it is vast almost beyond reckoning—might be measured by millions and millions of acres, upon which, if necessary, enough grain could be grown to feed a continent.

---

[1] The returns for 1898 show that the wheat area has increased to 2,102,220 acres, doubtless owing to the higher price which this cereal commanded during the winter of 1897 and the early spring of 1898.

Sir William Crookes's remedy for the famine which he foresees is that the water-power of Niagara should be used to produce nitrate to be employed in manuring the earth and making it more fertile. While Niagara and the Zambesi Falls are getting into harness I would suggest that the end required, namely, the accumulation of nitrogen in the soil, can be much promoted by the growth of leguminous crops, such as beans and vetches, which have the property of collecting nitrogen. I am afraid, however, that this plan sounds very humble and homelike after that of Niagara, yet it has merits, and with the help of a little farmyard muck will enable the farmer to produce forty or even fifty bushels to the acre upon sound and well-tended land. For the rest, as it is practically certain that if needful we can supply ourselves for many years to come with what wheat we want, I think that we may leave other nations to settle the question of their own shortage as may be convenient to them.

The Times also announces the death of Lord Winchilsea. Opinions may differ as to his schemes and ideas, which have been attacked by some, but there is no doubt that in him the agricultural interests, and especially the agricultural labourers, have lost a true and earnest friend. The last sentence of his will, ' God save Agriculture,' echoes the spirit that animated his life.

September 12.—The end of last week, like its beginning, was intensely hot. In this room on Friday night, with both windows and the door open, the thermometer stood at 75 degrees, which is high for England. Truly this is a strange climate, as a comparison between July 9 and September 9 will prove. The unfortunate harvestmen suffer much at their hard and incessant toil. From their appearance they might have been drenched with water, and they complain that they cannot eat their food. The 8th is said to have been the hottest September day of which a record exists in England. Perhaps this curious heat-wave has to do with the spot which has appeared upon the sun. Looked at through a piece of smoked glass, this spot appears to be the size of a bean, but I am informed that its real dimensions are about six times those of our own earth. Things in the sun happen on a considerable scale.

On Thursday at Bedingham I found that, except for about half the bean field, that still remains to get, they have finished harvest. When this is up, including the two hayricks, there will stand in the yard nine large stacks of produce gathered off this little farm, of which about half is pasture. I found also that the grass is withering in the intense heat, which has stopped the growth of the roots, and especially of the white turnips. But we must not grumble at the drought, which has done us a good turn this harvest.

To-day I went out shooting, but I cannot say that the sport was good. The birds are scarce and wild this year, and we had no luck with what we saw ; indeed, I do not think that personally I fired more than half a dozen shots all day. We often read accounts of a good day's shooting, but few people venture to publish the record of a bad one. In truth, there are not many things more dreary and depressing than the last two hours of an interminable trudge, in the burning heat, over ground like iron, after partridges which are non-existing or will not be found. On such occasions all the errors of your youth, all your rotten investments, all your worries, mistakes, doubts, and disappointments, all your earnest but misdirected efforts, all your least effective plots, marshal themselves in battalions within your mind as you drag yourself through fences and stumble across acres of roots and cornfields. Decidedly, walking up partridges when they are scarce in burning weather in September has its drawbacks, but luckily such days do not make up a season's sport.

The Ditchingham land being lighter, the drought here has got more hold than at Bedingham. As I trudged through the swedes to-day I noticed that they are beginning to turn mildewed and blue. The beet also are at a standstill and the grass is shrinking much. We have been obliged to bring the young cattle up from the marsh and turn them into the new pasture, No. 5, off which we had hoped to secure a second cut of hay. However, the splendid weather has been a great help this harvest, as without it I really do not know how we should have dealt with our heavy corn crop, much of which must have spoiled had the season proved wet. Farmers cannot get everything to their liking. We have had a good haysel and a good harvest, and the weather that suits the corn does not suit the roots and grass.

Certainly we have to fight against a tricky and a variable market. A few months ago wheat was as high as fifty-three shillings a quarter; to-day its average price is twenty-six shillings and tenpence, which is six and threepence lower than during the corresponding week last year. Barley is twenty-seven shillings and ninepence, and oats only seventeen shillings and tenpence the quarter. It would seem that those who manage the corn-market are not as much impressed as they ought to be by the jeremiad of Sir William Crookes.

September 14.—We expect to finish harvest to-morrow, after having been engaged on it for five weeks short of one day—a very long time considering that from first to last the work has only been stopped for two hours by rain. I hope devoutly that the cast of corn will turn out to be proportionate to the 'boolk' we have carried. To the labourers this 'boolk' is a positive nuisance. Very naturally they desire to win the harvest as quickly as possible, for the sooner it is done with the sooner they pocket the sum for which they have agreed, and are in a position to recommence the earning of their weekly wage. To them, therefore, a plentiful harvest is in fact a disadvantage. For this state of affairs co-operation seems to be the only remedy. It is in the air, we hear of it at every gathering, and read much about it in the papers. But is it practicable? I do not remember having seen any scheme which gives much prospect of its successful working—that is, where the land and its fruits are concerned.

Certainly, if a system of co-operation had been in force during the last ten years, by which I understand a system that would pay the labourer by assigning to him a certain share in the profits of the business, he must have starved, for in most cases there have been no profits. As it is, whatever may have happened to the landlord and the farmer, even during the most evil days week by week the labourer has received his wage. Of the three chief interests connected with the soil, his interest has suffered least. Should good times ever come again, he might be inclined to consider co-operation, but I believe that at present his class would scout the idea, unless indeed it was discussed upon the basis of a minimum wage not to fall below that obtainable at present, plus a percentage of possible profits. But would such an arrangement be acceptable to the other people concerned ? I doubt it.

In walking through the yard I noticed that on my farm at any rate—and others complain of the same thing—the stacking is now very inferior to what it used to be. Nearly every stack leans this way or that, and is propped up with boughs of trees and pieces of timber ; also they are roughly and untidily built. The old skill, upon which he used to pride himself, seems to be deserting the agricultural labourer. This is a fruit of the bad times. When a craft becomes unremunerative, its followers cease to take the same interest in their work, and all details that are not absolutely necessary begin to be neglected. Moreover, skilful and well-trained labourers are growing scarce. Only the old men really understand their trade. For instance, all my best hands, those who can be trusted to plough or thatch, are over fifty years of age. The pick of the young men are no longer brought up to these occupations ; they crowd to the towns to seek a living there, sometimes to succeed, sometimes to sink to misery or to the earning of bread by hanging about the dockyard gates upon the chance of a casual job. The labourer is leaving the land principally, if not entirely, because the land can no longer pay him what he considers a just reward for his toil. To me it seems a sad and unnatural thing that those whom the soil bore, and whose forefathers worked it from generation to generation, should now be driven to find a home in the teeming and unwhole-

some towns. But what is the remedy ? I suggest that perhaps it
may be found in the re-creation of the extinct yeoman class, which
incidentally, at any rate to a large extent, should solve the labour
problem. If they have a stake of ownership in the land, men will
not leave it ; they care nothing for it at present, because they have
no interest in it beyond the interest of the hireling. By way of a
beginning—but this is only a suggestion that may have been made
before—why does not the Government empower any suitable authority, such as the County Councils or the Board of Agriculture, to
buy up the glebe lands at a fair valuation and resell them on easy
terms to suitable applicants, to be farmed as small holdings ? At
present, in most instances, these glebes are only a nuisance to the
clergy, of which they would well be rid.

Time alone, however, can furnish the final answer to the question, unless Sir William Crookes has found it in the high prices
that he prophesies—a point upon which I am more than doubtful.[1]

September 17.—Last Thursday, the 15th, harvest being ended,
I left home to pay a visit to my friend Colonel Lorne Stewart, the
Laird of Coll, an island in the Hebrides. They farm in Coll ;
also the island is in many ways interesting, especially because
of Dr. Johnson's connection with it. Therefore, with the reader's
leave, I propose to set down briefly whatever things impressed me
on my travels. It is curious to read Boswell's 'Journal of a Tour
to the Hebrides' in 1773, and consider how the means of locomotion have improved in the short space of a hundred and twenty
years. What, I wonder, would the Doctor have thought of
a train that left Euston at nine o'clock at night and delivered him
at Oban at eight-thirty on the following morning ? 'Sir,' one can
imagine him saying to the obsequious Bozzy as he assisted him to
alight from the 'sleeper,' 'this is not *Travelling,* it is *Transportation.*'

But then, barely four generations ago not only were the

[1] Those of my readers who may be interested in this vital question of the
exodus of the rural population into the great cities are referred to the paper
published as an Appendix to this book.

methods of conveyance elementary, but, so far as I am able to discover, it never seems to have occurred to our forefathers that they could possibly be improved, except, of course, by mending the roads. This entire lack of imaginative foresight makes one wonder whether it is not possible that within another four generations the modes of voyaging of the civilised races will not be almost as much in advance of our own as ours are in advance of those available to Dr. Johnson. We know that before then many marvels will have happened ; that, for instance, individuals with half the world between them will be able to talk to each other across space by means of syntonised instruments that, of the millions pulsing through ether, will catch and record only those vibrations which are emitted by their own twin ; that the word spoken in Brighton will be instantaneously heard by the listener in Brisbane, and so forth. But what can it matter to us, who so long ago will have become inhabitants of a land where all things earthly are forgotten ?

From Oban to Coll the traveller goes by steamboat, a journey of six or seven hours, past the rugged heights of Appin, for so long the home of the Stewart clan ; past the rock where a particularly truculent Duart, desiring to be rid of his wife, hit upon the expedient, admirable in its simplicity, of taking her out for a day's sea-fishing and, just as the tide began to rise, finding that he had business on shore. Unfortunately for him the lady had good lungs and was rescued, but the rest of the story does not matter. Steaming along the Sound of Mull and leaving wooded Tobermory on the left, the vessel comes into Loch Sunart, over which tower the rude heights of Ardnamurchan, now, I am told, no longer owned by Highland chieftains. Indeed, the hereditary ' laird ' is rapidly becoming little more than a tradition in the sporting and more picturesque portions of the Highlands, where his place is filled by the successful southerner clothed in a very new kilt.

After Ardnamurchan Point is left behind come ten or twelve miles of open water, which, when the swell is pressing in from the Atlantic, have been known to interfere with the digestions of the hardiest. All this while lying before us can be seen the long low shore of Coll, a narrow island about thirteen miles long, very stony and desolate-looking, and at length, running round a point about which hang gannet and other diving birds watching for their prey from on high, we enter what is by courtesy called a harbour. I say 'by courtesy,' for if the wind is blowing hard, especially from the sou'-east, it is impossible for the steamer to communicate with the shore ; and even at the best of times she does not seem to care to undertake the adventure of mooring by the little stone pier, preferring to anchor a hundred yards or more away. Presently a broad-bottomed boat comes out, into which we are bundled with our luggage, some other passengers return-ing from the gathering at Oban, several black-faced rams, and a sheepdog. Unfortunately for himself, the dog was placed too near one of these rams, which, there on the bosom of the deep, proceeded to avenge the wrongs of its race upon his person until he retreated discomfited to another part of the boat.

Half an hour later we were driving towards the Castle, that is situated five miles away at a place called Breachacha, which, being interpreted, means Spotted Meadow. The Spots, it may be explained, are the lovely flowers wherewith it is adorned in spring, and especially a certain variety of wild geranium. Except that a good road now runs across it, with telegraph poles at the side, the landscape cannot have changed much since it was scanned by Boswell. There are the same low rough moorlands and the same dark lochs, while to the left heaves the same eternal sea. Pre-sently we pass a farmstead built of substantial stone and with its back turned to the ocean for protection from the roaring winds, but this house was not there in his day. Then we come to a sawmill driven by a water-wheel, and lying about it baulks of timber washed out of wrecks that have been ground to pieces on this stormy coast. Another mile and the Castle is in view—a three storied and naked-looking building coated with grey cement and backed by the massive ruin of the old home of the McLeans, who owned this island for many generations. Round about the Castle are lands more or less enclosed and improved, upon which wander some of the Laird's herd of beautiful Ayrshire cows—and a noble herd it is numbering 250 or more. Here also oats stand in stooks, and beyond them appears a field of magnificent swedes. Nowhere have I seen the swede thrive as it does in the damp, moist climate of Coll : the bulbs are splendid, and the leaves so tall and thick that it is a labour to walk through them. Another striking feature of the place is the great flocks of starlings that Boswell noted, which still frequent the island.

And so at last we come to the hospitable house that pleased Dr. Johnson so much when first he found shelter in it, although afterwards, when he grew bored, he described it 'as a mere trades-man's box with nothing becoming a chief about it.' The Doctor's and Boswell's bedchambers are, I believe, practically unaltered since their day, and in the former hangs the sage's portrait. Once I slept in it, but on this occasion Bozzy's chamber fell to my lot. It is recorded in the book that these twain disputed fiercely about those rooms, arguing as to which of them boasted the best curtains. Johnson's were proved to be the superior, being woven of linen thread, and giving up the curtains Boswell pointed out that his bed-posts were the finest. Thereon the Doctor retaliated, 'Well, if you *have* the best *posts*, we will have you tied to them and whipped.'

This does not seem a good specimen of the Johnsonian wit, or at least I cannot see its point. Boswell quotes it as illustrative of his hero's power of placing his adversary 'in a ludicrous view.' To my mind it is not the victim of the joke who is ludicrous.

After dinner we conversed about farming in Coll. There is no doubt as to the considerable capacities of the island, which is well suited to cattle and sheep, produces good hay where the land is improved, very fair crops of oats, and, as I have said, magnificent swedes and white turnips. Thirty, or even twenty years ago, when it was more highly farmed than it is now, it used to be a prosperous place. To-day, however, the blight of agricultural depression lies as heavy upon it as it does upon the Eastern Counties. Thus the cheeses that it produces can barely hold their own in the Scotch

market against the imported Dutch and American article, and as
it does not pay to ship young cattle to the mainland, the throats
of most of the pedigree calves are cut so soon as they are born.
When I told Hood this, by the way, he said little and turned the
subject, intimating thereby, I think, that it was of no use wasting
good travellers' tales upon a person of his experience. Yet the
thing is true. Another obstacle to the success of farming in Coll
is the deficiency of labour, which, if such a thing be possible, seems
to be even scarcer than it is becoming here at home.

To-day we went out shooting. Here I will stop to explain
that to a certain kind of sportsman, at any rate, Coll is a perfect
paradise, and, although I am but a moderate shot, I trust that I
may be numbered as one of that honourable army. Perhaps,
however, there is no name so vilely misapplied as this of 'sportsman.' The bruiser, the racing tout, the trap-shooter, and others
equally ignoble, are all 'sportsmen.' Sportsmen, also, are those
who take great 'shoots' with the object of killing the hugest
amount of game possible and seeing the reports of their prowess in
the papers. Woe be to the man whose poor performance diminishes
such a total ! Never shall I forget the story of a gentleman whom
once I knew, who, under some misapprehension as to the extent
of his skill with a gun, was asked to one of these colossal and
advertising 'shoots.' His very first stand happened to be at a spot
where, for about twenty minutes, pheasants and hares passed him
in an incessant stream. Furiously did he aim and bang, till, at
the conclusion of the beat, he found himself surrounded by a piled
up ring of cartridge cases, while almost at his feet lay an unfortunate hen-pheasant, the only thing that he had succeeded in
hitting, blown absolutely to pieces. He paused and mopped his
brow, and looking round him in the vain hope of discovering some
other trophies of his fiery labours, for the first time perceived a
little boy with a knife and an ash stick in his hand, sheltering
himself behind the bole of an oak.

'You beastly little boy,' he said, for his temper was somewhat
ruffled, 'what are you doing there ?'

'Doing?' answered that youth with a sour smile; 'I'm set to watch yer shoot, and *I'm a notching of yer misses !* '

The sportsman who would be happy in Coll belongs to none of these classes. He must be a person who does not mind hard work and who is a lover of Nature and its voices. To such a one there are few places like this island, for here wild things abound, and though the bags may not be heavy, they will certainly be varied. In the bogs are snipe, among the bents lie partridge, and yonder on the moorland grouse may be found ; both the partridge and the grouse having been introduced since Boswell's day, who, when *he* went out shooting in Coll, was content with starlings, which he ate. Then there are hares in great numbers, wild duck if you can get near them, golden and green plover, the last so plentiful that they are not shot, and in the winter woodcocks and wild geese.

Ravens may be seen also, and not far from them a pair of pere-grines hanging about the face of the Green Mountain, although, because of their destructiveness, neither of these birds are allowed to increase. Out of the caves, too, flash rock-pigeons with a noise of rattling wings, and from time to time a curlew, surprised in a hollow of the sandpits, twists away like a great snipe, filling the air with his ringing, melancholy notes ; while yonder on the sea-shore the gulls wheel and clamour. Indeed, if you will sit quiet and watch at certain places, there in the calm water under the shelter of a rock you may see a round head appear, a head adorned with whiskers and large soft eyes, followed presently by another. These are seals, pretty, harmless creatures, which in my opinion ought to be less shot at than they are, especially as for every one that is brought to bag about three sink down to die. They are comparatively rare here ; indeed, if the reader wishes to find seals he should visit the coasts of Iceland, where I have counted dozens of them, huge fellows, and apparently of different varieties, lying upon islands or disporting themselves within a few yards of our boat. I never shot at one, however, and of this I am very glad.

Shooting here is quite a different thing to shooting in Norfolk. To begin with, not more than two guns go out together. At a

quarter to ten o'clock or thereabouts a tall bearded figure with a
genial and weather-beaten face may be seen striding across the
golf-green towards the Castle, accompanied by a pointer dog or
dogs. This is the keeper, Lees, of whom I will say—and it is my
sole complaint—that his walking powers are simply demoniacal.
Not that he seems to go fast, but his length of stride is tremendous, and—he never stops. From ten o'clock in the morning till
seven at night, with the shortest possible interval for refreshment,
that stride will continue through snipe-bogs, over sand-bents,
across heather and peat-hags, with the fearful regularity of a
machine, till even the inexhaustible pointer dog begins to look
tired and to droop its tail. But Lees is not tired ; on the contrary,
having deposited a heavy load of game and cartridge bags at the
Castle, he just strolls back to his house a league or so away, has
his tea, and starts out for a spot several miles in another direction,
where he watches for flighting duck by moonlight. Nothing
makes any difference to him ; a few hares or an extra hundred
of cartridges he does not seem to feel. One morning, after a
tremendous trudge upon the previous day, I asked him if he
was not tired. 'Naa,' he answered wonderingly. 'Then I wish
to Heaven you were,' I said, much to his amusement ; but the
fact is that he never was, never is, and never will be tired ;
perhaps because he is a teetotaler. Total abstainers, please note.

On his arrival at the Castle he finds us waiting, for one of the
many merits of my companion is a remorseless and provident
punctuality which has become a proverb in the land, and off we
go. The arrangement is that we should begin with the snipe,
so we head for the big *Jheel* about two miles away, accompanied
by Lees and a satellite named Hector. A quarter of an hour's
walking brings us to a stretch of rough low meadows, which
were, I believe, reclaimed from the bog some years ago, but are
now once more becoming marshy. Just as we have climbed over
the stone wall of the first there comes a *ch—eep*, a flick of a
beautiful brown wing, a glimpse of a white stomach and green
legs, and a snipe—the first that I have seen for a year—is zig-

zagging up wind to my right. I manage to kill him, and at the sound of the shot others rise, which I do not kill, as I flatter myself, because I have made a mistake with the cartridges and am banging at them with No. 5. Then presently the air grows full of snipe, which appear in wisps in every direction, but their very number is confusing; also they are wild, being—so says Lees—just arrived from across the ocean and not yet settled in their winter quarters. It is charming shooting, but in a high wind, such as blew to-day, these snipe are terribly difficult and great absorbers of cartridges. This, however, makes it all the more satisfactory when you bag one of them.

With many men there comes an age when, although they still do the deed from force of habit or of circumstances, they begin to feel a very active dislike to depriving anything of life. At times I suffer sadly from this complaint, especially where hares are concerned; but my qualms seem a little difficult to explain, as I have small objection to shooting snipe, woodcock, duck, or any other creature that is downright and *bonâ fide* wild. Such things breed by the hundred thousand in vast swamps across the sea, and, after all, it does not seem unjust that those who protect them here should take a tiny tithe of their number for sport and food. Of course, however, that is the man's and not the creature's point of view. But the whole system of our inexplicable world is built up on this great corner-stone of death dealt out remorselessly by everything that lives to every other thing, and neither man nor beast can change its rule.

Having secured several couple of snipe in the meadows, we entered the *Jheel* or bog, that on its surface is a beautiful bright green with a substratum of oozy red mud such as snipe love, through which, however, it is both difficult and disagreeable to walk. Here, oddly enough, the birds were not so plentiful as in the meadows, though I am told that later in the season they are found in great numbers. When they are flushed from the swamp, after wheeling round and round high in the air, they settle about on little marshy patches among the hills, whither in due course we follow them. This is perhaps the prettiest shooting of all, for in these spots the snipe rise suddenly and unexpectedly. Nobody seems quite to understand their habits, or why they choose one place and not another to hide in ; thus, in Coll I have noticed on several occasions that on one side of a ridge they will be plentiful, whereas on the other, on what seems the most suitable and tempting ground, it is impossible to find a single bird.

Following the snipe ' lays,' by degrees we work round to the sand-bents near the seashore, where partridges make their home, strong and beautiful birds with a delicious flavour, but, as I think, a little browner in colour than our variety. They feed, I believe, on the young shoots of the bent. By the way, these tough sea grasses, of which the botanical name is *Elymus Arenarius*, play an important part in the natural economy of Coll, since except for them much of the island would be swallowed up in blowing sand. As it is, the aspect of the area of bent ground is strange and even fantastic. From year to year and from generation to generation the roaring winds of winter tear and delve among these sand-hills, here scooping out a huge pit fifty feet deep or more, there bevelling a ridge almost to the angle of a precipice. But ever during the more peaceful months the sand grasses are at work to repair the damage, matting and binding the shifting soil with their succulent white roots. It is another instance of the extraordinary providence of Nature, or the extraordinary nature of Providence !

At length we come to a little spring of water—water is not very plentiful in Coll, rain excepted, of course—and halt to lunch. The meal is frugal, for it must be carried—the heavy feed of an English shooting luncheon being represented by a few sandwiches and a bit of bread and cheese, flavoured with water-cress from the spring, and washed down with a little whisky. But how delightful it is to sit in that wild and lonely place, listening to the continual swish of the wind among the rocks and grasses, breathing an air like wine, and watching the billows as they roll in from the

Atlantic, while the gale catches their crests as they come, and drives them back in puffs of snowy spray.

Then the sport begins again, and is followed with varying success till evening is at hand. Here and there the pointer stands to partridges and we get a shot or two, but to-day our aim is snipe, so we do not follow up the coveys. Thus we work homewards across the lower land, till about six o'clock, thoroughly tired, we find ourselves back in the Castle, and murmur, almost in the words of Dr. Johnson, but, I hope, a little more politely : 'Now, Coll, if you could get us a dish of tea——'

Such is a day's shooting in the Hebrides ; bag, twelve couple of snipe and three brace of partridge. It ought to have been more, but on this we will not dwell.

September 18.—To-day is Sunday, and we rest from our labours. After breakfast I went to examine the old Castle where the McLeans lived for many generations, although I believe that it dates from long before their time. This ruin, massively constructed of great boulders gathered on the seashore, stands at a distance of about two hundred yards from the present house, which was built a few years prior to Dr. Johnson's visit. In his day the roof was still on the Castle, and the floors of the various stories remained ; but now roof and floors have vanished, and the place is tenanted only by numberless rock-pigeons. It consists of a square tower or keep, which was divided into four stories, and an attic covered in with a sharp-pitched roof, for its angle can be traced upon the stonework. Joined on to it is the dwelling-house, which was also of several stories, with wide fireplaces for the burning of peat and driftwood. All the arrangements of this abode, including those of a sanitary nature, seem to have been rude in the extreme, yet they proved sufficient for the needs of generations of chieftains and their families, till a certain McLean, the red McLean, built the present house, about 1730, and left the old sea-robbers' fortress to fall into ruin.

After leaving the Castle we walked to visit the tomb of the

McLeans. A more impressive or desolate resting-place for the bones of a departed family can scarcely be imagined, overlooking as it does the waters of Crossapol Bay, across which the winds moan without ceasing. No church or building is near it, the tomb, a stone enclosure of about twenty feet square, in the midst of which stands a sarcophagus, being the only trace of man's handiwork upon all the sweep of plain and bents. When I was here before the iron gate had rotted from its hinges and the cattle herded within the walls; but on learning of this Colonel Lorne Stewart, the present Laird of Coll, caused it to be replaced, with the result that, at the risk of impalement, my companion had great difficulty in clambering into the place—a feat which I did not attempt. On the wall of the tomb facing the gateway is a marble slab, which is so rapidly decaying and becoming illegible that I transcribe its inscription here. It runs :

THE LATTER CEMETERY OF THE FAMILY BEING NEARLY OVER
WHELMED BY SAND BLOWING, THIS WAS ERECTED, AND
THE REMAINS OF HIS FAMILY AND ANCESTORS REMOVED
TO IT BY ALEXANDER MCLEAN OF COLL, UPON THE
OCCASION OF THE LAMENTED DEATH OF HIS BELOVED
COMPANION, CATHARINA CAMERON, THE BEAUTY OF WHOSE
PERSON WAS ONLY SURPASSED BY THE VIRTUES AND
AMIABLE DISPOSITION OF HER MIND.
OBT. CLIFTON 10 FEB. 1802, AE. 46.

This is the first time that ever I remember seeing the personal appearance of the deceased alluded to upon a monument. I wonder how in those days, when there were neither railways nor steamboats, her husband contrived to convey the body of the beautiful Catharina Cameron from Clifton to Coll. I am told, however—for a piece of gossip of the sort lasts for a long time here—that while the tomb was building, and the bones of the old McLeans were being moved into it, her body lay for a year in a packing-case in some shed at the harbour without any one suspecting what the fatal box contained.

Leaving the tomb of the McLeans—all that remains to them of the island which they ruled for generations—we walked back to the Castle by the seashore, observing the ways of the seabirds as we went, and especially those of an old heron, who stood upon a rock looking out for little fishes until the tide rose to the height of his stomach and forced him to move on. By the way, on the top of the grass knolls in this part of the island are most curious little knobs of turf, almost bottle- or rather breast-shaped, and ending in a point. The suggestion is that these knobs are formed by the droppings of birds; but when I cut one off with my spud and examined it, I found that the peat of which it was composed is of the same character as that of the mound beneath. This seems to negative the bird-dropping idea, but what else can have caused the lumps is to me a mystery.

In the afternoon we accompanied our host to the Green Mountain to examine a mound which may have been a tumulus. Certainly it is placed in just such a spot as a sea-rover with taste would have chosen for his grave—elevated, airy, and commanding a magnificent view of the ocean, that beats incessantly on the gneiss rocks below, flying about and above them in clouds of glistening foam. Indeed, so choice a situation would commend itself to many even in these latter days; at least, did I dwell in Coll, it would commend itself to me.

September 20.—Yesterday we were shooting at Arinagaur and Gallanach. The day was beautiful, but rain with a high wind came on as we turned homewards. It was strange, in the gathering gloom, to see the plover borne past us on the gale, uttering their plaintive cries, and, now white, now black, as the breeze tossed them, looking for all the world like great wind-swept aspen leaves. I do not know the reason, but beneath that drear and sodden sky they seemed to add a wild touch to the landscape and to accentuate its loneliness.

As we passed Arinagaur I admired the dressed granite of which a chapel there is built, but Lees told me that this granite is very pervious to damp, which, unless they are cemented on the outside, will work through walls of it eighteen inches or more in thickness. In the cultivated lands I came across a new peat drain. These drains are cut several feet deep, and about a foot from the bottom upon either side of them a ledge is left in the turf. On this ledge, which supports them, are laid other turves, and thus a square channel is formed beneath, down which the water percolates. If made properly these drains will last for many years.

To-day was extraordinarily wet and windy, but in the afternoon it held up, and we managed to escape for a walk with our guns, but succeeded only in shooting a curlew and a rock-pigeon or two, which fell into crevices full of rushing yeasty water where we could not even look for them. To-day, also, I received a telegram announcing that we had taken a good many prizes, seven or eight in all, at the Mutford and Lothingland District Agricultural Show, which this year is being held at Bungay. First and second for cows, first for fat beasts, a first and a highly commended for butter, and so forth. It is very satisfactory, and I wired back to congratulate Hood. Here the telegraph, or rather the telephone, runs straight into the dining-room of the Castle. Nothing ever brought the marvellous nature of this invention more home to me than the despatching of a message to Ditchingham, five hundred miles away, and an hour or so later to be startled by a *ting, ting* on the bell and rise to listen to the answer. I think that the telephone, there by the lonely waters of Breachacha Bay, would have amazed Dr. Johnson even more than the 'sleeper.' How interesting it would be if by any miracle we could hear his reflections on the subject.

September 25, *Sunday*.—We have been shooting every day this week since the 20th. On Wednesday the 21st we killed about ten brace of partridges on the bents, lunching near to the farmhouse at Crossapol. Quite close by this house is a graveyard, which, after the curious fashion of Scotch burial-places, runs down to the rocks upon the sea-border. About this cemetery my host had a tale to tell, which will be interesting to the lover of collie dogs. Once, some years ago, he was living in the farmhouse at Crossapol while some repairs were going on at the Castle, and was greatly pleased by the daily visits of a most delightful collie that, from pure and flattering attention, came all the way across the island to see him at the farm. One fine morning, however, somebody chanced to walk into the neighbouring graveyard, where there had been a recent interment. The rest of the story may be guessed, but that clever doggie was knowing enough to fill in his excavations, and reopen them when necessary. The soil is sandy, and they do not bury deep at Crossapol.

Our best day's shooting this week was on the 22nd, at Cliad and Grissapol (not Crossapol), when we killed thirteen couple of snipe, one partridge, and two and a half brace of grouse. The last, however, were wild and hard to come by. Lees tells me that they are increasing on the island, which is very good news. I think that on that day I must have seen two hundred snipe in a single boggy turnip field, but for the most part they rose in wisps and out of shot. I remember that I had five down at once, which is not a common occurrence nowadays.

To-day we walked to service at the Presbyterian church at Clabac. People who grumble because they have to go half a mile to find a church door would scarcely praise the spiritual facilities of Coll, for from the Castle to Clabac is a good five miles, or an hour and a half of steady walking. The kirk, which belongs to the Established Church of Scotland, is joined on to the manse, and is a very plain building, whitewashed and shed-like in appearance. At the end of it, clad in a black silk grown, sat the minister, the Rev. D. Macechern, in a high pulpit, and beneath him were gathered a congregation of about twenty people. The service consisted of hymns, extempore prayers, two lessons, and a long, but on the whole a very good and well-reasoned sermon. The Psalms were sung from a metrical paraphrase, but why, instead of hacking them into rhyming couplets, the Bible or our beautiful Prayer-Book version of these unequalled poems is not considered worthy to be used in Scotland to me has always been a mystery. Another curious thing is the strange superiority of the ordinary Scotch over the ordinary English preacher. At one time or another I have attended various Scotch churches, and never yet did I hear a bad sermon ; indeed, some of those addresses struck me as masterly. I doubt whether the haphazard visitor to English village churches would be able to say as much. It is obvious, too, that the general intelligence of the average country churchgoers in Scotland must be much higher than that of the corresponding class in England. I am convinced that few members of an agricultural congregation in the Eastern Counties would follow the closely reasoned and often recondite arguments of the preacher with as much zest and understanding as do his hearers in the most out-of-the-world parts of Scotland.

Boswell talks of a lead mine in Coll, that must have been somewhere in this direction, which he actually visited with Dr. Johnson, although now all knowledge of it seems to have been lost. After church I asked the minister if he knew anything of such a mine. He said, No, but that he had some curious stones in his garden. I went to look at them, and among them found a lump of what appeared to be lead ore. It had been picked up on the sea-beach below the manse, which suggests that the vein cannot be far off. That afternoon on our homeward way, while walking down a hillside, I noticed a curious looking boulder, which, on examination, seemed to be permeated with lead, and so rotten that by the help of another stone I was able to break specimens off it. It looks, therefore, as though lead exists somewhere in the neighbourhood, though whether in workable quantity or not only an expert can tell.[1]

Having drank some water at the manse spring, we started to walk up Benhogh in order to visit the great stone which lies upon the top of it. This stone Boswell saw also, but not Dr. Johnson, who was too heavy to climb the hill. Boswell states that the stone

---

[1] I hear that analysis of the specimens does not confirm these hopes. Probably, like myself, Boswell and the people of his day were deceived by some mineral closely resembling lead in weight and appearance.

did not repay his examination of it, but, so far as I can gather, neither he nor the Doctor took the slightest interest in the curiosities and the beauties of Nature. Evidently they thought that 'the proper study of mankind is man,' and such things as scenery, or even the remains of past ages, they did not consider worthy of notice.

Unlike Mr. Boswell, I found that the rock repaid my trouble exceedingly well. It is a very curious object, weighing, I suppose, some twenty or thirty tons, and supported by three small stones of about the size of horses' heads. Its position where it appears to-day may be explained in several different ways. For instance, it might have rolled from the top of the mount, which is a little above it, and poised itself exactly upon these three stones. This, however, is very unlikely, for if once the boulder had started rolling, obstacles of that size would not have stayed its course. Or scores of thousands of years ago it might have been borne hither in the ice, and, when the glacial period passed away, deposited neatly upon its present supports. But neither do I put faith in this solution, for it is not a foreign rock, and I think that in the course of eons these three small stones would have crumbled away beneath the weight of its mass and the wearing of the weather. They are large enough and stout enough to bear the rock for a period of, say, two or three thousand years, but not for all those infinite ages. The third suggestion, which I believe to be correct, is that it was set where it is by the hand of man ; indeed, is not the legend. quoted of Boswell, as to its having been thrown there by a giant corroborative of this theory ?

Doubtless this rock, which is of the same character as the surrounding formation, lay from the beginning where it is to-day and by the aid of levers the primeval population of the island lifted it on to its supports. Could they have done so, probably they would have wished to set it upon the very top of the hill, a hundred yards or so away ; but to roll it thither proved beyond their strength, so, as it was eminently suitable to their purpose, they placed it where it stands. Within about sixty yards of it is another, smaller boulder, also set upon three stones, and at a distance a third boulder, likewise standing upon three stones—coincidences that can scarcely be accidental. Further, I observed that on all the highest points of the surrounding hills, where they could be most readily seen from the lowland, are other boulders of like character, though whether or no they stand upon three stones I cannot say, for I have never visited them. Lastly, I have seen a photograph of a similar rock which is to be found somewhere on the mainland, and is also arranged upon three stones. Why they were placed thus nobody can say with any certainty, but my own belief is that they formed the altars of Druids or Sun-worshippers, whereon the priests may have offered human sacrifices or stood to celebrate their rites.

While I am talking of the antiquities of Coll, I may mention that when laying a golf green my host discovered four skeletons buried beneath the turf. On investigation it was found that the ancient name of the site was Croc-na-Crochadh, or Hangman's Hill. Until the year 1745 the Lairds of Coll had power of life and death over its inhabitants, and without doubt these bones belonged to the victims of their justice or their vengeance.

In company with a brother, once I made a similar discovery. At Bradenham in this county is a furze-covered heath known as the Gibbet Common, and in the centre of it the spot where stood a gallows. Digging in the soil with our spuds here, we came upon the ancient irons, and the hook, nearly worn through, to which they hung. In the horrid cage that enclosed the head we found, moreover, a portion of the skull of the murderer who, so says tradition, killed his wife and child by throwing them downstairs. In his curious work, 'Hanging in Chains,' wherein these irons are described, Mr. Albert Hartshorne, F.S.A., states that there exists a legend in the neighbourhood that this man was hung up alive and watched until he died. I can prove, however, that this is not the case, for on the skull a mark of the searing of a hot iron could be seen distinctly, showing that the smith had set them there after death. Even during the last century hot irons would not have been welded on to a living man. I recollect that Miss Mason, of Necton Hall, an old friend of my family for several generations, whom I can very well remember, and who died at the age of ninety, used to tell a story of how, when she was young, she drove across the Gibbet Common while these bones were still swinging in their cage, and noticed that a robin or a starling—I forget which— had built its nest among the vertebræ. Some folk from Shipdham, it is said, came and took the young birds from their grizzly brooding-place. Another tale which I have heard in the village is that certain relations of the deceased, who lived upon the borders of the Common, were so disturbed by the constant creaking of the chains on windy nights that at last they cut the cage down and buried it. If so, to judge from the worn condition of the gallows hook, they must have borne the noise with patience for very many years. These remains of a barbarous but still recent age are now in the Norwich Museum.

From where we sat eating our frugal luncheon by the huge boulder that did not interest Mr. Boswell the view of Coll is very striking, and to all appearance arid. Beneath us lay thousands of masses of ice-rounded gneiss spotting the plains and hills in every direction, while beyond stretched the blue sea, and rising from it here and there, dimly outlined in the mist, the fantastic shapes of other islands. Also there are many ruins of stone houses which once were occupied by crofters. The most of these crofter folk were got rid of in the year of the great famine, or afterwards ; indeed, it is said that the Laird of that generation half ruined himself by the cost of shipping them away to America. In those days the population had increased beyond the capacity of the land to support it, and life was hard ; indeed, old folk who can remember something of them say that many a time have they been driven to seek their food among the mussels and limpets of the seashore. But all this is part of the Crofter Question, which is too large and intricate a subject for me to attempt to discuss here, even had I the necessary knowledge of its details. The gist of it seems to be, at any rate in the Highlands, and I have observed the same thing among the natives of South Africa, that the population has a tendency to increase to the extreme limit of the productive or feeding power of the land in good seasons, that is, if wars and epidemics are absent. Then come famines from failure of crops, or other distresses, and at once the problem presents itself in an acute form. With it arise also the inevitable quarrels between the owners and the occupiers of the soil.

September 27.—Yesterday was our last day's shooting. In looking for partridge on the Crossapol bents we came upon a spot so remarkable that it deserves mention. There, in the heart of the bents, with a ridge between it and the sea, lay a circular plain buried in white sand, which gave to it an appearance that can only be called weird. Indeed, were I an artist wishing to depict the site of the city from which Lot fled, I should find inspiration in that plain. Also here there was, if not a city, at least a dwelling-place of men, for the remains of houses are to be seen buried in the blowing sand, and, what is more curious still, the outlines of round huts. Who built these huts or to what age they belong nobody seems to know.

This morning we bid farewell to our host and departed south. But it is not always easy to escape from Coll, and in the grey dark of a winter morning many and anxious are the inquiries as to the strength and direction of the wind.

'I doubt ye'll no win to her. It's blawin' hard from the sou'-east,' said the old butler, 'her' being, of course, the steamer, which should be off Ardnagour about eight o'clock. However, we breakfasted and started. When we arrived at the harbour there were no signs of the *Fingal*, but presently along the cable came the ominous intelligence that she had been unable to communicate with Tiree, the island beyond us. Now we began to think that it would be our fate to stop on Coll for longer than we were expected.

There are terrible tales of the adventures of visitors attempting to quit Coll. One gentleman, who had most urgent reasons for reaching the mainland, is said to have driven to that harbour three times a week for a fortnight, only on each occasion to see the steamer go hooting past. It is told, indeed, that people have been detained for six weeks; but this was in the old days of the sailing packet, when there was no possibility of communicating with other shores even by telegraph. As the boatmen, however, were of opinion that the steamer would put in, we followed the mails and luggage into a large flat-bottomed boat and were rowed away across the harbour to the shelter of some rocks upon the further side. Here we lay for three-quarters of an hour or more, until, to our relief, we heard the *Fingal's* siren going beyond the point, and knew that thereby she was warning us to be ready.

Presently in she came and dropped anchor, and we started towards her, pitching and tossing across the stormy water. It requires a good deal of skill to bring a boat alongside without accident in such heavy weather, and when he jumps for the vessel as she rolls towards him the passenger needs agility and decision. However, we all scrambled aboard without mishap, and steamed to Oban in pouring rain.

And so good-bye to the Hebrides and holidays. 'Coll for my money,' said Dr. Johnson—before he had been there—and after experience heartily do I endorse his remark. It is a delightful spot, and, to say nothing of much kindness, he who sojourns there meets Nature face to face.

September 29.—Yesterday I arrived at Upp Hall, in Hertfordshire, and to-day I walked with my host, Mr. Charles Longman, to inspect a neighbouring farm. Leaving Oban in pouring rain, I find the home counties absolutely dried up by drought. The swede crop is blue with blight, few of the bulbs being larger than apples; a strange contrast indeed to the magnificent roots which I saw in Coll. The mangolds also are going back, and the land is so hard that no plough can work the fields. As we passed, two horses were dragging a harrow over a ploughed fallow, and I could see that they simply spent their strength in turning the lumps of soil without breaking up one of them. It is not, however, the lack of rain only that has caused this severe water famine in Hertford-shire, for, as Sir John Evans has pointed out in various letters to the *Times*, the London companies are responsible for a great deal of the trouble. I am told that by means of deep wells and in other ways they are literally draining the district, and if the present state of things is allowed to go on there is great risk that within a number of years, which can be reckoned, Hertfordshire will only have enough water for the barest necessities. Some people say, indeed, that it must become a desert. At least this is certain, that streams which used to run, run no longer, that ponds are drying up, and that wells in which was plenty of water are now dry and must be either deepened or abandoned. Indeed the process is going on at the back of this house, where, as the water suddenly showed symptoms of giving out, it has been found necessary to sink the bore another eighty or a hundred feet.

Undoubtedly the inhabitants of this part of Hertfordshire are becoming seriously alarmed as day by day they see the water upon which they depend being pumped away to London, but whether they will succeed in persuading Parliament to listen to their grievances is a matter about which I can express no opinion. Unfortunately, whenever one set of experts declare that a public catastrophe of the sort is owing to certain causes, another set of experts arise who explain in the largest possible print that the first set are donkeys, if not evilly disposed lunatics. Of this state of affairs the central authority, which does not want to be bothered, not unnaturally hastens to avail itself. 'If you gentle-men can't agree,' it says, 'you can hardly expect me to interfere,' and so the thing goes on till something happens, which, in the case of the Hertfordshire water supply, will not, I understand, be for very long.

From time to time there is much controversy in the Press and elsewhere as to the genuineness of the claims of the *Dowsers*, who assert that they are able to discover the whereabouts of water by means of a divining rod, that is a twig which they hold in the hand. This twig, under the influence of their magic or magnetic power, is alleged to bend whenever they pass over a spot where a spring lies hid. The experiment was tried here at Upp Hall, in 1894, in the presence of witnesses and with the following results. A noted *dowser* was retained and *dowsed* about the house. In the moat garden the twig tilted upwards so violently that it broke, indicating, so said the prophet, that a very strong spring existed near to the surface. On the faith of his guarantee a well was sunk, but, when it had reached a depth of sixty feet, as no spring either strong or weak was met with, the pit was filled in again. This authenticated story is instructive, and suggests that the supernatural powers of *dowsers* are not beyond question.

Compared with those which we see in our part of Norfolk, the fields here are enormous, measuring from twenty up to a hundred acres in extent. As a consequence, steam ploughs that are practically useless on much of our Norfolk and Suffolk land, because of the great amount of room which they occupy at the sides of the fields and their inability to deal with angles and corners, can in this district be used to extraordinary advantage. Just now, when the land is too hard for horses to be able to break it, these cultivators are in great demand. A pair of them were at work on one of the fields of this farm, and, seated on the drag, I made the journey from one steamer to the other, a distance of several hundred yards. It cannot be recommended as a luxurious method of locomotion, especially when the wire rope slips on the drum and when the cultivator starts forward with a sudden plunge ; but it is extraordinary to see the great hooks, dragged by a strength equivalent to that of fourteen horses, tearing up the iron soil to a depth of seven inches. The drag in use to-day is made on the same principle as our ordinary three-horse cultivator, but in addition to this the engines work a plough, or rather a bit of machinery, to the frame of which are attached five ploughshares arranged side by side, each one of them a little in front of the last. However, the land is too hard even for these giant ploughs, for in the next field lies the instrument, broken in the attempt to use it. I understand that under favourable conditions a pair of these steamers can deal with as much as twenty acres of land a day, working it first from end to end and then across, at a cost of about ten shillings per acre cultivated.

In this county the stacks are infinitely better built than those of my neighbourhood, being constructed much broader in the base and lower, which gives them a superior appearance and more stability. I do not know, however, whether this plan of erecting very thick stacks answers well when the corn is carried in a damp season, as the air can hardly penetrate so far to dry the sheaves.

The farming in these parts is chiefly of cereal crops, but I imagine that agriculturists here owe such prosperity as they possess to the nearness of the London market. Many of them keep large herds of cows and send up the milk by train ; also they supply hay and straw in great quantities to the liverymen, buying back manure from the London stables to fertilise the land. Some of these farmers have migrated from Cornwall, where rent is very high—as much as three or four pounds the acre, I am told—to this district, which, being for the most part heavy corn land, commands only from fifteen shillings to a pound an acre. I understand that at these prices energetic men are doing well. Labour here, however, seems to be growing scarcer every day, and without labour what is to become of the land ?

September 30.—To-day is cold and drizzly but there is no real rain. The method adopted to deepen the well here is one of great ingenuity. At the bottom of the pit, eighty or ninety feet down, stands a man, while at the top are several other men with a windlass. The deepening instrument is a steel chisel or cutter weighing about thirty pounds. The windlass is wound up for a certain distance, lifting the chisel. Then the rope is let run, and away it falls, cutting its way into the chalk and smashing any flints with which it may come in contact. When it has loosened the substances to a certain depth it is withdrawn, and a valved tube is dropped down in its place, which retains the chalk sludge that flows into it by a simple but effective action of the valve. Then the tube is hauled to the surface and emptied of its contents, and the process recommences. When a spring of water has been struck strong enough to fill the narrow bore thus drilled through the chalk and keep it full in spite of any reasonable amount of pumping, a pipe will be thrust down the cavity to a convenient depth and connected with the pump. As the London companies lower the level of the water in the moisture-bearing strata, the process described above can of course be repeated till a depth is reached at which it becomes impossible to work the tools.

This afternoon I went with a friend, who is the honorary secretary of a newly formed angling club, to inspect a trout stream in this neighbourhood which has recently been stocked with fish. Never before did I understand how arduous and expensive is this task of converting a coarse-fish river into a trout water. First the common fish, and especially the pike, must be captured, which, as the use of dynamite is illegal, is in itself no easy matter. I forget the number of pike which have already been removed from these few miles of brook, but it is not small. After most of the pike are extracted—for it takes years to be rid of them altogether—the bed of the stream must be cleaned. Then comes its re-stocking with thousands of young trout bought at a hatchery; the making of suitable spawning beds by the carting of gravel into the water, or the stirring up and washing of such stone as already exists there the sowing of water-weeds suitable to the collection of food such as trout love, and so forth. All these things are necessary if trout-fishing is to be enjoyed in such a stream, yet so much preparation gives a certain artificiality to the final result.

I am not a great fisherman, for the chance of much of that delightful sport has not come my way, but while my friend and the water-bailiff are discussing the advisability of the destruction of three herons that haunt the stream (poor herons!) my mind wanders back to certain experiences in Iceland when, towards midnight, the light turned ghastly blue, and for a while was so pale upon the foaming river's face that it became difficult to see the fly dancing in the black eddy of the fosse. Hark! the sound of whistling wings and there above a pair of wild duck travel like arrows from the sea. The water, too, roars in the cataract and murmurs against the stones, and now and again comes a splash as a heavy salmon or a sea-trout springs into the air and falls into the darkling fosse. But there is no other sound, no sound of man at least, and no sign of him either, for the little stead lies more than a mile away. Only the tremendous outline of the great mountains and the sweep of the flowery mead beneath, only the eternal rush of the river and the whisper of the perfumed wind, and, brooding about all, that blue and spiritual light—a light in which ghosts might walk their world again.

OCTOBER

October 4.—On my return to Ditchingham I find that the fierce drought still prevails, although the country here is not quite so much burnt up as is the case in Hertfordshire. The pastures are perfectly brown, almost as brown as the African veld in winter; indeed, if these seasons are to go on I believe that it would pay to sow with our mixtures a proportion of seed taken from the deep-rooted grasses which grow in the colder parts of the South African High Veld. The stock I find looking well, but although they are liberally supplied with cotton cake, the cows, or rather their milk supplies, are shrinking sadly in this bitter drought.

Since harvest about 250 loads of manure have been carted from the yards direct to the various fields where they are to be spread, and sundry dykes on the marshland have been drawn. Also a little thrashing has been done both here and at Bedingham, and we have sold some barley at sixteen shillings and fifteen shillings the coomb, according to its quality. A neighbouring farmer, whose land marches with my own, as I hear, realised eighteen shillings a coomb for barley which he thrashed upon the field; but I am told that his crop, although the sample was good, ran out only at the miserable total of four coombs an acre. This year there is a great deal of straw, but so far the cast does not seem to be heavy. The men with the thrashing engine complain much, as they are paid per the score coomb actually realised, and it takes them a long while to work this great bulk of straw through the machine.

Store cattle have dropped heavily in price, and I am glad that we bought none before harvest, as it is evident, owing to the wonderful variations of the British climate, that we shall be short both of feed and roots. The Bedingham ox, Royal Duke, which I have been cherishing all this year, is now in a box at the All Hallows farm. It is curious that he should have taken the first prize at the North Suffolk Association Show, as he is a nervous beast and, after being moved here several days previous to the competition, was so upset by the change and the heat that he refused to take his food.

As might be expected in such a season the mustard which I drilled on to the pease stubbles, No. 37 All Hallows and No. 43 Baker's, appears to be an almost total failure owing to the drought, although, being a stubborn crop, it may still pick up should we get rain within a reasonable time. Somewhat to my surprise, however, for it is a water-loving plant, the little piece of maize which was sown on No. 21, where the vetches were fed off by sheep, is throwing up a welcome breadth of green stuff. The vetches, which were harvested off the remainder of the same field, have been thrashed, but there seems to be no market for them this year.

October 5.—To-day we are ploughing on the bean stubble, No. 26, for wheat, and on Baker's, No. 42, for vetches, but with the soil in its present condition it is dreadfully hard work for the horses. This afternoon I went to Bedingham, and found Moore likewise ploughing for wheat upon the bean stubble, No. 14. Here the cattle look well; also the beet and the kohl-rabi, a most valuable crop in such a season, have stood the drought better than was to be expected. Young Moore and the new man, Whitrup, are engaged in clearing the brushwood rubbish from the sides of the dykes before they fill up with water, gathering it into heaps for the burning. The young things with the colts are feeding on the wheat stubbles, where they manage to fill themselves with the green weeds and the many ears of corn which seem to have escaped the attention of the gleaners. But perhaps none have been here, for nowadays I do not think that in these parts many people take the trouble to glean; I suppose corn is so cheap that the results are no longer worth the time expended.

The shed is not yet up over the cattle-yard, but the posts have been sunk into position to carry the roof.

October 6.—To-day is dull, but there is no break in the drought. Buck, whom I found hedge clipping, tells me that it is about thirty-two years since there was such an autumn 'dry' as that which prevails at present. In the season which he speaks of, however, a good rain fell in the middle of harvest, for he remembers that it started the potatoes into a second growth. After that rain the dry was so sharp that very few farmers succeeded in sowing their wheat before the following spring.

These are the results of the thrashing up to the present: From the three-and-a-half acre, Church Close field, No. 33, and two acres of the Milestone field, No. 25, fifty-one coombs of barley, or about nine coombs to the acre, of which forty-eight coombs were sold at sixteen and sixpence per coomb.

From the Glebe land five-acre, No. 40, forty-four coombs of oats, which we shall consume at home—not a bad return from this scaldy soil.

From about two acres of the Home Farm field, No. 26, twenty coombs of beans for seed and use, and from a little piece of No. 25, about twelve coombs of wheat for seed.

From six acres of the Vinery field, No. 41 on Baker's, forty-four coombs of barley. This is a poor return, but the barleys seem to have suffered from the wet and cold at the beginning of the year, and to have died too quickly owing to the summer drought, with the result that a good many of the kernels are shrivelled.

At Bedingham we have thrashed thirty-five coombs of barley off seven acres of land—only five coombs an acre—of which thirty-four coombs sold at fifteen shillings a coomb. From three acres of No. 13 we obtained thirty coombs of oats for home use, and from a little surplus stack saved from something over an acre of land about fifteen coombs of wheat.

Until all the corns have been thrashed and sold, however, it is difficult to estimate the exact results.

October 11.—A friend whom I met out shooting last Saturday told me that, since the beginning of this month, a hen pheasant has been found in the vicarage garden of his parish sitting upon six eggs. This seems a curious mistake for a bird to make, but I suppose that it is due to the extraordinary warmth of the season.

A big *D*—for drought—might be written across my diary. I can scarcely bear to go to look at the root-fields, it is so pitiful to see the bulbs shrivelling up to nothing and the sere leaves falling from them to the ground. A writer in the local paper estimates that owing to the scarcity of feed in Norfolk alone 20,000 fewer cattle will be fatted this year than last. Also all store animals are falling rapidly in price, and those who held their lambs begin to suffer from regrets.

We still plough, or try to, but the operation affords a curious side. The horses pant and sweat, the man struggles over the rough clods, and as the implement bumps and jumps through the iron soil a cloud of fine dust rises from its share.

To-day I was talking to one of my men as he dressed the barley in Baker's barn, and he tells me that for twenty years of his life he was a farmer and his own master. When he began farming with some capital that he had saved and, I think, inherited, he says that he paid 4*l.* the acre for his land. Even at this rent he did so well that he was able to put by enough to enable him to hire a larger farm. On this second farm he was still successful, and in course of time he took a third and yet larger farm at a low rent, but with the land in bad order. Then came the disastrous seasons and the floods, and, to make matters worse, he had a run of dreadful luck with his cattle. In short, everything went against him, and after twenty years of work all his savings and capital were lost and he was forced to return to the land again as a labourer.

There is nothing sensational about it, but this story strikes me as very sad, although of a sufficiently common order. It is wonderful how my friend manages to remain of so cheerful a disposition under the weight of such a disappointment in life, but I suppose that the back is fitted to the burden. Such toilers ought to have an old age pension to look forward to, collected from their earnings by insurance in the good time of strength, 'or ever the evil days come and the grasshopper shall be a burden.' As it is, unless they have been able to save, we know what they must expect.

October 12.—Some rain at last ! It fell last night, and thankful we were to see it. To-day I went to lunch at Earlham Hall, near Norwich. Although it is by no means large, to my mind this is in its way one of the most beautiful houses that I have seen in Norfolk. Its aspect from the road is disappointing, for one of the Quaker Gurneys whitewashed it, but on the garden side the mellow brick is left. The house is Jacobean, and still belongs to the Bacon family, but, oddly enough, it has been rented by successive generations of the Gurneys for about a hundred and ten years. One of the charms of this place is the river that runs below the lawns, with a heronry upon its bank. But the house itself, as readers of 'The Gurneys of Earlham' will know, is stored with memories. Here the sainted Elizabeth Fry, whose portrait hangs upon the walls, spent her youth. She died in 1845, but her memory will live on for many a generation as one of the half-angelic beings who, in pursuit of their mission of charity and love, did not shrink even from plunging into such an inferno as Newgate offered at the beginning of this century.

It is impossible to look at that old hall and the broad stairway of Earlham without imagining them peopled by Elizabeth and all her kin, whose young voices used to echo there. There is something terribly pathetic about these ancient houses.[1]

[1] Owing to recent deaths Earlham Hall, after its long lease of one hundred and ten years, is to let again at last. So I am told, at least, in June 1899.

October 14.—This afternoon we have been drilling rye, some by itself, and some mixed with vetches, in that portion of field No. 42 on Baker's which was under oats. This is a new crop to us, but we are growing it now to furnish early sheep feed. The land, which has not been manured, although it is very dry, seems to be in nice order now that the roller and harrow have been over it.

The papers are constantly talking of tuberculosis in cows and the tuberculin test. Till within the last year or so I do not ever remember hearing of the one or the other; but science is always revealing fresh horrors to our sight, and I have little doubt but that the experts speak truth when they say that a great deal of consumption is caused by tuberculous milk. For aught I know one consumes it daily in one's tea, and my best red-polls may be afflicted with this abominable disease. But how are we to find out? It is all very well to talk of tuberculin, but nine people out of ten have not the faintest idea what tuberculin is, and I imagine that even nine veterinaries out of ten would look a little vacant if suddenly asked to apply the test to a herd of cows. If these scientific operations are to be carried out, there ought to be in every county Government laboratories to which farmers could apply for instruction and assistance. Moreover, there ought to be Government inspectors to see that they did apply, and to assess damages when it became necessary to destroy affected animals. It is useless to leave it to the farmers them-selves to take the initiative, as not one in twenty would ever bother his head about the matter—indeed, I doubt whether some would stir if a scientific friend were to prove to them that their cattle were a walking mass of tuberculosis. I believe that there exist inspectors of dairies, though I never saw or heard of one of them inspecting my dairy, and I doubt whether the duty is half so efficiently or strictly performed as it ought to be. I know that when I took over this farm I found that into the pond from which the cows drank was led the entire sewage of a yard. I daresay that any inspector who took an interest in his work could make even worse discoveries in the Eastern counties.[1]

October 16.—Last night it was wet, and this morning very wet. The rain has come at last, and with it the autumn, for the beeches have turned suddenly sere and the wood-pigeons begin to haunt the lawn, although not in anything like the numbers in which I have sometimes seen them. Generally they appear at the dinner-hour, or on Sunday, when there are no gardeners about. First one flies down from the trees and begins to hunt for beech-mast among the fallen leaves; then comes another and another, until the whole lawn is dotted with their beautiful blue shapes; indeed, I have counted up to a hundred of them at one time. They do not mind the house, for they will strut about quite close to the windows, but their sentinels are set upon the surrounding trees, and the moment that a human being appears, off they fly with a mighty clapping of wings.

It is a dreary day—a day when the mind takes the colour of the sky and dwells, not on successes, but on failures, not on hopes of happiness, but on recollections of sorrow and dreary prognostications. The lesson that is hid in the turmoil of the tempest, the lashing of the rain, the falling leaves, the dying flowers, and the heavy ashen sky brooding over all, becomes painfully and persistently obvious. 'Summer has gone,' the raving wind seems to say—'*your* summer. You have seen your best days, you are wearing out with work and worry and responsibilities; and—do you hear?—you are not like these, there is no earthly spring to come for *you.*'

'Do not frighten the poor fugitive creatures,' answers the beating rain. 'I knew their kind a thousand generations gone, but they

---

[1] Retribution has overtaken me and I must pay for these remarks. An inspector (who knew them not) has just descended upon me and requested me to be good enough to alter a certain surface drain in one of my own cowhouses. I shall comply with much pleasure, delighted to reflect, indeed, that the sanitary authorities have developed such activity. They will, I think, find many worse things than my drain to occupy them. H. R. H., 1899.

were wrapped in skins and lived in a hole on the hillside yonder, not in a brick box. Yes, and I know the end of them all, for I drive upon their graves and wash their bones. Let them be! Winter is before them—beautiful, white, silent winter.'

Well, better perhaps the snow's peace and the bonds of the death-frost than this autumn rage of confusion and decay.

With what terror must our savage forefathers have looked forward to the coming of winter, with its dreadful darkness, its cold, its loneliness, its prowling enemies and ravening beasts? What must it have been even in the Middle Ages, and right down to the last century, when fireplaces in the houses were very few, and scant tallow dips furnished the only illumination; when the roads were such that it took four strong farm-horses to drag a coach along them; when there was no fresh meat for food, and cut-throat foot-pads lurked in the neighbouring thicket? To this day our highly civilised race has not got over its dread of winter and the gloom with which it is associated. Even among grown men there are few whom the horror of the dark does not take hold of from time to time, or even of the night when it is not dark. Not long ago I asked a friend, whose name would be known to every reader of this book, and whom one would certainly not associate with such fears, whether he ever felt afraid of being alone at night. He confessed to me that he did—that occasionally, when he sat working late, a panic would seize him, causing him to turn out the lights and slip away straight to bed. I believe that his experience is not by any means exceptional. We come of a Northern stock, and as all students of the Sagas, that magnificent but neglected literature, will know, to our Norse ancestors some few generations since the dark of the long winter was a fearful thing, peopled with malevolent, able-bodied trolls and with ghosts of the dead.

Last night Hood was knocked down by a heifer, although he escaped with nothing worse than an injured foot. The heifer was in difficulties with her first calf and actually fainted away. When she came to herself, either she had forgotten about the calf or—

with good reason—she attributed her discomfort to its presence. At any rate she attacked it fiercely, knocking the poor little creature and Hood into a corner of the hospital, and roaring so loudly that, although these events took place at the dead of night, people in the village got out of their beds and came to see what might be the matter. By degrees, however, she was quieted, and to-day seems to be quite reconciled to her offspring.

October 18.—Yesterday we drilled the Ape field, No. 37, with beans, which went in very well, as the rainfall, although considerable, has not been sufficient to clog the land. At night, however, heavy showers fell, with the result that we cannot sow wheat to-day as we intended. About a fortnight ago a poor boy, aged twelve, the son of a working man, while playing in Bungay, was so unfortunate as to swallow a tin 'squeaker,' a toy producing an abominable noise, which the lad was clever at manufacturing out of steel ribs taken from worn-out stays. The doctor and the father's employer urged his parents to send him at once to Norwich Hospital, where the obstruction could have been located with the Röntgen rays, or otherwise, and removed by operation. With the terrible blindness which affects so many persons in this class of life, they would not consent, and when at last their permission was obtained it proved too late, for the patient had developed peritonitis, of which he is now dead. It is very difficult to combat the hatred and mistrust of hospitals that so often afflicts such people. In this instance I believe that it cost his parents the life of a son to whom they were deeply devoted.

October 22.—The reader may remember my writing of an aged relative who in her youth assisted at the planting of the trees which grow about this house. To-day their autumn leaves fell upon her bier as she went by to burial. She was the last of her generation, and her death breaks another link with the past, for with her is buried much local history. Last Sunday I was talking to her in her own drawing-room, and within twenty-four hours she had passed away.

I have sold two of my red-poll cows, mother and daughter, to a gentleman in the neighbourhood for 35*l.* They are of a good milking strain, but rather long in the leg, so I weeded them out. It is not a very grand price, but nowadays one can only keep the best. On the farm and at Bedingham we have been drilling wheat and getting forward with the ploughing.

I have been reading a most instructive pamphlet sent to me by Messrs. Garton, of whose labours I have already spoken, dealing with the production of new types of clovers and grasses by selection and cross-fertilisation. Curiously enough, the results of their experiments with red clover do not at all coincide with those of other experiments carried out by Darwin. Whether they are right or Darwin is right it is of course impossible for me to say, but if it should chance that Darwin was wrong upon this point the fact is suggestive.

The weather is lovely, more like that of August than the end of October. Here, on the Norfolk coast, where I am staying for a few days at Kessingland, the autumns are frequently the finest part of the year. July and August are the fashionable months upon this shore, but if I were a town-dweller I should prefer those of September and October. This is very generally recognised in these counties, where people like to visit the sea at the fall of the leaf.

October 26.—To-day I was one of the party of guns at a pheasant shoot in a neighbouring parish, where we killed between four and five hundred birds, which, to my mind, is as many as anyone can want to see brought to bag in six hours. This particular shooting, although not by any means one of the largest, is certainly one of the best managed in Norfolk. The place to be occupied by each gun at every beat is arranged beforehand and marked with sticks; there is no delay; the beaters advance without shouting or unnecessary noise, and the birds are put over the guns in the best possible manner of which the lie of the land permits. The performance of some of the crack game shots—and there were one or two gentlemen present to-day who may be included in the list—is a thing to see. They seem rarely to make a mistake, and however high the bird may pass they always hit it well forward, killing it clean and dead ; not waiting, as bunglers like myself are so apt to do, till it is almost over the gun and sending an unavailing second barrel after it as it vanishes into space. Battue shooting, as it is popularly called, is a favourite target for the scorn of people who know very little about it, and who, to save their lives, could not bring down one high bird in twenty. As a matter of fact, it is a difficult art—indeed, like the poet, the really fine shot is born, not made. If any one doubts it, let him watch Lord Walsingham, standing away back behind the line of guns and bringing down pheasant after pheasant which appear to be almost out of the reach of shot, not picking or choosing, but taking them one after another as they come at every possible or impossible angle.

By the way, there is nothing more disconcerting to the ordinary sportsman than this process of being watched, anent which a gentleman once told me a most amusing story. He was taking part in some big shoot on a Yorkshire estate where it was the habit of miners to congregate to watch the sport. A number of these gentry attached themselves to him, following him from beat to beat and staring at him so hard that he grew nervous and began to miss freely. At length the last and great stand of the day was reached, when, just before the beat began, a ferocious and peculiarly powerful miner advanced and whispered hoarsely in his ear, 'Look 'ere, guv'ner, you're shooting h'orful, and I've lost three bob on yer. But I've backed yer double or quits, and, by gosh ! if I don't win this time *I'll knock yer bloomin' head off.*'

October 29.—All our wheat is now in except one piece at Bedingham, which if it is fine, we shall drill on Monday. We have begun lifting the beet from No. 22. On this field they are small, having been stunted first by the wet, when they were seedlings, and afterwards by the drought, when they had formed their bulbs, but the quality seems to be good. This is the process of beet lifting. Men go down the ringes drawing the roots from the soil, cutting off their leafy tops with a single swift and skilful movement, and throwing the bulbs together in a line in such fashion that room is left for a cart to travel without crushing them. Then comes the cart, drawn by one horse, and two men rapidly lift the beet, using both hands to the task, and throw them into it, the horse going forward and stopping as required at a word of command. When this cart is full another empty cart arrives with two horses, and the front horse is taken off and hitched on to the full cart, which is then dragged away to the hale, that, in this instance, is being made at the gate of the field. Here the cart is tilted up, depositing the beet at the end of the hale, where they are neatly arranged by hand into a long pile about four foot through at the bottom and sloping to a narrow ridge at the top.

As this pile grows, for fear of a possible frost it is loosely covered over each night with rubbish cut from the ditches and saved up for this purpose. In the old extravagant days, when farming paid, straw was frequently made use of, but now this is only turned to, at any rate on my farm, when there is no other material available. Ultimately the hale is earthed up, after having been ploughed round to a depth of about four furrows to provide a supply of loose soil with which to cover the roots. At first the crown of the ridge is left open, but after a while, when the beet are supposed to have finished heating, this is earthed in also, with the exception of pipes or holes placed at regular distances, which are stuffed with straw to provide for the ventilation of the heap.

To-day, with the usual formalities, one of the men approached me on the question of largesse, intimating that, as there were two extra hands employed this year, a slight addition to the accustomed sum would be acceptable. When I was a child I can remember how the harvestmen used to assemble at Bradenham Hall and,

standing in a semicircle facing the door, drink beer each in turn
and sing this song:

> Now supper is over, and all things are past,
> Here's our mistress's good health in a full flowing glass;
> She is a good mistress, she provides us good cheer;
> Here's our mistress's good health, boys—come, drink *half* your beer.
> She is a good mistress, she provides us good cheer;
> Here's our mistress's good health, boys—come, drink *off* your beer.
> Here's health to our master, the Lord of the feast,
> God bless his endeavours and send him increase,
> And send him good crops, that we may meet another year.
> Here's our master's good health, boys—come, drink *half* your beer.
> God send him good crops—come, drink *off* your beer.

ending with the cry of '*Largesse! Largesse! Largesse!*' uttered
by all in unison.

I remember that my mother noted down the music of the air
to which this quaint and ancient song was sung. I imagine that
it is not to be heard in Norfolk nowadays, and indeed never will
be heard again.

Talking of largesse reminds me that I have forgotten to say
that after harvest wages fell a shilling all round in sympathy with
the drop in the price of corn.

October 31.—To-day we have been thrashing barley from the
Ape field. The return is not very good, about seven coombs to
the acre, but the sample seems excellent.

This morning I was serving on the County Grand Jury. At
Norwich the Grand Jurors are crowded together in a kind of bird-
cage near the roof of the Court, while the learned Judge charges
them, or rather his blotting paper, down below. I found from
the papers afterwards, for it was impossible to hear what his Lord
ship said, that the subject of his address was the Criminal Evidence
Act, of which he does not seem entirely to approve. In this age
of change it is rather curious that Grand Juries should still survive
as an institution. One can well understand that in past genera-

tions they were a most useful bulwark between the subject and the Crown, but now their functions seem to be fulfilled by the benches of magistrates whose duty it is to investigate every case before it is sent to the Assizes. If Grand Juries departed into the limbo of antiquated but ornamental institutions, taking with them the office of High Sheriff, I do not think that the liberties of Englishmen would be imperilled. I believe, however, that a case in which the magistrates have declined to commit can be reopened before the Grand Jury by any party who considers himself aggrieved, although in practice I never heard of this being done.

NOVEMBER

November 1.—To-day we have been thrashing the barley off
No. 36, which gives a return of about seven coombs the acre.
To-day also Hood and one of the men have had a difference of
opinion, with the result that the said man has given notice to leave
(I am glad to say that he thought better of it later on). The cause
of war was an order issued by Hood to pile some straw from the
thrashing against a garden wall over which this man was in the
habit of climbing when going to attend to the cattle, with the
result that his nightly walk is prolonged by some few yards. The
grievance seems absolutely trivial, yet it was urged upon me with
an energy which may be called fierce. After all, bad quarrels
more frequently arise from small than from big questions; thus,
matters quite as absurd as this debated straw, as students of the
Northern Sagas will remember, often gave rise to feuds which lasted
for generations and cost whole families their lives. Of course, in
the present instance discipline had to be maintained, for without
it neither farming nor any other human enterprise could be carried
on ; but it is hard for an old man to be forced to bow the head
to his junior, especially when he has been 'his own master.' I
confess that I felt sorry for him.

This afternoon I went to Bedingham, and found Moore
making an end of harrowing in the wheat which has been drilled
on No. 13, while the men cleaned out the water furrows. On
No. 14 the wheat is already beginning to show in long lines of
delicate green ; the sprouting beans also are dotting the surface of
the soil of No. 5. So the eternal round of Nature has begun

once more. New oxen fatten in the byre, new corn springs in the fertile earth, and yonder through the fence new children watch the husbandmen at work as their forefathers watched them centuries and centuries ago, and as their descendants will watch them when we have been dead a thousand years.

The shed over the bullock yard is a great success although Moore complains that one of the posts will be in the way when he is carting manure. As it is necessary to the structure, however, this cannot be helped.

Since portions of this book began to appear serially various kind correspondents have written remonstrating with me for using galvanized iron as roofing material upon these rough sheds. Their allegation is that it is hot in summer and cold in winter, and that animals sheltering beneath it are liable to chills. Now, I have no doubt that there is truth in all these statements, and also that the vapours condense upon its inner surface, causing drip and damp. But after all the proof of the pudding is in the eating, and as one of these sheds has stood in a yard here for about fourteen years, and as the cattle have always done exceedingly well beneath its shelter, the iron cannot be so very unwholesome. It must be remembered in its favour also that it is cheap and most lasting; indeed, if kept coated with a suitable paint, I do not see why it should ever wear out. Doubtless the open boarded roof sheds, as one of my correspondents brings to my notice, are in many ways better, but are they as inexpensive and as durable? I may mention that these sheds of mine, if large, are ventilated by the lifting of a sheet above the others throughout their length, and that they are all of them lean-to sheds, so that the sharp through-draughts which some critics mention do not exist.

The kohl-rabi at Bedingham are a very fair crop, and have stood the drought marvellously. I believe that on these heavy lands it is far better to drill kohl-rabi than swedes, as the return is more certain, and they will flourish with half the amount of moisture. Also up till about Christmas-time they are excellent for stock. The white turnips, on the contrary, have suffered very severely from the drought, but the beet are as good as can be expected upon this land in such a season.

November 2.—To-day some friends came over from Kessing-land to lunch, and informed us that yesterday about midnight most of the Coastguard were telegraphed for with orders to mobilise at Harwich. When even Kessingland is robbed of its protectors in this fashion things begin to look serious, but for my part I do not believe that there will be any war—no, not if we annexed Egypt to-morrow, and for the simple reason that all Europe put together could not hold its own against us on the sea. If they wanted to fight us, they ought to have done so ten years ago, but even then I believe that we should have beaten them, although it would have taken longer and cost more money. Consider how vast is our strength, not only in money, ships, and guns, but in nations of mankind all the world over, sworn to our service, and in our colonial kindred, who, in most cases at any rate, would fight for us to the last ditch, if for no other reason because our fate must be their fate. The spectacle of the Empire defending itself against a combination of Powers, and putting out all its strength in men and money, would be the most tremendous that the world has ever seen. But although, doubtless, we should meet with reverses, for my part I should be sorry for the Powers, as I believe that within a year they would scarcely have a ship left between them, and not much British territory by way of consolation. One day the rest of the world, or most of it, I suppose, will fling itself at the throats of America and ourselves. That will be the day of Armageddon, after which may come the long peace. But the British Empire and the United States will dictate the terms of that peace. My only fear is one which I mentioned on a previous page, namely, that in the event of a prolonged war we might be driven to conclude it unsatisfactorily by the clamour of the electorate enraged at the price of bread and other necessaries. Doubtless this is a very real and grave danger, one more to be dreaded than all the fleets of France and Russia. However, these are only my private and quite unimportant opinions.

The weather to-day is very windy, with storms of rain, but the men are going on with the storage of the beet.

November 6.—On Thursday last Mr. Simpson came over to make the annual valuation on these farms and at Bedingham. I await the result with fear and trembling, for it may prove that after I have preached to others—&c. To be frank, it always has proved so hitherto, therefore a variation in the tale would be a most pleasant surprise. The corn is short this year; very few people have thrashed more than seven coombs an acre from their barleys in our neighbourhood, and a large proportion of this total is in some instances proving to be dross. Also there is the dead loss upon those ten Irish bullocks to be faced, and the poor return from the root-crop, so that, take it all together, we can scarcely hope for anything very encouraging.

On Friday and yesterday we were shooting the coverts on the Ditchingham Hall estate. The weather was beautiful, but Heden-ham Wood is still far too thick with leaf to be shot satisfactorily: indeed, it was quite impossible to see the ground game, and the pheasants were loth to rise. We lunched out of doors without cold or discomfort; in fact, judged by the green surroundings, the season might almost have been summer, a delusion that the presence of numerous wasps did not tend to dispel. The number of stops required makes the shooting of these large woods difficult and rather expensive, but without their help the pheasants would simply run from beat to beat and never fly at all. I think that it was last year an amusing incident occurred in connection with these stops. After luncheon was over, and as the beaters were about to get to work, a little boy was seen approaching, weeping as bitterly as though he had just lost his most intimate relation. When asked what was the matter, he sobbed out in a squeaky voice :

' Please, sir, *six of us little stops ain't 'ad no beer.*' Beer and food, it may be explained, have to be conveyed to stops at their posts, which they must not leave.

When I was alone at one stand, quite in the centre of the wood, I saw a beautiful specimen of the golden-crested wren picking insects from a bough literally within three feet of me. I never knew before that these friendly little birds haunted the interiors of large woods.

To-day the weather is of the most perfect stillness and beauty; so still, indeed, that the shed leaves float downwards softly as falling feathers. While we were at luncheon, suddenly, and without the smallest warning, a large piece fell off the bough of one of the great garden elms on to the path beneath. Had anyone been walking on that path under the tree he would certainly have been killed. It is this trick which elms have of shedding their boughs in perfectly still weather that makes them such dangerous timber to plant near houses. So far as my observation goes, these limbs come down in late spring or in autumn, that is when the sap is either rising or falling. On examining the wood of the bough, I found that it was absolutely rotten and devoid of all strength and virtue; indeed, it seems marvellous that it should have lasted so long.

This afternoon Hood and I came to the conclusion that it would be desirable to make a change in our farm policy. Heretofore we have been in the habit of fatting all the progeny of my red-polls which we have not actually required to rear as cows. In future I mean to alter this by keeping the best of the heifers till I can sell them as down-calvers, and the best of the male animals to be disposed of as young bulls. Of course, this presupposes a market for my stock, which is not quite easy to get in face of the competition of the large breeders. Already, however, there are inquiries; thus, this year I have sold four things, two cows and two heifers, to people who wish to breed from them. I cannot see why I should not in time establish a connection and get fair prices, as, after all, my cattle are practically as well bred as any other pedigree red-polls in East Anglia, nor do I think that their stamp is inferior to that of such herds as I have seen. Of course, however, one cannot expect much of this sort of trade frcm local sources, since the average East Anglian stock-keeper seems to me to be quite careless as to the class of animal he rears. The person who tries to buy young homebreds on the market for fatting purposes very soon finds this out, as it is almost impossible to get them of sufficient quality. This is the more strange since it has been proved over and over again that well-bred animals lay on flesh much faster and do better generally than those of low degree.

November 8.—Yesterday we began carting the beet from the top of the pit field, No. 23, and it is now that we see the results of that noble mixture, Bungay compost. I believe that there is half as much weight again per acre on this field as on any other root land which I farm. Moreover the roots, although not of the large, coarse variety, have defied the drought, and in some instances, at any rate, are perfect specimens of what high-class beet should be.

To-day the morning was very beautiful, nor during the whole year do I remember a scene of more singular and peaceful charm than that which I witnessed in the Buildings stackyard. Bright sunshine poured upon the meadows beyond me, and high against the tender blue of heaven wheeled the chattering daws. Perched on the surrounding trees, the loud-voiced rooks croaked solemnly, as is their fashion at this season, while a grey-breasted Royston crow, like the mischievous thief he is, sailed across the field searching the ground with his keen eyes in the hope of finding carrion or some sick and wounded thing which he could peck to death. At the sound of the gate as I shut it the ewes looked up and ran forward in the eager hope of being led to fresh supplies of food, but not recognising in me their accustomed guide, stopped and began to crop the grass with a redoubled energy to make up for the moment they had lost. Hopping on the ground between them were a flock of starlings, whose jewelled plumage shone in the sunlight.   Some of these were even perched upon the sheep's backs, and, declining to be frightened away, clung to the wool with their claws, their wings outspread to steady themselves while the creatures moved.   It was curious to see these industrious birds hunting for insects, ticks I presume, which were hidden in the fleeces of their hosts. One tick, I observed, was very obdurate and gave a starling much trouble, for he pulled at it as a thrush pulls at a worm upon the garden grass. Near to me also, poised upon a whitethorn bough covered with brilliant haws, sat a robin, watching everything that passed with his beady eye, his little head cocked on one side, in search, no doubt, of some opportunity of profit to himself.   It is strange, by the way, now that the foliage grows thinner and winter is at hand, how one begins to notice the red breasts of the robins.   In summer they catch the eye but seldom.

Then suddenly this brilliance of colour and these many sounding voices of beasts and birds passed away, for a cloud drifted over the face of the sun, and, behold ! all the landscape grew dead and ashen, and all the birds were still.   The daws ceased their chattering and the rooks croaked no more, the heavy shape of the Royston crow vanished from sight among the trees of the Vineyard slope, the Robin flew off with a disappointed chirp, and even the bright haws seemed to lose their brilliant hues and to become merged in the sombre tints of the autumn foliage. Only the sheep fed on eagerly, as they feed day and night, heedless of the season or the changes of the weather. Sheep are practical creatures, with no time to waste in sentiment.

On the road to-day I met an old fellow, a very handsome man with clear-cut features, whose face I know well although I forget his name.   He stopped me, and in a melancholy quavering voice said that he had a favour to ask. The favour was that he desired to be informed whether I could allot him parish relief. He was seventy-five, he told me, and could no longer work as his strength had left him, so that unless he could get relief he must take refuge in the House. I gave him such information as I could, and went away sorrowful. I have already commented on these cases, and there is nothing more to be said about them.

November 10.—Yesterday I was shooting with a friend at Earsham, and spent a very enjoyable day knocking through out-lying spinneys and doubling hedgerows for pheasants. We had one or two partridge drives also, the guns standing in large grass meadows, which in past times were a deer-park and belonged to the old Dukes of Norfolk. On a lovely day such as this was those great meadows look very beautiful, fringed as they are with tall, uncut hedgerows, wherein grow occasional stunted oaks and maple trees, now splendid in their yellow autumn dress. Here, too, the fieldfares chattered, congratulating themselves, doubtless, upon their safe arrival from over-seas.

To-day is fine, but misty, and we are getting off the root from the All Hallows field, No. 29. These beet are of a longer variety than those which we have grown elsewhere, and, being easier to grasp, are not dealt with in the same way. Instead of pulling them first and leaving them in lines to be tossed into the cart, a man goes down the rows, deftly cutting off the tops to the right and left with his sickle, but leaving the bulbs standing in the ground. After him follow the horses, and the pullers, dragging the beet from the soil with a quick and practised movement, throw them straight into the cart. This process is harder work, but, where the condi-tions make it practicable, it saves a good deal of time.

November 12.—Yesterday we were shooting in Tindale Wood, a great covert of about 120 acres, which even now, however, is very thick with leaf, some of the undergrowth being almost as green as though we were still in the month of June. This quantity of foliage, even if one can see the creatures, makes hare-and rabbit-shooting rather dangerous, as it is difficult to know when the beaters are close at hand. However, nobody was shot, perhaps because we had no clergymen among our party. Great as is my respect for the clergy, although there are exceptions (I myself know *one*), I confess that I am not fond of going out shooting with them, since on these occasions they are apt to display too active a trust in a watching Providence. When I was a young fellow there lived in our neighbourhood a retired naval chaplain, who in private life was a most delightful old gentleman, but who when armed with a gun became a perfect terror. On one occasion I was joining a party of shooters who were advancing up a turnip field, and, seeing among them my reverend friend, I was particularly careful to show myself and call out to him. When he arrived within about twenty yards of me, however, a partridge rose at his feet and flew straight past me, whereon, without the slightest hesitation, he sent the contents first of one barrel and then of the other slap into the fence within about a foot of my face.

'Mr. B. ! Mr. B. !' I exclaimed reproachfully, 'you very nearly shot me dead.'

'Oh,' he grunted in answer, 'shouldn't have been there, you know ; shouldn't have been there !'

On another occasion the same dear old gentleman nearly blew the middle out of one of my brothers, indeed he only escaped the charge by doubling himself up with a wonderful rapidity. After that experience we dared not ask him to shoot any more. This gave him great offence, as he believed that the omission was due to personal reasons. It is very difficult to make the dangerous man understand what a thing of fear he is to all his neighbours.

Here is a further reminiscence of a parsonic sportsman. The parson and another friend entered at the top of a long covert with a view to walking down it in line and shooting rabbits, while I stood at the bottom waiting for pheasants. There were a good many shots fired in the covert, varied by occasional shouts, and at last my friend staggered out at the end looking very hot and flustered.

'You had some shooting there,' I said.

'Shooting?' he answered in a fury. 'That infernal parson

had the shooting. He has been firing at my legs all down the Grove, and *I've been jumping the shot.*'

Afterwards this reverend gentleman very nearly slew me also in mopping up a low pheasant, at which no man ought to have fired.

Once, too, I knew another clergyman who went out ferreting with a companion and, turning suddenly, aimed his gun at that unfortunate's boot and—hit it. When remonstrated with he said that he thought it was a black rabbit. However, he was only a curate, from whom caution could scarcely be expected.

Next to the clergy I think that naval lieutenants are the most dangerous, for they return fresh from abroad, where they have been accustomed to shoot with nobody within a square mile of them. But perhaps the palm ought to be given to short-sighted and peppery old generals who chance to be jealous shots. I imagine, however, that sportsmen run more risk from their loaders than from companions, no matter how careless, who are rarely near enough to shoot them dead. I shall not readily forget one such experience.

Needing a loader, I retained for the next day's shoot a gentleman with a statuesque countenance and a beautiful white beard, who informed me that he had loaded for Lord Walsingham. At the first hot corner, as my second gun was not handed to me when I wanted it, I looked around, to perceive the party who had loaded for Lord Walsingham fumbling at the breech blindly with both hands, a loaded cartridge sticking out of each corner of his *mouth.* I ought to have dismissed him then and there, but accepted some explanation. At the very next stand, just as I had shot a high pheasant and was watching it fall, I heard an explosion at my side and saw a charge of shot strike the ground in front of my feet. My white-bearded friend had managed to discharge the gun which he was loading in such a fashion that the shot must have passed within an inch or so of my thigh.

For the rest of that day I used one gun only ; moreover I took to shooting with hammerless guns, which are much safer. On the other hand, the great carefulness of a loader under confusing circumstances, when a faulty gun exploded in his hands, once saved me from a terrible accident. No story that I know, however, of the mistakes of loaders can equal that authentic tale told to me by Lord Walsingham, of how, when shooting with three guns, the trigger of one of them was accidentally pulled while its loaded muzzle pointed at the small of his back. It may be asked how he survived. He survived because out of all the hundreds of cartridges he used that day this particular cartridge alone missed fire !

We bagged only one woodcock in Tindale and saw but two. In most seasons this wood is a favourite haunt of these beautiful birds, and I have known as many as eight or ten killed in going through the beats.

To-day, while we were partridge driving, I picked up on a field a bean seedling, self-sown no doubt, which had been harrowed out in preparing the land for wheat. It is very curious to observe the process of root formation in the bean. First the thick white root pushes from the seed, and then out of it and not from the bean itself, indeed about an eighth of an inch below it, starts the vigorous upward growth which develops into the plant. Although in this particular instance seedling and root were each about four inches long, the parent bean remained quite sound and unaltered in flavour.

I noticed that on the light lands the rabbits have done a good deal of mischief this year. They are numerous this season, and I suppose that the drought made them crave anything with a juicy substance. Talking of rabbits reminds me of an alarming tale which a friend who is staying here told me yesterday. A few weeks ago his brother, while riding a bicycle, was seized with the most frightful anguish in the region of the heart. He managed, however, to stagger to his home and send for a doctor. The seizure proved to be the beginning of an attack of *angina pectoris*, so severe that it nearly killed him. When he was better he went with all precautions to London to interview a specialist, who, to his enormous relief, for he thought himself a doomed man, told him that his heart was perfectly sound. Investigations followed, and he discovered that his attack was brought on by eating cold rabbit-pie, which produced some peculiar form of ptomaine poisoning. It appears that all pies if unventilated are dangerous, but that cold rabbit-pie in these circumstances is apt to be absolutely deadly.

We have sold the barley we thrashed the other day—about a hundred coombs—at seventeen shillings the coomb. I am rather proud to hear from the buyer, a gentleman of experience who handles a vast quantity of grain, that some of this barley—that which was grown on the Ape field (No. 27)—is in his opinion the best which our district has produced this year. He priced it at seventeen and sixpence, but as the rest was somewhat inferior, averaged the lot at seventeen shillings. With the exception of a neighbour who, as I think I have mentioned, realised eighteen shillings or eighteen and sixpence for a few coombs which he thrashed on the harvest field, seventeen and sixpence is, I believe, the highest price that has been obtained in my neighbourhood this season.

Among many other flowers heliotrope is still growing and blooming with vigour in the garden. For the 12th of November this is, I believe, unusual.

November 13.—To-day a friend, Mr. F. J. Jackson, who has just arrived in this country from East Africa, came to pay me a visit. Mr. Jackson, who is a Government Commissioner in the Uganda territories, played a very active part in the recent fighting with the Soudanese mutineers, in the course of which he was desperately wounded. The main battle, where he met with his hurt, which took place at a spot called Lubwa, must indeed have been one of the most fearful struggles that has happened in any part of our Empire for many years, and although in the end the white men came off victorious, their loss in killed and wounded was heavy. They held a position upon a slight slope, but without cover beyond what was afforded by a few bushes and ant-heaps. Here they lay supported only by seventeen Sikhs from an Indian regiment and a great mob of Swahili porters, who were expected to bolt at any moment.

The Soudanese enemy attacked them in enormously superior force—they numbered about three to one—and with all proper military precautions. Advancing up the slope, they partially out-flanked the Englishmen, so that for some hours the two forces seem to have been pounding away at each other at a distance varying from a hundred to forty yards.

Towards the beginning of this book I mentioned the extra-ordinary insensibility to pain and shock shown by animals and some races of men. Here is a strange example of it which occurred in this battle as it was told to me by Mr. Jackson. One of the leaders of the mutineers, a captain, whose name, I think, was Suleiman Effendi, made a rush at the opening of the fight and got quite close to the British position. Thereon Mr. Jackson and three other people fired at him from a distance of about thirty yards, and down he went. As the bullet which Mr. Jackson had discharged was a split sporting bullet that is used to kill game rapidly, and as he knew that he had hit the man fair in the middle, and other pressing matters claimed his attention, he troubled no more about him. Presently, however, his gun-bearer exclaimed, 'Look out, Sir, Suleiman Effendi is shooting.' He looked and saw the man resting on one elbow and drawing a cart-ridge from his belt with which to reload the rifle he had just dis-charged. Before he could fire again this unconquerable Soudanese was shot through the head. It will scarcely be believed that after the battle was over it was found that this man had four bullets in or through his vitals, any one of which must have caused death rapidly, as each of the wounds was mortal. Yet he had kept his presence of mind and courage, and had found strength to load and fire his rifle.

A while after this Mr. Jackson was struck himself. It seems that one of the enemy, who was a good shot, had crept round to a position a little behind him and about forty yards away, whence he is believed to have killed young Mr. Fielding, who, bravely but incautiously, exposed himself by climbing on to an ant heap.

Presently Mr. Jackson was aware of a bullet striking before his face and of a disturbance in his clothes. Thinking, naturally, that the shot had been discharged from in front, he lifted himself a little to search for the firer, when suddenly he felt a most frightful blow under the armpit, as though a very powerful man had kicked him with all his strength, and knew that blood was pouring from his mouth. The facts were that the first bullet also had come from behind and passed through his coat without touching his body, whereas the second, which was better aimed, struck him somewhere below the right shoulder-blade, flattened on the ribs and passed through him, piercing the lung, and falling out into his shirt, where it was found. This bullet he showed me ; it came from a Snider, weighs an ounce and a quarter, and in its flattened condition is of the size of a two shilling piece ; indeed, it seems a mystery how a man through whose lung it had passed could be sitting before me alive and well. He tells me, however, that in his own opinion he owes his life to a curious circumstance which, to my mind, is a strange instance of the triumph of the reason of man under conditions of unusual difficulty.

Mr. Jackson is a great sportsman and has killed large quantities of big game, from elephants down. Many of these animals were, of course, shot through the lungs, and he had noticed that when this happened, death frequently occurred through the creature trying to cough up its blood and choking in the effort. From the moment that he was struck at Lubwa, he was convinced that the bullet had pierced his lung, and remembering the example furnished by the game, he determined not to cough until the severed blood vessels had been given a time to close. This resolve, by agonising efforts, he succeeded more or less in putting into practice. The result was, that after lying in grave danger for some days, his wound healed, and in about two months he recovered.

As the subject has been touched on, a short account of the issue of the fight may be interesting. After hours of struggle during which the Soudanese made five separate advances, Major Macdonald, the officer in command, finding that the available ammunition was reduced to a few rounds per man, followed the example of the great Duke at Waterloo, and ordered a charge. The enemy, not being aware of our desperate straits as regards cartridges, gave way, and retired to the fort, where they brutally murdered their three white prisoners—Major Thruston and Messrs. Wilson and Scott. Thus victory upon that terrible field remained with the white men and those of the indomitable Sikhs who were left alive. It is another recent instance, if after Chitral one is wanted, of what Englishmen can effect when they are put to proof, whether they be trained to arms or mere undisciplined civilians. When it is needed, the innate martial spirit, the endurance and determination that are bred in their blood, answer to the calls of circumstance and duty, and they do what must be done or die in the effort. It is, I think, this resourceful and unquenched spirit which, from generation to generation, has made our race so great.

The man who shot Mr. Jackson, it is believed, was himself shot or very seriously wounded. Under the tree where he had taken up his station were found two heaps of cartridge cases—for he had a spare gun and a loader—and a pool of blood. His body, however, was not found ; probably he was severely hurt, and had been carried away by his comrades.

To turn to a subject which, if less warlike and exciting, has more to do with farming interests, Mr. Jackson gave me some very interesting details as to the working and ravages of rinderpest. This dreadful cattle disease, as many readers will remember, is supposed to have begun in East Africa, whence it travelled south, destroying kine, and even game, by the million, and spreading ruin with an even hand among Kaffirs and white men. The plague first struck East Africa in the year 1890, and having killed everything there was to kill—the Masai and other tribes were reduced to absolute starvation by its onslaught, and even the buffalo were practically exterminated—it passed southward. Last year, however, unhappily it was re-introduced by some infected oxen that were driven from the coast, and again killed off many thousands of cattle which had been bred up since the first pest. Mr. Jackson himself, who was living in the Mau district, possessed a herd of two hundred and fifty cows. The disease smote them, and, when it left, but twenty-five remained alive.

It is now so long since we have had rinderpest in England[1] that a description of its symptoms may be of value. They are— at any rate in East Africa—dry nose, with loss of cud and ulcerated gums, while post-mortem examination reveals inflamed and ulcerated intestines, and a gall bladder swollen to the size of a soda-water bottle, although the lungs appear to be quite healthy. This sickness does its work very quickly. In the morning the animal to all appearance will be in a state of perfect health and grazing as usual, indeed the stomach is generally found to be

---

[1] In the last century this or some similar disease seems to have ravaged England very sorely, as is testified by the following petition which I have discovered on a loose printed sheet in the leaves of a family Prayer Book bearing date 1743.

A PRAYER to be ufed Every Day immediately after the Prayer [*Wee humbly befeech the*, &c.] in the *Litany*; or when that is not ufed, after the Prayer, *For the Clergy and People.*

Gracious God, who in thy great Bounty to Mankind haft given them the Beafts of the Field for their Provifion and Nourifhment continue to us, we humbly befeech thee, this Bleffing, and fuffer us not to be reduced to Scarcity and Diftrefs by the contagious Diftemper, which has raged, and ftill rages, among the Cattle in many Parts of this Kingdom. In this and all other thy difpenfations towards us, we fee and adore the Juftice of thy Providence, and do with forrowful and penitent Hearts Confefs, that our manifold Vices and Impieties have defervedly provoked thine Anger and Indignation againft us. But we earneftly intreat thee Almighty Father, in this our calamitious State, to look down upon us with an Eye of Pity and Compaffiion; and if it be thy Bleffed Will, to forbid the fpreading of this fore Vifitation, and in thy good time to remove it from all the Inhabitants of this Land, for the fake of thy Mercies in Chrift Jefus our only Saviour and Redeemer. *Amen*

full of half-digested food. Suddenly it ceases eating, and stands awhile with a hanging head, after which it lies down, and about five hours later expires. I have myself seen cases of African horse-sickness run their course with equal swiftness, but I presume that, in both instances the fatal germs have been at work for some days, although they make no outward show. This, however, is pure conjecture, whereof the truth or falsity could only be proved by a frequent testing of the temperature of the animal, if, indeed, this precaution would suffice to establish the fact.

Although in the 1890 epidemic, in addition to the buffalo, eland, giraffe, lesser kudoo, and wart-hog died in great numbers throughout East Africa, curiously enough, so far as can be ascertained, the last outbreak does not seem to have affected these animals.

November 16.—Yesterday I received a cheque value 7*l*. 12*s*., being the net amount due to me for prizes taken at the Lothing-land Agricultural Show. This sum, after deducting the expenses to which wc were put in sending the animals for exhibition, I propose to divide among Hood, his wife, Moore, and the men and boys who were employed in looking after the cattle.

The weather is very damp and quiet, and we are now engaged in getting off the mangolds on Baker's, No 44.

As he showed no signs of recovery, the old Southdown tup, which, as I think I have said, was injured by a rival ram some time ago, was despatched yesterday to graze in the Elysian fields. His mortal remains are now being distributed among the farm labourers at a cost of threepence the pound, and I dare say that, if boiled long enough, they will make very good soup. Although his shoulder is found to have been dislocated, it cannot have troubled the creature much, or prevented him from feeding, as his condition is good.

Two pigs have accompanied him to the Shades. A pig is the only animal which looks more attractive dead than alive ; then, for the first time in his guzzling career, he is white, cool and clean.

At Bedingham, to-day, I found that the beet have all been lifted and haled. The men are carting flashings from the hedge-rows into heaps for burning, as it is useless to keep them till another year to serve as stack-bottoms, since by that time they would have rotted. Moore is ploughing up the root land, the two young horses, which have 'come in' very satisfactorily, working half a day apiece. This is as much as they ought to do at present.

November 18.—To-day I went to Norwich to see the Agricultural Show. I cannot pretend that an agricultural show held under a roof is a particularly pleasant place to linger in; there are too many smells and too much noise. The red-poll classes were strong, the fat steers being, some of them, magnificent animals. As was to be expected, the executors of the lamented Mr. Colman took a large proportion of the prizes. Out of their great herds they are able to pick and choose; moreover, in such establishments the rearing of cattle for show is almost a business. From birth till they appear upon the bench, every delicacy which they can be persuaded to eat is crammed down the throats of these pampered animals, together with liberal draughts of new milk. Hood tells me that when he was in the service of a gentleman in the Shires, they reared a short-horn steer that took the first prizes at some of the largest shows in England. In addition to all his other nutriment, this creature was accustomed to swallow a bucket of new milk every day, with admirable results upon his condition. Such treatment means a large expenditure, with a very problematical return in the way of advertisement; indeed, as I believe I have written elsewhere, I doubt whether it pays the small man to compete at these great shows, however good may be his stock.

At first sight to-day an observer in the Show might have thought, as I did, that the condition of the various cattle exhausted the possibilities of fat, until a visit to the pig department proved him to be utterly mistaken. What monsters are these ! And how in the name of Barley-meal do they manage even to move under such a weight of adipose deposit? Perhaps they do not move. Perhaps they are carried; anyhow, the operation had tired them, and they were all asleep. By the way, it is a fact worth recording that the ancients could boast an excellent breed of pig. This I know, because I have an Etruscan vase in my possession on which is painted a picture of what I take to be the hog that, on some occasion before the founding of Rome, secured the cup, or rather the bowl, at a local show in Etruria, a supposition that seems to be borne out by the garlands of oak leaves and acorns with which he is encircled, and the rosettes that are painted above his noble snout. At least, if he did not score the prize, he ought to have done so, for really he is an admirably proportioned animal, in magnificent condition; short and thick, with a regular Berkshire head, a tail like a corkscrew, and pure white in colour.

In one of the galleries of the Hall the Queensland Government has a stall, set there doubtless to attract the intending emigrant. I must say that it attracted me. Such heads of Indian corn, such samples of wheat and barley—the latter a little pale coloured perhaps. The gentleman in charge of the stall gave me a bundle of literature, which I perused all the way home, with the result that before I reached Ditchingham I felt inclined to book a passage for Queensland by the next steamer. A country which is twice the size of the German Empire, with a nice warm climate, and a death-rate of only 12·10 per thousand; where anything will grow, from a pine-apple to a cabbage; where horses, sheep, and cattle flourish; where, in short, naught is lacking except the many and varied plagues of Africa—what could a man want more? Moreover, there the land is dirt cheap and arranged in lots to suit all purses; and—best of everything—the British flag flies over it, with nobody to question its supremacy.

What says the little book which was presented to me? 'Foreign competition, high rents, bad seasons, &c., &c., render the cultivator's life here an unending effort to keep his head above water. Why not close the conflict, and go to a land where labour and

money properly invested are sure to return good interest?'
Many will be inclined to echo the question. Why not, indeed?

But I hold no brief for Queensland, of which I know little.
Doubtless it has its drawbacks, like other places. Within the
giant circle of the British Empire are several such favoured lands,
whose fertility and wholesomeness literally cry aloud to man to take
his profit from them.

What I *do* hold a brief for, what I *do* venture to preach to
almost every class, and especially the gentle-bred, is emigration.
Why should people continue to be cooped up in this narrow
country, living generally upon insufficient means, when yonder
their feet might be set in so large a room? Why do they not
journey to where families can be brought into the world without
the terror that if this happens they will starve or drag their parents
down to the dirt; to where the individual may assert himself and
find room to develop his own character, instead of being crushed in
the mould of custom till, outwardly at any rate, he is as like his
fellows as one brick is like to the others in a wall?

Here, too, unless he be endowed by nature with great ability,
abnormal powers of work, and an iron constitution, or, failing these,
with pre-eminent advantages of birth or wealth, the human item has
about as much chance of rising as the brick at the bottom has of
climbing to the top of the wall, for the weight of the thousands
above keep him down, and the conventions of a crowded and ancient
country tie his hands and fetter his thought. But in those new
homes across the seas it is different, for there he can draw nearer
to nature, and, though the advantages of civilisation remain un-
forfeited, to the happier conditions of the simple uncomplicated
man. There, if he be of gentle birth, his sons may go to work
among the cattle without losing caste, instead of being called
upon to begin where their father left off, or pay the price in social
damage; there his daughters will marry and help to build up
some great empire of the future, instead of dying single in a land
where women are too many and marriage is becoming more and
more a luxury for the rich. Decidedly emigration, not to our over-

peopled towns, but to the Antipodes, has its advantages, and if I were young again I would practice what I preach.

When I had satisfied myself with a vision of fat beasts, I went on to the Chrysanthemum Show at St. Andrew's Hall. I suppose that it is my bad taste, but although I am a great lover of flowers, and grow them to the best of my ability, I cannot say that I am attracted by prize chrysanthemums. They seem like our society—too highly cultivated, too much developed from the primitive type, and, with all their infinite variety, to me they still suggest a curious sense of sameness.

As one may as well do a thing thoroughly while about it, after the chrysanthemums I marched to the Poultry Show. It was my first visit to one of these exhibitions, and, unless for some very special purpose, I incline to the opinion that it will be my last. Here the odours are very pungent, while the noise is absolutely deafening, for every cock in the place is fiercely set upon crowing down about three hundred and fifty other cocks. One of these birds showed extraordinary intelligence. There he stood in his box with his head laid sideways on its floor. I thought that he must be very sick, and watched him ; but presently he lifted himself up and crowed most furiously. Clearly the creature was like the deaf adder that stoppeth her ears, only he stopped his ears to make himself deaf, being, like myself, overpowered by the execrable noise.

I never knew before that cocks grew to such a size—indeed, some of the birds at the Norwich show reminded me of young ostriches, fowls with which I am acquainted, for I have farmed them. Once, with a friend, I rode to a distant stead in the Transvaal, where we invested our little all—or most of it—in ostriches, of which a shrewd and progressive Boer wished to be rid. There were six or eight of them, and they cost about three hundred pounds, for at that time the ostrich market was tight—in the Transvaal. For the same sum, or a little more, I have no doubt that in those days of cheap land we might have bought the whole farm. Had we done so, I suppose, if a plethora of wealth had left me still alive, that instead of writing books in the country

I should now be entertaining foreign Royalties in a marble palace in Park Lane, for that farm lies in the centre of the Rand district, and I have heard that the best reefs run through it.

And yet, although my vision failed me in this instance—why are there not gold *dowsers* as well as water *dowsers* ?—I must have been a youth of some foresight. Here I quote a passage written by me in 1876 when I was a lad of twenty. For a first effort in prophecy it has proved fairly accurate, especially as I cannot have had much to go on, for in those days few people looked upon the bankrupt and unvisited South African Republic as a country of any value :

' It is very difficult to convey an impression of the intense dreariness and monotony of the great Transvaal wastes, " where wilds immeasurably spread seem lengthening as we go." Day after day the traveller passes over vast spaces of rolling veld stretching away north, south, east, and west, without a tree, a house, or any sign of man, save here and there a half-beaten waggon track. And yet those wastes, now so dismal and desolate, are at no distant date destined to support and enrich a large population , for underneath their surface lie all minerals in abundance, and when the coal of England and of Europe is exhausted, there is sufficient stored up here to stock the world. Those plains, too, which for centuries have lain idle and unproductive, will before long supply the greatest corn markets with grain ; for, save in some places where water is scarce, the virgin soil is rich beyond comparison. Yes, before us lies the country of the practical future, of the days when the rich man will have his estate in Switzerland to gratify his eyes, and his estate in the Transvaal to fill his pockets. *This vast land will one day be the garden of Africa, the land of gems and gold, of oil and corn, of steam-ploughs and rail-ways. It has an assured and a magnificent future.*'

Ostriches are disappointing birds. Ours steadily declined to lay eggs, but by way of compensation their kicking powers were perfectly unrivalled, indeed I have seen one of them cause a strong man to perform cart-wheels like a street arab. Also they were subject to unreasonable panics, in the course of which they charged fences and broke their expensive necks. Once, under pressure of necessity, we performed tracheotomy on an ostrich—a terrible and exhausting operation. The creature had swallowed a bone about eight inches long, which became fixed across his gullet. As it would move neither up nor down, with the help of four picked Kaffirs and a razor we held him and hewed out the obstruction. Strange to say, he recovered from this delicate surgical feat, but by an evil fate a few months later he swallowed another bone, which stuck in the same place. This we were unable to remove, and that ostrich died.

One of the most beautiful sights which I ever saw is that of a flock of these birds in their wild state floating away across the vast plains till their snowy plumes were lost in the dim blue of the sky-line. This and the spectacle of the Transvaal veld black with thousands upon thousands of trekking game are things that I am glad to have beheld, especially as the latter of them will never be seen again. And so farewell to ostriches, which to me furnish no happy memories.

On the farm we are still getting off beet, in much colder weather, for the wind has turned to the east.

November 19.—The beet on Baker's, No. 44, have proved a better crop than might have been expected, when the poor state of the land and the rather thin plant are taken into consideration. From the seven acres of them we have carted about one hundred and forty loads, which must represent not far short of twenty tons to the acre, or, to be on the safe side, let us say eighteen tons—a not unsatisfactory return.

We have begun digging the carrots—for the soil is too tight to allow of their being pulled—which have grown upon the Thwaite field. There are an acre and three quarters of them, with some parsnips mixed in, and I reckon the weight at about thirteen tons. A good crop should run to ten tons the acre, so, if this estimate is correct, we are five or six tons short of what we might have hoped to get, which shortage is due mainly to the ravages of the accursed rabbit, that persistently ate out the crowns of the young plants. Also the summer has been too dry for the successful growth of carrots, which show the result of a lack of rain in the fanginess of the root, caused by their starting into fresh growth when moisture fell after a long period of drought. For the same reason a good many of them have run to seed. A carrot cannot grow top and bottom at the same time, therefore when they go to seed there is little or no root, all the virtue of the plant being absorbed in the reproductive process. Even if left to stand, this seed would come to nothing. To secure it in a fertile condition, the carrots should be lifted and haled in autumn, for, if left in the ground, a severe frost will perish them. In the spring they must be taken from the hale and replanted in good soil, when they will produce a plentiful crop of seed.

The tops of the carrots are being cut off and left upon the ground, on which, as it was not manured last year, we propose to fold the sheep, that devour them greedily, together with the swede heads from the top portion of this field, which will be carted down to provide them with a little extra sustenance.

To-day we are delivering the barley which we sold to the maltsters.

The last stalks of our green maize have been eaten. It has furnished us with a very valuable bite of succulent food, and that it should have lasted so long in good condition is a striking testimony to the openness of the season, for mealies fall easy victims to the attack of frost.

November 21.—To-day is dull with a drizzling rain, not heavy enough, however, to prevent us from drilling wheat on the little bit of land which has been ploughed after the maize was cleared. We are carting grit also gathered from the highway to spread about upon the surface of the seven-acre pasture, No. 10. This stuff seems to be a perquisite of the road-scraping men, at any rate when it is collected in the streets of the village, as we buy it from them at eighteenpence the load. If, on the other hand, it is laid up against the banks it belongs to the owner of the adjacent soil. Road-grit, containing as it does all manner of finely pulverised refuse, is very valuable as a dressing for pasture land. Also it can be put to good advantage by using it in the holes where young apple-trees are being planted, especially if the soil beneath is clay, as the roots find it very 'kind' to work in.

The score or so of lambs which, with the help of a little cake, have been fatting on this pasture, No. 10, are now all sold to the butcher, as we have come to the conclusion that the cross with the Southdown produces an animal too small to breed from. The largest of them fetched thirty-eight shillings, and the smaller, which are pure Southdown, thirty shillings. It is not a very high price, but on the whole we are well rid of them.

November 24.—Yesterday and the day before the weather was a good deal colder, but this morning it is rough and mild. Two ploughs are going on the farm, while the carrot-lifting and the earthing up of the beet still continue.

At the Bench to-day we had our first experience of the new Criminal Evidence Act, of the provisions of which the defendant elected to avail himself in each case, with the result that one and all they proceeded to give themselves gracefully away. I have seen this Act a good deal criticised, but my own opinion, for what it is worth, is that it will prove a very useful measure, and ensure the conviction of a great many guilty people who would otherwise have been acquitted, and the escape, or, at any rate, the complete clearing of the characters, of some innocent people who might otherwise have been left under a cloud of suspicion. Few accused persons, at least among the classes with which magistrates have to deal, will, I believe, be able to resist the temptation of going into the box and giving evidence on oath, however guilty they may know themselves to be. Once there the result is sure, for my experience is that such persons break down at once under a cross-examination conducted by a trained intellect. The two objections to the Act seem to me to be that it will cause an enormous amount of extra perjury, and that if a defendant elects not to go into the box, having had the opportunity of so doing, whatever judge or counsel may urge, the mind of the jury will very likely be prejudiced against him.

As to the first of these two points, it may be answered that people who perjure themselves, even on their own behalf, are liable to prosecution and penal servitude. But will such prosecutions be instituted, and, if they are instituted, will any jury be found to convict a man who, on his oath or out of it, has told lies to save his liberty? I am convinced that they would acquit him on the general principle that it is only to be expected that a rat in a corner will try to escape by any means it can discover.

The view of Mr. Justice Hawkins, whose opinion is entitled, I suppose, to as much or more weight than that of anybody else in England, seems to be that the prisoner charged before the magistrates with an indictable offence ought not to go into the box in their court, insomuch as they are not trying him, but merely investigating the charge to see whether there is a case against him strong enough to be sent for trial. This is all very well, though some great authorities take a much wider view of the duties of magistrates—but, under the words of the Act, if a defendant insists upon giving evidence at petty sessions, or anywhere else, I do not quite see how he is to be prevented. Then, of course, arises the question as to whether or no his cross-examination should be allowed. However, I suppose that all these points will be settled sooner or later by the wisdom of those above.

One man amused me to-day. He was before us for an indictable offence, and having elected to be dealt with under the Summary Jurisdiction Act, expressed a wish to give evidence.

' Well,' I asked him, when he had been sworn, ' what have you to say ? '

' If you please, sir,' he replied gravely, ' *I stole the fowl.*'

November 25.—The mild and open weather continues, and we have three ploughs at work, two of them on No. 22 and one on Baker's, No. 43. After breakfast, I walked down to the All Hallows field, No. 37, half of which, it may be remembered, was under layer hay, while the other half bore a crop of pease. Some mustard seed was harrowed in on to the pea stubble, but when I returned from Scotland it looked to me as though it would not furnish a day's bite for the sheep. Still, it lived through the drought, and now, under the influence of the recent rain, has thrown up quite a fair crop, on which the ewes are being penned at night. In the daytime both they and the cows run on the hay stubble alongside the mustard, where there is still a good deal of excellent feed, although two crops have been cut from it. It is most amusing to watch these animals, which one and all naturally wish to get to the mustard, with the result that the boy in charge has an exceedingly lively time. First the cows make for it with quiet determination. He rushes to turn them, whereon the sheep see their opportunity and slip in at the other end of the line. I think that by nightfall this boy must be very tired, for it is almost impossible to restrain a flock of experienced ewes which see something tasty in front of them. Indeed, ours had to be removed from the Pithole field, on to which they were turned to clean up the beet tops, as, notwithstanding the herd's efforts, they broke continually into the swedes and white turnips, doing them a good deal of damage.

It was funny also to note the behaviour of a little terrier dog named Di that accompanied me. Di is terrified of sheep, which chase her (she will kill *lambs* if she gets the chance), but in order to avoid showing her fear by beating a humble retreat, she bolted to the fence and began to hunt an imaginary rabbit all the way round it, being careful to keep on the further side until she reached the road again. For cunning humbug few animals can beat a dog, which is a creature that hates to be laughed at. Talking of Di reminds me of her evilly disposed companion Dan, that, it may be remembered, was given to a friend after the wicked little beast had tried to kill a ewe in Flixton Park. Recently I have seen this friend and heard the sequel. In London Dan behaved well, piously even. Then he went on a visit to the country for the benefit of his health. That same evening he was reported missing. Next morning he reappeared, accompanied by a furious farmer and—*a large dead sheep.* Now unhonoured and unwept Dan hunts the shades of sheep along the fields celestial. Moral—but it can be guessed.

On my way home I noticed that, owing to the indifferent stacking, the large wheat rick in All Hallows yard has sunk so much that it is on the point of falling over. Indeed, the poles by which it is supported have pushed up the roof in bulges, so great is the weight upon them.

I hear to-day that the man whom we hired at Bedingham is leaving again, having found a place as groom and gardener to a clergyman. I am glad for his sake, since the work is easier, and the pay—probably—better ; but where we are to find another I know not, as the young men in this year of grace absolutely decline to labour on the land.

November 29.—Saturday and Monday were very wet and wretched, but for my part I am glad to see some rain. To-day I have been out shooting in a charming natural covert among the marshes, by which I mean a wood that does not seem to have been planted by man. The holly trees in it look especially beautiful, and are covered with brilliant red berries.

We have bought six little steers from a neighbouring farmer, aged from ten months to a year old, at the price of 4*l.* 10*s.* apiece. This strain of animals has some of our own blood in it, and therefore I prefer them to promiscuous home-breds. They have gone to Bedingham for the winter. To-day also I handed over the 7*l.* 12*s.* that we won in prizes—or rather 5*l.* 2*s.* of it, for the rest went in expenses—to be divided up according to scale.

As I was walking from one stand to another while out shooting this afternoon I came across a mole which, on hearing us—for I believe that these creatures cannot see—instantly began to burrow into the bank. In from two to three seconds its fat black body had nearly vanished, for it seemed to disappear into the soil much as a hot iron sinks into snow. To pull it out needed considerable force, and I fear gave the poor little thing a great fright, for, after this experience, it just covered itself with loose soil and began to squeak loudly. I asked the beaters not to kill it, so I hope that by now it has recovered its nerve.

My host told me a good story. At a big shoot a guest of his was given an old keeper as a loader—a man of somewhat caustic wit. The guest was not shooting well that day, and although he fired freely very little happened. After a hot corner the groom with the game-cart asked the disgusted loader if he wanted any more cartridges.

'Keertridges,' he was heard to reply, 'no bör ; take 'em away. Keertridges ain't no use to *us* !' Half the joke, however, lies in the Norfolk intonation, which it is impossible to reproduce, rising *crescendo* till the last word is uttered in a modified scream.

DECEMBER

December 3.—December has opened with rough weather, and yesterday the wind rose steadily, till at nightfall it blew a gale, before which, at sunset, gorgeous-coloured clouds went driving past like the chariots of a heavenly host.

To-day I went to Norwich to attend a meeting of the Norfolk Chamber of Agriculture, of which I am a member. The subject under discussion was that of 'Better methods of remunerating skilled agricultural labour,' which was introduced in an interesting speech by Mr. Lee Warner, and dwelt upon in its various aspects by other gentlemen.

If I may criticise, however, it seemed to me that the debate turned too much upon such matters as technical instruction, benefit societies, ploughing matches, &c. Piece-work also was discussed, some of the speakers being in favour of and some against the system. As regards ploughing and thatching competitions, my experience has been that it is not easy to persuade labourers—who are a suspicious folk—to enter their names for them. I remember a good many years ago that, with some difficulty, one of my own men was induced to compete for a prize in stack-building. It never even entered his mind that there was a possibility of fair dealing about the matter.

'I doubt they'll give that to their own people'—'they' being the the judges—he said to me, shaking his head; and, as it happened, by bad luck, I believe that they did. My friend did not seem in the least surprised, but I do not think that he will enter for any more competitions. Kissing, in the opinion of the agricultural labourer, goes very much by favour. Moreover, as a class, they are sensitive, and dislike the idea of failing. ' But how dreadful it would be if I didn't win,' said a certain good lady to me the other day when I urged her to show her butter. Fortunately she did win.

Before the meeting broke up I ventured to point out that in my view these questions went much deeper than had been suggested, being rooted indeed in the prevailing agricultural depression. Surely the matter of skilled labour is economic, and it is leaving the land, not for lack of technical instruction, benefit societies with money prizes, or flower-shows, but because the land can no longer compete against the towns and pay the able-bodied and active labourer a sufficient wage to tempt him to stay at home. It must never be forgotten that the lot of the agricul-tural labourer is part and parcel of the lot of agriculture. There used to be plenty of labour upon the land when the land was prosperous ; now that its prosperity has departed, there is little, and the inference is plain. The young men are not learning the trade ; they are drifting to the cities or elsewhere, leaving the old or the unfit to do the work, and ultimately to increase the rates.

That this is no fancy can be proved by any one who takes the trouble to walk over my own or other farms and see how large is the proportion of elderly men employed upon them. The young fellow who can plough, and thatch, and milk, as his father did, is indeed a *rara avis* to-day. This cry of the want of labour is to be heard in every direction—one can hardly open a country news-paper without seeing some allusion to its scarceness. Some try to explain this as consequent on the lack of cottages in certain districts. Cottages do not pay to build, and there may be a basis of fact in this argument ; but it is not the kernel of the question, for even where the dwellings exist the men are wanting, Thus : a cottage of mine with a good garden has been standing vacant for a year because I cannot find a labouring tenant. Indeed, I am told that in one small village a few miles away no less than forty cottages are unoccupied.

Mr. Philip Bagenal, the Local Government Board inspector for these counties, has very kindly sent me his ' Report on Pauperism and Distress for 1898,' in which he points out that the Census returns show that between the years 1871 and 1891 one-tenth of the agricultural labourers of Norfolk had left the land ; adding : ' There is too much reason to believe that since 1891 the rate of decrease has been accelerated.' This rate, by the way, is slightly higher in Suffolk than in Norfolk.

Among the reasons given by Mr. Bagenal for this emigration are : the inability of farmers to employ as many labourers as formerly ; the conversion of arable land into pasture ; and the desire of the young men to lead a less monotonous life. The results he sums up in very few words : ' A constant drain of the best class of wage-earners is thus going on. The old and infirm are left, and these necessarily come on the rates.'

What is to be the end of it ? Mr. Bagenal says in his report that we appear to have touched bottom in the matter of the conversion of arable into pasture. But if the exodus is to continue, I can see no other way of meeting it than by the multiplication of machines and the laying down of grass, which absorbs less labour than ploughland. Of course, however, this matter of the inconvenience ensuing to those employed in agricultural pursuits is but one side of the question, which involves other and even greater interests of a national character, and affecting the well-being of the whole race. ' The inhabitants of the village ceased,' is a sad record for any generation to write down, but the results may prove still sadder to its descendants.[1]

While waiting in Norwich for my train I took a walk to the cattle market. The sight of all those poor beasts crowded in their pens brought the memory of my ten departed Irish bullocks back to my mind with a force which was quite painful. Indeed, in one or two lots I could almost imagine that I saw the brutes before me—gaunt, slab-sided, and hungry-eyed. I think that

[1] For a fuller discussion of this question see Appendix I.

these unfortunate animals—especially those of them that are brought from overseas—must suffer more than most people imagine ; at any rate, I am sure that I saw suffering written large on some of them to-day. But they cannot complain, and if they try to resist, the stout ash stick of the drover is waiting for them. Indeed, the brutality of these men, or some of them, especially when a little in liquor, is shocking. I saw them again and again striking the cattle in their charge without the slightest necessity and generally about the head, I suppose because experience teaches them that there animals are most sensitive to pain. Indeed, in one case a passer-by appealed to me to put a stop to the thing, but as there was no policeman in sight, what could I do ? I presume that the Society for the Prevention of Cruelty to Animals has local inspectors. Where were they ? But at best it might be difficult to secure conviction in such a case, as the offenders would swear that it was necessary to thrash the beasts in order to keep them in their places.

A week or two ago, through the kindness of a friend, I had the opportunity of tendering for, and very probably of obtaining, a large contract to supply hay, straw, roots, &c., to an Institution in London to the value perhaps of about 1,000*l.* a year. The prices that the Institution was willing to pay seemed to be quite satisfactory, the only question being whether or no the cost of carriage would absorb any profit which it might be possible to make. I have now made inquiries to find that this is absolutely prohibitive. To deliver hay in London from Ditchingham—that is at Liverpool Street, not reckoning the expenses of cartage—involves a charge of 19*s.* 2*d.* a ton, whereas straw figures out at no less than 1*l.* 2*s.* 9*d.*, although roots can be carried at 6*s.* 6*d.* if a truckful is sent. So there is an end of that scheme, which is a pity, since, if the carriage had been cheaper, many others besides myself would have benefited by it, as I should have bought up considerable quantities of produce in the neighbourhood. A gentleman to whom I was talking at the Norwich Club to-day told me that, in his capacity of trustee or executor to a large

East Norfolk estate, he had an opportunity of selling a great quantity of wind-felled timber to be used for mining purposes in the North of England. The carriage which he was prepared to pay upon this timber amounted, I understand, to no less a sum than 6,000*l*., but the railway companies concerned declined to transport it at that price, with the result that the business fell through, and the trees are now being disposed of locally for what they will fetch as firewood and fencing.

I may add that in my own case I made inquiries also as to delivery by water-carriage, but this too proved impracticable.

This question of transport is one of the gravest that the agriculturist has to face, for here he must compete against the preferential rates granted to foreign produce by the railways. I will quote a single instance. The Rev. J. Valpy, of Elsing, in this county, writing to *The Times*, states that one of his parishioners receives a hundred apples delivered by rail from California, U.S., at a cost of 3*s*. But when the same person sent a hundred apples to be delivered in Leicester, by the Midland or Great Northern Railway, he was obliged to pay 2*s*. 10*d*.—that is to say, twopence less than the charge for the carriage of exactly the same quantity of fruit from California. This example speaks for itself. At the same time it would be unjust not to acknowledge with gratitude the offers which are now being made by the Great Eastern Railway to convey small parcels of farm and garden produce to London at greatly reduced rates.

December 7.—For the last few days we have been ploughing and fence trimming on the farm, in weather that, for the time of year, is extraordinarily fine and mild. It appears, indeed, according to a letter to *The Times* from Mr. G. J. Simmons, that the nights of the 5th and 6th of this month were the warmest recorded in the notes of meteorological observations made during forty years. On the 6th the reading reached 63·9, which is nearly twenty degrees above the average for a December night. This temperature was milder than that of any night during last May, while in July there were twenty-one days when the night readings were less. Wonderful are the ways of the British climate !

To-day the rain is falling in a steady sheet, which is unlucky, as Royal Duke and two other of my fat animals have gone to the Harleston auction, and beasts never look or handle so well if they are draggled with wet. My consolation is that all the other creatures on show will suffer from the same cause. Now is the time that we find the advantage of roofed-in yards. It is a pleasure to see the stock standing warm and dry beneath them, and the litter unwashed by a drop of water.

In such weather work is slack upon the farm, but one man is employed in white-washing the cow-sheds, another in cleaning harness, and so forth. To-day, for the first time since early spring, the ditch leading into the garden pond is running with water.

December 8.—The weather is now fine again, so that we are able to resume our ploughing. For the last three days I have been plunged in a controversy on that thorniest of all subjects— Free Trade. It began by my yielding to one of the most unwise of human impulses, and correcting a statement about myself in a newspaper. Last Saturday, at the meeting of the Norfolk Chamber of Agriculture, of which I have spoken, in the course of my few remarks—according to the reporters—I said that agriculturists should urge upon Governments, or those responsible, the necessity of doing something to help the general state of agriculture, for in helping agriculture they would also help the general state of the labourer. Thereupon a leading local paper of advanced views devoted an article to me, in which it was stated that ' by doing something' I meant the introduction of protective measures. In actual fact I meant nothing of the sort. Protection was not in my mind ; indeed, at the moment, speaking in a very cold room in a hurry and entirely without premeditation to a meeting that was eager to escape to lunch, I had not even formulated to myself what this 'something' ought to be, although generally I was alluding to the equalisation of rates on real and personal property

and to the necessity of really effective measures for the protection
of farmers against fraud.

Under these circumstances I corrected the local paper, which
thereupon in another article replied that in 1895, when I was
standing for Parliament, I urged the imposition of a tax upon imported flour and barley. This is true : in common with many other
people I did urge the absolute justice of such a tax, which, if looked
into, however, will be found to mean a very infinitesimal measure
of protection. Barley is not used as a food for men, and I think
that I was careful to exclude from my proposal crushed barley
destined to be devoured by pigs. Further, when that grain was
much dearer than at present I believe that the price of beer was
practically the same as it is to-day. Therefore the drop in the
price of barley has not benefited the consumers of malt liquors,
but has found its way into the pockets of brewers and middlemen.
The duty on imported flour would only mean that the corn must
come whole into this country, there to be ground by our millers.
I have never urged that any duty should be charged upon wheat
or upon sea-borne meat, which, under present circumstances, in
the opinion of many might be against the interest of the community
as a whole. At any rate it would be contrary to its wishes.

One of the dangers of a newspaper correspondence lies in
its seductiveness. The controversialist, seeing things stated about
himself to which he objects, is led on to reply and explain, whereby, in nine cases out of ten, he makes matters worse than they
were before. I replied and I explained—amongst other things
that, although I still held the same opinions as to the justice of an
import tax upon foreign barley and flour, the whole question had,
in my view, become purely academical on account of the strong
opposition of the people of this country, and that I did not think
it likely that I should again publicly advocate the imposition of a
duty upon foreign foodstuffs. I added, however, that I did hold it
desirable that under certain circumstances a bounty should be given
to growers of wheat. But here are the exact words :

'I do, however, think it desirable that whenever wheat falls below a certain unprofitable price—say 30s. a quarter—a moderate bounty should be paid from the Imperial Exchequer to those who continue to grow it. Probably it is futile to expect that such a measure will be adopted except under the stern compulsion of conditions which we cannot foresee, and perhaps this also may be held to savour of Protection. Still, it will be admitted that in view of national and other contingencies, it is not to the interest of the country that wheat should go out of cultivation, or indeed that the present area under that crop should be further contracted. Nor is it to the interest of the country that the classes who were wont to be employed in its production at a profit, and who for generations have been the backbone of England, should, for the lack of a reasonable wage, which under present circumstances it is impossible to pay them, be driven from the land that bore them and herded together in the towns.'

This letter has produced a third article, wherein I am held up as one reprobate, and told that 'a noble scorn of consequence' is preferable by far to 'a spirit of stealthy opportunism.'

Well, I am a person acquainted with criticism; indeed, there are few epithets, angry or disparaging, that have not at one time or another landed upon my appointed head, but never before has it been suggested, as I understand this writer to suggest, that I am a stealthy opportunist. From no such failing as this, O Scribe, have I suffered chiefly in the past, but rather from a tendency to enter on rash ventures and crusades and to indulge in speech undiplomatically plain. Surely, too, as a matter of argument, my position could better have been defined as stealthily opportunistic if, hiding my real views, for this reason or for that, I had pretended to change them. But I make no such pretence; I say only that it is useless to continue to urge publicly—by which I mean in platform speeches, and especially in addresses to rural audiences—what the electorate rejects; and further, that the advocacy of any measure of protection, however just it may seem to some, is so misinterpreted and exaggerated, that it is perhaps best to leave the thing alone. For instance, during my election campaign in 1895, it was persistently put about in the constituency that I supported the imposition of a tax upon wheat and meat. This, as I have said, I had never even thought of doing.

My letter, I am further informed, 'is mainly interesting as an index to the true inwardness of the Conservative mind on subjects of economic policy.' I do not quite see what the purely private views of a purely private person who is not engaged in standing for Parliament have to do either with the outwardness or the inwardness of the Conservative Mind. Probably, if it were asked, the Conservative Mind would decline to be identified with my personal opinions, which are, to be frank, of a somewhat independent order.

But this is not all of it, for my suggestions as to the advantages of a bounty are next discussed. It is pointed out that a bounty 'designed to prevent the cost of home-produced wheat falling below 30s. a quarter, is a tax on the consumer to the extent of the difference between 30s. and the price at which wheat can be produced by other peoples.'

Quite so, and what then? Nobody can say that 30s. a quarter is a high price to pay for wheat; indeed, in this country it cannot be grown to profit at that figure. If a thing cannot be grown at a profit, sooner or later it ceases to be grown at all, and the real issue is whether or no it is desirable that wheat should be cultivated in England in the future.

I do not pretend to any certainty of view upon the subject—mine is only a pious opinion. It may be wise that we should learn to depend entirely upon foreign supplies of corn, though many declare that this would be the reverse of wisdom. But at least there are two sides to the question, and a time might come when, under the pressure of foreign complications, home-grown grain would be wanted. The issue therefore arises whether—if this supposition be correct—it is not better to violate the strict letter of a doubtful dogma than to expose the country to what may be a national risk? Lastly, to come to the root, out of which all this controversy grew—how about the labourers who live upon the land? Are they or are they not to receive a decent wage? At present their pay is inadequate, and therefore they are leaving the land, neither, as I believe, to their own ultimate benefit, nor to the good of our country. Is this to go on or is it not to go on? And if not, how is it to be prevented without the aid of measures which will restore the soil to its prosperity? That is the problem to which wiser men than I am must find an answer, and within the next generation.

What I have never been able to understand is why those who, owing, let us suppose, to some mental twist, are unable to accept as wise or advisable all the strict and far-reaching consequences of the Cobden doctrines should be spoken of almost as if they were evil-doers? Why indeed others, possibly more enlightened, should wag the head and point the finger at them even as though they were persons who, conceiving, rightly or wrongly, that they had a message to deliver and a duty to perform, have dared to write a novel with a purpose? Scarcely without exception, these doctrines in their entirety are to-day repudiated, or at any rate not acted upon, by the other civilised peoples of the world, those of our own colonies included, most of which communities are not without intelligence, and may indeed be supposed to be competent, like ourselves, to form an opinion as to what is or is not prudent and to their advantage. Also they are questioned by a great many thinking men in this country, as is evidenced by the articles which now often appear in some of the leading papers. And yet, if an individual ventures openly to express the belief that a tax upon imported barley and foreign-ground flour is just, or that it would be desirable to give a bounty to home-grown corn, behold what happens to him. Perhaps, however, the local paper does not really think that I am so very wicked, or wish to throw strange lights upon my views; indeed, I venture to believe, if all the truth were known, that we part good friends.

Hood tells me that the weather at Harleston yesterday was fearful, but, wet or fine, the show and sale had to be held. All my three beasts were disposed of. Royal Duke fetched 26*l*., turning the scale at 93 st. 12 lb. live weight, which is estimated to produce about 63 stone dead weight. The young bullock and the heifer, aged about eighteen months, sold respectively for 17*l*. 5*s*. and 17*l*. Although he took first prize at the Lothingland Show, Royal Duke has never quite come up to expectations, as throughout his—for a bullock—considerable career of two years ten months, he has proved himself but a second-class 'doer.' Ultimately he was bought by our local butcher for the same sum that the said butcher offered before he left my yard, and as his journey to Harleston and the sale expenses will come to at least 1*l*. 1*s*., it is clear that we have lost money by our enterprise. Still, it is a good thing occasionally to sell stock at a public auction, as it advertises the fact of the existence of a herd. For instance, the two young things went away to Colchester, and those who bought them may come back for more.

December 9.—The weather to-day remains mild and windy. On the farm there is little or nothing of interest to record. The ploughs move from place to place, and throughout the grey December days steal up and down the dripping fields. Beyond the daily routine of stock-feeding, root-cutting, &c., that is almost all. It is the dead of winter, in which few things grow, and yet I suppose that vegetation does increase whenever the temperature is above 42 degrees, for almost imperceptibly the tender wheat shoots lengthen, and the young bean plants look sturdier at each visit; also the green leaves of weeds spring in the shelter of the hedges.

To-day a widow visited me to enlist my interest, such as it is, in the Royal Agricultural Benevolent Institution, to which admirable charity I am a small subscriber, and asked me to sign her certificate of recommendation. For thirty-four years her husband farmed no less than 680 acres of land in this neighbourhood, for which he paid an annual rent of 930*l* Now she is penniless. The causes to which her present distress are attributed, as they appear upon the paper, are 'loss of capital, bad seasons, etc.' As in all such cases, and their name is legion in the Eastern Counties, that 'etc.' covers a great deal. It includes, for instance, the practical ruin of the agricultural interest. Is it a permanent ruin, I wonder, or will it pass like other sorrows?

To-day, too, I visited a man who has now been bedridden for about five years. He was a soldier who served in Egypt and took part in some of the desert battles—a broken Arab spearhead is one of the ornaments of the tidy room where he lies from year to year with no sight but the topmost boughs of an apple tree to cheer him. In spring he sees that tree grow green with leaf and pink with blossom, in summer and autumn the fruits swell and ripen before his eyes, then comes winter and the boughs are bare again. This is all he finds to look at, all that remains to tell him of the passing of the seasons.

This man was born at Bedingham and knows the Moat Farm well. Oddly enough, I found his wife and himself reading this diary in the magazine in which it is being published, and he talked to me with interest of the condition of the Moat Farm as he remembered it, he who, as I suppose, will never see the face of earth again, although his life may be prolonged for years. He suffered from fever in Egypt, and a while after he left the Service paralysis seized his legs, affecting all one side of him including his left eyelid. At first it was thought that he would die, but he did not die, on the contrary he has grown somewhat stronger. What strikes me most about him is the gentle patience with which he endures his terrible affliction. I congratulated him upon the improvement in his health since my last visit, to which he replied that this did not lessen the burden 'of those who had to bear with him.' Many of us who worry and repine at our ailments and troubles might surely learn a lesson from this quiet sufferer. But I think that patience and a kind of divine courage often characterise those who are thus smitten. A while ago I was interested in a paralytic of the name of Flintoff, a native of

London, who passed the last years of his life in the Ditchingham Hospital, and whose story would be worth the telling if I had the space to write down human documents. One day a message was sent to me to say that he was dying, and I hurried to the place to bid him farewell. He received me with a beaming smile.

'Thank God, dear friend,' he gasped in a broken whisper so low that I could scarcely catch his words, 'at last I am "shuffling off—this mortal coil."'

He was a man of considerable reading, and enjoyed quoting Shakespeare to the end.

With reference to the controversy of which I wrote yesterday, I am interested to see in the paper where it has been carried on a letter from a gentleman who signs himself 'An Old Radical.' The Old Radical, after stating that he is strongly opposed to myself in politics—I should like to hear his definition of my politics —adds that 'in this instance, if he will allow so unworthy a subject to join hands with him, I will.' He then says that he has passed the allotted span of life, that he was born a farmer's son, and became a London tradesman, and has been the witness of a great deal of misery, with the result that 'the very thought of Protection makes me shudder.' He adds that after forty-five years of absence he returned to his native country. Now I will let him speak for himself:

'What did I find? Well, I looked about for my old schoolboy friends, sons of men of good position in those days. I found most of them dead, and, if not dead, certainly "dead-broke." Several of them are paupers. I seek for the cause. I find it all put down to Free Trade. I say that we cannot afford to have our wheat lands thrown out of cultivation. Then don't kill the farmer, but give him a bounty. Let the loaf be cheap, and if the foreigner wants to swamp us with his corn, let him. Let's have a cheap loaf, and no reasonable taxpayer will object to help the farmer.'

A bounty on wheat when it falls below 30s. a quarter may be an economical iniquity—possibly it is, and certainly it is not a remedy of which, personally, I am enamoured—but at least, even if its arguments are slightly illogical, a letter like this, coming from such a source, is a curious sign of the times.

December 10.—Standing on the new pastures at Bedingham this afternoon just before the fall of night, the scene looked very desolate, wet as it was with rain and torn with wind. Above the flat, bare fields hung a singularly lurid heaven, which the background of black woodlands almost seemed to touch, while low down, sinking to the horizon between two lids of angry cloud, a red sun stared like some fearful, watching eye. To the left, and strangely white in hue against this veil of gloom and fire, appeared the naked arms of a tall windmill. Then suddenly the cloud-lids close ; the fierce eye sleeps, the pale mill vanishes, the drear landscape turns dull, and in the distance disappears ; while among the leafless oaks the wind moans the requiem of another winter's day.

On my homeward path I met Moore travelling from Ditchingham with three horses and a waggon, whereon was piled a towering load of thorn bushes to be used in the draining of the Denton field, No. 22. The horses stepping along merrily as they neared the stable, the rugged face of their driver, the swaying burden of the rope-held thorns, the faded colours of the waggon, made together a homely but a striking picture as they advanced down the deserted road in the gloom of a short twilight. Why I scarcely know, but in my eyes Bedingham is a spot endowed with a peculiar charm, perhaps because it is so very rural and so unvisited. Here at least, among its wet and dreary fields more than in any other place in England with which I am acquainted, do I seem to discover Nature's actual face and presence.

The want of bushes is becoming a serious question on the Moat Farm. Of late years we have drained with such vigour that scarcely a fence is left to cut, so that now most of the necessary stuff must be brought from Ditchingham. By the way, a gentleman reviewing an early instalment of this book in an agricultural paper, pointed the finger of enlightened scorn at a passage in which I talk of pipe-draining as a waste of money on such land as that with which we have to deal at Bedingham. And yet, with deference, I, and not my critic, am right. A neighbour who owns some still heavier land, within the last few years spent a large sum of money in pipe-draining it in the best possible manner. About a week ago, however, he told me he believed that this tenacious clay had caked down so hard above and around the pipes that the storm water, instead of running through them, hangs about on the almost impermeable surface. I think that few very heavy land farmers in our part of the country would go to the expense of using pipes upon such soil. After all, the experience of generations generally tells us what is the best and most effective method of dealing with any particular class of land.

December 12.—Both yesterday and to-day the weather has remained of extraordinary mildness. Roses are still in bloom, and I hear that a plateful of ripe raspberries have been gathered in the Lodge garden. But as this state of things can scarcely be expected to continue indefinitely, we are getting off the swedes as fast as we can and carting them straight into the sheds. Usually, we hale up swedes, but this year, owing to the shortness of the crop, we have been saved that labour. Oddly enough, those that we are carting to-day off the light glebe land, where one might have expected that the drought would hit them hardest, are the best which we have grown this season.

About a week ago, in the remarks that I made at Norwich, I said incautiously that although I had been looking for a long while, I was quite unable to find a young and skilled farm-labourer to take into my employ. This statement seems to have been reported throughout England, with the result that post by post applications pour in from gentlemen who appear to desire a place as *bailiff*. Alas! I can assure them that were any person with land on hand merely to whisper that he wanted a farm-steward, next morning he would probably find his bag crowded with letters, and very possibly several applicants awaiting him in the garden. There are but too many unfortunate farmers who, having conspicuously failed in the management of their own affairs, would be rejoiced to obtain such a place, where they have light work, no risk, a position of authority, enough to live on and a good house to live in. It is the labourer who is scarce, not the overseer who looks after him.

One of these letters shows so extraordinary a misapprehension of the facts connected with English farming that I cannot refrain from comment.

The writer, who appears to have passed through agricultural colleges &c., says that finding a post as an estate agent difficult to obtain, he has decided to take up 'ordinary agriculture,' any branch of which he is ready to follow. His suggestion is that I should employ him, I suppose as an 'ordinary agriculturist,' and in return for his services pay him *150l. a year*, although he intimates that to begin with he might take a smaller wage.

Now, this gentleman must have known perfectly well that I was speaking of the scarcity of skilled labourers, for in his letter he has written 'farm labourers,' although it is true that he has altered the words to 'farm managers.' What wage, then, does he suppose that we pay labourers in the Eastern Counties? Even if it is a post as manager that he seeks, his ideas are liberal. With the exception of one very great estate, I know of none which pays so much as he asks, or indeed more than 100l. a year. These are not the times when even an ordinary working bailiff can expect to draw 3l. a week.

Talking of post-bags, I wonder if everybody in my modest station is the recipient of quite so many begging letters and appeals of all sorts as fall to my lot, among them such trifles as requests to do literary work for nothing—these are frequent—or to entirely re-write the lengthy novels of strangers.

I imagine that nearly half the correspondence I receive, which is considerable, comes from people who want things of one sort or another; indeed, I am beginning to believe that a very large proportion of the world is engaged in a perpetual and frantic struggle to get something for nothing out of the remainder. Nor are these people always either grateful or courteous. Take the common example of autograph collectors, for instance—I do not suppose that more than three per cent. of them think it worth while to say thank you to the person who, on his part, has taken the trouble to gratify their peculiar form of weakness.

Occasionally, also, one has fallen into temptation, and, in re sponse to piteous appeals, sent such money as could be afforded. According to my experience, however, this is not a practice to be recommended. Once it involved me in a three days' journey to Manchester and back, to appear as a witness against a miserable scoundrel who had imposed upon me by pretending that he was a poor young wife about to be laid by, with a sick and starving husband dependent upon her efforts. Often I have sent letters of this nature to that splendid institution, the Charity Organisa- tion Society, and it is a fact that never in my recollection have the cases detailed in them turned out to be genuine. Only the other day through it I was avenged upon a female who has pestered me for years. This time—she has done it before— she sent me the usual pawn ticket with a request for a remittance. I forwarded it to the local branch of the Charity Organisation Society, intimating to my correspondent that she might call there. She did call, doubtless expecting a remittance, and as she was well known to the official in charge, I gather that the visit proved quite lively.

Impostors like these to my mind are truly wicked people, for they poison the very fount of charity, make the trustful suspicious, and, worst of all, give an excuse to rich men of niggardly nature (*'penurious retainers of superfluous wealth'*) to shut their purse- strings to many a good cause, 'for fear lest they should be imposed upon.'

Curiously enough, however, the cases which seem the most suspicious are sometimes honest. Here is one instance that I remember. A lady, who was a total stranger to me, wrote, telling this tale : That she and her husband were earning their livelihood by some form of literary work ; that so soon as their gains were sufficient they had felt justified in marrying and buying their furniture upon the hire system ; that they did very well, but when some small sum only was left to pay upon the furniture, they were both stricken by scarlet fever, and both rendered deaf or blind, I forget which ; that they had prospect of recovery, but were friend-less, and unless the required assistance was forthcoming, their goods would be seized and they must be reduced to utter ruin. To all appearance this case presented every symptom of fraud, but as I happened to have a friend, who is a solicitor, living in the same town, I asked him to be so kind as to make inquiries. It turned out to be genuine in every particular, and by a little timely help the persons concerned were enabled to turn the corner of their trouble, or so I gathered from a letter subsequently received. What has become of them now I do not know, but the lady pro-mised that when she was 'a famous woman' I should hear from her again.

In conclusion of this subject : *Final Notice*. To the vast Something-for-Nothing Public. This agricultural scribe is not a successful playwright and as yet farming has been his most fortunate speculation ! Try——or—or—*Verbum sap*.

To-day there was a meeting at this house, with one of the medical gentlemen of our neighbourhood in the chair, to discuss the possibility of establishing a Queen's nurse to attend on the sick in Ditchingham and adjacent parishes. I trust that the usual money difficulties may be overcome, for I am convinced that these properly trained and qualified nurses are one of the greatest boons that can be bestowed upon a rural district. Within my own experience in this village alone, I know of several cases in which the patients have died for the lack of timely ministrations from such a person, and to-day the doctor who was in the chair gave other instances. If the money which is so often taken from the proceeds of ancient charities, such as we have in this place, to be distributed in the form of coals, were devoted to this end, it would, in my view, be far more advantageously employed.

Personally, I dislike these fuel doles, which are most troublesome to distribute, lead to a great deal of bitterness, and come to be regarded, not as a means of relief to the very poor in cold weather, but as an endowment in which everybody has a right to share. Thus in past years I have found men in my own employ, who were in every way well-to-do for their station, applying for and receiving an allowance of coal. Surely the pious founders of the charity, who died so many centuries ago that even their names are not known to-day, can never have intended that their gifts should be put to such a purpose. They must have wished to help the poor, and to the poor that portion of the fund which is allocated to them ought to go. Surely, also, the money cannot be better employed than by providing thoroughly competent nurses in time of sickness, and especially in maternity cases, when the labourers' wives are too often left to the tender mercies of a neighbour, or of a well-meaning, but ignorant, Gamp.

December 14.—Yesterday the weather was almost ideal for the time of year, mild, windless, and sunny, and in it we made good progress with our ploughing and root-carting.

To-day I went with a friend, who is one of the guardians of the poor for this district, to visit Heckingham Workhouse, where I have not been for about fourteen years. Once I was a guardian there myself, and in that capacity used to sit upon the Board, but after a year or two's experience of it I resigned the office, which I confess I did not find congenial. There are few things more depressing than to listen, fortnight by fortnight, to the tales of utter poverty and woe poured out by the applicants for relief from the rates.

Heckingham is the workhouse for the Loddon and Clavering Union, in which are included forty-one parishes, with a total population of about thirteen thousand five hundred. The large and rambling red-brick erection, that is of the accustomed ugliness, was built about 1763, when it was called a House of Industry. In 1836 it became the Union Workhouse, with accommodation for five hundred and ten inmates, although the present total of its occupants is only ninety-two, which means, of course, that the district has to keep up a much more extensive building than is necessary. When I was a guardian, I think that we had a roll-call of about one hundred and thirty.

It astonished me to-day to see how greatly the conditions of existence at Heckingham have been improved of late years. Now it resembles an infirmary for the aged poor, rather than the last shelter to which the destitute are driven by necessity. In the old days, indeed, it was a dreary place; for instance, I remember the sick ward, a cold and desolate room, where two children, to whom I used to carry toys, a twin brother and sister, lay dreadfully ill of some scrofulous disease, with no fire in the grate, and, so far as I recollect, no trained nurse to wait upon them. To-day that ward is bright and cheerful, with a good fire burning in it and a properly certificated attendant to minister to the wants of its occupants. By the way, this afternoon I heard the fate of those stricken twins. The girl died almost immediately after I knew her, but the boy recovered sufficiently to emigrate to America.

The only people in the workhouse to-day who were there in my time are the master, an inmate named Sam Reeder (who used to put up my pony when I visited the place), and another aged and imbecile man. All the rest have gone, a good many of them underground, I suppose. Reeder I found laid up with asthma, but he knew me again at once. With several intervals he has inhabited this house for about a quarter of a century. In the same room there was another old fellow lying in bed with a great roll of flannel tied round his throat. I asked him what was the matter with him, and he replied that he was suffering from ' poll-sickness,' which, as he alleged, he had caught from a horse by sleeping in a rug belonging to the said horse. Poll-sickness, it seems, is a kind of sore or abscess which horses get from knocking their heads against low doorways, and is commonly supposed to be incurable. Therefore the old gentleman, whose name is Lawes, assured me that, as he had taken it from a horse, his ailment also was incurable. He told me too that he had cut up hayricks for me before now, and that his daughter was servant in this house eighteen years ago, when I married.

Never shall I forget my early experiences of Heckingham Workhouse. Having been elected a guardian, I attended the Board in due course, and, as is too often my fortune, at the very first meeting fell into controversy. At that date all children in the house, including infants, were fed upon skimmed milk. Owing to some illness, however, the doctor ordered them a ration of fresh milk, which ration the master had neglected to discontinue when the sickness passed. Consequently there arose trouble, and with the doctor he was brought up before the Board to be questioned and reprimanded. Thereon, with all the courage of inexperience, I rose and announced boldly that I considered new milk to be a necessity to infants, and that, if I could find a seconder, I would propose that the allowance should be continued to them until they reached the age of nine years. Somewhat to my astonishment a worthy clergyman, now long dead, seconded the motion, and there followed a great debate. Soon we found that it would be absolutely hopeless to carry the innovation in its original form, and were therefore obliged to reduce the age limit from nine to five years.

The argument of the opposition was that the children were not fed upon new milk in their own homes, to which I replied that even if they were starved at home, it was no reason why they should be starved when in the public charge. Ultimately the Board divided, and to my surprise I carried the motion by a majority of one vote, so that thenceforth the infants at Heckingham were rationed with fresh milk instead of 'blue skim.'

Now I hear that the age limit has been raised to what I originally proposed, namely, nine years.

I remember that in those days I thought the condition of the graveyard not all that it should be. It lies in an open meadow of about two acres, on which cows were grazed, and the visitor, standing at the top and looking down it, could, and indeed can still, see long lines of little mounds, some of them sunk below the level owing to a collapse of the coffin beneath, and some in process of being trodden flat by the hooves of cattle. There, with never a stone or even a wooden cross to mark their place, rest the bones of those unclaimed paupers who, for the last century, have passed through the portals of Heckingham. On the occasion of my first visit to this dismal spot, the pond at the bottom of the field had been fyed out and its contents strewn about the graves to enrich the grass. History repeats itself, for to-day, after many years, I find the pond again being fyed out and its mud used for the same fertilising purpose.

Otherwise, however, there is great improvement, for that part of the field where interments have been made during the last twenty years has been fenced off with posts and barbed wire. I confess it is a question to my mind whether a place that is full of dead—even if they be pauper dead—should be used at all as a common grazing ground for cattle, although to this it might be answered that it is useless to waste the feed of an acre and a half of land, and that Boards of Guardians are in no position to indulge in sentiment. The improvements notwithstanding, it cannot be said that the spot has become attractive, and personally, although I am neither exclusive nor particular, I should prefer not to lay my bones in the burial-field of Heckingham Workhouse. Indeed, it strikes me that the Crematorium has great advantages over the most sumptuous and select of graves. The pity is that those among us who think thus must be carried so far to reach its purgatorial fires.

In truth, to whatever extent it may be brightened and rendered habitable, one cannot pretend that a workhouse is a cheerful place. The poor girls, with their illegitimate children creeping, dirty-faced, across the floor of brick ; the old, old women lying in bed too feeble to move, or crouching round the fire in their mob-caps, some of them stern-faced with much gazing down the dim vista of the past, peopled for them with dead, with much brooding on the present and the lot which it has brought them ; others vacuous and smiling—'a little gone,' the master whispers ; others quite childish and full of complaints , all of these are no more cheerful

to look on than is the dull appropriate light of this December afternoon. The old men, too, their hands knobbed and knotted with
decades of hard work, their backs bent, their faces often almost
grotesque, like those caricatures of humanity we see carved upon
the handle of a stick, come here at last in reward of their labours
—well, as the French writer says, '*cela donne furieusement à penser.*'
It is not the place that is so melancholy, it is this poignant example
of the sad end of life and all its toilings ; it is the forlorn, half-dazed
aspect of these battered human hulks who once were young, and
strong, and comely.

Year by year fewer people seem to drift into the House, I
suppose because of the shrinkage of the population, coupled with
an extension of the system of outdoor relief. This system is one
that, without precautions, lends itself to fraud and the waste of
public money, although I believe in it myself if it is properly and
carefully administered. In some cases, however, when they are
alone in the world and too helpless to do much for themselves, the
aged poor are doubtless much better off in the House than dragging
out the dregs of a miserable existence with the help of two shillings
a week and a stone of flour. Here at least they are kept warm and
clean, and find suitable nursing and attendance until the end comes.
The food also is much better and more plentiful than they can
hope to enjoy at home.

And yet how they hate it, most of them. In this parish dwells
a vacuous but amiable old fellow called Turk Taylor, who has no
belongings and picks up a living heaven knows how, for beyond a
parish cottage which he occupies, and some small allowance from
the rates, supplemented by an occasional job of pig-herding, he has
no visible means of subsistence. Five or six years ago, in the
course of a very hard winter, I heard that poor Turk Taylor had
been found lying on the floor of his cottage at death's door from
cold and starvation. He was attended to and his wants relieved,
and afterwards an attempt was made to remove him to the workhouse. If I remember rightly the relieving officer actually came
to fetch him, but the poor old man, getting wind of his designs,

hid himself in a ditch until that official had departed, with the result that he still continues his free but precarious existence.

After all, his terror is not to be wondered at when we remember that were we suddenly to be deported to America to end our days, it would scarcely be a greater break to us than his removal to Heckingham, seven miles away, is to such a person.   Once there he cannot get out of the place, for he is too feeble to visit his former haunts, and even if he has descendants or relatives, they very rarely come to see him—perhaps never until they are summoned to fetch away the body, for few care to 'keep up' with a relation in the House.   In short, he is divorced from the old surroundings, to which he has been accustomed for sixty or seventy years, and caged among strangers in a strange land ; doomed, when the bread of charity has been eaten to its last bitter crumb, there to die and be thrust away, perhaps beneath one of those nameless mounds in the grave-field, where, staring vacantly through the fence, he can see the Union cows at grass.

Better, argues such an one as Turk Taylor, is freedom than such a fate as this, although to be free may mean starvation in a fireless house.   Perhaps, under similar circumstances, some of us would come to a like conclusion.

What do these old fellows think about, I wonder, as they hobble to and fro round those measureless precincts of bald brick? The sweet-eyed children that they begot and bred up fifty years ago, perhaps, whose pet names they still remember, dead or lost to them to-day for the most part ; or the bright waving cornfields whence they scared birds when they were lads from whom death and trouble were yet a long way off.   I dare say, too, that deeper problems worry them at times in some dim half-apprehended fashion ; at least I thought so when the other day I sat behind two of them in a church near the workhouse.   They could not read, and I doubt if they understood much of what was passing, but I observed consideration in their eyes.   Of what ?   Of the terror and the marvel of existence, perhaps, and of that good God whereof the parson is talking in those long unmeaning words.   God !   They know more of the devil and all his works ; ill-paid labour, poverty, pain, and the infinite un-recorded tragedies of humble lives. God ? They have never found Him. He must live beyond the workhouse wall—out there in the graveyard—in the waterlogged holes which very shortly——

Or perhaps their reflections are confined to memories of the untoothsome dinner of the yesterday and hopes of the meat pudding and tobacco to-morrow. Who can tell? It would be useless to ask them.

At Heckingham there is a yard where tramps, in payment of their lodging, are set to break granite to be used in road repairs. To-day I had a try at this granite breaking, and a poor hand I made of the task. I hit hard and I hit softly, I hit with the grain and across it, I tried the large and the small hammer. As a result flakes of sharp stone flew up and struck me smartly in the face, but very little granite did I succeed in breaking. My companion tried also, and after him the master, who said that he understood the game, but neither of them did any better. I have come to the conclusion that even in breaking stones there must be a hidden art.

If I remember right, this tough northern granite was first introduced in my own days of office, or just before them, to provide occupation for a really remarkable rogue—a 'master' rogue, as they say here—who, in those times, lived upon the rates. This man, who was as strong as a horse, absolutely declined to do steady work. Numerous were the attempts of the guardians to be rid of him ; once, for instance, they paid his passage to Hull, whence he promptly tramped back again to Heckingham. Then some inventive genius bethought him of this hard granite, which proved effectual, for he took his discharge. Not long after he reappeared, and with him a widow whom he had married in the interval, and *eight* of her children. That was his repartee to the granite. Needless to explain the House was forced to extend its hospitality to his ready-made family at the expense of the ratepayers of the Union.

Many stories are told of the misery that existed before the passing of the present Poor Laws, but here is a fact illustrative of the feeling of the labouring classes when workhouses were first built, about sixty years ago. My friend, who conducted me over Heckingham, tells me that not long ago he visited the House of the Depwade Union, which is situated, I believe, at Pulham St. Mary, in order to inspect the hot-water system in use there, and was astonished to see that it is loopholed for musketry. On inquiring the reason, he heard that when it was built, about 1836, the feeling among the poor of the neighbourhood grew so bitter that they came at night to pull down the brickwork which had been set during the day. So determined were their efforts that at last a guard armed with rifles was placed behind these loopholed walls to protect the rising fabric.

The whole question of Poor Law relief—at any rate in our rural districts—is very complicated, and one which I will not attempt to discuss in the narrow space at my disposal. It seems quite open to argument, however, whether in our days of dwindling population, instead of keeping up these great buildings for the accommodation of but a small percentage of the number of inmates that they were designed to contain, it would not be more economical and satisfactory to institute some well-considered system of local parish homes.

The mild weather holds, and on the farm we are still ploughing and carting root.

December 15.—To-day the weather remains very fine, although it has turned more chilly. The sky this afternoon was exceptionally clear, and through it the sun sank large and red, betokening frost. Seldom have I seen its light look more beautiful than it did this evening on the brimming river and the rich green common, as I viewed them from the crest of the Vineyard Hills. Above the sinking orb hung one long cloud, whereof the upper edge was tinged with fire. The appearance of this wavering line of flame was exactly similar to that of a distant grass fire crawling forward over the African veld at night ; while, to complete the resemblance, against the blue sky above it floated dark streamers of vapour like smoke borne backwards by the wind. This mild and open weather is very favourable to the cows and cattle, which can run upon the pastures all day, saving the hayricks by filling themselves with grass, and at the same time finding healthy exercise.

To-day another magistrate and I held a special sittings of the Bench to try the case of a girl of sixteen years of age who was accused of the crime of attempted suicide. She ran away from the farmhouse where she was in service, and on being sent back by her parents, as it is alleged, tried to drown herself in a pond. The case was chiefly remarkable for the curious discretion shown by this child. When cautioned by the police-constable on her arrest, she made no statement whatsoever; also when the option was given her, under the provisions of the new Act, of giving evidence, she declined to go into the box or to say anything; with the result, I am glad to say, that there was practically no legal evidence upon which she could be committed for trial. In the end, with the consent of her father, on the application of a representative of the Police Court Mission, a society to whose admirable work, after some years of experience, I wish humbly to testify, she was handed over to its charge, to become an inmate of a training home.

December 17.—Yesterday and to-day we have been shooting cock pheasants in Hedenham and Tindale woods, in weather more mild, I think, than any that I can remember at this time of year.

When standing in silence at the far end of a long beat it is curious and strangely interesting to watch the behaviour of the various beasts and birds which it contains. Every one of these creatures hears the beaters the moment they set foot in this section of the wood, and while they are still a quarter of a mile or so away at once devote their minds—or instincts—to escape.

When the Gun at the far end of the fell takes up his stand there, a complete stillness will probably reign about him, broken only at intervals by the aggressive chatter of a golden-billed blackbird,

or the sound of a squirrel, which is still abroad in this warm
season running over the dead leaves, or scampering up the trunk
of an oak-tree with an acorn in its mouth. Presently, however,
from far away the keeper's voice can be heard in the still air
asking the beaters if they are all ready, followed by the answering
' Ayes ' of the men and a faint rattling of sticks.

A swift-winged wood pigeon passes high over head, quite out
of shot indeed ; then there is a rustling sound amongst the sere
twigs and mosses, and the watcher, if he be quick-eyed, may catch
sight of something brown moving to and fro in front of him.
What it is he cannot see, for the creature keeps itself hidden
behind the brown hazel-stubs or the grey-green growths of ash,
but he knows from the motion, which seems to rise and fall,
and also from the sound of the disturbed leaves, that it is not
a bird.

The thing vanishes, then appears again, and at last comes forward more boldly, and shows itself to be a hare. Catching sight of
its arch-enemy, man, who cuts it off from the retreat which it was
seeking, it stops suddenly, and perhaps sits up as though it were
begging for its life, its beautiful soft eyes fixed upon that dread
and unexpected vision. Then probably the man, following his
instincts, lifts the gun and shoots it, turning its happy breath,
perfect shape and smooth fur into a screaming, kicking, gory heap,
for that is what man—gentle, beneficent man—is out to do. Or
perhaps he does not shoot, from compunction or because he
thinks the game too near, whereon, taking fright, the hare wheels
round and dashes off at speed, trying the boundaries of the beat
here and there, till at length, let us hope, it finds a place where
it can creep through unobserved, and, unmaimed by shot, speed
away, safe until another season.

Next there comes a quicker pattering among the dead sticks
and foliage, and another brown thing runs up and crouches,
vanishing altogether except for a bright and beady eye. This
is a hen pheasant, that presently rises and flies away, but so
low that even the youngest or most ardent sportsman dare not

shoot it, fearing lest he should hit some other sportsman in the face.

Again comes the pattering, and with it a gleam of green and gold, and this time an old cock appears bent upon escape, whoever else may fall a victim. He runs up, a gorgeous-looking bird, catches sight of the Gun, runs back again and tries the little leg of underwood to his left, only to find himself face to face with a boy who has been placed there for the express purpose of stopping him and his fellows. Then he turns and rushes down the fell like a race-horse, till presently, with a crow and a sound of beating wings which it is almost impossible to describe, he bursts his way through the undergrowth, perhaps to come over high and die rocketing as a good pheasant should; perhaps to be happily missed; or perhaps to slip away with such cunning that no one gets a shot at him.

Now the ear catches a rapid scampering noise, and yonder, badly frightened by the cock pheasant, which has almost trodden on it, a grey rabbit, that has crept forward stealthily, runs back again at full tilt, only, alas! to be caught by a charge of shot and sent tumbling over stone dead. There it lies, its little mud-stained paws pointing upwards, and the white fur of its stomach making a patch of light which catches the eye as it travels to and fro over the dull carpet of sere leaves where poor Coney is stretched out.

Before the beaters got to work the hoarse cries of jays could be heard echoing far down the quiet covert, but from the moment that they found themselves surrounded, these cunning birds have changed their tactics, for not a single scream now issues from their painted throats. Up and down the beat they move in short dipping flights, refuging in every convenient tree, and travelling for preference almost on the tops of the brushwood. At last they draw near the end and determine to make a dash for liberty. On comes the boldest of them, till, suddenly catching sight of the shining gun-barrels, weapons of which he seems quite to understand the use, he turns in a wide wheel and once more attempts to hide his too conspicuous self among the bushes. Presently, with the first burst of pheasants, these jays will rise and cross in their company, for they know well that jays, which, by the way, notwithstanding their slow flight, are very hard to hit, are only shot in moments of idleness and waiting, and will be overlooked when the cocks are flying fast.

The jays have gone, and for a minute or two there is nothing to study except the light falling on to the boles of the oaks so clearly that the watcher sees every little frond of the grey lichen which grows upon their rugged bark, when suddenly far away, in and out among the trees, passes a swift brown shadow. It disappears, it appears again, it comes near, rocking from side to side on those wide wings which move so silently and carry it so fast. This is a woodcock, one of the most beautiful birds that flies, although coloured in a sombre key. So close does he pass that now the strong light can be seen shining between the mandibles of his tapered bill and on his brown, searching eye. Too late he perceives his danger and twists wildly, but without avail, for the shot catches him and robs him of his life and beauty. Never again can the lovely creature hope to flit across the moon-illumined Norway moss, hugging its young against that pencilled breast.

Then the pheasants begin to rise in bouquets, so that, for the next five minutes, all is noise and gore and feathers, and some are missed and some are killed and some, I fear, are wounded. When the slaughter is done with and you have time to look round you again, close by, on an oak tree to the right, may be seen a tomtit busily searching for insects among the crevices in its bark. He was there before the firing began and he is still there, for he knows that all this fuss and fluster does not concern him, since no reasonable being wants to shoot a titmouse, and to the fate of the great bullying pheasants he is quite indifferent.

To-day while I was walking up a ride of Tindale Wood, as it happened without a gun in my hand, a woodcock rose absolutely at my feet, so near indeed that I could observe its every feather. I mention this, because as it flew away the bird did what, personally, I have never heard a woodcock do before—uttered a low double note not unlike that of a snipe, but much less shrill. As nearly as I can copy it on paper this was the noise it made, *cheep-cheep.* By the way, once I saw a curious incident occur in this covert. I was walking down one of the long tunnel-like drives when a woodcock sprang from the brushwood exactly in the same fashion as the bird of which I have been writing. So close did it pass that my loader put out his hand and caught it, much as a clever field might take a ball at point. This bird, I remember, showed no outward signs of having been wounded.

There were about a dozen woodcocks in the covert to-day, but from one mischance or another, very few were shot. Indeed, no bird is more frequently missed than the woodcock, or indirectly, I may add, more dangerous to those who try to shoot him. Under the cover of a jest there is wisdom in the latter half of the old sporting axiom which tells the beginner when he hears the cry of 'Woodcock' to fire both barrels straight at his nearest neighbour and throw himself flat on to his face. Once I was shot through the hat by a gentleman intent upon bagging a low woodcock.

I suppose that shooting as a sport comes in for more contempt and abuse than almost any other form of outdoor recreation. While I was waiting at one of my stands to-day, however, and listening to the long line of beaters as they approached, it occurred to me that it would be a very great misfortune if, through the abolition of the game-laws, or any other cause, it ceased to be possible in this country. I imagine that in the Eastern Counties alone such a thing would mean the loss of tens—I almost venture to say of hundreds—of thousands of pounds, which are now distributed annually amongst the owners and occupiers of the soil, gamekeepers, beaters, gunmakers, grain and patent-food dealers, liverymen, hotel-keepers, parish authorities (shootings pay rates), and a hundred others who directly or indirectly benefit by the spending of money in a place Some years ago I shared with two friends a moderate-sized shooting in Norfolk, which otherwise might have remained untenanted. A careful estimate of the amount disbursed showed that the people living in that village benefited to the extent of 600*l.* a year by the re-opening of this shooting upon a suitable scale; that is to say, there were 600*l.* to spend in the place annually which before it had to do without.

Another of the good sides of shooting is its companionable opportunities. Many men come to know each other at shooting parties who, although near neighbours, otherwise would remain strangers all their lives. Also as a by-product it provides an enormous supply of cheap food for the dwellers in towns. These, together with the healthiness of the recreation, are some of the advantages of the sport; indeed, to my mind its only disadvantage is that it involves the necessity of putting a large number of creatures to a death which is sometimes lingering. Personally I salve my conscience—or try to—with the thought that were they not destined to be shot, they would never live at all, and that until they are shot their fortunes are excellent. Do away with shooting and in twenty years scarcely a game-bird would exist in England, except such of them as stress of weather or the instinct of migration might drive upon our shores.

The shortest day has passed. Nature, her despair outworn, turns her face again towards light and life. Little wonder that our Norse ancestors made a great Yule feast to celebrate the birth of the new season—the season of the lengthening days and kindling sun.

Christmas Day.—Upon the 22nd fell the first frost of the year, which rendered the land so hard that on the following day the ploughs could only just manage to get through with the work of breaking up the stubble land, as ploughing for crop was out of the question. We have made up our minds the next time we thrash at Baker's to keep the engine half a day or so longer in order to steam-cut as much chaff as we can stow away. This will save us a great deal of time and labour which is otherwise lost, first in carting the hay and straw up to the machine at the Home Farm, and secondly in carting them back in the form of chaff.

My correspondence to-day contains a letter from that rare person, an agricultural enthusiast. This gentleman, who is earning a very handsome salary in an office, proposes to abandon it in order to commence farming, apparently on borrowed capital. And what, my reader, do you suppose has led him to his resolve? No, not the earlier pages of a certain book, but—*the teachings of Carlyle and Ruskin*. If a study of these leaders of thought tends to such amiable insanity, which I confess has never struck me in reading them, surely so far as the young are concerned, they should be placed upon the *Index Expurgatorius*.

I have written imploring my correspondent to forsake these false lights and stick to his safe and gilded stool, but if he declines to listen to me, I can only hope that he will reap the reward of his pluck and succeed in this difficult adventure.

Yesterday, as the frost continued, we were obliged to give up the ploughing and take to the carting of manure. While I was walking along a hedgerow I saw a sight that I have never seen before. Suddenly, about fifty yards ahead of me, a cock pheasant sprang from the fence and lit upon the ground with an angry crow, flicking up one wing in a very curious fashion. Next second I learned the reason, for after him came a medium-sized black and white cat, which evidently had tried to pounce upon him in the hedge. On seeing it the pheasant took to his legs, and the disappointed cat slunk back to shelter. I did not know before that a cat would attack so powerful a bird.

Royal Duke, the prize ox, made his last appearance at Ditchingham this evening in the shape of sirloin of beef. The meeting was painful to me who had known him from a calf, but I must admit that he was excellent eating. Oh! what carnivoræ we are!

Yesterday the frost broke, with the result that this Christmas has not the beauty of that of last year, the weather being dull and mild, towards nightfall softening into rain. In the afternoon I went to hear some carols sung in the neighbouring church of Broome. Afterwards a friend of mine, who lives there, gave me some curious facts illustrative of the decrease of population in that parish. It is his habit to make a present of meat at Christmas to every cottage inhabitant of Broome, and he informed me that the difference in its cost owing to the shrinkage of population between this year and last is something really remarkable.

I wonder what must be the result of this exodus if it continues? Will the most of the land have to be put down in temporary pasture and cultivated more roughly? When travelling in the United States of America I have seen a mule and a cow harnessed to a plough, which was being directed by a woman across a great expanse of plain studded with tree stumps, and roughly fenced with their tops dragged into a kind of zeriba. Is that a possible future to which our agriculture may look forward? And if most of the land is to go down to grass, will grass continue to pay? Heretofore the graziers have had the best of it, but is not their bad time coming? I have a friend connected with Argentina who tells me that a frozen meat company in which he is a shareholder is able to sell excellent chilled mutton at twopence-halfpenny the pound.

How are British graziers to compete against mutton at twopence-halfpenny a pound? Moreover, as appliances improve and rates of carriage lessen, will it not come in at a still lower price from a country of endless and fertile pastures, where they pay their labour in paper and depreciated silver, which must be taken at face value, and are paid for their produce in good British gold? The prospect is so melancholy that I do not care to study it further. Perhaps the world may fill up, or perhaps drought and locusts will take a hand in the game. We must put faith in our old friend—the Unexpected, for we have no other.[1]

December 26.—The ordeal is over, my balance sheets are made out and here they be:

See Appendix II.

DITCHINGHAM FARM

DR.   *Balance Sheet, Michaelmas,* 1898   CR.

	£	s.	d.		£	s.	d.
To Covenants, Michaelmas, 1897	283	4	6	By Covenants, Michaelmas, 1898	416	10	0
,, Horses	187	0	0	,, Horses	210	0	0
,, Stock, &c.	611	2	6	,, Stock, &c.	724	16	0
,, Implements	145	0	0	,, Implements	145	0	0
,, Corn	276	8	0	,, Corn	485	4	0
,, Covenants (Carr)	101	15	6	,, Live Stock sold	596	18	0
,, Live Stock bought	272	12	7	,, Dairy produce sold	265	7	2
,, Cake, Seeds, &c.	157	3	6	,, Corn sold	203	11	9
,, Tradesmen's Bills	116	13	9	,, Miscellaneous produce sold	40	18	10
,, Rent paid for land hired and payments for Rates and Tithe	215	3	10				
,, Labour	388	16	5				
,, Balance available for Rent of own land in hand, Interest, and Living Expenses	333	5	2				
	£3,088	5	9		£3,088	5	9

DR.   *Cash Account*   CR.

	£	s.	d.		£	s.	d.
To Capital	1,300	0	0	By Valuation at Michaelmas, 1898, Covenants, Horses, Stock, Sheep, &c., Implements, Corn	1,981	10	0
,, Balance from Profit and Loss Account	540	13	7	,, Cash at Bank	192	8	9
,, Profit, 1898	333	5	2				
	£2,173	18	9		£2,173	18	9

BEDINGHAM FARM

Balance Sheet, Michaelmas, 1898

DR.   CR.

	£	s.	d.		£	s.	d.
To Balance brought forward	16	18	6	By Covenants, Michaelmas, 1898	157	12	0
,, Covenants, Michaelmas, 1897	130	16	0	,, Live Stock and Implements, Michaelmas, 1898	346	10	0
,, Live Stock and Implements, 1897	335	9	0	,, Corn, Michaelmas, 1898	176	5	0
,, Corn, 1897	189	12	0	,, Live Stock sold	118	9	0
,, Seeds and Corn bought	61	8	4	,, Miscellaneous produce sold	23	15	4
,, Live Stock bought	28	0	0	,, Corn sold	206	4	6
,, Tradesmen's Bills, &c.	43	16	4				
,, Labour	133	5	6				
,, Balance available for Rent, Interest, &c.	89	10	2				
	£1,028	15	10		£1,028	15	10

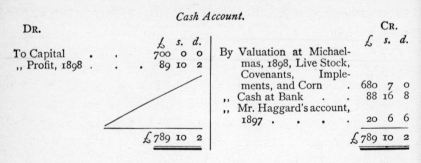

Cash Account.

DR.	£ s. d.		CR. £ s. d.
To Capital . .	700 0 0	By Valuation at Michael-mas, 1898, Live Stock, Covenants, Implements, and Corn .	680 7 0
,, Profit, 1898 . . .	89 10 2	,, Cash at Bank . .	88 16 8
		,, Mr. Haggard's account, 1897	20 6 6
	£789 10 2		£789 10 2

I, Robert Thomas Simpson, of Bury St. Edmunds, in the County of Suffolk, Auctioneer and Valuer (a member of the firm of Salter, Simpson, and Sons, of Attleboro', Norfolk, and Bury St. Edmunds, Suffolk), hereby certify that on the 3rd day of November last I made Valuations of the Live and Dead Farming Stock, Corn and Covenants, upon the Ditchingham and Bedingham Farms as occupied by Henry Rider Haggard, Esq., the amounts of such Valuations being £1,981 10s. and £680 7s. respectively, and that to the best of my judgment such Valuations are fair and reasonable, and that the said amounts would have been realised had the Farms actually passed from one occupier to another at that date.

As Witness my hand this 30th day of December, 1898.

R. T. SIMPSON.

From these documents it will be seen that my profit on the two places for the year amounts to 422*l*. 15*s*. 4*d*., a round sum which at first sight is enough to make the half-starved farmer almost delirious with joy. After the first shout of triumph, however, comes reflection. Among my readers may be persons who, in search of new experiences of life, have gone upon the Boards of public companies. If so, they will perhaps have discovered that the chief advantages accruing to the director appear to be—that he enjoys nights sleepless with anxiety and works like a slave for no pay, since at the first pinch 'the Board' is expected to jettison its fees ; and that, although his pocket may be bare of gain and his conscience white as the snows on Hecla, day by day he runs the risk of seeing his conduct held up to the British public in some strange and unexpected light. For in practice the director seems to be responsible to everybody for everything that happens, whether he is to blame for it or not.

Yet there is a great deal to be learned from this fearsome occupation. For instance, he who has gone through that mill will know how futile are the schemes which from time to time have been advanced of carrying out agricultural enterprises on a large scale by means of companies. I cannot conceive a great farm, or group of farms, being successfully worked by a Board of directors, meeting, say, once a month or a fortnight, to pass resolutions already prepared by the secretary or one or two ruling spirits.

Another piece of knowledge to be acquired in Board-rooms—and this is my immediate concern—is that you can call nothing a profit until all previous trading losses are worked off. Of course if this test is applied to my farm accounts, the profit shown for 1898 vanishes utterly in the total loss which I have incurred since I began to farm. (See pages 38–40.) Moreover, there must be deducted from this sum of 422*l.* 15*s.* 4*d.* rent on say 250 acres at 1*l.* an acre, and interest on 2,000*l.* capital at 4 per cent. amounting to 80*l.* plus management expenses—let us say 20*l.*, or in all 350*l.* This leaves a total of 72*l.* 15*s.* 4*d.*, upon which the farmer would be supposed to exist, that being the living profit left after the satisfaction of outgoings and charges. As a matter of fact, however, he would not be able to exist thereon, because it would scarcely be possible to draw out of the farm account every farthing returned as profit. To begin with, it is, immediately at any rate, available only to the extent of the cash balances in the bank ; the rest being represented by corn taken at a valuation but not yet sold. Even when it is sold the farmer could scarcely put the whole proceeds into his pocket and spend them, inasmuch as a certain sum must be left to meet unexpected expenses, enough to 'veer and haul on,' as sailors say. Thus, in practice, out of this 422*l.* shown as profit I shall be fortunate if 300*l.* can be transferred to the estate account.

It will be seen therefore, that after all the gingerbread, although it is composed of costly materials and has taken long abaking, is not so very richly gilded.

Such as it is, however, I am grateful for it, especially as I find that I have done better than some of my neighbours. In one case, for instance, of a farm a little larger than my own, whereas last year there was a handsome profit, this year it is practically nil, only a small sum being available towards rent and interest.

It may be asked, then, how I have managed to succeed even to this moderate extent—a question which needs some lines to answer. Largely, I think it is owing to the advice and experience of my agent, Mr. Robert Simpson, and to the constant hard work and attention to detail of Hood. Also I may, perhaps, claim as a factor in the result my own interest in the land and the daily thought and care I give to everything that happens in or about these holdings. So much for personal considerations, which, however, would help little were it not for the fact that the soil itself is gathering a better heart, and that my young pastures are beginning to come into value—that, in short, I am reaping the result of the outlay and labour of past years. But it is my belief that without the help of the little flock of ewes all this would have availed nothing. From the beginning I was a constant advocate of trying a few sheep, and ever since those sheep were bought, about three years ago, things have begun to improve. The reason is plain ; comparatively speaking they cost little to keep, for they will devour anything down to thistles or ivy off the trees, and practically much of what they eat would otherwise be wasted. Then they are productive animals, and, as old Tusser says, 'good lamb is worth gold.' Lastly, their presence is of extraordinary benefit to the land, especially where young pastures are being built up into sound productive meadows.

One swallow does not make a summer, and one fairly successful year at farming certainly does not prove that this industry can be made remunerative. Still, it does go to confirm me in the opinion, which I think I expressed in the beginning of this book—that with plenty of capital, inexhaustible patience, a real love of the thing, and the exercise of about as much general intelligence as would be necessary to move an army corps up the Nile, a moderate rent, an interest on the money invested, and possibly a small living profit, if the labour and other conditions are fairly favourable, and in the absence of any special ill-luck or calamity, may still be wrung out of the land in our Eastern Counties.

That is my view of the matter after a good many years of experience, and I trust that others better qualified to judge may not think it misleading or too sanguine. This, if I live and continue to farm, I suppose I shall learn in the future, but I hope even by adhering strictly to my plan of lessening the corn acreage in every possible way, cultivating soundly, and increasing the number and the quality of the stock to the utmost limit that we can carry, to do somewhat better in future years.

But even if I succeed in this endeavour, I fear that it will not alter my estimate as to the general position of the farming interest in the Eastern Counties. On every side we hear new complaints, such as those that Mr. Clare Sewell Read utters in his agricultural summaries and elsewhere ; whereof I quote a specimen extracted from a letter written by him to the *Times*, as it seems to me to sum up the present situation in a few sentences. 'We have to pay more for labour, manures, and feeding stuffs. Yet we are selling the best wheat England ever produced at 25*s*. per quarter, wool has reached the lowest price ever recorded, and, notwithstanding the poor root crop, beef hardly averages 6d. per lb. But there is another feature of the farming outlook which is very sad to contemplate, and that is the decreasing influence agriculture has upon Parliament or even with a friendly Administration. . . . We might possibly have been spared the melancholy spectacle of the President of our Board of Agriculture defending and upholding one of the greatest frauds upon British produce by granting a legal *status* to colouring margarine to represent butter.'

I know that this much respected gentleman and great agricultural authority has been accused of taking too gloomy a view ; he has even been called 'Jeremiah.' Yet if a very minor prophet may venture an opinion, I must say that I agree with almost every inspired wail which he has uttered. Indeed, short of the entire stoppage of the industry, it is difficult to see how things could change greatly for the worse.

In these parts, for instance, as a fruit of this dreadful depression, the labourers are melting away, and, practically, the old stamp of tenant farmer is ceasing to exist. In his place has arisen a new style of person, who, unless the land be in tip-top condition, when he may venture on a four years' lease, will only farm from year to year. I say 'farm,' but in many cases it cannot be called farming, for, without capital, without sufficient stock, without insight and the determination to make that spot a home for years and by skill and adaptability to force the land to yield a living, how can a man farm in such times as these? He had better give it up and take to tax-collecting, after the shrewd example of an ex-tenant of my own.

According to the Agricultural Summary in to-day's *Times*, which is admirably done, this view—that it would be better to give it up—seems to have been largely shared throughout the kingdom. Thus I find it stated there that this year 76,079 acres have been entirely lost from the previous cultivated area, as against a loss of 13,546 acres in 1897. Further, this cheerful fact is recorded —that in 1898 the aggregate area of all corn crops, cereal and pulse together, is absolutely the lowest on record. This is a situation on which it is quite unnecessary for me to comment: it speaks for itself.

The extraordinary mildness of the season continues. This afternoon I saw a perfect red rose—not one of the very hardy varieties— in bloom upon the garden wall. It is curious to find a flower that would have done no disgrace to June unfolding its petals in the death days of December.

December 27.—To-day a fierce gale is blowing from the sou'-west, and against it—having business there—I struggled to

Kessingland, accomplishing most of the journey upon a bicycle. The ride from Lowestoft, in the very teeth of the wind, was the hardest I have ever undertaken. Very frequently, indeed, I was obliged to dismount and push behind, a duty that was not made more entertaining by the vision of a curate, cigarette in mouth, sailing past me in the opposite direction, his feet reposing on the rests. I wonder why it is, by the way, that most curates and many clergymen ride bicycles so madly? Thrice have I nearly fallen a victim to their rage—the last time, indeed, I just escaped being run down by a coasting covey of six of them at once.

At length I turned down the lane which leads to Cliff Grange, the very easternmost dwelling, I suppose, in the whole kingdom, and as the wind was now upon my side, got along much better, until a sudden and ferocious gust blew me and the bicycle several yards into a ploughed field. The sight from the cliff was very grand—a sullen, tempest-fretted sea raging beneath a low and sullen sky. But a gale from the sou'-west is not that which does damage on the eastern coast—it is the nor'-easter that we dread, especially if it be accompanied by very high tides. This was what happened in the great storm of last December, when the tide and the sea rose higher than they are believed to have done for the best part of a century. The damage at Lowestoft, Southwold, Pakefield, &c., was enormous, and as I had recently come into possession of this Kessingland property, my state of mind until I heard that it had taken no harm can be imagined. I think, however, that if our cliff will resist the worst onslaught of two generations, for the future we may sleep at ease. As a matter of fact, indeed, the beach at Kessingland is increasing in width; in front of my house it has risen more than five feet in height during a single year. This is consoling, but he who has to deal with the sea can never be quite certain of anything. If old Ocean wishes to have a thing he will take it, and at present he is taking Southwold and Pakefield, with other places; also large stretches of marshland are being ruined by the continual advance of the tide along the rivers.

But the inhabitants of East Anglia still do little or nothing—or at least nothing concerted. Every man for himself is the cry, and let the sea take the rest.

Even the December gale, however, so far as violence is concerned, was but a small thing compared to the tempest of last March three years. That frightful storm came up one Sunday afternoon from the nor'-west, and when the full fury of it struck this house, which is an exceedingly solid building, the whole fabric rocked and tottered till I feared lest the great mass of chimneys should fall through the roof. Everywhere trees were going down. They just bowed and vanished. One instant they were standing, the next they were gone. In the worst of the gale I went out and struggled into Bungay. Out of the front gate I dared not go because of the rocking elms, fear of which forced some of the Hood family in the farm which stands by it to take refuge among the cowsheds, so I was obliged to break my way to the road through the lawn fence. The streets of Bungay were an extraordinary sight, being strewn with broken tiles and chimney-pots, much as though the place had been bombarded, and as I walked I saw one woman lifted quite off her legs by the wind and thrown into the middle of the road.

All of this, however, though our damage was great enough, seemed as nothing to what happened in East Norfolk and in other parts of the county where the soil is light. There the trees fell literally by the ten thousand, and such a sight as the woods presented after the hurricane was done with I never before witnessed. In some instances they were perfectly flat—a tangled heap of boughs and timber, and here and there, standing above the *débris*, a deep-rooted oak with the top twisted out of it, or a great Scotch fir snapped in two like a carrot. A friend told me that he stood in the middle of a little park and watched the surrounding woods go down, just as though they were being pressed to the earth by the power of some mighty hand. First the outer trees would fall, then line by line those that stood within till little or nothing was left. And the most curious feature of this marvellous spectacle was that no noise could be heard. Although forests were crashing to the earth all about, no sound reached the ears of the watcher except the sound of that howling tempest.

Only one other such gale do I remember—at any rate in this country. It happened, I think, in the year 1881, when I was coming home from Africa in a disabled ship. Luckily we won shelter in the mouth of the Thames before it burst; and there we lay, for we could not go up the river because most of the water was blown out of its bed. Two powerful tugs tried to get our head round, and I saw one of them caught by the wind and dashed into our side as though it were but a little sailing-boat. Also I saw ships one after another carried from their moorings, and other things too long to mention.

Here, however, is a little story connected with that gale which it is, perhaps, worth while to preserve. Shortly after it my late father accompanied me to North Walsham to visit some property in that town which belongs to this estate. After our business was completed he expressed a wish to look over the grammar school, which he had not seen since he was a scholar there as a little boy some sixty years before. By the wall of the playground grew a line of poplar-trees which the gale I have spoken of had thrown down, so that they lay upon the wall, whereof all the upper part was destroyed by their weight. Looking at this curious sight brought to my father's mind the recollection that there was a brick in this wall upon which Nelson, who was also a scholar at North Walsham, had cut his initials. He asked those who were showing us over the school about this brick, but no one seemed to know anything of it—indeed, I fancy that since his time the tradition of the thing had died away. But the more he thought of it the more positive he became of its existence, and as he expressed a belief that he could find it, a lantern was brought—for the autumn evening had now closed in—by the light of which he began to search the wall. And there, certainly, he found the brick with the weatherworn initials H. N. cut upon its face. Curiously enough, although this particular brick was quite uninjured, one of the fallen trees that rested on the wall had ground everything above it to powder. I believe that it has now been taken from its place and is preserved in the schoolhouse.

I suppose that there are not very many people living who have known a person who knew Lady Hamilton, but as it chances I am one of them. In or about the year 1804, Mrs. Bolton, who was Nelson's sister, and her husband hired Bradenham, my brother's house, where I was born, and here Lady Hamilton used to visit them. Indeed, there is a large cupboard in the Red Room that was dedicated to her dresses, whereof the exceeding splendours are still recorded in the traditions of the village. At that time a man of the name of Canham, whom I knew well in his age, was page boy at the Hall, and more than once has he talked to me of Horatia and Lady Hamilton, the former of whom he described as a ' white little slip of a thing.' I asked him also what Lady Hamilton was like. 'Oh,' he replied, in the vigorous Norfolk vernacular, 'she wör a rare fine opstanding . . . she wör.' The missing word is scarcely suited to this page polite, but may easily be guessed. In effect it is a curious piece of contemporary criticism from a source likely to be unprejudiced if outspoken.

After Nelson's death all his sea-going belongings were sent to Bradenham; a piece of mahogany furniture from his cabin still stands in one of the bedrooms. Also it was Canham's duty from time to time to take out the coat in which he was killed at Trafalgar and to air it on the lavender bushes that grow by the kitchen garden railings.

Only the other day I came across a curious souvenir of Nelson. On his death a patriotic club was founded at Norwich in memory of him, and called the Nelson Club. This Club, after an existence of about fifty years, finally became extinct, or was merged into the present Norfolk Club; the last member of it, the Rev. Henry Lombe of Bylaugh, dying less than a year ago. It was a dining club, and owned two very curious pewter platters, which passed into my possession through the agency of that pedlar whom I have mentioned upon an earlier page. First, I bought one, then the other was traced and obtained from London, where it had descended in a different branch of the vendor's family.

These platters, which must have served the purpose of meat dishes, measure twenty inches in diameter, and about sixty-two in circumference. Round their rims are cut in bold letters, *Copenhagen*, *The Nile*, *Trafalgar of glorious memory*, the arms of Norwich, and the date 1806. In their centres appear the full armorial bearings of Nelson, his motto *Palmam qui meruit ferat*, and an inscription, *The Nelson Club*.[1]

December 28.—The gale has been followed by a morning that was indeed lovely. Against a vast dome of tender blue the naked trees were outlined with a wonderful clearness, while the whole landscape lay steeped in a bath of sunshine. Indeed, the scene when I walked through it this forenoon might almost have been such as is common on an autumn evening, for it was pervaded by the same gentle light, and so low lay the sun that the shadows of the trees stretched away upon the grass, as in the summer at the death of day shadows are wont to do. On the purple, new-turned plough of the fourteen-acre at Baker's were feeding many glossy-plumaged rooks, and with them a flock of green-backed plover, driven inland by the rough weather. In that light these peewits were almost invisible upon the plough, but when by some unseen disturber they were frightened suddenly from the ground, the white of their under-wings and breasts shone in the sun's rays like discs of polished metal. Then down they went, and once more disappeared. Taking off my hat I waved it, which startled them in good earnest, for they mounted high into the air and circled round me in wide sweeps, looking most beautiful in the sunshine, till, fearing lest I should scare them quite away, I hastened to another field.

How extraordinary sweet and wholesome is the odour of fresh ploughed earth ! To my mind there are few fragrances so pleasant. Yet this is only the case after man has cultivated the same soil for many years, for, if my recollection is right, virgin

---

[1] See Note on pp. xiv–xvi of preliminary matter.

land when broken up smells somewhat sour. Certainly it is most unwholesome ; witness the fevers contracted by white men employed in cutting canals and railways in Africa and other semi-tropical places.

Already we have been obliged to begin upon our beet, mixing them for the food of the seven young oxen at Baker's with the few remaining swedes, as to put cattle upon a sudden diet of lush mangolds would be too violent a change. Owing to the drought swedes are very scarce this year ; indeed, my experience of them upon our soil is that they are the most uncertain of all crops. Very generally they suffer from mildew, or stunt of one kind and another, especially in such dry seasons as we have experienced of late. I should like to grow more kohl-rabi, a most valuable root, but Hood is of opinion that this Ditchingham land is too light for the needs of that vegetable. White turnips also, he thinks, have not more than half the feeding value of swedes. Yet with humility I venture to believe that it would be wise to lessen the acreage of this crop as much as possible.

December 29.—This has been a most miserable day, very wet and windy, indeed one of the darkest of the dying year. Throughout its gloomy hours, however, two ploughs have been going upon the light glebe land, although, as Peachey pointed out, such soil, on account of the gravel in it, is apt to set very hard if turned up in the wet. In the present case, however, as we are not ploughing for crop, this does not greatly matter.

To the observer standing on the crest of the rise by the corner of the cemetery—a fitting spot for such a study—the scene, as it appeared beneath the pall of slaty flying scud this morning, was one of singular desolation. In the far background, piercing the wreaths of vapour like some lone beacon upon a dreary coast, stood the tower of Broome church, and to the left of it, but nearer, the gaunt framework of a thatchless, ruined barn. Below this skeleton came lines of dim elms, now hidden and now revealed as the driving wrack of rain lifted or closed in about them.   Near at hand, forming the dip of a little valley, lay the brook pasture, looking blue rather than green in colour beneath the leaden clouds, and beyond it, right up to the sombre mass of Tindale Wood, stretch upon stretch of rusty stubble and sullen plough.

Let the eye roam where it would, there was but one cheerful thing at hand to catch it, the garlands of bright ivy clinging to the hedgerow pollards, and at times in the thickest of the rain-storms even these grew black.   Then, to complete the picture, patient and solemn, the ploughmen wrapped in their thick capes, toiled forward side by side, heedless of the lashing sleet, heedless of the savage wind; up and down, continually up and down the grey length of field, with the striving horses before them and the complaining ploughs beneath their hands, very embodiments indeed of the dignity and the doom of labour.

December 31.—Yesterday was a day of sharp sleet-storms, varied by intervals of sunshine, through which our ploughing went on as usual; but the dawn this morning, the last of the year, was also, I think, the most beautiful.   A white rime of frost covered the ground, for at night it froze sharply, while the air was so quiet and windless that no twig even stirred upon the trees.   One great loveliness lay upon the eastern sky, as though there some vast and wondrous flower was bursting into bloom— a perfect but ever-changing colour scheme of pink and yellow laid upon a groundwork of pale and tender greens and broken into lines and petals by streaks of fire pouring upwards from the rim of the appearing sun.   Strange to say, however, over against this glory, as though at war with it, lay an ominous and gloomy sky, which, while the sun rose, invaded and conquered the splendour in the east, till the whole heaven grew dark and pregnant with rain or snow to come.

To study such a sight is to understand the hopelessness of art. This morning's sunrise would have been enough to drive a painter mad with envy and despair.

I hear that the tithe rent-charge for 1899 is down to 68*l*. 2*s*., a further drop on last year's averages. The poor parsons—how will they manage to live, I wonder? I wonder also if it has ever struck any one how intimate is the link between the fall of agriculture and the welfare of religion in this country, or at least of that form of it which is represented by the Church of England. It is undoubtedly to the advantage of his parish that a clergyman should be able to keep up a modest position; that he should not at least be notoriously struggling with debts and visibly out at elbows. Yet in eight cases out of ten how is he to do so in these days, with the rates mounting higher and higher, the demands upon him increasing, as they do generally while time goes on, and with an income that lessens like a *peau de chagrin*? If a man has a thousand a year, and it comes down to seven hundred, the pinch is perceptible, but if he has three hundred a year, which shrinks to under two or less, it is overwhelming, and there are very many benefices in these counties that do not return 300*l*. clear per annum. Also the losses of country clergymen in these days are not confined to the wasting of their tithe. In the majority of cases the glebe land is either thrown on to their hands or must be re-let at a great reduction. So it cannot be said that the average country rector will begin the new year with prospects so rosy as this morning's daybreak.

Later in the day the omen of a red dawn was fulfilled, for the rain came down in torrents, but through it all the ploughs ploughed on. With them, as the steaming horses are unyoked, leaving their sharp shares buried in the half-turned furrow, ends my record of farming and thinking in 1898.

On the whole it has been a favourable year so far as climatic conditions are concerned. Last winter was mild and open, the spring very late, cold, and wet, but leading us on to an excellent haysel; the harvest, one of the most splendid times that has happened within the memory of man. After that came drought, which almost destroyed the swede crop, although the mangolds stood it marvellously. At last this broke, and thenceforward the weather has been all that could be desired, enabling us to get more forward with the ploughing than might have been expected. Such of next year's crops as are above the ground, wheat, winter beans, tares, &c., all look well and vigorous, but a spell of frost would now be welcome if only to kill the grubs and make the heavy lands tender and friable. Perhaps we shall have it yet, since even in my own day the English climate has changed very greatly—now it is common for autumn to stretch almost up to Christmas, while winter often prevails from February to June.

But if the difficulties and variableness of our weather and climate were all which he had to face, the farmer might wish his neighbour a happy New Year after church to-morrow with a reasonable belief that, the decrees of Fate apart, his invocation would be fulfilled. The facts, however, point another way, for it cannot be denied that, taking the country through, the farming outlook has seldom been more gloomy than it will be at the beginning of 1899. Wheat, our staple product, has fallen again to a figure at which it is not remunerative to grow; meat does not, and some think will not rise, while wool is, I understand, lower in price than it has ever been before.[1] What then is the farmer to do and where is he to turn for aid? Protection, at any rate upon wheat and meat, is at present but a dream, and he will be wise if he dismisses the hope of it from his mind. A bounty on corn might help, but will there ever be a bounty unless some great war has first taught the people how necessary it is that a certain proportion of our acreage should be kept under wheat? I doubt it.

What remains then? In addition to considerable and very necessary changes of the system and subject matter of elementary education in country districts I can only suggest: help from the State in the shape of (1) monetary aid advanced on the security of the property to persons of approved character who wish to purchase small holdings, thus fostering the growth of a new yeoman class,

---

[1] Since the above was written, owing to a shortage, probably temporary, of the foreign supply, meat has risen a little, while corn has fallen still further in price.—April 1899.

(2) the removal or remission of the unjust land tax, (3) the equalisation of the rating and other burdens upon real and personal property, and (4) the passing of a thorough-going and really comprehensive Act inflicting severe penalties upon dishonest traders who, amongst other frauds, sell foreign meat for British, and colour the fat of animals and kindred substances in such a way that the public buy them believing them to be butter. That some adequate and necessary legislation of this sort has not been enacted long ago is, as many of us think, nothing less than a scandal. Also, if it is not so already, it should be made illegal for the keepers of restaurants and hotels, when asked for butter and paid for butter, in its place, as they often do, knowingly to supply margarine to their customers; and if it is so already, then the law should be enforced. But what hope is there of most of these reforms? Very little I imagine.[1]

The house of the agricultural interest is a house divided against itself, therefore it cannot stand, and those who dwell in it are a feeble and a frightened folk. Moreover, owners of land and tenants of land muster but a few votes between them, whereas the labourers, who really hold the balance of political

---

[1] As these proofs leave their author's hands the Sale of Food and Drugs Bill is passing through the report stage in the House of Commons, and, presumably, will soon be law. Such as it is agriculturists will accept it with gratitude, and in the pious hope that it may not become a dead-letter through a lack of the enforcement of its provisions, especially, as I trust may be the case, if it makes it punishable to palm off foreign meat as British fed and provides machinery to detect the fraud. It does seem lamentable, however, that this opportunity was not taken to make it illegal to colour margarine to represent butter. Such colouring can have but one object. To urge that under the law margarine cannot be sold as butter scarcely touches the point, since in its tinted condition it can be, and is, supplied to the customers of eating-places who are paying for butter and would not, for the most part, knowingly consume margarine. In its natural, uncoloured condition this and other tricks would be impossible, and it is no consolation to the unwilling absorber of margarine to be told that the dishonest person who passes the stuff off on him as butter bought it from a tub labelled Margarine, and not from one labelled Butter. Nor is it any consolation to the British farmer, whose produce is thus exposed to a competition manifestly unfair.

power, only too often believe that salvation lies in attacking what they are taught to consider the interests of the farmer, the parson and the squire, rather than in insisting that the ancient industry of British agriculture, by which their forefathers have lived for centuries, should at least receive fair treatment in its struggle for existence. They forget—speaking broadly—that all those who live by the land must swim or sink together, that if the farmer falls the landlord will fall, and if the landlord falls the labourer must follow him, since under our system and customs, if one cannot wring a living from the soil neither can the others, so that it becomes almost valueless to all. The worth of land depends fundamentally upon the value of what it will produce, and if, from any given causes, its cultivation ceases to be remunerative, then all who took a return from the fields, whether in the shape of rent or crops or wages, must go empty away. To suppose if the landlord were abolished (which is impossible under any scheme of tenure that I can conceive, since it can scarcely be made unlawful for an individual, a corporation, or the State to own and hire out land) that the others concerned would necessarily flourish is a pure fallacy, as many a person has found out who farms his estate, and thus becomes his own landlord. Putting aside other questions that arise—capital is necessary, and profits can scarcely be cut so fine.

Well, these be great matters, which I suppose no words of mine may move for good or ill. A still greater matter is the desertion of the land by the labourer. To my mind, under present conditions which make any considerable rise in wages impossible, that problem can only be solved by giving to the peasant, through State aid or otherwise, the opportunity of transforming himself into a small landowner, should he desire to do so, and thus interesting him permanently in the soil as one of its proprietors. But to own acres is useless unless their produce can be disposed of at a living profit, which nowadays, in many instances, at any rate in our Eastern counties, is often difficult, if not impossible. Will steps ever be taken sufficient to bring the people back upon the land ; and to .mitigate the severity of the economic and other circumstances which afflict country dwellers in Great Britain to such a reasonable extent that those who are fit and industrious can once more be enabled to live in comfort from its fruits? In this question with its answer lies the secret, and, as I think, the possible solution of most of our agricultural troubles. But to me that answer is a thrice-sealed book. I cannot look into the future or prophesy its developments. Who lives will see; these things must go as they are fated—here I bid them farewell.

As I write the year is dying. In a few minutes its glass runs out and 1899 must come, the last year but one of an eventful and a wondrous century. With 1898 this humble record of passing thoughts and little things is finished, and it remains only for me to offer my thanks to each reader who has found patience in my company to wander through its devious pages. If any idea, passage or reflection in them has pleased him, I am rewarded; indeed, to speak truth, the writing of them has brought its own reward, since to me it is a joy to tell day by day of this earth which is at once 'our mother and our monument,' of its fruits and of the creatures that dwell thereon.

Now, above every time and season, in this moment of midnight while the world beneath us leaps to the pathway of another year, to Him who, with an equal hand, makes the Star, the Child, and the Corn to grow, and, their use fulfilled, calls back the energy of life He lent them; to the Lord of birth and death; of spring, of summer, and of harvest, let us make the offering of a thankful spirit for all that we have been spared of ill and all that we have won of good, before we rise up in quietness and confidence to meet the fortune of the days to be.

THE END

APPENDIX

I

THE RURAL EXODUS

NOTE

The following paper is the substance of an address delivered by the author before the Norfolk Chamber of Agriculture at Norwich on May 6, 1899, when, after discussion, the resolution proposed in it was carried unanimously.   He reprints it here because it has occurred to him that it is as well to give the great subject with which it deals somewhat more adequate treatment than it has received in the foregoing pages, and still more because he hopes that in future generations some readers may be interested in learning the condition of the agricultural labour market in the Eastern Counties in the year 1899.   He may add that on May 30 he moved a very similar resolution —the alteration in its terms being merely verbal—before the Central and Associated Chambers of Agriculture in London, where, after criticism and discussion, it was also carried unanimously; a fact, he ventures to submit, which shows in how serious a light this matter of the depopulation of the rural districts is regarded by representatives of the agricultural interests gathered from every part of England.   That the state of affairs in the Eastern Counties is in no ways exaggerated in this address will be proved by the following paragraph cut from the 'Norfolk Chronicle' in August 1899:

'A sale of standing crops of wheat and barley under circumstances unprecedented in Norfolk, and, perhaps, in England, has taken place at Wacton. On Monday Mr. Robert Borrett, instructed by Mr. Robert K. Fisher, offered for disposal by public auction the growing crops of wheat and barley upon about 170 acres of land in the parishes of Moulton St. Michael, Pulham Market, Tivetshall St. Margaret, and Wacton.   The land is in Mr. Fisher's occupation, and the official notice of the sale stated that the crops were offered in consequence of there being a scarcity of labour.'

Could any domestic occurrence be of much more evil omen to agriculture and all connected with the land than this strange sale of unreaped crops—or, indeed, had we but ears to hear, and eyes to see, to our country and its inhabitants?

By the permission of the Chamber obtained upon a previous occasion I beg to move the following resolution :

'This Chamber respectfully calls the attention of her Majesty's Government to the continual and progressive shrinkage of the rural population in the eastern counties, and especially of those adult members of it who are described as skilled agricultural labourers.

'In view of the grave and obvious national consequences which must result if this exodus continues, the Chamber prays that her Majesty's Government will as soon as may be convenient make its causes the subject of parliamentary inquiry and report with a view to their mitigation or removal.'

Before going further I propose to prove that 'the continual and progressive shrinkage of the rural population' of which I speak in this resolution really does exist ; that it is not a mere bugbear created by grumbling farmers. The foundation-stone which I will lay in this wall of proof that I hope to be able to build is that of our common experience as farmers, proprietors, and others connected with the land. Probably there are few gentlemen present who would not be able to tell the Chamber from what they themselves know that the supply of agricultural labourers is much less than it used to be ; that to-day it is largely furnished indeed from the ranks of elderly and old men who at their time of life can turn to nothing else, or by those who for some reason or other, such as mental weakness, are unfit to do anything else. Most of those present could tell us also that the young men are no longer going on the land in anything like the same proportion as used to be the case, and, further, that when they do go on the land their great desire is to get off it and into some other employment as quickly as possible.

I myself farm about 370 acres, and of the four ploughmen whom I employ, not one is under 50, and two must be between 60 and 70, or so I judge their ages. Indeed, it is a question to me, if anything were to happen to these men, where I should look for others of sufficient skill to till the soil, and what I say of ploughmen applies equally to the other classes of agricultural labour, such as milking, drilling, thatching, and ditching, in which training and judgment are required. For more than a year I have been looking for a young skilled labourer to whom I could offer the advantage of a good cottage, but have been unable to find one. Most of those to whom I have spoken upon the subject in my neighbourhood make the same complaint, and the other day when going over a farm not far from Halesworth, the man in charge of it told me that the labour on a neighbouring farm of nearly two hundred acres had been reduced to that of the bailiff in charge of it and one horseman through all the winter months, the place being kept going only by its owner or tenant occasionally sending over men from another farm at a distance.

Now I pass on from personal observations, which, after all, must be very partial and limited, to those furnished by Parliamentary and other records, or by gentlemen in neighbouring counties who have kindly answered my questions upon the matter. First I quote from the report of the inspector of the union counties of Norfolk and Suffolk with parts of Essex and Cambridge, Mr. Philip Bagenal, for 1897–8, as made by him to the Local Government Board. In it he says :—

'In the years 1871–91 the census returns show that one-tenth of the agricultural labourers of Norfolk had left the land. There is too much reason to believe that since 1891 the rate of decrease has been accelerated. For the same period in Suffolk the decrease in the same class was a fraction over 10 per cent. . . . . a constant drain of the best class of wage-earners is thus going on. The old and infirm are left and these necessarily come on the rates.'

The next document I shall quote from is the ' Report by Mr. Henry Rew (Assistant-Commissioner) on the county of Norfolk,' published in 1895. In paragraph 73, page 39, he says :—

'That the number of labourers employed upon the land in Norfolk has decreased, and is decreasing, goes almost without saying.' Then he quotes figures, and adds, 'in the twenty years 1871-91, therefore, one-tenth of the agricultural labourers of Norfolk have left the land. . . There is good reason to believe that since 1891 the decrease has been accelerated.'

Further on he shows that between 1871 and 1894 in fourteen Norfolk union districts there has been a net decrease in population of 11,235, whereas between, 1871 and 1891 the population of England and Wales increased by over six millions, showing that the diminution is in agricultural districts alone. Further, in paragraph 76 he quotes the following striking allegations :

'The majority of farmers consider that the quality of the labour has deteriorated. They especially alluded to the lack of interest in their work exhibited by the men, and particularly by the younger men. "The young men," said one witness, " will not learn farmwork, and will be of no use on the land when they grow up." Another said he did not know a man under 50 years of age who knew how to lay a fence or underdrain. Another said that in his district (North-east Norfolk) the first prize in a thatching competition was awarded to a man 70 years of age.'

In his report on the county of Suffolk published in 1895, the Assistant Commissioner, Mr. Hugh Fox, on page 75 points out that between 1871 and 1891 the number of male agricultural labourers in the county has fallen from 40,751 to 36,202. In his report, published in 1894, Mr. Hunter Pringle, the Assistant Commissioner for parts of Lincolnshire and Essex, points out that between 1871 and 1891 there has been a decrease of 17·2 per cent in the rural population.

Now I will leave official records and come to those of a more private character. To begin with, I may state that in my own neighbourhood I am informed that in a single small parish 40 cottages are standing empty. Next I quote from a letter written by a large estate agent in Hertfordshire, in reply to queries made on my behalf. He says :

'I do not know of any statistics as to the migration of labour from Herts to London or elsewhere, but I believe it to be a fact that the labour question is becoming very serious, and in order to induce men to remain on the land, farmers have already raised their wages, in one case 2s. a week and in others 1s., and I think that they will have to make a still further rise ; and I fear that they will get very little, if any, more work done. . . . There is a large well-to-do farmer in this district who is giving up his holding this next Michaelmas, and he assures me that the only reason for his doing so is the fact that he cannot get labour. . . . If any one attended our local markets at the present time he would find that the " labour question is the chief topic of conversation." . . . I am afraid the true and serious facts of the case are as follow : All the young men have or are quitting the land for the Army, Navy, towns, railways, police and large nursery grounds near London, leaving only the idle young men and those of weak intellect (who are of no use anywhere), the middle-aged and old men, to work the land, and as these die, or become incapacitated through illness, there is no one to take their place, and, therefore, it is only a matter of time and there will be a very few hands left for agricultural work. I am afraid that nothing short of a very substantial rise in wages will induce the young men to remain and work in the country, but at present prices I do not see how the farmer can afford to meet this extra call on his expenses. I fear that there is a good deal of truth in the remark a farmer made to me yesterday, "Education has done it all, sir."'

Here, too, are some extracts from a letter written to me by a large landowner in this county, Lord Walsingham, from which he has given me leave to quote :

'April 13, 1899.

. . . 'I observe that you are about to introduce a discussion in the Norfolk Chamber of Agriculture on the dearth of agricultural labourers, and to suggest a Government inquiry into its causes. This dearth is much felt here, and although for many years I have been cultivating land at a loss under the impression that it was at least a charity to find employment for the agricultural population, I have now seriously to contemplate the prospect of allowing farms which do pay to go out of cultivation for want of hands to carry on the work. Better education makes every young man desire to wear a black coat, and the drift is towards the towns, where clerks are superabundant already, and the brain market is overstocked. Mechanical contrivances may come to the rescue to some extent. I send a lot of milk to London, and shall probably be obliged to milk the cows by machinery, for the men here dislike the job, and the women won't do it. Yet are they likely to be so much better off that they can afford to decline a healthy country life and rural labour ? High wages will not mend matters, for farming is very uphill work at present prices, and if the labour bill runs high no profit can be made, and the light lands must go back to rabbits. Already many farmers prefer to pay their rent out of these rather than to run the risks of higher cultivation. . . .'

Lord Walsingham informs me also that the population in the villages on the Merton estate showed a marked diminution at the last census and that allotments there are found to have no attraction, as they have been tried and failed. I add another instance that suggests a rapidly decreasing population. From the report made by the Officer of Health to the Bosmere District Council in Suffolk, it would appear that in 1898 the marriages of the district were about 33 per cent. less than those of 1897, and 14 per cent. less than the average of those in the previous decade. Out of a total of 205 deaths in the same district it would appear also that no less than ninety-eight were those of persons of over sixty years of age, the great disproportion of the figures being explained by the absence of that section of the population whose ages vary from twenty to sixty.

Commenting on these facts in an article the *East Anglian Daily*

Times, the paper from which I cull these statistics, adds : " It is the same everywhere, and yet this, the most urgent of all social problems, receives practically no attention from our legislators.' It was my intention to quote from other communications, but as their tenour is very similar to those that I have already given, and as time is short, I will not do so. I think that it will be admitted, however, that I have now proved my point that there is a shrinkage, a large shrinkage of the rural population going on, and that such shrinkage is progressive ; that if indeed it continues at the present rate, within a time which our children might live to see, there would be practically no rural population in certain parts of the Eastern Counties.[1] My own belief, which is based upon death entries in registers, is that at the present time the population of many of our villages is smaller than it was in the middle ages, the enormous increase which is revealed by the census having taken place in the towns.

Now I go on to my second point—namely, What are the causes of this shrinkage ? I have heard various reasons given, all or most of which have some weight : That the spread of education makes labour on the land distasteful to the young—though, by the way, one would think that, other things being equal, true education, the education which teaches us how great and good a thing it is to be in daily contact with Nature, and to breathe the pure air undefiled by the reek of cities, might have led to a different conclusion. That the housing of labourers is in many cases insufficient—although here I may remark that the housing of similar classes in large towns is not all that could be desired, and the rent is very much higher. That the desire for music halls and

---

[1] The following letter, received since this paper was read, seems illustrative of this unpleasant suggestion :

Welborne Rectory, E. Dereham : May 17, 1899.

DEAR SIR,—Having read with interest your paper on the ' Exodus of the Rural Population,' I think the example of this small parish may interest you as showing what is going on in the way of exodus. In 1881 there were 56 names on the school register—31 boys and 25 girls. Of the 56 only two are left in the parish. All the boys are gone.

In 1890 there were 36 names on the register. Only eight of these are now living in the parish.

At the present time, 1899, there are 23 names only on the register.

Yours faithfully,

(Signed) H. B. JOHNSON. *Rector.*

H. Rider Haggard, Esq.

other forms of entertainment draw the young from dull country places, which is doubtless true.

Such are some of the reasons, but I maintain that the true first cause of this emigration is purely economic : that the labourer leaves the land because the land cannot pay sufficient wage to keep him upon it, and that if it could pay him sufficient he would soon get over his longing for the music halls, or his dislike of labour in the fields, or even the insufficiency of house accommodation in his neighbourhood. This can easily be proved ; if any one of us wants a groom, or a keeper, or an under-gardener, there is no lack of applicants for the post, because the work is comparatively light and the pay a few shillings a week better. Again, you will find that gentlemen in business, such as maltsters, who can afford to pay good wages, can find plenty of labour and of the very best class.

I think then that we may take it as a proposition beyond all reasonable doubt that the labourer is leaving the land because in the present depressed state of the great agricultural industry in our part of England the cultivator of the land cannot by any possibility manage to pay him a better wage and live himself. Into the vexed question of whether or no the young fellow who thus departs to find employment elsewhere really betters his position at 'the far end' I have no time to enter at length. Still it must be remembered that 18s. or 1l. a week always sounds a good deal better than 12s. or 14s., and however the thing may work out at last the young man who strives to secure the higher wage is actuated by a very proper and laudable ambition. We cannot expect him to stop here and turn himself into a ploughman if he thinks he can do better elsewhere. He has his own interests to consult, like every individual among us, and he must not be blamed for consulting them.

Well, as this emigration is going on, and if some way is not found to check it, is likely to go on, it may be worth while to glance at its probable results. As regards the land they seem to be that within the next twenty years or so a great deal of the poorer soil—the very heavy and the very light—will go out of cultivation ; the grass area will be largely increased, while such lands as remain for arable will have to be cultivated by machinery directed by a few highly paid mechanics. This in its turn would mean that small fields must be done away with, since steam ploughs, &c., cannot be used in them to advantage. You can form your own opinion as to whether this prospect is pleasing to agriculturists, or advantageous to the villages and small country towns which are in process of desertion.

The next question is : What will be the effect upon the large towns towards which the migration flows, and especially upon London ? I have from time to time been credited with some powers of imagination, but I confess that they fail me when I think of this England of ours, spotted with huge overgrown cities, surrounded each of them by market gardens, and beyond by great stretches of what in Africa we should call veld, that is unimproved or scarcely improved country, broken here and there by the mansions of rich colonials or city men, encircled by their areas of sporting lands. Yet appalling and in some ways almost ludicrous as is the picture, it is one that human eyes may see unless the country folk cease rushing to the towns, and agriculture once more becomes a paying pursuit, or rather, unless this last happens, since all these questions hinge upon the prosperity or non-prosperity of the agricultural interests.

Behind these which I have touched upon remains the largest question of all. What will be the effect upon the national health and physique, and, therefore, upon the national character, of the trans-planting of the sturdiest classes of our inhabitants, the dwellers in the rural districts, from their wholesome country homes to the crowded courts of sweltering cities ? I dare say that the immediate result has been exaggerated by some thinkers and writers, for the stamina of the race will hold out against the influence of surroundings for one generation, or perhaps for two. But, by way of example, look at the pure-bred Cockney—I mean the little fellow whom you see running in and out of offices in the City, and whose forefathers have for the last two generations dwelt within a two-mile radius of Charing Cross. And then look at an average young labourer coming home from his day's field work, and I think that you will admit that the city breeds one stamp of human beings, and that the country breeds another. They may be a little sharper in the towns, but after all it is not mere sharpness that has made Great Britain what she is, it is the thews and sinews of her sons which are the foundation of everything, and the even, healthy minds that dwell in healthy bodies. Take the people away from their natural breeding and growing grounds, thereby sapping their health and strength in cities such as nature never intended to be the permanent homes of men, and the decay of this country becomes only a question of time. In this matter, as in many others, ancient Rome has a lesson to teach us. That is why this question of the depopulation of the country is a question of national interest.

And now one word as to the possible remedies for a state of affairs which I think most people will be inclined to admit is not natural, and which may prove disastrous.   First, I will say that in my humble opinion what a speaker in this Chamber a month or two ago very aptly called sugar-plum cures are no cures at all, though in certain instances they may be palliatives, and after all palliatives are not to be despised.   I mean that such things as better housing, more technical education, more rural holidays, such as flower shows and ploughing matches, more coffee-rooms and games of draughts, &c., will never suffice to keep the labourer on the land unless you are able to raise the labourer's wages.   No, if you offered him a house with hot and cold water laid on throughout, and lit with electric light, and took him to and from his work on a motor-car, and had a coffee stall erected upon every farm, and brought him to a lecture three times a week, it would not persuade him to accept 12s. or 13s. a week when he knows, or believes, that by transferring himself and his family to two or three squalid rooms in the dingy courts of a great town, he can earn 20s. or 25s., for, as I said before, wages, and nothing but wages, to speak broadly, is at the bottom of this movement from the country to the towns.

Another remedy which in my opinion is no remedy is the semi-Socialistic legislation that is advocated by some, by which I mean legislation whereof the real, if not the ostensible, object is to better the position of the labouring classes out of the pockets of the owners and occupiers of land and the allied sections of society, as by forcing them to build houses that cannot possibly be remunerative at their own cost, or to become responsible for anything and everything that may happen to a man in their employ, however entirely it may be his own fault.   It is no remedy, as I think, for this reason, that you cannot get blood out of a stone.   The land, or at least our Eastern Counties land, can bear no more burdens.   As it is, with wheat from 24s. to 25s. per quarter, it does not pay, and another straw or two upon the camel's back will break it.   Governments, it is probable, would like to solve the trouble in this fashion, namely, by spoliation of certain classes for the benefit of other classes, for Governments naturally attack the weak—that is those who have few votes—and offer them up as a sacrifice to those who have many votes, and from whom they hope to win support.   But although the agricultural interest, with its seven or eight millions of people who are connected with it, is, I suppose, because of its suicidal divisions, its timidity, and its want of political organisation absolutely the weakest in the kingdom, it has this protection—the protection of its utter poverty, so if money is wanted for more experiments in popular legislation it will have to be found elsewhere.

Then what is there that could help the land, and therefore help the labourer? I venture to suggest one or two things : very stringent measures, which would make it impossible for the farmer to be defrauded by the sale as his produce of that which he never grew ; the equalisation of rates and taxation upon real and personal property, thereby lessening the burdens that now fall upon the land ; and the making it impossible, in fact as well as in name, for carriers to transport foreign goods at cheaper rates than they grant to British produce.

But I do not go into this subject at length, for after all it is not our province to decide upon the remedies. I suggest that what we have to do is to call the attention of those in authority to a certain grave state of affairs, and ask them to deal with it, for a Government is immeasurably more clever and full of ideas than all the Chambers of Agriculture in the country put together can be ; moreover, it has the power of translating its ideas into some practical and useful action. For my part I do not suppose, however, that the agriculturist for its mere love of him, would be likely to get anything from this or any other Government, since it is our common experience, as Mr. Clare Sewell Read told us the other day, that when he asks for bread he receives a stone, and I may add that he is fortunate if that stone is not violently thrown at his head. But this is not a question that affects the agriculturist only, although in my opinion it is the gravest which he has to face, or will shortly become so, graver even than foreign competition. Nor is it in any sense a party question, or merely a local question, as if I had time and you had patience I could easily prove to you from an unimpeachable authority, the *Labour Gazette*. In the April issue of that journal, which is published by the Board of Trade, are reports of the state of the agricultural labour market from all over England. In every county the cry is the same, and this in the face of a rather general rise in wages. In the article with which these reports are prefaced the editor says :

'Reports from correspondents in nearly every county refer to the increasing difficulty of getting extra hands, and complaints come from some districts that sufficient labour to do the necessary work cannot be obtained.'

It is, I repeat, a national question, and the state of affairs upon which I have dwelt constitutes a national danger. We have therefore a right to ask that it should be inquired into, and dealt with by the national authorities. At least that is my view, after some study of the matter, and I hope that it may prove to be the view of this Chamber. I know that some landowners and farmers say : 'Oh! leave it alone'—they wish, for reasons that seem to me absolutely futile, and in these days of newspapers and universal publicity, unwise and even dangerous, to try to keep the facts secret ; to adopt the policy of an ostrich, and hide their heads in a ditch while the labourer and the more vigorous members of his family tramp past them to the railway station, leaving the sick, aged, and incompetent to swell the rates. But I do not believe in that policy. I believe that it is much better to be frank and look matters in the face, even if it does involve the discussion of economic questions with which they have a perfect right to be acquainted by the classes chiefly concerned. Also I believe that, nowadays more than ever, if you want a thing looked into and remedied you must make a stir about it, for who is to move if the people primarily interested do not? This belief is my excuse for troubling you to-day.

I hope that this may be your opinion also, and as now, to my own satisfaction at any rate, I have proved : 1. That there is a progressive shrinkage of the rural population in the Eastern Counties. 2. That such shrinkage constitutes a grave national danger. 3. That its causes ought to be inquired into by Government with a view to their mitigation or removal, I beg to move the resolution which has already been read to you.

[I

NOTE

As an almost perfect illustration of the effect of unfettered foreign competition upon the prospects of the British Producer, I reprint here a very striking letter, written by Mr. Frederick Marryat, an Argentine farmer, which appeared in the *Morning Post* of June 17, 1899. I wish to call attention particularly to Mr. Marryat's statements as to the British butcher and 'home-grown' meat, and to his *débonnaire* summing up of the situation in the last sentence of his letter. Little wonder that he—kind and altruistic competitor—puts up the pious prayer that free trade may long continue, in view of his own conclusion that in face of it '*the revival of English agriculture is an utter impossibility.*'

To the Editor of the 'Morning Post'

SIR,—I have read with much interest the various theories propounded both for and against the revival of English agriculture wondering much at the hopefulness of some contributors, and at the 'baseless fabric of a dream' on which they rely. I have been for nearly twenty years a breeder of cattle, sheep, and horses, a fattener of stock, and a grower of wheat, maize, hay and barley, in the Argentine Republic, and I can say with confidence that as long as Free Trade exists—and long may it do so—the revival of English agriculture is an utter impossibility. England cannot compete with new countries in producing any of the things enumerated above, and time will only add new obstacles. We have everything in our favour. Millions of acres of virgin soil from one to four feet deep to be rented or bought at a nominal valuation ; a climate where stock of all kinds can remain in the open paddocks all the year round with no artificial fattening food except, perhaps, a little hay in exceptional droughts ; labour of ploughing, &c., far below European wages, the cost of harrowing, ploughing and sowing by contract, coming out at about 1*s.* 6*d.* an acre, the owner supplying horses and implements ; one man, with a double furrow plough and four horses, doing about four acres of ploughing per day, and the cost of transport so low that freights from Buenos Ayres or Rosario to Liverpool are but little more than those from Liverpool to London. Above all, everything is done on an enormous scale, and the economy of supervision and management is therefore minimised, and an owner can afford to get less profit, because it is a question of a small gain on large quantities.   May I be allowed to quote my own case, not as being an exceptional one—quite the reverse.   My *estancia* contains about ten thousand acres.   Between 1892 and 1897 it consisted of about four thousand acres of arable land, and the remainder in paddocks of lucerne or *alfalfa*, laid down after several crops of wheat had been taken from the ground. We sow about a bushel to the acre of wheat, and average about fifteen for one in good years and ten in bad ones—say twelve all round.   The reader can calculate the result and deduct probable expenses, if he is an expert, and if not, he can take my word that English farmers are out of the running. As regards stock, we had given up breeding, except a fine stock point of about five hundred head. We bought store cattle from up country, and passed through about four to five thousand fat stock yearly, rarely making less than 30 per cent. increase on the purchasing price. Horses 'breed themselves,' and are no trouble to any one, running out all the year through.   We bred 'vanners' from Shire stock.   We had a small stock of two thousand Lincoln sheep, which in three years gave me over 100 per cent. in wool and wethers, but I sold the flock, as it took up so much time in keeping down the scab.   How, then, can the English farmers compete with us?   Of course, drought, disease, and locusts often do terrible damage, but, taking all things into account, we can 'win as we like,' and time only strengthens our position, as we continue to improve the class of stock and open up more country with new railways.   Thousands of fine beasts and tens of thousands of sheep are annually sent alive to England and there killed and sold as 'home grown.'   The Army and Navy Stores may differentiate between 'fresh killed foreign' and 'home grown,' but not the British butcher.   No !   English agriculture is a thing of the past, and land in England has to-day practically little more than a prairie value as far as the farmer is concerned.

Yours, &c.,

FREDERICK MARRYAT.

16 IDDESLEIGH MANSIONS, WESTMINSTER :

June 16.

INDEX

A NOTE TO READERS

We hope you have enjoyed this Cresset Library edition and would like to take this opportunity to invite you to put forward your suggestions about books that might be included in the series.

The Cresset Library was conceived as a forum for bringing back books that we felt should be widely available in attractively designed and priced paperback editions. The series themes can be loosely described as social, cultural, and intellectual history though, as you can see from the list of published titles at the front of this book, these themes cover a broad range of interest areas.

If you have read or know of books that fall into this category which are no longer available or not available in paperback, please write and tell us about them. Should we publish a book that you have suggested we will send you a free copy upon publication together with three other Cresset Library titles of your choice.

Please address your letter to Claire L'Enfant at:-

> Century Hutchinson
> FREEPOST
> London
> WC2N 4BR

There is no need to stamp your envelope.

We look forward to hearing from you.

THE CRESSET LIBRARY